ENTER PURS

THE UNKNOWN PLAYS OF

SHAKESPEARE-

NEVILLE

John Casson

for Nial with special thanks for the music!

Yours

John Casson

ENTER PURSUED BY A BEAR

THE UNKNOWN PLAYS OF
SHAKESPEARE-
NEVILLE

John Casson

MUSIC FOR STRINGS

Published by MUSIC FOR STRINGS LTD
9 Hambledon Place, Bognor Regis, West Sussex, United Kingdom, PO21 2NE
Email for orders and enquiries: sales@musicforstrings.com
website: www.musicforstrings.com

Cover design by Kaspars Vilnitis

ISBN: 978-1-905424-06-1

for **Diane Adderley**,

a brave, creative woman,

psychodrama psychotherapist,

sociodramatist, playback theatre director,

and my enthusiastic supporter in these discoveries.

Contents

Book cover illustrations

Front cover:
The Ursa Major (The Great Bear) Constellation from the ceiling fresco of Mappa Sala del Mondo in the Villa Farnese. Edmund, the bastard in *King Lear*, states that he was born under this constellation (see chapter 2).

Phaeton falling from the sky: the ceiling fresco of Mappa Sala del Mondo in the Villa Farnese in Caprarola, Italy, painted by Giovanni de Vecchi and Raffaellino da Reggio 1574-5. Neville was in Italy in 1581, just six years later: we do not know if he saw this room but the party travelled from Venice to Rome and so may have passed this villa (see chapter 1).

Back cover:
The Phoenix: from Whitney's *Choice of Emblemes* 177: Unica semper avis (see chapters 2 and 7).

Illustrations in Chapter 3

Whitney emblems:

32: In poenam sectatur et umbra

75: O vita, misero longa

183a: Qui me alit me extinguit

Foreword

BY BRENDA JAMES

I am sad to say that I believe Dr. John Casson's book concerning the apocryphal plays of Shakespeare is unique. My regret stems from the fact that there should have been a book like this years ago. It concerns a subject upon which many scholars have thought fit to write the occasional learned paper, but not one, to my knowledge, has ever before presented us with an overview of so many of these anonymous plays, coupled with a thorough analysis and inter-linking of their themes and linguistic contents.

Not since 1853 has such a comprehensive assessment been even attempted. This former attempt was in a three-volume work edited by Henry Tyrell, entitled 'The Doubtful Plays of Shakespeare: Revised From The Original Editions With Historical And Analytical Introductions And Notes Critical and Explanatory.' However, as its title suggests, Tyrell was satisfied with re-printing, introducing, collating and annotating the plays rather than with assessing their vocabulary, relating them to each other, or trying to trace them all back to the same recognisable, individual author.

Dr. Casson's book is therefore indeed unique. But why has it appeared only now, after centuries of debate concerning the young Shakespeare's apprentice hand? I think the answer is twofold. Firstly, the possibility of accessing the texts of these plays via electronic copies has afforded an opportunity that linguistic analysts of the pre-computer age could only have dreamt about. These erstwhile little-known texts are now accessible and searchable, so their vocabulary, phrases and style can be readily and quickly compared with the *known* Shakespeare canon. Secondly, the identification of Sir Henry Neville as the true author of the plays has made it possible for the works which Dr. Casson here assesses so expertly to be traced back to a feasible source. This enables him to perceive a logical train of development, and a holistic pattern of thought within their themes - for the first time. Dr. Casson demonstrates not only how the erstwhile doubtful works tie in with the accepted Shakespeare canon, but also how Henry Neville's life, knowledge, and general world-view unifies and illuminates their meaning.

It is sometimes said that when we read Shakespeare, or his apocrypha, we should not consider an authorial identity. And I accept that there is much to be said for linking any work of art with the cultural circumstances surrounding its production. As Roland Barthes declares, "The death of the author heralds the birth of the reader". But we readers are all individual human beings, just as the artist who created the works is also an individual. We each inevitably exist in our own time and space. Some points within that same time and space are of course shared, but some are also uniquely personal. Yet even the *shared,* collective circumstances surrounding our existence are mediated by our personal situation, affecting the way we deal with what we undergo. The knowledge of other people's life struggle constantly re-forms and transforms us. Great Art communicates such knowledge on many levels and in a powerfully-condensed structure. Thus is the transformational effect of art achieved by the artist communicating his personal outlook to his or her many receivers. The corollary of Barthes' remark is therefore that artist *never* dies but is reborn within his audience.

But if the artist's identity is mistaken or completely unknown, the important elements of empathy and true understanding may very well elude the receiver. To appreciate this, we only have to think how difficult it is to study *movements* and *patterns* in history without studying the *individuals* who initialised and/or worked under the freedoms and constraints those movements afforded them.

The true author of Shakespeare's works lived in a time when the movements and patterns within society were very different from our own. How much more important is it, then, that we have a real, individual identity through which to perceive those far-off times. Only then can we truly understand, and empathise with, the concerns, culture and problems of the era in which that individual had to work. By clothing an individual creative artist - Henry Neville - with the little-known texts of Shakespeare's doubtful plays, John Casson is able to make sense of them and thus make them at last accessible to every reader.

An important aspect of testing any theory is to put it to work in as many different circumstances as possible and see whether it explains and illuminates those circumstances or whether, on the contrary, it causes more problems and illogicalities. In *Enter, Pursued by a Bear,* Dr. Casson has successfully shown how Henry Neville's presence illuminates the hitherto unlit coners of both the Shakespeare apocrypha and the Shakespeare canon. Moreover, his extensive linguistic research and methodology sets a pattern for all future investigations of every aspect of the plays and poems. His book is therefore an outstanding achievement on these levels alone. But it is lively and readable too. Dr. Casson is able to tell the story of each individual play in a succinct and clear fashion. He also engages the reader in such a multiplicity of investigations that readers from many different disciplines will find much of interest in his book.

Most of all, it is a book which every reader will find informative and entertaining. If you enjoy solving puzzles, then this is a book for you. If you enjoy Shakespeare but wish there was more, then read this book and then go on to read the plays with which Dr. Casson has now succesfully enlarged the Shakespeare canon. Without his guidance these apocryphal plays may have seemed difficult to approach; with this book by your side, I guarantee that you will read through them with enjoyment and understanding.

Brenda James, October 2008

INTRODUCTION

In the 1990s I developed an interest in the Shakespeare authorship question after reading a book about the Earl of Oxford. Later I read other books and this interest assumed the nature of an occasional pastime. Although intrigued as one might be with any whodunit, I was not entirely convinced by any candidate and kept an open mind. Increasingly however I was aware of an authorship problem: that the evidence did not seem to support William Shakespeare, the Stratford man. However it was one thing to have doubts, it was another thing to accept implausible candidates who either died too soon (Oxford and Marlowe), had very different writing styles (Bacon and Marlowe) or who were just too speculative (Derby and Elizabeth I). In 2005 I came across James & Rubinstein's *The Truth Will Out: Unmasking the Real Shakespeare*, which revealed that Sir Henry Neville, politician and diplomat, was the hidden poet who used the nom-de-plume 'William Shakespeare'. I read it and re-read it, immediately realising that here was a real candidate who was meticulously researched and credible. I contacted Brenda James and began to correspond with her, to ask questions and follow up bits of information. She was very patient at this stage when she might easily have found my simple questions irritating!

I went to look at the volumes of Winwood's (1725) *Memorials of State* (which contain many letters by Henry Neville) in Manchester's John Rylands Library. Almost immediately I found words and phrases that reminded me of Shakespeare. I arranged to meet Brenda and Howard James in London and we went to see the Henslowe Diary at Dulwich College. I was now researching alongside Brenda and decided to focus especially on the apocryphal plays to see if there was any evidence for Neville as their author.

I focussed my attention on Brenda's brief mention of *Cardenio* and the intriguing possibility it had survived in Theobald's version, *Double Falshood* (James & Rubinstein, 2005, 199). I discovered a facsimile edition in Manchester's Central Library. I found evidence not only that *Double Falshood* was the real remnant of a Shakespeare-Fletcher text but that there was within it material pointing to Neville as the hidden author. The result was a paper, which was published in the first Journal of Neville Studies, and that has now become chapter 7 in this volume (Casson, 2007a). I then went on to look at *Arden of Faversham* and my paper on that play originally appeared in the second Journal of Neville Studies (Casson, 2008, see chapter 4).

I am a psychotherapist so I am aware of the mental habit of projection: namely of seeing in complex, vague material (such as clouds, lichen or oil on puddles), patterns, pictures and faces that have some meaning to the viewer. Hamlet teases Polonius on this very phenomenon. I was also aware of the "self serving bias": the tendency we have to find things that confirm our own ideas. I was therefore very keen to ensure that I was not seeing what I wanted to see. This has led me to search the plays and writings of other authors to satisfy myself that I am not projecting onto the vast Rorschach test of the bard's plays what I want to see. However despite my caution so much evidence tumbled out that I was making a discovery a day: this was extraordinary given the amount of time that had gone by and the number of scholars who had studied the material. Each discovery has led to another. The Phaeton sonnet led me to *Mucedorus*. One word in *Mucedorus* led me to look at *A Yorkshire Tragedy*; other rare words and image clusters in *Locrine* also linked into *Thomas of Woodstock* and *A Yorkshire Tragedy*. The Phaeton sonnet in particular has been like a Rosetta Stone so I do not apologise for starting a book about unknown plays with a chapter on a poem.

A good theory explains many facts that have previously been difficult to understand. The identification of Henry Neville as the real writer behind the name 'Shakespeare' solves many mysteries. I tested this theory by applying it and made so many discoveries, so rapidly, I became convinced that it was true. Brenda James suggested I consider *Locrine*. I started out very much doubting that *Locrine* was really by Shakespeare-Neville. Meticulous examination of the text eventually showed me that it was not only possible but also likely, until the mass of detail convinced me it was an early play by Shakespeare-Neville (see chapter 3). My aim has not been to 'prove' that these apocryphal plays are by Shakespeare-Neville but to present the evidence I have found and leave the reader to decide whether it is as compelling as it seems to me. I know that using parallel passages as evidence of authorship is controversial but when these occur so often I am bound, as Sams (1986) and Egan (2006) were, to say that Occam's razor suggests the simplest solution: namely that when a passage by an unknown writer is similar to that by a known writer then the simplest inference is that they **may** have been written by the same person. If there were no parallels, no echoes, no shared vocabulary, no recurrent themes, images, plot lines, it would be clear that these works were probably not by the same author. However when such similarities repeatedly recur they are evidence of a literary fingerprint, a continuity of identity behind the texts. If I had not found clear evidence consistent with Neville being the author I would not have continued my research.

There is a degree of snobbery in Shakespeare studies: some plays have been looked down upon as inferior. *Locrine* has certainly suffered from this fate: Lucas, in 1921, calling it 'worthless' (Lucas, 1972, 116). Maxwell (1969, xxiv) wrote of "the consummate ineptitude of *Mucedorus*" (this really is snobbery: it was the most popular play of its time). I directed *Pericles* many years ago and love the play yet it was long excluded from the canon and considered poor, even hack work. It was amongst a number of plays excluded from the First Folio that were later admitted to the canon, including *The Two Noble Kinsmen* and *Edward III*. Now *Edmund Ironside, The Troublesome Raigne of John King of England* and *Thomas of Woodstock* hover on the threshold of the canon. I have been convinced by Sams (1986) that *Edmund Ironside*, and by Egan (2006) that *Thomas of Woodstock* were written by the bard. *The Troublesome Raigne of John King of England* is clearly a first version that, after revision, became Shakespeare's *King John*. For me it is not scientific to dismiss a play because of a judgement on its inferior quality. A writer's early works are bound to be less skilled than his later, mature creations and no artist consistently achieves masterpieces. *A Yorkshire Tragedy* may well be by Shakespeare-Neville despite being short and not of the transcendent quality of the plays that surround it (see chapter 6), but then neither is *Timon of Athens* up to the standard of *Macbeth* and *Antony and Cleopatra*. I have not written separate chapters on *Edmund Ironside* and *The Troublesome Raigne of John King of England* because I regard the case for them being early plays by Shakespeare as effectively proven. I have examined them carefully and integrated my discoveries and reflections into the relevant chapters.

William Shakespeare was born in 1564. Henry Neville's birth date is mysterious: he was born at some time between 1561-4, probably in 1562. This gives him a head start. The earliest works I will examine date from about 1583 onwards, when Neville was 18-22. Shakespeare did not leave Stratford until after the twins were born in 1584 (when he was 19-20) and he did not appear in London until 1592 (aged 28): the gap between these dates being the "lost years" for which no certain evidence exists, though many have grasped at straws and constructed a biography that has been accepted as part of the orthodox myth. In contrast we know what Neville was doing during this time: everything the young Shakespeare needed to do in order to write the plays! Indeed he travelled to Vienna (*Measure for Measure*), Padua (*The Taming of the Shrew*), Venice (*The Merchant of Venice, Othello*), Glamis Castle in

Scotland (*Macbeth*) and possibly also Elsinore (*Hamlet*: see James, 2008b, 214). What is incredible is that Shakespeare from Stratford could arrive in London, unknown and poor, with the vast script of a three-part epic, *Henry VI*, as his first stage work and get these plays put on. Clearly these were plays by someone who had written before and developed a style. We therefore have to look at the anonymous plays of the 1580s to discover the earliest writings of the bard, whoever he was. When those anonymous works show possible traces of Neville and the bard, they become of special interest. This quest has motivated the research on which this book is based. I have extended the search to include *Thomas of Woodstock* written in the early 1590s, *A Yorkshire Tragedy* of 1605 and *Double Falshood* of 1613 to demonstrate the links between the forgotten early works and the whole canon. A continuity of images, ideas and language revealed when we put the Neville key into the rusty padlock that prevented us realising their true significance.

I have mentioned projection as a mental mechanism. Writers project into their creations aspects of their own experience. This is virtually unavoidable. Even when asked to imagine something utterly different, indeed to lie about oneself, aspects of one's personality will colour the story created. Knowing that Neville was the writer enables us to find in the plays hints of his personality and experiences recorded in his letters and reports by his contemporaries. Brenda James has previously shown this in the main canon: I now present the discoveries I have made in several apocryphal works. As we get to know Neville's letters and notebooks we can also find him using words and phrases that occur in the poems and plays. This area of study is still in its infancy: as yet no fully searchable database is available, so I have not been able to make a complete search of Neville documents. This book presents the state of the evidence thus far.

Given that his father, son and grandson shared Henry Neville's name I have chosen to call the playwright Neville or Shakespeare-Neville and identify when I am referring to any other person of the same name, such as specifying Sir Henry Neville (Neville's father).

This volume will be best read after *The Truth Will Out* (James & Rubinstein, 2005) and/or *Henry Neville and the Shakespeare Code* (James, 2008b) as otherwise the reader may well be startled by the idea of Henry Neville as the author of Shakespeare's works.

Acknowledgements

Without Brenda James' discovery and careful scholarship I would not have written this book. She has contributed a great deal to it, offering me evidence, information and notes to complement my discoveries. She is a prodigious scholar and it has been my privilege to work alongside her. I am grateful for all her support.

I am very grateful to Ms. Cynthia Lees and the librarians of Uppermill, Oldham and the British Library, including Mr. Malcolm Marjoram of the Rare Books Reference Service and Mr. Giles Mandelbrote, curator of pre 1800 British Printed Collections, for their help. Thanks are also due to Professor Anthony Jackson and John Rylands University Library of Manchester for granting me access to the Literature on Line database (LION), to Winwood's *Memorials* and other works of reference. I am also grateful to the staff at Chetham's Library (Manchester) and at Lincolnshire Archives, including Mrs. Anne Cole. I am grateful to Mr. Christopher Hunwick, archivist, Alnwick Castle, Northumberland for information on the Northumberland Manuscript.

Special thanks are due to Mr. Andy Smith for his thorough help with my text and images. I am also grateful to Di Adderley for her careful reading of the book and her advice. Thanks also are due to Mr. Ben Pitman and Mr. Combiz Moussavi for helping to identify the painting used on the book cover, and to Mr. John Harris for his assistance.

I am grateful to Dr. Katherine Duncan-Jones and Mr. Philip Watts for their opinions about the Phaeton sonnet. I am also grateful to Mr. Geoff Evans for making me aware of Joseph Sobran's paper on the sonnet.

Last, but not least, special thanks to my daughter Anna for her suggestion that led to the title: **Enter pursued by a bear**.

Chapter 1

THE PHAETON SONNET

John Florio's 1591 book of Italian-English language lessons, *Second Fruits*, presents readers with a series of dialogues, with the Italian on one page and the English version opposite. These dialogues are little naturalistic dramas, which are not only exemplars of language but also of manners, with references to contemporary life, fashion and literature. The dialogues are full of proverbial sayings, myths and images: this is not simply a textbook but an elegant exploration of language. The book opens with a sonnet.

Phaeton to his friend Florio

Sweete friend whose name agrees with thy increase,
>How fit a rivall art thou of the Spring?
>For when each branche hath left his flourishing,
>And green-lockt Sommers shadie pleasures cease:

She makes the Winters stormes repose in peace,
>And spends her franchise on each living thing:
>The dazies sprout, the little birds doo sing,
>Hearbes, gummes, and plants doo vaunt of their release.

So when that all our English witts lay dead,
>(Except the Laurell that is ever greene,)
>Thou with thy Frutes our barrenness o'er-spread,
>And set thy flowrie pleasance to be seene.

Sutch frutes, sutch flowrets of moralitie,
>Were nere before brought out of Italy.

Phaeton

If this sonnet, published in 1591, is by Shakespeare, it was possibly written before any of the later published sonnets. This poem was published two years before the name 'Shakespeare' first appeared (in 1593 with the publication of *Venus and Adonis*). The bard was already writing his first history plays but had not published anything. If it were by Neville then it would be his very first published poem. He had not adopted his pseudonym 'Shakespeare' yet and therefore the name 'Phaeton' can be seen as his first nom-de-plume. Sams (1988) suggested that *The Troublesome Raigne of John King of England* is Shakespeare's first version of *King John*: it was also printed in 1591, with no author named, and was therefore his first published play. As we shall see these two works are connected by the myth of Phaeton, in a way that points to the hidden author's identity. A list of plays made in 1669 allotted Shakespeare's *King John* to Thomas Killigrew, a relative of Henry Neville (Braunmuller, 1989, 81).

The Phaeton myth

Phaeton was a young man whose mother had told him that his father was the Sun, Phoebus. Bragging about this, he was teased by Epaphos, who said he was giving himself airs: that Phoebus was not his real father. Ashamed, Phaeton demanded his mother prove that his father was indeed the Sun (and not Merops). She sent him to seek his father in the Eastern palace of the dawn. When they met, Phoebus acknowledged his son and promised him anything he wanted. Phaeton asked to drive the chariot of the Sun. Knowing how impossibly dangerous this task was, Phoebus begged his son to ask for some other gift but the young man insisted and the father felt duty bound to fulfil his oath. Unable to restrain the powerful horses in their race across the sky and so losing control of the chariot, Phaeton was destroyed by a thunderbolt from Zeus and the Earth scorched by the careering, out of control solar car. It is a story of a boy seeking recognition from his father, of youthful ambition and dangerously arrogant over-confidence, of the disaster awaiting hubris. (Innes, 1955, 49) The myth is told in Ovid's *Metamorphoses*.

Phaeton in English Literature 1560-1600

Thomas Norton and Thomas Sackville wrote *Gorboduc*: it was the first English tragedy, being performed in 1561-2 and published in 1565. In it there are three references to the Phaeton myth:

> Too soon he clamb into the flaming car,
> Whose want of skill did set the earth on fire.
>
> (1.2.330)

> This did the proud son of Apollo prove,
> Who, rashly set in chariot of his sire,
> Inflamed the parched earth with heaven's fire.
>
> (Chorus Act 2, 16)

> As was rash **Phaeton** in Pheobus'car;
> Ne then the fiery steeds did draw the flame
> With wilder random through the kindled skies...
> Then traitorous counsel now will whirl about
> The youthful heads of these unskillful kings...
>
> (2.1.204)

The first two references are to the issue of the inheritance of the crown. The first scene is reminiscent of the start of *King Lear*. The third use of this myth reveals a wider political meaning concerning the dangers of ill-advised governance. The myth is central to the theme of the kingdom being burned by the fires of civil war because of an arrogant young usurper's folly (see 3.1.163 and Act 4 Chorus, 19). The writers were warning Elizabeth that not to have a clear, single, mature heir to the throne was to risk civil war. Here the Phaeton myth is a political metaphor: a warning. Whilst this work may seem remote, being written over thirty years before the Phaeton sonnet, nevertheless it is significant: Thomas Sackville's daughter Mary married into the Neville family (see below). Sackville had also referred to Phaeton in his Induction (line 36) to *The Mirror for Magistrates* (1563): a work which was later to be a source for Shakespeare's history plays.

Written between 1578-80 Sidney's *Arcadia* contains two brief references to Phaeton (Duncan-Jones, 1999, 232, 131; Evans, 1987, 718, 299). It was first published in 1590. Sidney also referred to the myth when describing a decorative image of a chariot drawn by flaming, winged horses, "as if she had newly borrowed them from Phoebus", thus hinting at Artesia's ambitious nature (Evans, 1987, 43, 157). *Mucedorus*, which is partly based on *Arcadia*, was a very popular play. In Act 3, scene 1, 19, the hero says:

> Ah, luckless fortune, worse than **Phaeton**'s tale,
> My former bliss is now become my bale.

I believe the play was written before 1591, and so before the Phaeton sonnet. In 1598 the first quarto of *Mucedorus* was published anonymously (it was attributed to Shakespeare only in 1656: see chapter 2).

Christopher Marlowe mentioned Phaeton once in *Tamburlaine II* (1587, i.e. before the Phaeton sonnet was written), "heaven's coach the pride of **Phaeton**" (5.3.244) and again in *Edward II* (1592, after the Phaeton sonnet). Speaking of Gaveston, Warwick says:

> Ignoble vassal that like **Phaeton**
> Aspir'st unto the guidance of the sun...

John Lyly in his *Midas* (1588-9) wrote, "desiring things above my reach, I be fired with **Phaeton**." (1.1.15-16). Robert Greene referred to "fond-conceited **Phaeton**" (5.2.57) in his play *Orlando Furioso* (first printed 1594, probably written by 1591, possibly as early as 1588). Thomas Lodge briefly mentioned Phaeton in his 1590 *Rosalynde* (the source of *As You Like It*). The image was also used by the writer of *The Troublesome Raigne of John King of England* "as sometime **Phaeton** mistrusting silly Merop for his Sire..." (1.341). Merop is briefly mentioned in *The Taming of A Shrew* (13.58), which was published anonymously in 1594 (Miller, 1998, 114) and in *The Two Gentlemen of Verona* (see below). Edmund

Spenser used the myth in *The Faerie Queene* (Book 5, Canto VIII, Stanza XL), published in 1595, but he was referring more to the horses that drew the sun's chariot than to Phaeton himself. Thomas Nashe also referred to Phaeton twice but long after the Phaeton sonnet was published: in *The Unfortunate Traveller* (1594): "**Phaeton** his chariot did misguide" and in *Summer's Last Will and Testament* (1600): "Dead **Phaeton's** three sisters' funeral tears." Francis Bacon mentioned Phaeton once in his essay on *The Vicissitude of Things* (written between 1597-1625): "**Phaeton's** car went but a day."

Shakespeare mentioned him **five** times in canonical works (and by implication a sixth time). The name of Phaeton/Phaethon appears **only** in the early plays. In *Henry VI* part 3, first performed 1590-91, (and therefore most likely written before the Phaeton sonnet; but only published in 1594) there are two references: in the first of these Clifford is speaking to Richard Plantagenet, Duke of York, (who was married to Cecily Neville).

> Ay, to such mercy as his ruthless arm,
> With downright payment, show'd unto my father.
> Now **Phaethon** hath tumbled from his car,
> And made an evening at the noontide prick.
>
> (1.4.31)

Later the wounded Clifford laments:

> O Phoebus, hadst thou never given consent
> That **Phaethon** should cheque thy fiery steeds,
> Thy burning car never had scorch'd the earth!
>
> (2.6.11)

As he lies dying Edward, Warwick, Richard, George and Montague, who were all Nevilles, enter and triumph over him. In this latter scene the following words, that are in the Phaeton sonnet, occur within the first 50 lines: 'summer', 'peace', 'dead', 'friend', 'branch', 'sweet(ly)', 'spring'.

Thus by the time the Phaeton sonnet was published in 1591 eight known contemporary writers had used the myth: Norton & Sackville, Sidney, Marlowe, Lyly, Greene, Lodge and Shakespeare who had done so twice in one play.

In *The Two Gentlemen of Verona* first performed about 1593-5 (and so probably written **after** the Phaeton sonnet) the Duke says:

> Why, **Phaeton**, - for thou art Merops' son, -
> Wilt thou aspire to guide the heavenly car
> And with thy daring folly burn the world?
>
> (3.1.153)

18

Just two lines before this reference to Phaeton Valentine promises, "Silvia, this night I will **enfranchise** thee" (3.1.151). The word is actually used twice in the play (see also 2.4.85). In the Phaeton sonnet the word '**franchise**' is used in line 6. (Shakespeare uses 'franchise' once, in *Cymbeline*: 3.1.55.) There is a glancing reference to the Phaeton myth in *Titus Andronicus* when Titus speaks to Tamora:

> ...thy chariot-wheels;
> And then I'll come and be thy **waggoner**,
> And whirl along with thee about the globe.
>
> (5.2.47)

The word '**waggoner**' is used in *Romeo and Juliet* (first performed 1594-5 and published in 1597) when Juliet wishes time away:

> Gallop apace, you fiery-footed steeds,
> Towards Phoebus' lodging: such a **waggoner**
> As **Phaethon** would whip you to the west,
> And bring in cloudy night immediately.
>
> (3.2.1)

In *Richard II* first performed 1595-6, (published in 1597) the king compares his fall to that of Phaeton:

> Down, down I come; like glistering **Phaethon**,
> Wanting the manage of unruly jades.
>
> (3.3.178)

In the same scene there are the words 'summer', 'green', 'friend(s)', 'peace', 'spring', all of which are in the Phaeton sonnet; there are also the words 'infranchisement, 'barren', 'flower', 'larks should sing', 'tempest', 'thund'ring', that recall the words 'franchise', 'barrenness', 'flowrie/flowrets', "birds doo sing" and 'stormes' in the sonnet.

Whilst not naming him there is a Phaeton image in *Venus and Adonis* (see below). This myth then was important to the young playwright, yet after *Richard II* he ceases to use it. In 1598 *Love's Labour's Lost* was published as by 'W. Shakspere' and the same year *Richard II* and *Richard III* were identified as by 'William Shakespeare'. The implication is that once the name 'Shakespeare' was established as that of the playwright, the image of Phaeton ceases to appear in the plays. I hypothesise then that 'Phaeton' was Neville's nom-de-plume before he chose the pseudonym 'Shakespeare'.

Thomas Dekker had written a play called *Fayeton* (*Phaeton*)[1] by 1598 (the year after the last of 'Shakespeare's' Phaeton images

---

[1] See Ward & Waller (1907–21): this play was mentioned in Henslowe's diary. The Henslowe family knew Neville, as Henslowe's father was the keeper of Ashdown Forest, which the Nevilles still partly owned and which was situated near to Henry Neville's home in Mayfield, East Sussex.

appeared in *Richard II*). Sadly it is now lost. It was presented at court in December-January 1600-1, during the build up to the Essex Rebellion. I hypothesise that Dekker was aware of the possible political significance of this myth, about the fall of a man who tried to drive the Sun's chariot. Indeed the appearance of this play, with its possible political content, may have been one reason why Neville stopped using the Phaeton myth after this date. There is a strong probability that Dekker knew Neville. Dekker's ancestry, though uncertain, was Dutch.[2] Not only was Gresham (Neville's great uncle) trading from Antwerp, but also he was actually one of the main merchants featured in Dekker's plays.[3] Neville took over Gresham's iron works as soon as he returned from his continental and Scottish touring, and by 1585 - the year after his marriage - settled in Mayfield[4], taking on the serious business of manufacturing and merchanting his cannons. Ironmastery, with the need to control fire and molten metals, might well have suggested the Phaeton image to the young poet.

The Troublesome Raigne of John and the Phaeton sonnet
This anonymous play and the Phaeton sonnet were both published in the same year: 1591. In the play the Phaeton reference is not to his dangerous career as solar driver but to his questionable parentage: "**Phaeton** mistrusting silly **Merop** for his Sire..." (1.1.342). As already noted, Phaeton's earthly father, Merop, is also mentioned in the early Shakespeare play *The Two Gentlemen of Verona* (3.1.153). The myth is taken from Shakespeare's favourite classical source, Ovid. There is a quotation from the Latin of Ovid's *Metamorphoses* in *The Troublesome Raigne* (6.106). This myth is integral to the play both psychologically and politically. Philip, who uses it, speaks of how his "mounting minde doth soar too high" (1.1.264), and of "honor's fire" (1.1.278). In the following scene King Philip of France refers obliquely to the Phaeton image:

> Twice should not Titan hide him in the west,
> To coole the fet-locks of his wearie team,
> Till I had with an unresisted shock
> Controld the **mannage** of proud Angiers walls...
>
> (1.2.9)

---

[2] ODNB, 2004, Vol 15, 697, Twyning, J. See also James, 2007c, 73.
[3] McVeagh (1982)
[4] See the Couthorpe ms. ref. (discovered by Tim Cornish.)

Here the Sun (Titan) is equated with kingship and the management of unruly horses with the task of the ruler. (This is precisely the usage Richard II makes of the Phaeton image: of "glistering **Phaethon**, Wanting the **manage** of unruly jades" 3.3.178). The theme is integral to the play and many passages refer to the dangers of "overdaring arrogance" (Scene 8, 5), such as:

> Peter: Clime not overhie [= Climb not over high]
>   For from aloft thy fortunes stands in hazard thou shalt die.
>
>   (6.124)

The myth opens with Phaeton asking his mother whether his father really was the Sun, Phoebus, and not Merop. In the play Philip Fauconbridge chooses this image as he begins to question his mother about who his real father was. In the first scene we see his dispute with his brother, Robert Fauconbridge, the legitimate son of Sir Robert and Lady Margaret Fauconbridge, for his inheritance. It is then revealed that Philip is the illegitimate son of Richard I, the Lionheart. King John resolves the dispute and knights Philip as Sir Richard Plantagenet. Holinshed recounted that Richard Cœur-de-lion had a bastard son, Philip, who avenged his death by killing the Viscount of Limoges (Honigmann, 1954, xxii). McLynn (2006, 93) confirms that Richard I "certainly had one acknowledged bastard, named Philip, born in the pre-1189 period who is said to have become lord of Cognac later in life." In *The Troublesome Raigne of John*, 'The Bastard', is called Fauconbridge; in *King John* he is Faulconbridge. This name however is an unhistorical invention by the playwright. There was a Philip de Falconbridge who, as Archdeacon of Huntingdon in 1222 (after King John's death), was the successor to William Cornehill, one of John's right hand men and he may have been a receiver of Church goods seized by John, like his namesake, the Bastard in the plays, but he was not the son of Richard the Lionheart (Honigmann, 1954, xxv).

The name 'Fauconbridge' conceals a Neville connection: Thomas, Bastard of Fauconberg, was an illegitimate son of William Neville, Lord Fauconberg and Earl of Kent. (An alternative spelling of Fauconberg was Falconbridge.) The Fauconbridge sub-plot in *The Troublesome Raigne of John*, and again in *King John*, highlights the issues of the transmission of property, power and legitimacy from generation to generation: an issue especially close to Henry Neville as he was most probably born illegitimate (see James, 2008b, chapter 11). This secret shame may indeed be one of the factors behind Neville's decision to remain a hidden author. The bastard Fauconbridge can be seen as an alter-ego for Neville: "the character is changed from a witty, detached, even self-interested commentator into an increasingly thoughtful participant in, and eventually a major director of, the political action" (Braunmuller, 1989, 72). Furthermore by knighting the bastard as Sir Richard Plantagenet, Neville also points to the fact that his family were of royal blood: he was related to the Plantagenet kings (see below, *Henry VI* part 3 and also James and Rubinstein, 2005).

Honigmann (1954, xxiv) in a footnote pointed out that, "The Faulconbridge title came to England with Belasius, Lord Faulconbridge, in 1066. In Shakespeare's day the Belasius family of Yorkshire (for which the title of Fauconberg was revived in the 17th century) would be *the* Faulconbridges. Their circle included the Northumberlands, Rutlands, Lord Burghley and the Archbishop of York." The Nevilles had extensive property in Yorkshire and were also related to the Northumberlands, and to Lord Burghley.

There are five other Falconbridge/Fauconbergs in the canon. The Falconbridge name appears in *Henry VI* part 1 (4.7.67) where it is used as a title - "thrice victorious Lord of Falconbridge" - awarded to the heroic Talbot. In *Henry VI* part 3 (1.1.239): "Stern Falconbridge commands the narrow seas": a clear reference to the real, illegitimate Thomas (Neville) Fauconberg, a sailor who received the freedom of the City of London in 1454 for his part in removing pirates from the North Sea and the English Channel. He was made Vice-Admiral of the Fleet by his cousin Richard, Earl of Warwick (another Neville) of whom he was a zealous supporter. He had also played an active part in placing Edward IV (another Neville) on the throne in 1461 and stayed with Warwick when the 'Kingmaker' changed allegiance. In the ensuing debacle he was arrested and finally beheaded in 1471.

A Jacques Falconbridge is mentioned in *Love's Labours Lost* (2.1.42). In *The Merchant of Venice* (1. 2. 66) Falconbridge is a young English baron who is a hapless suitor for Portia's hand. Fauconberg (or Fauconbridge) occurs twice in *Henry V*, (3.5.44 and 4.8.100) where he is listed as one of the French lords before the battle of Agincourt and then as one of the dead afterwards. In Hall's *Chronicle* an "erle of Fawquenberge" is listed as present at the battle and also, just as in *Henry V*, "the erle of Fauconberge" is a casualty of the battle (Hall, 1965, 65, 72). What is striking when looking at this, Shakespeare's source, is that he chooses to name Fauconberg out of all the other possible names listed by Hall.

Thus between c1588 – 1599 'Shakespeare' was unaccountably using the name of an illegitimate member of the Neville family in his plays!

Indeed there is another figure related to Neville in *The Troublesome Raigne* who announces himself as "I, **Thomas Plantagenet**, Earle of Salisbury" (Scene 11, 221) King John reigned from 1199-1216. During this time the Earl of Salisbury was William de Longespée ('Long-Sword', c 1170- 1226), an illegitimate son of Henry II. His half-brother, King Richard I, married him to a great heiress, Ela, Countess of Salisbury in her own right, and daughter of William, 2nd Earl of Salisbury. By his wife Ela, countess of Salisbury, he had four sons and four daughters, including: Ella, who first married Thomas de Beaumont, 6th Earl of Warwick, and Ida, who first married Ralph de Somery, and then William de Beauchamp.[1] (Henry Neville was related to the Earls of Warwick, Salisbury, and the Beauchamps.)

Who then might **Thomas Plantagenet** of *The Troublesome Raigne* be? The Earldom of Salisbury was granted in 1337 by Edward III to William de Montacute, Lord Montacute (1301-1344), in whose family it remained till 1400, when John, 3rd Earl of this line, was attainted and his titles forfeited. His son **Thomas** (1388-1428) was restored in blood in 1421 and married twice: his second wife being Alice Chaucer, grandaughter of Geoffrey Chaucer the poet. Thomas' daughter (of the first marriage) and heiress, Alice, married Sir Richard Neville (1400-1460), a younger son of Ralph Neville, 1st earl of Westmoreland and a grandson of John of Gaunt, who sat in parliament in right of his wife as Earl of Salisbury.[2]

There are the following 32 words in *The Troublesome Raigne* that are used in the Phaeton sonnet: <u>sweete</u>, **<u>friend</u>**, **<u>name</u>**, **<u>agree(s)</u>**, **spring**, **branch**, **flourish**, **<u>sommer</u>**, **shade**, **<u>pleasure(s)</u>**, **<u>cease</u>**, **<u>winters</u>**, **<u>storme</u>**, **<u>peace</u>**, **<u>living</u>**, **<u>thing</u>**, **<u>little</u>**, **birds**, **doo**, **<u>sing</u>**, **plant**, **vaunt**, **<u>English</u>**, **<u>wits</u>**, **<u>dead</u>**, **lawrell**, **<u>ever</u>**, **<u>greene</u>**, **frute/<u>fruite</u>**, **barraine**, **flower/flowre**, **Italy**. I have retained the spellings used in *The Troublesome Raigne* (Sider, 1979) and for comparison underlined those words that also occur in 'Shakespeare's' *King John*. From this it is evident that the playwright cut some words that are in the Phaeton sonnet from the later version of *King John*, which is believed to date from 1596-7. He also cut the reference to Phaeton. In *King John*, however, the word 'th'enfranchisement' is used: this contains a rare word that does occur in the Phaeton sonnet. What is especially significant about the occurrence of these words in *The Troublesome Raigne* is that there are more Phaeton sonnet words in this play than any other 'Shakespeare' work except *Richard II*. Above all there are three particular words: branch [16], vaunt [4] and laurel [3] (the numbers in square brackets being their occurrence in the whole canon). 'Laurel' is only found in two early plays, written about the time of the

---

[1] From: http://en.wikipedia.org/wiki/William_de_Longespee,_3rd_Earl_of_Salisbury [Accessed 2008]

[2] From: http://www.1911encyclopedia.org/Earls_of_Salisbury [Accessed 2008]

Phaeton sonnet: *Henry VI* part 3 (4.6.34) and *Titus Andronicus* (1.1.77) and the much later *Anthony and Cleopatra* (1.3.101).

The use of the Phaeton myth in *The Troublesome Raigne*, so entirely integrated with the name and parentage of a hidden Neville, does a number of things:

1) It points to Henry Neville's authorship;
2) It strengthens the hypothesis that the Phaeton sonnet is by Shakespeare-Neville;
3) It reveals the meanings behind the use of the Phaeton myth for Neville.
4) It solves the puzzle of which came first: *The Troublesome Raigne* or 'Shakespeare's' *King John*. The former can now be understood to be an early version of the latter, which Neville entirely re-wrote in the mid 1590s (after he had started using the 'Shakespeare' nom-de-plume), cutting out the Phaeton reference to further hide his authorship.
5) The scene of Philip Fauconbridge confronting his mother can be seen as an early version of the Hamlet-Gertrude scene and might even be based on a real scene in which Henry Neville confronted his own mother about his legitimacy. The Hamlet-Gertrude scene begins with Hamlet saying, "Now, mother, what's the matter?" (3, 4, 7) In *The Troublesome Raigne* Lady Fauconbridge starts their conversation with, "What's the matter Philip?" (1, 320).

Neville, Phaeton, Phoebus and Phoenix

In his political career Neville did aspire to hold the reins of government: he came close on two occasions to the highest political office; he also had the greatest artistic ambition, seeking

> ...a Muse of fire that would ascend
> The brightest heaven of invention,
> A kingdom for a stage, princes to act,
> And monarchs to behold the swelling scene.
>
> (*Henry V*, Prologue)

Neville must have known that this 'career' of writer was a potentially dangerous one. His own grandfather had been executed and writers who transgressed were subject not merely to censorship but to mutilation, torture and imprisonment. Sams (1986) suggested that the early play *Edmund Ironside* might have been banned by the censor (it contains an 'unseemly' fight between bishops on stage!). Right from the start then Neville would have had forebodings - which in real life turned out to be

24

accurate: he did fall at the height of his career and ended up in the Tower under threat of execution. It was indeed the play *Richard II*, which contains the last of the Phaeton images, that was performed just two days before the Essex rebellion (February 6th 1601). Sir Thomas Hoby, hearing of Neville's arrest, blamed his impatient ambition: "Neville was ambling towards his preferment, and would needs gallop in all the haste, and so stumbled and fell." (Bruce, 1868, 135) Hoby's imagery of galloping horses and falling recalls the Phaeton myth.

Whilst Phaeton vanishes from the plays and poems after *Richard II*, Phoebus (9 times in the canon) and the Sun (234 times) continued throughout the plays to be an important image symbolising many things including kingship and the Neville family. The three suns image that occurs in *Henry VI* part 3 has been identified by Brenda James as the sign on the banner that the Plantagenet-Nevilles carried into battle (James & Rubinstein, 2005, 260). On seeing three images of the sun (caused by a rare, natural phenomenon, a parhelion) Edward Neville-Plantagenet speaks these lines:

> …we, the sons of brave Plantagenet,
> Each one already blazing in our meeds,
> Should not withstanding join our lights together
> And overshine the earth, as this the world.
> Whate'er it bodes, henceforth will I bear
> Upon my target three fair shining suns.

(2.1.35)

This is the future Edward IV with his brothers, George, Duke of Clarence and Richard, Duke of Gloucester (later Richard III), the sons of Richard Plantagenet. The Nevils are mentioned by name in *Henry VI* part 2 **eight** times (1.1.198 [this first reference is only in the Quarto, not the First Folio]; 1.1.241; 1.3.73; 2.2.8; 2.2.79; 3.2.214; 4.1,90; 5.1.203: this play being written about the same time as the Phaeton sonnet). The above passage about the three sons/suns has at least a hint of Phaeton in 'blazing' and 'overshine'. The sons of Cecily Neville would rise to be rulers of the kingdom, but George and Richard were to fall from the zenith of their power.

Phaeton and Phoebus also echo in the Phoenix. Indeed in *Henry VI* part 3, immediately after Clifford mentions Phaeton, York speaks of a Phoenix rising from his ashes (1.4.35). The Duke of York was Richard Plantagenet, married to Cecily Neville so the phoenix is the Neville line. (I further trace the development of the phoenix image through the Shakespeare plays in chapter 7; see also below). I suspect a connection between these: the Phaeton image is one of burning up in the Sun (Phoebus); the Phoenix is an image of resurrection out of the fire. As such this binary image is a key for Neville's life: the ambitious young man, daring to rise as high perhaps as secretary of state; the older man dying through the disaster of imprisonment and disgrace, to be reborn in his later years and beyond, with intimations of immortality as a playwright and poet. In sonnet 19 he refers to the Phoenix and ends with:

> Yet do thy worst, old Time, despite thy wrong,
> My love shall in my verse ever live young.

The vocabulary of the Phaeton sonnet

Let us now return to examine the Phaeton sonnet for traces of the young 'Shakespeare'. The sonnet opens with the words **'Sweet friend'**: these words are used together in *The Taming of the Shrew*[5], *A Midsummer Night's Dream* and *The Winter's Tale*.

In the sonnet the seasons are mentioned in the following sequence: Spring, Summer, Winter, Spring: despite the mention of fruits there is no Autumn. This is slightly odd. The plays written after the date of this sonnet (1591) were *The Two Gentlemen of Verona* (written 1592-3), *Richard III* (1592-3), *Titus Andonicus* (1593-4), (1594), *Love's Labour's Lost* (1594-5), *Romeo and Juliet* (1595) and *Richard II* (1595-6): all have spring, summer and winter but no autumn. *Titus Andonicus* contains two passages which have the same sequence of seasons without any mention of autumn:

> O earth, I will befriend thee more with rain,
> That shall distil from these two ancient urns,
> Than youthful **April** shall with all his showers:
> In **summer's** drought I'll drop upon thee still;
> In **winter** with warm tears I'll melt the snow
> And keep eternal **spring**-time on thy face,
> So thou refuse to drink my dear sons' blood.
>
> (3.1.16)

> Here stands the **spring** whom you have stain'd with mud,
> This goodly **summer** with your **winter** mix'd.
>
> (5.2.170)

Perhaps more significantly, as we are examining a sonnet, is Sonnet 98, which again has the seasons without mentioning autumn:

> From you have I been absent in the **spring**,
> When proud-pied **April** dress'd in all his trim
> Hath put a spirit of youth in every thing,
> That heavy Saturn laugh'd and leap'd with him.

---

[5] This play also contains some lines, which had already appeared in Marlowe's *Tamburlaine*, in which play the Phaeton reference also occurred.

> Yet nor the lays of birds nor the sweet smell
> Of different flowers in odour and in hue
> Could make me any **summer's** story tell,
> Or from their proud lap pluck them where they grew;
> Nor did I wonder at the lily's white,
> Nor praise the deep vermilion in the rose;
> They were but sweet, but figures of delight,
> Drawn after you, you pattern of all those.
> Yet seem'd it **winter** still, and, you away,
> As with your shadow I with these did play.

In both the first *Titus Andronicus* passage and this sonnet, summer is personified and possessive (having an apostrophe in modernised texts) as is 'Sommers' in the Phaeton sonnet. Between Sonnet 98 and the Phaeton sonnet there are a number of common images: birds, flowers, the poet addresses another person whom he values and sees as a rival attraction to the spring; both poems rhyme 'spring' with 'thing'; both have a hyphenated word (a characteristic device of Shakespeare). Clearly the Phaeton sonnet is a very early work but it is comparable with this later poem.

Again in *Venus and Adonis* (1593) there is no autumn:

> Love's gentle **spring** doth always fresh remain,
> Lust's **winter** comes ere **summer** half be done;
>
> (801-2)

Similarly, whilst winter, spring and summer are all mentioned in *The Rape of Lucrece* (1594) there is no autumn. Given the occurrence of Phaeton in *The Troublesome Raigne of John,* which I have suggested is an early work by Shakespeare-Neville, it is interesting to note that the words '**spring**', '**sommer**', '**winters**', occur in that play but not autumn.

Why no autumn? The word 'autumn' occurs in six plays (*Henry VI* part 3, *The Taming of the Shrew, The Merchant of Venice, A Midsummer Night's Dream, Troilus and Cressida, Antony and Cleopatra* and two sonnets – 97 & 104). All references to autumn appear in mid to late plays, except in *Henry VI* part 3 ("autumn's corn", 5.7.3) and *The Taming of the Shrew* when the lusting Petruchio says:

> ... I will board her, though she chide as loud
> As thunder when the clouds in **autumn** crack.
>
> (1.2.94)

The early plays and poems are the work of a young artist who connects youth, spring, summer, pleasure and lust. Later, as in sonnet 73, he connects autumn with aging. In *Romeo and Juliet* Capulet says:

> Such comfort as do **lusty young** men feel
> When well-apparell'd **April** on the heel
> Of limping **winter** treads, even such delight
> Among fresh female buds shall you this night
> Inherit at my house...
>
> (1.2.26)

At the end of *Love's Labour's Lost* there are songs of Winter (Hiems) and Spring (Ver). The Spring is associated not only with new life but also with lust: when husbands fear the cuckoo (cuckoldry). The words, '**daisies**', '**summer**', '**birds**', occur: they are also in the Phaeton sonnet. Again autumn is not mentioned. The words 'daisy/daisies' occur in *Love's Labour's Lost* and *The Rape of Lucrece*, where the flower is connected with April, in *Hamlet* (4.7.168) and *The Two Noble Kinsmen* (1.1.5). In all these latter cases the daisy is associated with lust. In *As You Like It* there is a song which includes the Phaeton sonnet words "**birds do sing**" (repeated four times: 5.3.19, 25, 31, 37) in the context of '**spring**', and '**sweet**' (and by implication, young) lovers.

Sonnet 12, in the *Passionate Pilgrim*, states:

> Crabbed age and youth cannot live together:
> Youth is full of **pleasance**, age is full of care;
> Youth like **summer** morn, age like **winter** weather;
> Youth like **summer** brave, age like **winter** bare.

Shakespeare uses the word '**pleasance**', which is in the Phaeton sonnet, twice: here and in *Othello*, where it occurs in a context that reminds us of Ovid: Cassio says, "We should, with joy, **pleasance** revel and applause, transform ourselves into beasts!" (2.3.287)

In sonnets 5 and 6 the seasons of Summer and Winter are contrasted as youth and old age. Sonnet 15, in which youth and plants (with their rising sap) are connected with Spring, contains three words that occur in the Phaeton sonnet:

> When I perceive that men as **plants increase**,
> Cheered and cheque'd even by the self-same sky,
> **Vaunt** in their youthful sap...

In *Henry VI,* part 3 (probably written just before the Phaeton sonnet) George says:

> But when we saw our sunshine made our **spring**
> And that thy **summer** bred us no **increase**
> We set the axe to thy usurping root...
>
> (2.2.163)

We see the same words recurring with associations that lead to images of pruning/cutting trees. In the Phaeton sonnet Florio is compared to the

Spring, and by implication a tree, spreading its flourishing branches, flowers and fruits for others' pleasure. The idea of men as plants/branches is a common conceit in the early plays, which use gardening/pruning metaphors. In *Richard II* the Duchess uses the word **'branches'** repeatedly:

> Edward's seven sons, whereof thyself art one,
> Were as seven vials of his sacred blood,
> Or seven fair **branches spring**ing from one root:
> Some of those seven are dried by nature's course,
> Some of those **branches** by the Destinies cut;
> But Thomas, my dear lord, my life, my Gloucester,
> One vial full of Edward's sacred blood,
> One **flourishing branch** of his most royal root,
> Is crack'd, and all the precious liquor spilt,
> Is hack'd down, and his **summer** leaves all faded,
> By envy's hand and murder's bloody axe.
>
> (1.2.11)

Later in *Richard II* the Gardener continues the pruning metaphor:

> O what pity is it
> That he had not so trimm'd and dress'd his land
> As we this garden! We at time of year
> Do wound the bark, the skin of our **fruit-trees,**
> Lest, being <u>over-proud</u> in sap and blood,
> With too much riches it confound itself:
> Had he done so to great and growing men,
> They might have lived to bear and he to taste
> Their **fruits** of duty: superfluous **branches**
> We lop away, that bearing boughs may live:
>
> (3.4.55)

Here the word 'over-proud' recalls Phaeton (and it is in *Richard II* that the image of Phaeton occurs for the last time in the plays). Furthermore, in *Richard II* the following 38 words reminiscent of the Phaeton sonnet occur: "sweet, friend, whose, name, agreed, rival, spring, summer, winter, (no autumn!), branch, flourishing, shadow (of these trees), pleasure, storm, repose, peace, spend, enfranchisement, each, living, thing, singing birds, herbs, plants, release, English, wits, dead, except, ever, green, barren, spreading, pleasure, fruit, flowers, Italy". In fact, virtually every word in the sonnet! The next nearest plays in these terms are *The Two Gentlemen of Verona* (19 key words), *Titus Andronicus* (18 words), *Henry VI* part 3 (17 words), *Love's Labour's Lost* (16 words), *Richard III* (15 words): the earlier the play and the closer to the date of the Phaeton sonnet, the higher the incidence of these words.

In *The Rape of Lucrece*, which is closer in date (published 1594, so probably written in 1593) than *Richard II* (first performed 1595-6 so probably written 1594-5) to the Phaeton sonnet (1591), there is an interesting sequence of images, which echo that sonnet. As Tarquin talks with Lucrece we have the following words in succession: "**birds, moralise, wanton, fruitful Italy, wreaths, stormy, slumber, rest**" (88 - 125). These can be compared with: "**birds, moralitie, pleasures/pleasance, frutes, Italy, laurell, stormes, repose in peace**", in the Phaeton sonnet. These last words "repose in peace" suggest both sleep and death: indeed four lines later the 'English witts lay dead'. In the opening scene of *Titus Andronicus* (1593), laying to rest his dead sons, Titus says:

> In **peace** and honour rest you here, my sons;
> Rome's readiest champions, **repose** you here in rest,...
> Here grow no damned grudges; here are no **storms**,
> No noise, but silence and eternal sleep...
>
> (1.1.153)

The early sonnets, encouraging a young man to become a father, oppose death/barrenness to fruitfulness/fertility, as the Phaeton sonnet does. The very first of Shakespeare's sonnets begins with a line that ends, as does the first line of the Phaeton sonnet, with the word 'increase':

> From fairest creatures we desire **increase**,
> That thereby beauty's rose might never die...

(See also Sonnet 15, which uses the word '**increase**' in relation to the fertility of men and plants.) Sonnet 1 uses the words '**Spring**' and '**sweet**', also found in the Phaeton sonnet, includes flower images (rose and bud) and contrasts famine with abundance, just as the Phaeton sonnet contrasts flourishing with barrenness.

In the Phaeton sonnet the poet uses the word 'flowrets'. This rare word is used just twice by Shakespeare: in *A Midsummer Night's Dream* (1595-6: 4.1.54) and *Henry IV* part 1 (1596: 1.1.9). Brooks (1990, lxii) suggested this word originated from Spencer's *Shepheardes Calendar* (1579). Spencer may be the "ever green" poet in the Phaeton sonnet (see below).

Flowers take us further into gardens and to herbs: as when, in *Richard II*, a servant helping the gardener says:

> ...our sea-walled garden, the whole land,
> Is full of weeds, her fairest **flowers** choked up,
> Her **fruit**-trees all upturned, her hedges ruin'd,
> Her knots disorder'd and her wholesome **herbs**
> Swarming with caterpillars?
>
> (3.4.43)

Friar Laurence in *Romeo and Juliet* (1595), out collecting herbs, says:

> O, mickle is the powerful grace that lies
> In **herbs**, **plants**, stones, and their true qualities:
> For nought so vile that on the earth doth live
> But to the earth some special good doth give...

> (2.3.11)

Just as in the Phaeton sonnet (1591) where the words, 'hearbes', 'gummes', and 'plants' are together, so in *Venus and Adonis* (1593) there is a line:

> Herbs for their smell, and sappy plants to bear...

Within four lines of this the word 'increase' (used in the first line of the Phaeton sonnet) occurs twice. Within a further six lines is a Phaeton image:

> Titan, tired in the midday heat,
> With burning eye did hotly overlook them,
> Wishing Adonis had his team to guide,
> So he were like him and by Venus' side.

> (177-180)

(Titan was another name for Phoebus, the sun, who here is wishing Adonis was Phaeton, taking over the solar chariot so that Titan would be free to embrace Venus!)

Thus the words, images and themes of the Phaeton sonnet echo especially through the early plays and poems: further suggesting a common authorship.

Finally let us also compare the association of the following words from the Phaeton sonnet: "**Sweet friend, green-lockt Sommers shadie pleasures, storms, repose in peace, birds doo sing, ever greene**" with a speech in *Titus Andronicus* where Tamora describes to her friend summer pleasures in a shady spot, where birds sing, and they may sleep:

> The **birds chant melody** on every bush,
> The snake lies rolled in the cheerful sun,
> The **green** leaves quiver with the cooling wind
> And make a chequer'd **shadow** on the ground:
> Under their **sweet shade**, Aaron, let us sit... (five lines cut)
> The wandering prince and Dido once enjoy'd,
> When with a happy **storm** they were surprised
> And curtain'd with a counsel-keeping cave,
> We may, each wreathed in the other's arms,
> Our pastimes done, possess a golden **slumber**

> (2.2.12-26)

I submit that these two pieces of poetry were written by the same writer at about the same time: 1590-93.[3]

As long ago as 1885 W. Minto suggested the Phaeton sonnet was by Shakespeare (Yates, 1968, 130). Only when I had completed the above did I come across Joseph Sobran's 1996 paper on the Phaeton sonnet. Sobran has many, though not all, the points I have made and others I had not discovered. I draw the reader's attention to the following from his paper:

> "**Lines 11-14 - fruits, barrenness, pleasance, Italy**: The antonym of increase, barrenness is a theme of the *Sonnets*, which use the word barren six times... And in Shakespeare, barren is often accompanied by fruit. Compare *Venus*, where fruitless chastity (751) is followed by barren dearth (754). Or see *A Midsummer Night's Dream* (1.1.72-3), where a barren sister is imagined chanting hymns to the cold fruitless moon. What is more, Phaeton's association of fruit and pleasance with Italy in the concluding section of this poem calls up several passages in Shakespeare. *Lucrece* yields us barren skill (81) and, four stanzas later, fruitful Italy (107). *The Taming of the Shrew* (1.1.3-4) gives us fruitful Lombardy, The pleasant garden of great Italy.
> And in *Antony and Cleopatra* (2.5.23-5), Cleopatra welcomes the messenger from Rome with a sensual image:
>
> > O, from Italy!
> > Ram thou thy fruitful tidings in mine ears,
> > That long time have been barren.
>
> The Phaeton sonnet should be studiously compared with Sonnets 1, 5, 11, 12, 13, 15, 18, 54, 68, 73, 97, 98, 102, and 103 for theme, style, sentiment, imagery, vocabulary, rhyme patterns, and other affinities. Sonnets 97 and 98 are surely the work of the same hand that wrote the Phaeton sonnet, which they echo in the words winter, pleasure, bareness, summer's, increase, decease, fruit, birds, sing, spring, sweet, flowers, shadow, and various synonyms and paraphrases.
> If internal evidence alone can prove authorship, Shakespeare wrote the Phaeton sonnet. It certainly deserves at least parenthetical inclusion in the canon. Its early date certainly poses a problem – but only for those who assume that 'Shakespeare' must mean the Stratford man born in 1564."
>
> Sobran, (1996)

---

[3] Brenda James has also pointed out to me that 'Golden Slumbers kiss your eyes' appears in a play by Dekker - the playwright who seems so likely to have known Neville and the Greshams, and who wrote the now lost *Fayeton*.

Sobran however concluded that Shakespeare was the Earl of Oxford! He does however state that Florio later referred to an unnamed "friend" of his as "a gentleman" who "loved better to be a poet than to be accounted one." This could of course be Neville: I shall explore the connections between them below.

In *The Life and Times of William Shakespeare*, Peter Levi (1988) stated that the Phaeton sonnet: "is surely by Shakespeare: he certainly knew Florio, though we don't know when they met, and no other poet in 1591 could have written the sonnet." He added: "No other writer of sonnets is as good as this except Spenser, but Spenser would have signed it. The humour is Shakespeare's, and so is the movement of thought, so is the seasonal coloring."

One further theme is implicit in the Phaeton sonnet that ties it into the Shakespeare canon: the relationship between Art and Nature. This is especially explored in *Love's Labour's Lost, The Winter's Tale* and *The Tempest*. In this early sonnet Art and Nature are related through images of Florio's productivity being as creative as the Spring. One could see Phaeton himself as the artist, attempting to rival Nature in driving the chariot of the Sun.

Sonnet Form

Philip Watts and Katherine Duncan-Jones both pointed out to me that this sonnet does not conform to Shakespeare's normal sonnet form and rhyme scheme:

abab cdcd ef ef gg

It can better be described as a variety of Petrarchan (Italian) sonnet form, with the rhyme scheme:

abba abba cdcd ee

To say that because it is not in normal 'Shakespearean' sonnet form means that he could not have written it, is to deny that the poet could write in other forms. This is patently absurd since the bard was able to write in any form he chose and used different forms for his other poems. Even within the sonnet sequence, we have Sonnet 145, with its quatrameters instead of pentameters, and Sonnet 126, with its twelve lines and **aa bb cc dd ee ff** rhyme scheme. Furthermore Minto (1885, 373-380) pointed out that the English sonnet form was only established by Daniel and Drayton in 1592 and 1594, after the Phaeton sonnet was published. "Before that Sir Philip Sidney, who set the fashion of sonnet-writing at the time, had followed the Italian model" (Cockburn, 1998, 162). "Whoever 'Phaeton' was I should guess that he was someone fluent in Italian…" (Duncan-Jones, personal communication, 26/2/07). Neville and his father had both spent time in Italy before 1591. Both could read and speak Italian. It is entirely appropriate that this sonnet, addressed to an Italian, be in an Italianate form. Furthermore there was an active dispute at the time between Petrarchists and anti-Petrarchists and this is rehearsed in the twelfth dialogue in Florio's *Second Fruits*. In his *Eroici Furori* (1585) Giordano Bruno, an anti-Petrarchist, used a Petrarchan sonnet to address Sir Philip Sidney on Neoplatonic love. Florio quotes from Bruno on the Petrarchan controversy in the twelfth dialogue of *Second Fruits* (Yates, 1936, 109-14).

Sonnets 1591-98
Sir Philip Sidney's sonnet sequence *Astrophil and Stella* was published in 1591 (he had written these in 1580-3; he died in 1586). In 1591 John Clapham, one of Burghley's secretaries, dedicated a Latin poem 'Narcissus' to the Earl of Southampton; this was part of a poetic campaign to persuade the young man to marry Burghley's granddaughter. (Bate, 1993, 98) In 1593 Shakespeare dedicated his *Venus and Adonis* to the same Earl. Other sonnets by the bard were also on this topic. However it is not possible to date the sonnets exactly or to be sure of a definite earliest date: scholars have suggested Shakespeare started writing sonnets between 1591 – 1594 (Duncan-Jones, 2005, 17-19). The Phaeton sonnet must have been written in 1590 or the first quarter of 1591 (Florio dates his own address to the reader April 30th 1591 so we can presume it was written before then). There is a continuity with the sonnets addressed to young Southampton: the Phaeton sonnet celebrates Florio's productivity, his fruitfulness. The poet uses the word 'increase' in the first line. He contrasts flourishing Spring with barrenness.

We know from Francis Mere's *Palladis Tamia* (1598) that Shakespeare's sonnets were circulating amongst his friends in manuscript long before they were published. *Love's Labour's Lost* (probably first performed 1594-5, published 1598), contained four sonnets. The earliest these might then have been written would be 1593: between *Venus and Adonis* and *The Rape of Lucrece*, when Shakespeare's poetic skills were in full flower. Therefore we must consider the *Love's Labour's Lost* sonnets are perhaps the closest in date to the composition of the Phaeton sonnet. They are different in kind, being parodies of conventional love sonnets. In two of them the Sun and Jove (Jupiter, whose lightning bolt killed Phaeton) are mentioned. The Phaeton sonnet has an element of parody - the final lines:

> Sutch frutes, sutch flowrets of moralitie,
> Were nere before brought out of Italy.

contain an implicit suggestion that previously Italy had only exported immorality! There may even be a hint here that the poet was gently sending up Florio, who was of Italian parentage. The general view of Italy as a land of licentiousness was then a commonplace among Englishmen, who even spoke of venereal disease as being Italian in origin. Shakespeare used the word 'morality' just once: in *Measure for Measure* (1.2.110).

Did Florio know Henry Neville?

From his letters to his brother Robert in 1578 and 1580 we know that Sir Philip Sidney knew Neville (mentioning him twice by name) and that it is highly likely that Neville had access to an early copy of his *Arcadia* (Duncan-Jones, 1991, 171). From late 1583 Neville was involved in the manufacture of ordnance and it is possible that Sidney had, by the autumn of 1583, gained a role in the office of Ordnance: he certainly worked in that office in 1584, and in 1585 was made joint Master of Ordinance. In 1584 Neville had become an MP. The very next year, in 1585, Sidney became the Member of Parliament for Kent, and this was the same year that Neville settled in Mayfield, East Sussex. Therefore in poetry, parliament and ordnance and through his contact with brother Robert, it is highly likely that Neville knew Sir Philip Sidney. Moreover, Neville's father was a friend of Henry Sidney, father of Philip and Robert. In a letter to his son Robert, dated 1578, Sir Henry Sidney wrote: "There can be no greater love than of long time hath been and yet is, between Sir Henry Neville and me; and so will continue to our lives end" (Duncan, 1974, 16). It is highly likely that John Florio also knew Sidney: he had been Italian tutor to Sidney's best friend Fulke Greville, whose mother was Anne Neville, daughter of the 4th Earl of Westmoreland. Florio may have helped Fulke Greville with the 1590 publication of Sidney's *Arcadia* (Evans, 1987, 13). Fulke Greville and Neville were both M.P.s and members of the Mitre Club. Neville mentioned meeting Greville in a letter dated 13/8/1609 (James, 2008b, 179-180).

Sir Philip Sidney is mentioned in the twelfth chapter of Florio's *Second Fruits*: a nighttime dialogue about woman and love. Sidney's works definitely underlie *Love's Labour's Lost* (Yates, 1936, 150). Florio's father had lived in Burleigh's house and as Sidney was Burleigh's ward after his father's death, it is possible that Florio had met Sidney early in his life.

Florio lived in Oxford from 1576: as Neville was at Merton College, Oxford, from 1574 it is possible they met even at this time.

When, in 1578, Neville left Oxford for his European travels, Florio also left and then lived in London for 2 years (1578-80) before returning to Oxford and becoming a scholar at Magdalen College until 1581 (Yates, 1968, 27-8, 53).

In the spring of 1583 Neville returned from his travels. On April 13th 1583 Giordano Bruno arrived in London. Bruno travelled to Oxford in the hope of gaining a post and took part in academic debates. In June, the Polish Prince Albert Laski came to Oxford with Sir Philip Sidney and on the return journey they visited Dr. John Dee (who had been Sidney's tutor). Bruno met John Florio in Oxford and they became friends: they then lived together at the residence of the French Ambassador, Castelnau, in London where Florio was employed as a language tutor. Bruno wrote a number of books during his two-year stay and he may have worked for Walsingham as a spy (Bossy, 1991). It is also possible that Florio worked for Walsingham as a spy (Yates, 1936, 36). From August – October 1583 Walsingham and Neville went to Scotland (thereby missing Sidney's wedding to Walsingham's daughter) and there is clear evidence that Neville was involved in intelligence work (James, 2007c).

In 1584 February-March, Bruno wrote about a meal ('Cena') with Fulke Greville. Florio himself is mentioned in the 'La Cena de le Ceneri' as a friend who accompanies Bruno to the meal (Yates, 1968, 48, 92). In July that year Sir Philip Sidney helped Bruno revise his 'Cena'. Therefore through his contact with Greville and Bruno, Florio would have come into contact with Sidney. Yates (2002) suggested that Bruno's Neoplatonic ideas influenced Shakespeare. Before he had come to England Bruno had written a comic play, *Candelaio*, which Florio knew well (Yates, 1968, 111). It is therefore possible that Neville met Florio and Bruno during this period. Indeed, it would be strange had he not done so, for Bruno was an enthusiastic adherent of the Copernican theory so Neville, who majored in Astronomy at Merton, would surely have sought him out.

If *Second Fruits* was probably written in the years 1585-90 (being published in 1591) it must have been in preparation for some time; (the *First Fruits* had been published in 1578). Neville was travelling in Europe from 1578-83. His early writing would have been developing perhaps from 1587 if not earlier: the first plays were certainly on the stage from 1590. So *Second Fruits* was published right at the start of Neville's career as a writer.

Lady Jane Grey was a pupil of John Florio's father (ODNB, 2004, Vol 20, 165, O'Connor, D.). Neville's father had been instrumental in promoting her as monarch, so it is probable the families already knew each other. Further evidence of Florio's possible contact with Neville is that at some time from 1591, and certainly before 1594, when the Earl of Southampton would have been 21 years old, John Florio was Southampton's tutor, appointed by Lord Burghley (Yates, 1936, 192). Neville knew Southampton as a boy in Burghley's house, so he could hardly have avoided meeting Florio. During this period Shakespeare-Neville published his poems *Venus and Adonis* (1593) and *The Rape of Lucrece* (1594) dedicated to Southampton. In 1598 Florio dedicated his *World of Words* Italian-English Dictionary to Southampton. Not only was Florio Southampton's tutor, he later became Prince Henry's (James I's eldest son), and Henry Neville often spoke to the Prince. Indeed, he wrote of him to Winwood. Southampton and Neville were not only related but also shared their friends and relations. For instance, Southampton became Governor of the Isle of Wight, and his deputy was a Worsley - brother of Neville's son in law. Neville is reported by John Chamberlain as being a frequent visitor to the Isle, after his daughter, Frances, went to live there with her husband, Richard Worsley. Neville and Southampton were known as 'Damon and Pythias' because their relationship was so close, and they later spent two years together in the Tower of London following the Essex rebellion.

In 1600 Florio's translation of Montaigne's essays was registered. There is some evidence that this book influenced Shakespeare (Yates, 1968, 244-5; see also chapter 2). It was published in 1603 and dedicated to Mary Neville (daughter of Sir Thomas Sackville, Lord Buckhurst – later first Earl of Dorset - and author of Gorboduc, the first English tragedy). She had married Sir Henry Neville, the 7th Lord Abergavenny, cousin of our Henry. She was thus related to Henry Neville through marriage, and Neville had been a neighbour of his cousins, the Barons Abergavenny, when he lived in Mayfield from 1585 - 1598. Mary Neville was also called Moll and was a friend of Anne Clifford, wife of Richard Sackville, 3rd Earl of Dorset (grandson of Sir Thomas). She was Richard Sackville's aunt. Mary Neville took part in court theatricals, dancing in the Masque of Beauty on 10th January 1608 (Chambers, 1923, Vol 3, 380). The Sackvilles had a portrait of Florio painted by Mytens, (mentioned by the 6th Earl of Dorset in 1690:Yates, 1968, 241).

Florio was a friend of Ben Jonson who created the First Folio. Jonson wrote a poem to Neville: "Who now calls on thee, Nevil, is a muse" (James & Rubinstein, 2005, 251). Florio was also a tutor, friend and protégé of William Herbert, 3rd Earl of Pembroke to whom the First Folio is dedicated. Neville was, latterly, also a friend of the Earl of Pembroke. Florio also knew TT: Thomas Thorpe, publisher of

Shakespeare's sonnets and probably part author of the dedication code that was eventually to reveal Neville's identity. There is a report that Florio later lived in Mitre Court, Fleet Street, where Neville attended the Mitre Inn Literary Symposium between 1608-11 (Yates, 1936, 14; Gayley 1914, 146).

Florio and Shakespeare

Yates (1936) established that Shakespeare was parodying Florio's *Second Fruits* (1591) in *Love's Labour's Lost* (1593-6). I agree with her that no one person can be seen as the original of any character in the plays: as a creative artist the bard drew his characters from many sources. Yates however found good evidence that traces of Florio can be found in that play in its pedantic and verbose figure of Holofernes and that Shakespeare was parodying various literary crazes of the day including Petrarchism, sonneteering, and the mania for proverbs. Florio's *Second Fruits* is stuffed with proverbs. One of them, about Venice (which is in the sixth dialogue about travel, see Simonini, 1977, 106-7) is directly quoted by Holofernes:

> I may speak of thee as the traveller does of Venice:
>> Venetia, Venetia,
>> Chi non ti vede non ti pretia.

(4.2.93-98)

Both Neville and his father had spent time in Venice.

In the last dialogue in *Second Fruits*, Florio "sets out arguments for and against love, the Petrarchist and anti-Petrarchist dispute which was a commonplace of the Italian Renaissance" (Yates, 1936, 24). Furthermore Yates reminds us that Florio is alluding to the anti-Petrarchan tirade that Giordano Bruno addressed to Sir Philip Sidney, the latter being mentioned by name in this dialogue. Yates continues: "I am convinced that this dialogue was carefully studied by Shakespeare and that there are undoubted echoes of it in the arguments for and against love and sonnet-writing in *Love's Labour's Lost*" (Yates, 1936, 24). She provides much more detailed evidence for Florio's influence than we have space for here. She shows how important a source *Second Fruits* was for *Love's Labour's Lost* and so Shakespeare must have read it. The Phaeton sonnet is in a Petrarchan form. If Henry Neville were Phaeton he would have had access to the book even before it was published!

Phaeton and Phoenix

In *Henry VI* part 3, written about the same time as *Second Fruits*, immediately after the first mention of Phaeton is a phoenix image:

> York: My ashes, as the **phoenix**, may bring forth
> A bird that will revenge upon you all...

> (1.4.35)

This image recurs when Sir William Lucy says:

> ...from their ashes shall be rear'd
> A **phoenix** that shall make all France afeard.

> (4.7.92)

In chapter 12 of *Second Fruits*, in a dialogue about love, the Phoenix is mentioned:

> "There is but one **Fenix** in the world, and she is female, nature apt to all the world is a woman: so is her imitatour arte, is not the mistres, nay the princes(s), nay the foundres(s) of good artes Minerva onely of all that ever were born of a man, not of a woman, not of the thigh or ribbe of a man, but of the brayne of highest Jove, is she not a woman? A woman shall I say, or a goddesse? A Goddesses indeed: for such women are deservedly called Godesse, who for their excellencie and goodnesse have bin deified, as Diana for chastity, and Ceres for her needful huswiferie.
> Why add you not Venus to them for letchery? The mother of your love, & mistris of your mistery? Belike your count is soone cast with a cipher of nothing, adding nought unto nought: for as you condemne none, so you commend but one, and **one is none unless it be in opinion,**
> > For as the **Phenix** still doth live alone,
> > Because that more than one was never seene,
> > So is there none nor never was but one,
> > That hath a virtuous woman beene..."

The dialogue continues about women in general. The above passage is interesting because of Shakespeare-Neville's use of these images, of the phoenix, Venus and the personification of art as a woman (Hermione in *The Winter's Tale*: the statue becoming woman). This passage of Florio's was written just before *Venus and Adonis* was written. Adonis dies but is resurrected in the flower (the violet). Phaeton is the ambitious young artist who dares to ascend the brightest heaven of invention; the Phoenix is the immortal artist who is reborn from the flames of the creative process, his works of art the flowers of his creativity. The poet Phaeton praises Florio's dialogues as 'flowrets'. Furthermore, as Shakespeare-Neville continues through the plays to use the image of the phoenix, it gradually evolves until it is a woman: Iachimo compares Imogen to "the arabian bird" in *Cymbeline,* (1.6.17), meaning the phoenix. The flower imagery also develops concurrently: Imogen is also a lily ("fresh lily", 2.2.15 and "O sweetest, fairest lily!" 4.2.202). The phoenix and the lily are again linked in *Henry VIII* as images of Elizabeth I (5.5. 40 & 61). (For an analysis of the Phoenix image in the late plays see chapter 7.)

Finally, Florio's reference to '**one is none** unless it be in opinion' is directly echoed in Sonnet 136:

> In things of great receipt with ease we prove,
> Among a number **one is reckoned none**.
> Then in the number let me pass untold...

which latter sentiment also accords with Florio's remark that a friend of his loved being a poet more than being *accounted* one. Furthermore, if Brenda James is correct in suggesting the Sonnets contain some significant numbering, then with the number 136 we have $1+3+6 = 10$, and $1 + 0 = 1$, and $1 \times 0 = 0$, which result both underlies the subject of the poem, and attests to the fact that its writer was interested in mathematics (which we know Neville was).

Henry Neville in *Second Fruits*

Real people are behind at least some of the named figures in Florio's dialogues. In the very first chapter he introduces Nolano as he gets up in the morning. Giordano Bruno called himself 'the Nolan'. Florio and Bruno lived together in the French embassy 1583-5 so Florio would have known what Bruno was like first thing in the morning! The dialogue shows us a Nolano who is an early riser, a rather demanding companion who rouses his sleepy friend. He is also something of a poet: he says, "You should rise with Aurora who is a friend to the Muses."

I believe that Henry Neville himself appears in the second dialogue of *Second Fruits*: identified by his first name. Three men John, Thomas and **Henry** meet in the street. John is probably John Florio himself: this latter identification is supported by Yates (1968, 126). (John is G for Giovanni, Italian for John.)

> G. Good Lord, see whether master Henry is comming towards vs.
> T. It is even he. O master Henrie you are verie well met.
> H. I kisse your worships hands.
> G. What shall we doo until it be dinner time?
> H. Any thing pleaseth me, so we may doo something.
> T. As for me I referr my selfe to the companie.
> G. Let vs make a match at tenis.
> H. Agreed, this coole morning calls for it.
> T. And afterwards we will dine together.
> G. And then after dinner we will goe see a plaie.

H. The plaies that they plaie in England, are not right comedies.
T. Yet they doo nothing else but plaie every daye.
H. Yea but they are neither right comedies, nor right tragedies.
G. How would you name them then?
H. Representations of histories, without any decorum.
G. Go to, let vs determine some thing to auoyde idelnes.
T. Let vs goe plaie at tennis.

This tantalising exchange provides us perhaps with a fragment of a real conversation between the young playwright and his friends. A number of things are clear. Henry is called **master** Henry: Neville was not knighted until 1596 (James & Rubinstein, 2005, 119). Henry is a young man with a serious and critical interest in theatre. He is interested in the correct way to write plays, using the words 'right' and 'decorum'. He speaks of "representations of histories" at precisely the time when Shakespeare was writing his first history plays. His early comedy, *The Comedy of Errors* was very much based on a classical model (Plautus). He uses the word 'decorum' in a technical sense.

> "In classical rhetoric, the principle of **decorum** controlled what was appropriate to each of the main styles into which Hellenistic and Latin rhetors had divided written literature: the grand style, the middle style and the low (or plain) style. Certain types of vocabulary and diction were considered appropriate for certain stylistic levels. In the Renaissance the term was used more widely to suggest the appropriate or 'fitting' style for particular subject matter. Thus a strict neo-classicist would regard laughter in tragedy as a breach of decorum"
>
> (personal e-mail communication 6/2/07 from Jonathan Bate, Professor at Warwick University).

As a young artist Shakespeare-Neville would be interested in form and style: what was correct and what was innovative. "He practiced the recognised Renaissance ideal of decorum, suiting the style to the action..." (Cairncross, 1965, xxxii). Bate (1993, 3) however sees many similarities between Shakespeare and Ovid, including "a refusal to submit to the decorums of genre..." Whilst at first Shakespeare-Neville looked to classical models of Ovid, Plautus and Seneca, he very soon developed his own style and departed from narrow 'decorum' to mix comedy and tragedy. In Florio's dialogue however Henry laments the state of English theatre. Furthermore there is here a link with the Phaeton sonnet: the poet there complaining of the barrenness of the English literary scene and that "all our English witts lay dead". Indeed Sir Philip Sidney had died in 1586: a disaster for the English literary renaissance. Cockburn (1998, 162, note 1) believed that 'the Laurell' (in the Phaeton sonnet) that is 'ever greene' was Edmund Spencer. Florio praised Spencer in his dedicatory epistle. In Sonnet 8 of *The Passionate Pilgrim* (1599) Spencer is mentioned by name. Brenda James believes this to be addressed to Anne Killigrew, Neville's wife, who loved music. Significantly for this context sonnet 8 mentions Phoebus. Alternatively this 'ever greene' Laurel could be a reference to Robert Greene, a prolific writer who, the very next year, attacked 'Shake-scene' in his *Groatsworth of Wit*! The spelling of 'greene' with a final 'e' is perhaps significant here. Greene travelled extensively between 1578 and 1583 (Halliday, 1977, 247), precisely the years during which Neville toured the continent, so they may have met. Greene died in 1592, the year after the Phaeton sonnet was published. Greene's *Pandosto* was, 18 years later, to be the source for *The Winter's Tale*. However, given that the laurel crown was awarded to distinguished poets (Greene wrote prose works and plays) I think Spencer is the likelier candidate. His *Faerie Queene* was published in 1590: just a year before the Phaeton sonnet. A book of Spencer's poems (*Complaints*) was published the same year (1591). Spencer probably met Sir Philip Sidney at some time between 1577-80: during these years Neville was at Oxford and travelling abroad. Spencer then went to Ireland from whence he returned with the manuscript of *The Faerie Queene* in 1590. If Neville ever met Spencer it would perhaps have been at this time, just before the Phaeton sonnet appeared, possibly at a literary soiree in his father-in-law's house in London.

There is another view of the Henry-Thomas-Giovanni dialogue on theatre available to us: Yates (1936, 37-38) thought that it expressed Florio's own pedantic views. "He remained an adherent of the 'classical', a supporter of Jonson's 'art' rather than Shakespeare's 'nature', throughout his life." Of course since Florio is the writer of this dialogue he may well have projected his own views into the mouth of his speaker. Indeed in the *First Fruits* the first dialogue contained a criticism of the theatre from a Puritan standpoint: "I believe there is much Knavery used at those Comedies…" This may also relate to Stephen Gosson's attack on the stage, *The School of Abuse*, which prompted Sidney's *Defence of Poesy* (Yates, 1968, 42). In the *Defence*, which was written in 1581 but only published in 1595, Sidney criticised English theatre for not observing the Aristotelian unities of place, time and action. Florio then in *Second Fruits* was following up a current controversy about theatre. However this could still be seen as the remnant of a real conversation between Henry Neville and John Florio: the response to his question,

John: How would you name them then?
Henry: Representations of histories…

is telling, given that Shakespeare-Neville was writing history plays at the time. Yates further suggested that this little dialogue and the subsequent caricature of Holofernes, the pedant, could be taken as evidence of a public argument between Florio, Shakespeare and others including John Eliot and Thomas Nashe. Her suggestion is that Florio felt wounded by the satire in *Love's Labour's Lost* and complained bitterly in the preface to his 1598 dictionary:

> "Let Aristophanes and his comedians make plaies, and scowre their mouths on Socrates; those very mouthes they make to **vilify**, shall be the means to amplifie his virtue."
>
> (Yates, 1936, 48)

The Comtesse de Longworth Chambrun suggested the Henry of this dialogue is in fact Henry Wriothesley, Earl of Southampton (Yates, 1968, 125). In 1591 he would have been 18 years old so this is not impossible but perhaps improbable, given that *Second Fruits* would have been written in the years before 1591 when Southampton was but a lad. Neville however had been writing plays from about 1587 so would have had time and motive for discussions with Florio about theatre. Moreover, there may even be a pun included in the above extract: '**vilify**' could be meant to represent part of Ne**vil**le's name. (Similarly, the title page of *Venus and Adonis* begins with a quotation from Ovid '**Vil**is vulgus...')

Who then might the Thomas in this dialogue have been? This could be Thomas Nashe, pamphleteer and satirist. Some scholars think he wrote parts of the *Henry VI* plays (1590-2), so his appearance with Neville in *Second Fruits* (1591) would fit the chronology exactly. He certainly wrote about the death of Talbot in *Henry VI* part 1 in his *Pierce Peniless* the very next year (1592). "Nashe's favourable mention suggested that it was written by a friend of his" (Cairncross, 1965, xxix). Other scholars see Nashe as an enemy of Shakespeare and a follower of Greene in his attacks on the young bard. The problem vanishes when we consider there were two men: the actor Shakespeare and the playwright Neville: Nashe may then be a satirist of the former and a friend of the latter (just as Ben Jonson was). He may not at this time have known that Neville was the hidden writer. In Florio's dialogue, Thomas doesn't say anything about theatre except a joke. It is noticeable that Thomas makes other jokes during the dialogue and Henry is serious: Neville was known as a serious young man, though the son of a sometimes merry father. Neville and his family were later to be referred to as 'a merry crew' by Robert Cecil, but it is indeed probable that Neville's very early 'book-learnedness' came from a serious attitude to his studies, especially when young. Nashe however was a satirical humourist and had already been mentioned by Florio in the dedication to *Second Fruits*, though under a pseudonym he had used in writing an amusing astrological tract published the same year (Yates, 1968, 128). In *Pierce Peniless*, Nashe explicitly dissociated himself from Greene's attack on 'Shake-scene':

> "Other news I am aduertised of that a scald triuial lying pamphlet, cald Greens groatsworth of wit is giuen out to be of my doing. God neuer haue care of my soule, but vtterly renou[n]ce me, if the least word or sillable in it proceeded from my pen, or if I were any way priuie to the writing or printing of it."

If Nashe were a friend of Neville, he would want to publicly disassociate himself from the attack on 'Shake-scene', especially if he knew that Neville was about to use William Shakespeare as a pseudonym (although this name did not appear until the next year, 1593). In 1591 Nashe wrote a preface to Sidney's *Astrophil and Stella*: as Sidney's and Neville's fathers were best friends it is likely that Neville knew the man who wrote this preface. Nashe dedicated his *Unfortunate Traveller* (1594) to the Earl of Southampton, Neville's best friend. Nashe also wrote poetry dedicated to the Earl of Southampton. Nashe was a friend of Ben Jonson too, and Jonson knew Neville - firstly through Neville's and Savile's friendship with Camden (who was Jonson's headmaster and private tutor) and secondly through the Mitre Club. Some scholars think Moth in *Love's Labour's Lost* is Nashe. Nashe is named in the Northumberland Manuscript: the only contemporary document which brings together the names of Neville and Shakespeare. Probably scribbled in 1597 it includes several versions of his first name, Thomas, and the title of a play by him:

		Thomas
Ile of Dogs frmnt	Thom	Thom
by Thomas Nashe	inferior	plaiers[4]

Brenda James believes at least some of this is in Neville's handwriting and Burgoyne (1904) thought the Northumberland Manuscript had originally belonged to Henry Neville. *The Isle of Dogs* was a satirical comedy written by Nashe and Jonson and acted in July 1597 but then suppressed as slanderous and thus lost to us. Jonson and others were imprisoned (Cockburn, 1998, 168). That Neville should have once owned a copy of a banned play by Nashe is suggestive of some contact between them. Nashe's name has also been found by Brenda James in the Dedication code to Shakespeare's Sonnets. Thus with *Second Fruits*

---

[4] An alternative reading of the word 'plaiers' (players?) is 'places': so it may mean the text was "inferior in places".

we have three occasions when Neville and Nashe are (more or less visible) in the same text. Furthermore as I explored rare words in Shakespeare's vocabulary, again and again I have come across Nashe using the word at about the same time or shortly afterwards.

After the theatre dialogue in *Second Fruits* the three men go on to play tennis: John/Giovanni watches Thomas and Henry play a match which Henry wins. (Might this be Florio's metaphor for Neville eventually winning over the satirist?). In 1591 Neville would have been a healthy young man of 29, not yet subject to the gout that plagued him and later made him lame (Falstaff complains of gout in *Henry IV* part 2 (I, 2, 254) and that play was written 6 years later. Falstaff was Henry Neville's nickname about that time.) Nashe referred to tennis in his *Pierce Peniless* (1592). Neville showed his interest in tennis in his letters and plays. After returning to England for his break from Ambassadorial service in 1600, he wrote a letter dated 2/11/1600 (Winwood, 1725, Vol 1, 271) stating that the only place the Earl of Essex and Robert Cecil could meet was at a game of tennis, presumably because the Queen wished Cecil not to invite Essex into any part of her court once she had banished him from her presence. Tennis is mentioned in *Much Ado About Nothing, Henry IV part 2, Henry V, Hamlet, Pericles* and *Henry VIII*.

In *Hamlet* Polonius instructs Renaldo to spy on Laertes, suggesting that he enquire of his behaviour and hint to others that he might gamble or visit brothels, to check on his reputation, speaking thus about him:

> I know the gentleman;
> I saw him yesterday, or t'other day...
> There was a' gaming; there o'ertook in's rouse;
> There falling out at **tennis**...

(2.1.55-9)

This might recall a famous dispute in the late 1570s between the aggressive Earl of Oxford and the young Philip Sidney, whom the Earl called a 'puppy' and threw off the tennis court (Duncan-Jones, 1991, 23). As Neville knew Sidney he had probably heard of this incident.

Conclusion

The nom de plume 'Phaeton' was Neville's first pseudonym. This exploration has shown Neville to be in the network of figures who influenced the young 'Shakespeare'. Florio's *Second Fruits* offers us therefore a fascinating glimpse of the young bard.

Chapter 2

MUCEDORUS

We are used to the idea that Shakespeare's creative development began with the first history plays and comedies: *Henry VI, The Two Gentlemen of Verona, The Taming of the Shrew* and *Titus Andronicus*. We see them as, to some extent, 'crude', and we pass on in anticipation of the more sophisticated works beginning with *Richard III* and culminating in the towering tragedies. The early plays then seem pale beginnings compared to such transcendent masterpieces. However *Henry VI* is in itself a masterpiece: a huge trilogy, which reaches across kingdoms and reigns to chart an entire period in the nation's development. Are we really to believe that this was Shakespeare's first play: that he leapt onto the stage, aged 26, with a staggering three part epic? Writers develop over time. Shakespeare's skills as a dramatist, and as a writer, evolved; yet his early brilliance seems to appear without any precedent in juvenilia. If we are to discover such earlier writing we must look at the anonymous plays and poems of the period immediately prior the *Henry VI* trilogy: 1580-1590. In doing so we would have to consider works that are necessarily simpler, more naive in the style of writing and theatrical imagination but nevertheless which contain the seeds of language, images, action, plot, character that might offer hints of material later developed by 'Shakespeare'. We have already looked at the Phaeton sonnet (chapter 1). Sams (1995) also pointed to evidence that Shakespeare began his writing in the early to mid 1580s.

With the emergence of Henry Neville as the real writer behind 'Shakespeare' we can begin to wonder at his development as a writer, based on what we know of his life and thus possibly rediscover his early writings. This chapter then is a heuristic, hermeneutic exploration of an anonymous text, which, like speculative archaeology, seeks to reconstruct the development of an area from the anonymous fragments left behind.

A heuristic starting place
Heuristic research focuses on personal experience and meaning. I am a playwright: I have been a writer since I was 10 years old. My recent play, *Voices and Visions*, is undoubtedly my most complex, mature work. It is based on my PhD and a future researcher would have little

difficulty finding its sources in my research thesis. However I now know that there are older sources that were invisible to me whilst I was writing it, indeed until some time later, when I looked at my earlier writings - going back over 30 years. Take for example the metaphor of Punch and Judy in the play: I now realise I had unconsciously used this in three other plays, in *Back from the Brink* written in the early 1990s, a giant Punch and Judy puppet show I created in 1982, and *Play About Play* which I wrote as an undergraduate in 1973: so over a span of 30 years I had used the same idea in four plays. In that early piece I created a role for a mad doctor and a scene of the psychoanalysis of Mother Earth. Thirty years later I wrote a scene in which a psychiatrist hears the voice of the Devil and a woman with bi-polar disorder says, "I thought I was the Earth giving birth."

This realisation that my own created works contain images that gradually emerge and re-emerge as leitmotifs, offers a possible method of looking at anonymous texts that predate the 'Shakespeare' canon, for evidence of Henry Neville's juvenilia. Whilst conclusive proof may forever elude us, this archaeology of 'Shakespeare's' imagination, could illuminate the emergence of our greatest writer. In looking at these plays then, my search is not simply for words, phrases, images and plot structures that can later be seen in known 'Shakespeare' plays, but for examples where a 'Shakespearean' passage echoes an aspect of Neville's life. This double focus would be stronger evidence than mere word echoes, which can be dismissed as commonplaces or borrowings.

Henry Neville's early life as a writer

Just as I have looked at my own life and writings and noticed antecedents to my later work, so it is also possible to look back and find psychological antecedents in Neville's life for the origins of his later theatrical creativity. His grandfather and father both took part in court masques: indeed his grandfather improvised verses. Neville's father "devised court entertainments along with his life-long friend Henry Sidney, who was father of Sir Philip Sidney..." (James, 2008b, 64) and entertained Elizabeth I at his Sunning Hill house in August 1583 (Rowse, 1962, 99).

In 1574 Neville, aged about 13, went to Merton College, Oxford. For five years from 1578, Neville travelled though France, Germany, Italy, to Prague, Vienna and Venice. In 1583, aged about 21, he arrived back in England. Whilst the earliest known plays came into existence five years later, from 1588 -1590 (*Edmund Ironside*, *Henry VI*), Neville could have begun writing between 1577 and 1588, though he might have written from an even earlier age: Mozart wrote music from the age of 7, though he was studying composition from the age of 4. Leonardo's earliest extant drawing, dated 1473, (when he was 21) cannot have been his first! (Nicholl, 2005, 50) As his father was a writer, Neville would have been encouraged from an early age. Theatrical children often create little shows from a very early age. However I am placing a limit on this study and focussing on the years after Neville's return to England in 1583 and I have been looking for works that would have been written in the following five years: precisely the period where we would expect earlier writings to show traces of his emerging style. We would expect any such early works only to be published years after they were written, so the plays that might be by young Neville would be published in the 1590s but have been written much earlier. From the anonymous plays of the period I have chosen first to examine the comedy *Mucedorus*. It was very popular, being published in more editions than any other play of its time: between 1598 and 1668, 15 quartos were printed.

The plot of *Mucedorus*

Mucedorus is a prince, the son of the King of Valencia. He decides to travel to the neighbouring kingdom of Arragon to see the beautiful princess Amadine, but does so in disguise as a shepherd. He arrives just in time to save her from a bear! Amadine had been walking in the forest with her suitor, Segasto, when the bear attacked: the cowardly suitor ran away, leaving her to fend for herself. Amadine falls in love with Mucedorus but the jealous Segasto tries first to have him murdered (by Tremilo, whom Mucedorus kills in self defence), then executed for that offence (the princess pleads for his life as her rescuer) and then banished. Mucedorus goes into the forest. Amadine pledges to follow him and they arrange to meet by a well. In the forest a wild man, Bremo, captures Amadine. Mucedorus, now in disguise as a hermit, tricks Bremo and cudgels him, rescuing the princess. There is a happy ending when Segasto gives up his claim to marry Amadine and she is free to wed Mucedorus, who is now revealed to be a prince. Mouse, who becomes Segasto's clown-servant, provides comical word play.

External evidence

In 1598 the first quarto (Q1) of *Mucedorus* was published anonymously. The epilogue makes it clear it was performed before Elizabeth I at court. The third quarto, (Q3) 1610, stated that it was performed by the King's Men (and therefore before James I), the company who performed 'Shakespeare's' plays (Peachman, 2006). Tucker Brooke (1908, xxvi) thought the play was by a member of the school of university wits. Some have suggested it was by Robert Greene but that has been discounted recently. Additional scenes were written between 1606-1610, which, Tucker Brooke said, "are of greater poetic merit and somewhat more in Shakespeare's manner," but not up to the standard of his writing at that time and so probably by someone imitating his style. I speculate that Neville was responsible for the 1610 additions but deliberately disguised his writing style to fit the earlier, juvenile text. The play was attributed to Shakespeare in 1656. This was just 41 years after his death: we should not simply dismiss this attribution, which was made within living memory. In examining the text of the play I have distinguished between the two versions by putting (Q1) or (Q3) after quotations to make clear whether a word, phase or section is from the first 1598 version or the amended 1610 version. The second quarto, 1606, (Q2) was a reprint of Q1 so the additions that appeared in Q3 were probably written between 1606 - 1610. Q1 and Q3 were published by William Jones. The play was only listed in the Stationers' Register in September 1618.

The Tragical History, Admirable Atchievements and *Various Events of Guy Earl of Warwick* was first printed in 1661 but is believed to have been written in the early 1590s (Peacham, 2006). According to the title page it was written by B.J. (Ben Jonson). It contains much material from *Mucedorus* and so must have been written after that play. So remarkable however are the implications of this play that I will discuss it further below.

I have also discovered echoes of *Mucedorus* in George Peele's *The Old Wife's Tale*, which was written about 1593, being first printed in 1595. If *Mucedorus* was a source for *The Old Wife's Tale* then it must predate it. I will examine this play further below.

In *The Knight of the Burning Pestle* (1607) by Francis Beaumont, one character, Rafe, is said to have played the role of Mucedorus.

The date of *Mucedorus*

The name 'Musidorus' is used in Sir Philip Sydney's *Arcadia*, which was written 1579-81. From his letters to his brother Robert in 1578 and 1580 it is clear that Sidney knew Neville (mentioning him in both letters by name: Robert and Neville were travelling through Europe together). In the 1580 letter he mentioned his "toyful book" (the Old *Arcadia*, written between 1577-80), which he said he would send to Robert by February 1581 and so it is highly likely that Neville had access to an early manuscript copy of this *Arcadia* from 1581 (Duncan-Jones, 1991, 171). As *Arcadia* is thus a source then the earliest date for the writing of the play *Mucedorus* must be after this time. If written by

Neville, the play would probably have been written after his European travels: he returned to England in 1583 aged about 21. The play is believed to have been written before 1590 (for further textual evidence that this is so see below). I suggest therefore that the play was written between 1581 – 89. Bevington (1962) noted that the printing of a cast list at the start of the Quarto was common up through the mid 1580s, but increasingly rare thereafter (Jupin, 1987, 3). Bevington also noted that in the late 1580s, allegorical figures were relegated to roles outside the play proper, as Comedy and Envy are relegated to the Prologue and Epilogue.

The writer of *Mucedorus* transposed the setting from Arcadia in Greece to **Arragon** and Valentia in Spain. However the fact that it is set in Spain would suggest a date before 1588, as the Spanish Armada would not make that country a popular place to set a comedy after that date[5]: indeed Shakespeare did not set a play in Spain until *Cardenio* in 1613. In *Much Ado About Nothing* there is Don Pedro, a Prince of **Aragon** and his bastard brother, Don John, but that play takes place in Messina, Sicily. (Neville was probably in Spain briefly during the Earl of Essex's Cadiz expedition in 1596. He was considered for the role of English Ambassador to Spain by James I. He could read and speak Spanish.) With this in mind and the presumption that Neville did not write *Mucedorus* during his travels round Europe, but on his return, we can move the date to between 1583-7: in other words before he wrote any of his later poems or plays. The lack of any iron imagery in the play argues for an early date of composition: Neville took over the Mayfield iron works in late 1583 so *Mucedorus* might have been written during 1583. From further evidence on vocabulary presented below I refine this to between 1583-5 (though the play did go through revisions and additions for Q3, 1610). *Leicester's Commonwealth*, (1584) may also be a source for the play: this would suggest 1584-5 as the date for *Mucedorus*.

Only after I had independently arrived at this dating did I discover that Arthur Acheson had also suggested the date as 1584-5 (Jupin, 1987,1). I accept Sams' (1986) conclusion that *Edmund Ironside* was written by Shakespeare. Sams convincingly dated *Ironside* to 1588, after the Armada. A humourous link is to be found between the plays: in *Edmund Ironside* (1133) and *Mucedorus* (2.2.66) the gluttonous clowns, respectively Stitch and Mouse, both want "beef and brewis". I believe *Mucedorus* pre-dates *Ironside*. The word 'steel' is used in

---

[5] Kyd's *Spanish Tragedy*, set in Spain, was written between 1585-90, probably before the Armada.

Ironside, which also points to it being written after Neville had taken over the Mayfield iron works. There are other links between these two plays which I explore below.

If this very early date (1584-5) is correct we would expect the text to be simpler than the mature works; but if it is a genuine piece of 'Shakespeare' juvenilia it should exhibit elements that are recognisable, that in later years we see again, developed and mature in canonical plays. We should also be able to detect elements that would fit known facts about Neville's life and experience. If Neville was the author of *Mucedorus* he was aged between 21-24 when he wrote it. Thus the very fact that the name Mucedorus can be seen as emerging from Sydney's *Arcadia* and we know that Neville knew Sydney and his work, is an example of such evidence. Indeed Musidorus is one of two friends: the other being Pyrocles (who does not appear in the play *Mucedorus*). Pyrocles might be an alter ego for Sydney so perhaps Neville chose to focus on Musidorus, thus placing himself as the friend of the poet. Sydney's father and Neville's father were great friends so Philip Sidney and Henry Neville, two of the greatest English Renaissance poets, must have met. *Arcadia* and a number of Shakespeare's plays belong to the genre of 'friendship literature'. At the start of the play Mucedorus is talking with a friend, **Anselmo** (Q3). This is very typical of Shakespeare who often opens plays with friends talking together. In *Romeo and Juliet* a list of guests for Capulet's party includes "County **Anselm**" (1.2.65). Sydney's *Arcadia* was later to be an influence and source for Shakespeare's plays including for *The Two Gentlemen of Verona, Love's Labours Lost, King Lear* and *Pericles*. Indeed the choice of the name Pericles may have been influenced by the name Pyrocles (Warren, 2003b, 18). Yates (1975, 79) noted "the pervasive influence of Sydney's *Arcadia* in all the Last Plays" of Shakespeare.

The sources of *Mucedorus*
The writer of *Mucedorus* did not simply dramatise *Arcadia* but selected elements and transposed them into a new story. In the *Arcadia* Musidorus rides out at the tilt dressed as the "Black, or Ill-apparelled Knight", with "his armour of as old a fashion (besides the rusty poorness) that it might better seem a monument of his grandfather's courage." (Duncan-Jones, 1991, 135) Neville's grandfather Sir Edward Neville, took part in tilting at Henry VIII's court and in France. Musidorus, in *Arcadia*, also disguises himself: as a shepherd. In the play, Mucedorus deliberately chooses an "obscure, servile" disguise, using a shepherd's costume from a masque, which Anselmo gives him,

for his journey to see the princess Amadine. Sir Edward Neville, disguised, took part in masques with Henry VIII (see chapter 5).

In *Arcadia* Musidorus elopes with Pamela and kills Amphialus. In the play Mucedorus elopes with Amadine and kills Tremelio and Bremo; but the circumstances are very different: the *Arcadia* has inspired the playwright, who has developed his own story. Jupin (1987, 19) pointed to further parallels: in both *Arcadia* and *Mucedorus* the lovers elope into a forest, are captured (by a wild man in the play, by a band of brigands in the romance), are discovered by a search party, return to her father's court and eventual betrothal, when the hero's true identity is revealed.

There are two versions of *Arcadia*, the Old and the New: the latter also being called *The Countess of Pembroke's Arcadia*. It was this later version that was first published in 1590, having been prepared by Fulke Greville, Sydney's best friend, after his death in 1586. The Countess of Pembroke (Sydney's sister) brought out another edition in 1593. The Old *Arcadia* existed only in manuscript and was lost until it was rediscovered in 1907 and published in 1912. There is clear evidence that the play *Mucedorus* is based on the Old *Arcadia* and thus the playwright must have had access to this early manuscript version. For example, in the play Amadine describes the bear that chased her as, "That fowle deformed **monster**" (1.3.13) and "A **monstrous ugly bear**" (2.4.34). Amadine tells us:

> Then I amazed, distressed, all alone,
> Did hie me fast to scape that **ugly bear**,
> But all in vain, for, why, he reached after me,
> And hardly I did oft escape his **paws**...
>
> (2.4.50)

Segasto also calls it "an **ugly bear**" (1.4.10). Sidney, in his Old *Arcadia* used the words: "**monstrous** she-bear", "**ugly bear**" and "**ugly paws**" (Duncan-Jones, 1999, 46-7). The words '**ugly**' and '**monstrous**' are not used to describe the bear in the New *Arcadia*. In the latter a lion is called '**monstrous**', the bear, "a foul, horrible bear" (Evans, 1987, 176-7). Thus whoever wrote *Mucedorus* did so from the Old *Arcadia* and probably before the New *Arcadia* was published in 1590. One person whom we know had access to the Old *Arcadia* manuscript from 1581 was Henry Neville. The word '**ugly**' is used 30 times in the Shakespeare canon but two thirds of these usages can be dated from the 1590s: the earlier part of Neville's writing career. In *A Midsummer Night's Dream* Helena says, "I am as **ugly** as a **bear**, for beasts that meet me run away for fear." (2.2.93) Is this a memory of Mouse in *Mucedorus* fleeing the bear?

Bears had already appeared on the stage in Italy: intriguingly in works of the early 1580s when Neville was there. In 1582 Bernardino Pino's *L'Eunia, ragionamenti pastorali* was published in Venice: in it Nippio escapes from a bear and Mindio is falsely reported to have been devoured by one (Clubb, 1972, 22). Neville visited Venice in 1581. There was always a delay between a play being performed and published so it is entirely possible that Neville saw Pino's play and the bear on stage.

Dametas in Sidney's *Arcadia* is obviously the source for the clown Mouse in *Mucedorus*. Both make an entry with multiple weapons to protect themselves (Duncan-Jones, 1999, 39 and 2.2.1). Musidorus provokes Dametas' wife to sexual jealousy, but Dametas is more interested in cheese than a woman. Mouse is equally interested in his food. In the *Arcadia* Dametas misunderstands Cleophila when she says to herself, "O spirit of mine, how canst thou receive any mirth in the midst of thine agonies?" Dametas responds, "Thy spirit, dost thou think me a spirit? I tell thee I am the duke's officer..." (Duncan-Jones, 1999; Evans, 1987, 143). This joke is entirely relocated by the playwright:

King: I will make thee a knight.
Mouse: How a spright? No, by ladie, I will not be a spright.

This is an example of the way Mouse mishears words said to him, as if he were slightly deaf. This is not the case in the *Arcadia*: Dametas hears exactly what Cleophila has said, he just misunderstands. I am slightly deaf in my left ear and sometimes mishear things. The brain compensates by guessing the nearest word to what has been partially perceived and the effect is often comic: the other day my neighbour said, "I'm going to meditation." I heard this as, "I'm going to vegetation." Mouse seems to have this same comic facility of mishearing words. Henry Neville's uncle, the Lord Abergavenny, was famously deaf and Neville himself complained of deafness in a letter dated 29/11/1599: "an **indisposition and infirmitie** befallen me in my hearing" (Winwood, 1725, Vol 1, 133). Neville here uses a hendiadys (a pairing of nouns joined by 'and'), a device characteristic of Shakespeare.

"On New Year's Day, 1574, Elizabeth I watched a masque portraying six Foresters dressed in green satin, with Wild Men in moss and ivy as torch bearers." (Egan, 2006, 98) Given that he was a Forester, and took part in writing such entertainments, Sir Henry Neville (Neville's father) may have been one of these performers. Neville would have been aged between 10-13. The very next year it is possible that Neville went with his father to see the Kenilworth entertainments given by the Earl of Leicester for Elizabeth I in 1575.

These court masques were possible sources for the wild man Bremo in *Mucedorus*: at Kenilworth the Queen was met, on her return from the hunt, by a wild man "with an oken plant pluct up by the roots in his hande, himself forgronc all in moss and ivy." The wild man was charmed by Elizabeth's nobility just as Bremo is charmed by the princess Amadine's beauty. The part of the wild man was written and performed by George Gascoigne[6] (Jupin, 1987, 64). Gascoigne had, in 1566, written a play, *Supposes* (based on Ariosto's *I Suppositi*), that later provided the source for the stories of *The Taming of The Shrew* and *The Comedy of Errors*.

There is other evidence that the bard may have seen the Kenilworth entertainments of 1575: in *Twelfth Night* the Captain describes Sebastian's survival of the shipwreck as he swam, "like **Arion on** the **dolphin's back**" (1.2.15). One of the spectacular entertainments at Kenilworth involved a man representing "**Arion** upon a **dolfin's back**". Interestingly, rather like the lion in *A Midsummer Night's Dream* ("know that I as Snug the joiner am a lion" 5.1.218), the actor took off his disguise and revealed his identity, much to the Queen's amusement, as he swore he "was none of Arion, not he, but e'en honest Harry Goldingham" (Jupin, 1987, 64 and Duncan-Jones, 1991, 97).

Whereas it would be extraordinary for an 11 year old country boy from Stratford, like William Shakespeare, to have access to these courtly shows, Neville, given his father's position, would have been welcome. Alternatively he may have received reports from his father or others who were present. We do know that Sir Henry Sidney (Neville's father's best friend), his wife, Lady Mary, and his son, Philip Sidney were present. Philip's sister, Mary, and his brothers Robert (aged 11) and Thomas (aged 6) were also there. Robert may already have been Neville's friend: they later travelled the continent together (1578-83). Thus even if Neville was not present to see the wild man charmed by the queen, he knew people who could tell him the story.

I will also present new evidence that *Leicester's Commonwealth*, (1584) the banned work attacking the Earl of Leicester, may also be a source for the play.

Evidence for Shakespeare-Neville: the bear and the boar
In Sidney's *Arcadia* there is a lion and a she-bear. In *Mucedorus* the playwright cut the lion from the story, preferring just to have a bear on stage. This was probably an actor in costume: Mouse describes the bear as "some devil in a bear's doublet" (1.2.4). The bard refers to lions 84 times in the canon: many of them being a symbol for royalty; bears are

---

[6] From: http://www.luminarium.org/renlit/gascbio.htm [Accessed 2008]

mentioned 49 times. The bear was a symbol for the Earls of Warwick, who were Henry Neville's ancestors. In *Henry VI* part 2, Warwick says:

> Now, by my father's badge, old **Nevil's** crest,
> The rampant **bear** chain'd to the ragged staff...

(5.1.202)

Here Warwick (Richard Neville) by his father, means his father-in-law, Richard Beauchamp: it was through his wife, Anne, Beauchamp's daughter, that Richard became the Earl of Warwick. The mistake however reveals the **Nevil** connection. Earlier in the same play the Duke of York, (who married Cecily Neville) says:

> Call hither to the stake my two brave **bears**,
> That with the very shaking of their chains
> They may astonish these fell-lurking curs:
> Bid **Salisbury** and **Warwick** come to me.

(5.1.144)

The Earl of **Salisbury** was Richard Neville (1400-60) and his son the Earl of **Warwick** Richard Neville (1428-71: the King Maker). Clifford replies:

> Are these thy **bears**? We'll bait thy **bears** to death.
> And manacle the **bear**-ward in their chains,
> If thou darest bring them to the baiting place.

(5.1.148)

Again in *Henry VI* part 3 King Edward refers to: "two brave **bears**, **Warwick** and **Montague** that in their chains fettered the kingly lion" (5.7.10). Both men were Nevilles: Richard Neville (The King Maker) the Earl of **Warwick** and his brother, John Neville, Marquis of **Montague**. Richard, Duke of Gloucester, (soon to be King Richard III, a Neville (who will marry Anne Neville), calls himself, "an unlicked **bear-whelp**" in *Henry VI* part 3 (3.2.161). Edmund the bastard in *King Lear* says he was born under Ursa Major (the Great **Bear** constellation: 1.2.127). Bears continue to appear occasionally in other plays: in *The Comedy of Errors* (written between 1589-94) Dromio of Syracuse says,

> As from a **bear** a man would run for life,
> So fly I from her that would be my wife.

(3.2.153)

This, in one of Shakespeare's earliest plays, sounds like a memory of Segasto and Mouse fleeing the bear in *Mucedorus* or of Dametas fleeing the bear in the *Arcadia*. All this is comic but there may be a serious reason for fleeing a bear if that bear is murderous. In *Leicester's Commonwealth* (1584) Robert Dudley, the Earl of Leicester, is referred to as such directly: "my Lord of Leicester (whom you call the **Bearwhelp**)..." (Peck, 2006, 61). Neville had two copies of this banned document, which were discovered by Brenda James amongst the Worsley Manuscripts at the Lincolnshire Archives. Neville annotated *Leicester's Commonwealth* with references that link up with Shakespeare's history plays. Two of these annotations pick out the bear:

> "You know the bear's love, said the gentleman, which is all for his own paunch, and so this **Bearwhelp** turneth all to his own commodity, and for greediness thereof will overturn all if he be not stopped or muzzled in time."
>
> (Peck, 2006, 53)

Here, in the margin, Neville has written '**Beares**' (Worsley MSS 47). Furthermore the politics of this **bear** image are further developed in the document:

> "my Lord of Leicester is very well known to have no title to the crown himself, either by descent in blood, alliance, or otherways... he **will play the Bear** when he cometh to dividing of the prey and will snatch the best part to himself."
>
> (Peck, 2006, 86)

Robert Dudley was not only linked with a bear by the authors of *Leicester's Commonwealth*. The prey Dudley was after was of course Queen Elizabeth herself. In 1573 Dudley gave Elizabeth I "a fan of white feathers set in a gold handle decorated with emeralds, diamonds and rubies, on each side a **white bear** and two pearls hanging a lion ramping with a white bear at his feet." Dudley had received a gift of "**white bears**" from the Muscovy Company in 1571 (Haynes, 1987, 100). In *Mucedorus* we find:

> Segasto: Thou talkest of wonders, to tell me of **white bears**.
> But, sirra, didst thou ever see any such?
> Mouse: No, faith, I never saw any such, but I remember
> My father's words: he bade me take heed I was
> Not caught with a **white bear**.
>
> (1.4.39)

This dangerously political warning (the play was performed before Elizabeth I) is disguised in a pun on 'wight' = person/woman = white and bear − bare/naked, and is delivered by a seemingly innocuous clown. Neville's father did warn his son about Robert Dudley's ambitions. Dudley was believed to have poisoned the Earl of Essex, murdered his own wife and to have ambitious designs to take over the kingdom. Mucedorus saves the princess Amadine from a dangerous bear and from the unwanted suitor Segasto: the princess stands in for Elizabeth I. This identification is further suggested by the following from *Leicester's Commonwealth* which describes Robert Dudley's "hasty preparation to rebellion and assault of her Majesty's royal person and dignity... she should once fall within the compass of his furious **paws**, seeing such a smoke of **disdain**..." (Peck, 2006, 92) Just ten lines later the name Amadis occurs in the text. Is this a possible source then for the name of the princess Amadine? She speaks of:

> that ugly bear,
> But all in vain, for, why, he reached after me,
> And hardly I did oft escape his **paws**...

(2.4.53)

Furthermore at the start of the play Comedy (a woman) confronts Envy (a man):

> Thou, **bloody,** Envious, **disdain**er of men's joy,
> Whose name is fraught with **bloody stratagems**,
> Delights in nothing but in spoil and death,
> Where thou maist trample in their luke warm blood,
> And grasp their hearts within thy cursed **paws**...

(Induction, 41)

In *Leicester's Commonwealth* the words '**disdain**', '**paws**', '**bloody**' and '**stratagems**' all relate to Robert Dudley. In the Shakespeare canon a **paw** just once belongs to a baited **bear** – who is none other than Richard Neville, the Earl of Warwick (in *Henry VI* part 2, 5.1.153). Ambrose, Robert Dudley's brother, became Earl of Warwick in 1561 and so the bear and ragged staff were his emblems. Neville had an argument with Ambrose in 1583. I have suggested *Mucedorus* was written 1584-5. A story in which a bear is killed and a proud, unwanted suitor is displaced might well express Neville's feelings towards the Dudleys.
Furthermore the writer of *Leicester's Commonwealth* warns:

> "Hastings, for aught I see, when he cometh to the scambling is like to have no better luck by the **Bear** than his ancestor had once by the **Boar**"

(Peck, 2006, 90).

As William Hastings, the Lord Chamberlain, goes to his execution in Shakespeare's *Richard III*, he recalls a dream of a **boar** (3.4.87). Richard III is symbolised by the **boar** repeatedly in the play. Bremo, the wild man in *Mucedorus*, asks:

> Who knows not Bremo's strength,
> Who like a king commands within these woods?
> The **bear**, the **boar**, dares not abide my sight,
> But hastes away to save themselves by flight.

(2.3.6)

This inclusion of the boar is especially significant. Scherer pointed out that the name Bremo is derived from 'bream', 'breme' or 'brim': a boar. Breme could also mean "fierce, raging, furious, stern, wroth". Brimming was the sexual act of a boar. Mucedorus speaks of a time when men were wild: "a rude unruly rout". "The word 'rout' can refer to a rummaging pig as well as a disorderly crowd" (Scherer, 1999, 59). This then fits into the archetypal scheme which Ted Hughes (1992) discovered underlying the Shakespeare canon and which is first revealed in *Venus and Adonis* (a poem which has 16 of the 30 boars in the canon) and *The Rape of Lucrece*. (See chapters 4 & 7 for further material on Hughes' analysis.) The boar later symbolised Richard III. Richmond announcing Richard's death, calls him, "The wretched, bloody, and usurping **boar**..." (5.2.7). That play contains 10 boars. Richard III was a Neville thrice over: being the son of Richard Neville (Plantagenet), the Duke of York and Cicely (Cecilia) Neville and having married Anne Neville. Hughes' archetypal scheme has the usurping boar at its core and so this ties *Mucedorus* into the canon: we can now recognise that the play fits into that scheme of rival lovers (Mucedorus and Segasto); the rapist/killer, (boarish Bremo); the rational versus the irrational (Mucedorus versus Bremo). Hughes' tragic equation is not yet in place: Mucedorus does not reject Amadine, as Adonis will reject Venus, nor is Amadine a rape victim, though she is threatened by Bremo; but the symbolic elements are emerging in Shakespeare-Neville's poetic vocabulary. Gibbons (1990, 217) noted that the "episode in *Cymbeline* in which the would-be rapist Cloten is challenged and beheaded by a prince disguised seems to recall *Mucedorus*." In *Venus and Adonis* there are "the blunt **boar**, rough **bear**, or **lion** proud..."(884) and in *A Midsummer Night's Dream* (a play of lovers lost in the forest) the lion, bear and boar are all mentioned by Oberon (2.1.180 & 2.2.29). In *As You Like It* Rosalind runs away to the forest and dresses as a man, carrying a "**boar** spear" (1.3.117).

These developing parallels of emerging themes and metaphors will be further explored below.

Shakespeare's vocabulary and *Mucedorus*

In my examination of the text I have looked at unusual words. This survey has shown me that some *Mucedorus* words occur throughout the 'Shakespeare' canon. What is perhaps especially interesting is the fact that a number of these words recur only in the early part of the canon. If *Mucedorus* is an early work by Shakespeare-Neville this would be expected. It may be argued that this might show one of three possibilities:

1) These words were current at the time so any writer might use them;
2) Writers were seeing each other's plays and reading each other's works so parallels prove nothing;
3) The use of similar words and phrases suggest the same writer wrote both texts.

1) is certainly possible and I explore other contemporary texts for the *Mucedorus* vocabulary.
2) *Mucedorus* is anonymous and may have been written and revised by more than one writer. However there is clearly one main authorial voice: from the vocabulary used is it possible to detect this main writer?
3) is only possible where the work is anonymous and no other author has been convincingly shown to have written the play.

I suggest therefore we now focus on rare words and phrases. For the purposes of controlling for item 1) above I have chosen to check the following texts for all the words/phrases examined in this section below: Jasper Heywood's translation of *Thyestes* (1560); Thomas Norton & Thomas Sackville's *Gorboduc* (1565)[7]; *Leicester's Commonwealth* (1584); Lyly's *Campaspe* (1581-4), *Sappho and Phao* (1584), and *Endymion* (1591); George Peele's *The Arraignment of Paris* (1584); Kyd's *The First Part of Hieronimo, The Spanish Tragedy* (probably written between 1585-7, published 1592[8]) and *Soliman and Perseda* (1592); Sidney's *An Apologie for Poesie* (1581, first printed 1595), *Astrophil and Stella* (written 1582-3, published 1591); Marlowe's *Tamburlaine The Great* parts I & II (1587), *Dr. Faustus* (1589-93), *The Jew of Malta* (1592), *The Massacre at Paris* (1593), *Edward II* (1593-4) and *Dido Queen of Carthage* (1594); Robert Greene's *Alphonsus King of Arragon* (1587-8, printed 1599), *A Looking Glass for London and England* (written with Thomas Lodge between 1587-91, printed 1594), *Orlando Furioso* (1588, printed 1594), *Friar Bacon and Friar Bungay* (1589, printed 1594), *James IV* (1590, printed 1594); *Edward III* (1590-6), which was recently accepted into the

---

[7] Thomas Sackville's daughter, Mary, married Henry Neville, 7th Lord Abergavenny.
[8] The date of *The Spanish Tragedy* is debatable: Cairncross (1967) suggests 1585-7, or Edwards (1974) offers 1582-1592 with a preference for a later date, probably about 1590-2.

Shakespeare canon. I have also looked at the anonymous texts of *Edmund Ironside* (1588); *Arden of Faversham* (1592: see chapter 4) both of which I believe to be by Shakespeare-Neville. Where I do not mention these texts it is because the word or phrase is not used. If the early date of 1584-5 for Mucedorus is correct only *Thyestes* (1560); *Gorboduc* (1565); *Campaspe* (1581-4), *Sappho and Phao* (1584), and possibly *The First Part of Hieronimo* and *The Spanish Tragedy* (probably written between 1585-7) would pre-date it and therefore be possible sources of vocabulary.

Amadine describes Segasto as '**cowardlike**' (Q1: 2.4.46). This word is used in *The Rape of Lucrece*: "But **coward-like** with trembling terror die" (231). The word had been used by in a translation of Euripides' *Jocasta* (by George Gascoigne and Francis Kinwelmersh) which was performed in 1566 at Gray's Inn.[9]

Segasto fears Amadine will accuse him of '**disloyaltie**' (Q1: 1.4.22). The word '**disloyalty**' occurs in two early comedies: *The Comedy of Errors* (3.2.11) and *Much Ado About Nothing* (2.2.48).

Segasto then says: "A trustie friend is tride in time of neede." (Q1: 1.4.23) Again these two words are used only in an early play when, in *Henry VI* part 3, Gloucester says:

> Brother, this is Sir John Montgomery,
> Our **trusty friend**, unless I be deceived.
>
> (4.7.40)

These words appear in Marlowe's *Tamburlaine* I, once as "**trusty friend**" (1.2.227).

Segasto sarcastically responds to Mouse, who is fleeing from the bear, with "A **lamentable tale**." (Q1: 1.4.46) In *Richard II* the King, who has just responded to the Queen talking about the lion as the king of beasts says: "Tell thou the **lamentable tale** of me" (5.1.44).

Mouse uses the rare word '**hoodwinked**' (Q1: 1.4.). The word '**hoodwink**' is used in *All's Well That Ends Well* (3.6.25), *Macbeth* (4.3.72) and The *Tempest* (4.1.206); '**hoodwinked**' occurs in *Cymbeline* (5.2.16); '**hoodwink'd**' in *All's Well That Ends Well* (4.1.83) and *Romeo and Juliet* (1.4.4).

In reply to Segasto's demand that Mucedorus be executed the King says:

> when the sisters shall decree
> To cut the **twisted thread** of life...
>
> (Q1: 2.4.77)

---

[9] From: http://encyclopedia.jrank.org/EUD_FAT/EURIPIDES_48o4o6_BC_.html [Accessed 2008]

This same image is used by the Bastard in *King John*:

> ...if thou want'st a cord, the smallest **thread**
> That ever spider **twisted** from her womb
> Will serve to strangle thee...
>
> (4.3.127)

At the start of *Mucedorus* Envy says:

> Why then, Comedy, send thy actors forth
> And I will cross the first steps of their tread:
> Making them fear the very **dart of death**.
>
> (Q1: Induction, 71)

Later Segasto says:

> In living thus, each minute of an hour
> Doth pierce my heart with **darts** of thousand **deaths**.
>
> (Q1: 1.4.17)

Thomas Newton had used the "**dart of death**" in his 1581 translation of *Thebais* by Seneca (LION). Sydney, in his *An Apologie for Poesie* had written: "**Death**'s ugly **dart**" (line 3000). This was written between 1581-3. If Neville did pick up this image from Sidney it would further refine the date of *Mucedorus* to 1584-5. I have found another verbal link between *Mucedorus* and Sidney's *Apologie* (see below). *An Apologie for Poesie* certainly influenced *Love's Labour's Lost*. In *Romeo and Juliet* the heroine refers to "the **death-darting** eye of the cockatrice" (3.2.45). Tamburlaine speaks of "The ugly monster **Death**...with his murdering **dart**" (part II, 5.3.67-9). In Kyd's *Soliman and Perseda* Death has a dart (1.1.Induction, 28).

Mucedorus says, "banishment is **death**, aye, **double death** to me..." (Q1: 3.1.72). This repetition of the word 'death' occurs in *Henry VI* part 2 when the king says:

> For in the shade of **death** I shall find joy;
> In life but **double death**, now Gloucester's dead.
>
> (3.2.54)

The words "**double death**" also occur in *Titus Andronicus* (3.1.246) and in *The Rape of Lucrece* (1114). The Chorus in Act 4 of *Thyestes* speaks of "**double death**" (215).

Mucedorus, lamenting his exile from Amadine, calls on the forest to provide "**wholesome herbs** and **sweet smelling savours**" (Q1: 3.1). In *Richard II* a servant uses the words "**wholesome herbs**" (3.4.46). "**Sweet smelling**" occurs in *Venus & Adonis* (1177). In *The Taming of*

The Shrew Induction, Scene 2, Sly says, "I **smell sweet savours**." In *A Midsummer Night's Dream* Bottom makes a mistake in his lines:

> Bottom: Thisby, the flowers of odious **savours sweet**...
> Quince: 'Odorous' ! 'Odorous' !
> Bottom: Odorous **savours sweet**...
>
> (3.1.78)

Bremo says, "The **crystal waters** in the bubbling brooks" (Q1: 2.3.10). He goes on to say, "Thy drink shall be goat's milk and **crystal water**" (Q1: 4.3.34). The King of Valentia says, "The **crystal eye** of Heaven shall not thrice wink" (Q3: 4.1.38). Shakespeare's sonnet 46 has "**crystal eyes**"; King Ferdinand in *Love's Labour's Lost* says, "her hairs were gold, **crystal** the other's **eyes**..." (4.3.139); in *Venus and Adonis* there is "**crystal eyne**" (633) and later the bard combines 'eye' imagery with 'water' imagery in:

> She vail'd her eyelids, who, like sluices, stopt
> The **crystal tide** that from her two cheeks fair
> In the sweet channel of her bosom dropt...
>
> (957)

In *A Midsummer Night's Dream* Demetrius says, "shall I compare thine **eyne? Crystal** is muddy" (3.2.138). The bard uses the word 'crystal' 17 times: all are in early plays and poems written before 1596 except one (*Cymbeline*). They mainly refer to eyes and tears. In four uses of the word it is connected with water and rivers.

Bremo, eyeing up Amadine as his prey, says:

> A happy prey! now, Bremo, feed on flesh.
> **Dainties**, Bremo, **dainties**, thy hungry **panch** to fill!
>
> (Q1: 3.3.17)

He repeats this word when offering Amadine "all the **dainties** that the woods afford" (Q1: 4.3.36). '**Dainties**' occurs four times in the canon, all in early works: *The Taming of The Shrew* (2.1.189); *The Comedy of Errors* (3.1.21); *Love's Labour's Lost* (4.2.24); *Venus & Adonis* (164) and in *Edmund Ironside* (5.2.252). All are to do with food. '**Dainties**' is used in *Thyestes* (1.123); *Astrophil & Stella*, *Tamburlaine II* (612); *Dr. Faustus* (1717); *The Spanish Tragedy* (1.4.176); and *Friar Bacon and Friar Bungay* (3.3.130). Greene often uses the word 'dainty' but not the plural 'dainties'. Keen discovered a copy of Hall's *Chronicle*, in the margins of which some 16th Century student had made notes. Keen saw this annotator as Shakespeare. One of the annotations brings together the idea of cannibalism and the word '**dainties**':

"Scottes in fraunce dyd eate men and wom(en) his fleasshe for **daynti(es)**" (Keen & Lobbock, 1954, 137).

James has found evidence that the book belonged to Neville (James & Rubinstein, 2005, 232-3).

Bremo here refers to his 'hungry **panch**': this is an old spelling of 'paunch'. I have found the word '**panch**' in *The Taming of A Shrew* (printed in 1594): "empty your drunken **panch** some where else" is line 2 of the Induction. **Paunch** occurs in just two canonical plays: twice in *Henry IV* part 1, referring to Falstaff (2.2.62 & 2.4.141). Interestingly Bremo also refers to his "greedy guts" (3.3.19): the word 'guts' is used 14 times by the bard: 8 of these belonging to Falstaff! '**Paunch**' occurs again in *The Tempest*, when Caliban says,

> Why, as I told thee, 'tis a custom with him,
> I' th' afternoon to sleep: there thou mayst brain him,
> Having first seized his books, or with a log
> Batter his skull, or **paunch** him with a stake,
> Or cut his wezand with thy knife.

> (3.2.85)

This is especially interesting as the murderous cannibal Bremo is the ancestor of Caliban (I will discuss this further below). The word '**paunch**' was used three times in *Thyestes* (1560: 1.21; 5.4.60 & 69). In *The Spanish Tragedy* Horatio speaks of a horse being '**paunch'd**' (i.e. stabbed in the belly, 1.4.22 - the same usage as Caliban's above). '**Paunch**' also occurs in *Locrine* (see chapter 3) and in *Leicester's Commonwealth* (Peck, 2006, 53).

Bremo threatens Amadine that he'll "suck the sweetness from thy **marie bones**" (Q1: 3.3.30). There are six references to '**marrow**' in the canon: but only once is it associated with the word '**bones**' in the early play, *Henry VI* part 3 (3.2.125). '**Marrow**' is used twice in *Arden of Faversham* but not with the word 'bones'. It is also used in *Soliman and Perseda*, again, not with 'bones', but as "marrow-burning" (5.2.14). In *Venus and Adonis* the words "my marrow burning" occur (142). In his play *Edward I*, (printed in 1593 and so, by my dating, probably written after *Mucedorus*), George Peele wrote of "marrowbones" (scene XVIII, line 4: Bullen, 1888, 189).

In *Mucedorus* the King exclaims, "**Oh, impudent**! a shepherd and so insolent!" (5.2.49). In *Edmund Ironside* the King likewise exclaims, "**Oh impudent**, ungodly wretch!" (5.1.32). There is a particularly extraordinary link between *Mucedorus*, *Edmund Ironside* and the canonical plays. In Act 3, scene 1, a messenger enters to tell Mucedorus he has been banished. He greets the disguised prince with, "**All hayle**, worthy shepheard." To which Mouse adds, "All rayne, lowsie shepheard" (Q1, 3.1.6). Mouse is punning on hail and rain. Jupin (1987, 45) pointed out that Mouse parodies the Messenger and Mucedorus, deflating their formality: he quips on our hero's "My former heaven is now become my hell" with: "The worse ale house that I ever came in, in all my life" (3.1.24). Yet under this comic parody there is another level and this reference to hell we will soon see is significant. Behind the "All hail" is the jealous Segasto's plot to get rid of Mucedorus. This resonates through the canonical plays. In *Henry VI* part 1 a French Messenger greets the English with, "**All hail**, my lords!" (2.2.34). He has been sent to entrap Talbot into becoming a prisoner of the duplicitous Countess of Auvergne. In *Richard III* Tyrell, who has just come from the murder of the princes in the Tower, greets King Richard with, "**All hail**, my sovereign liege!" (4.3.23). Thus a pattern is emerging where the salutation "**All hail**" alerts us to villainy. Indeed Sams (1986, 198) pointed to an "*idée fixe* about the words '**all hail**', which persistently connote an evil force working for the destruction of hero or king." He cited other examples including in *Henry VI* part 3 when Richard (at this point merely Duke of Gloucester, but later Richard III) says to King Edward:

> And, that I love the tree from whence thou sprang'st,
> Witness the loving kiss I give the fruit.
> [Aside] To say the truth, so **Judas** kiss'd his master,
> And cried '**all hail**!' when as he meant all harm.
>
> (5.7.31)

In *Edmund Ironside*, when the villainous flatterer Edricus meets King Edmund, his greeting is ironically commented on by the clown Stitch, just as Mouse parodied the Messenger.

> Edricus: **All hail** unto my gracious sovereign!
> Stitch: Master, you'll bewray yourself, do you say
>   'all hail' and yet bear your arm in a scarf?
>   That's **hale** indeed.
> Edricus: **All hail** unto my gracious sovereign!
> Edmund: **Judas**, thy next part is to kiss my cheek
>   and then commit me unto Caiaphas. ...
>
> (5.1.30)

Sams (1986, 198) referred also to *Richard II* and the king's speech:

> Yet I well remember
> The favours of these men: were they not mine?
> Did they not sometime cry, '**all hail**!' to me?
> So **Judas** did to Christ.
>
> (4.1.167)

Likewise Julius Caesar (2.2.58) and Macbeth (1.3.48) are betrayed, with this same greeting, by evil forces. With Judas as emblematic of evil and the prototype of betrayal, we can see why Mucedorus goes on to mention hell! *Mucedorus* again fits into the development of patterns that come to fruition in the later works.

My final example of the play's vocabulary is when Mucedorus uses a rare word about a tree's shade:

> Down in the valley where I slew the bear:
> And there doth grow a fair broad branched beech,
> That **overshades** a well...
>
> (Q1: 3.1.106)

In *Titus Andronicus* (1592-3) this word recurs in a very similar context to the use in *Mucedorus*, when Saturnus reads in a letter:

> Look for thy reward
> Among the nettles at the elder-tree
> Which **overshades** the mouth of that same pit...
>
> (2.3.271)

In *Henry VI* part 3, Warwick says, "Dark cloudy death **o'ershades** his beams of life" (2.6.62). In *Richard III* (1592-3) Anne says, "Black **night o'ershade** thy day, and death thy life!" (1.2.131). This image of night is also used in *The Taming of A Shrew* (printed 1594): "And darksome **night oreshades** the christall heavens" (Induction, 14). In *The Winter's Tale* (1611) Polixines says, "Fear **o'ershades** me" (1.2.446).

This list is not exhaustive but I hope substantial enough to show that the *Mucedorus* playwright used a number of rare words that 'Shakespeare' also used, especially in his early plays. Whilst some of these words/phrases are also used by other writers, others are only used by the bard: **'cowardlike'**, **'disloyalty'**, **'lamentable tale'**, **'hoodwinked'**, **'bloodthirsty'**, **'twisted thread'**, **"wholesome herbs and sweet smelling savours"**. All these are in Q1. This could either mean that Shakespeare devoured words from many sources including *Mucedorus*, or that in fact he wrote this early play.

Neville's vocabulary in his letters and *Mucedorus*

James (2008b, 246-252) provides a list of characteristic words and phrases used by Henry Neville in his letters. These include the words: **'procure'**, **'pretence'**, **"like enough"**, **"open eyed"**, **"cold comfort"** and words beginning with **'dis'**-. The word **'procure'** is used three times, **'pretence'** twice in *Mucedorus*:

ENTER PURSUED BY A BEAR: THE UNKNOWN PLAYS OF SHAKESPEARE-NEVILLE

> ...I will **procure** his banishment for ever.
>
> (2.4.92)
>
> it is only Segasto that **procures** thy banishment.
>
> (3.1.85)

Two of these words occur within two adjacent lines:

> God grant my long delay **procures** no harm
> Nor this my tarrying frustrate my **pretence**.
>
> (3.3.1)
>
> But other business hindered my **pretence**.
>
> (3.4.3)

Neville's frequently used '**like enough**' occurs just two lines before one of the above uses of '**procure**' and is followed by one of 34 words beginning with '**dis-**'.

> Yet **like enough** where there is no **dis**like.
>
> (3.1.82)

The words beginning with 'dis-' include: Disturbance/disturbed, disdainer, disgrace, disloyalty, dissuasion, disguise, disposition/disposed, dislike, distress, dismayed, displeasure, disclose, distilled, discourse, and discretion.

Whilst the words '**open eyed**' do not occur we do have "In **open sight**" (1.3.66).

Echoing Neville's '**cold comfort**' there is: "And thou bright sun, my **comfort** in the **cold**..."(3.1.55).

The third quarto of the play (1610) opens with a speech to James I, which ends in the words: "may our Pastime your **Contentment** find." Whilst the word 'contentment' was never used by Shakespeare it is used by Neville in his letters from 1599 (Neville Journal, vol 1, no 2). Of the 7 times the word is used in these diplomatic letters, 5 are about a King or Queen's contentment. Tucker Brooke (1967) and others have considered the additional scenes of the 1610 Quarto are "in Shakespeare's manner." I have found the word 'contentment' in Spenser, Nashe and Jonson but none of these uses are in relation to royalty.

Further research deserves to be done in this area: these are just the first hints of links between the vocabulary of Neville's letters and *Mucedorus*.

Neville and the forest

Neville's father was the royally appointed forester of Windsor forest. In fact his ancestors had been foresters back as far as Henry II in the

12th Century (James, 2008b, 48). Forests were to play an important role in a number of Shakespeare's plays, including that of Windsor in *The Merry Wives of Windsor* (James, 2007a). Much of *Mucedorus* takes place in a forest, which is not the case in his source, Sidney's *Arcadia*. On one occasion Neville's father taught the young princess Elizabeth to shoot deer (James & Rubinstein, 2005, 124). This incident is replayed in *Love's Labour's Lost* (4.1.7-35). It is also alluded to in *Mucedorus*: Bremo, the wild man of the woods, says to princess Amadine:

> And I will teach thee how to kill the deer,
> To chase the hart and how to rouse the roe…
>
> (Q1: 4.3.53)

The playwright also uses the metaphor of stock grafting, which Shakespeare uses. Mucedorus says, "My mind is **grafted** on an humbler **stock**" (Q3: 1.1.48). **Graft** occurs near **stock** and the name **Nevil** in *Henry VI* part 2 when Suffolk says:

> Thy mother took into her blameful bed
> Some stern untutor'd churl, and noble **stock**
> Was **graft** with **crab-tree** slip; whose fruit thou art,
> And never of the **Nevils'** noble race.
>
> (3.2.212)

Here we have a direct connection with Neville's anxiety about legitimacy. The **crab-tree** links us back to *Mucedorus* as Bremo hands the hero "a knotty **crabtree** staff" (Q1: 5.1.55) which Mucedorus promptly uses to kill him. Scherer (1999, 64) pointed out that the Oxford English Dictionary (OED) defined a crab-stock as "a person or thing of wild unreclaimed nature" (1625). In *Coriolanus* Menenius says, "We have some old **crab-trees** here at home that will not be **grafted** to your relish" (2.1.184). In *Richard III*, Buckingham uses this metaphor:

> Know then it is your fault that you resign
> The supreme seat, the throne majestical,
> The scepter'd office of your ancestors,
> Your state of fortune and your due of birth,
> The lineal glory of your royal house,
> To the corruption of a blemished **stock**:
> Whilst, in the mildness of your sleepy thoughts,
> Which here we waken to our country's good,
> This noble isle doth want her proper limbs;
> Her face defaced with scars of infamy,
> Her royal **stock graft** with ignoble plants…
>
> (3.7.116)

In *Henry V* the Dauphin says,

> Our scions, put in wild and savage **stock**,
> Spirt up so suddenly into the clouds,
> And overlook their **grafters**…

(3.5.7)

Neville had an interest in forests, legitimacy and the hereditary and legitimate transmission of kingship: the Neville family had a claim to the throne. I will later track this metaphor in *The Winter's Tale* (see below). I believe *Edmund Ironside* (1588) is also an early work by Shakespeare-Neville so it is interesting to see the complex of metaphor and words in the following passage from that play (which includes the rare word '**sprout**' – also to be found in the Phaeton sonnet). Canutus says:

> A traitor may be likened to a tree,
> Which being shred and topped when it is green,
> Doth for one twig which from the same was cut
> Yield twenty arms, yea twenty arms for one,
> But being hacked and mangled with an axe,
> The root dies and piecemeal rots away.
> Even so with traitors. Cut me off their heads,
> Still more out of the self-same **stock** will **sprout**,
> But plague them with the loss of needful members
> As eyes, nose, hands, ears, feet or any such; …

(2.3.40)

The young Shakespeare was often concerned with bodily mutilation (see chapter 4) and I link this to the execution of Neville's grandfather for treason. Below I will also look at the forest in other plays of the 1590s.

Plots, characters and themes

If *Mucedorus* is an early work of Shakespeare-Neville I would expect it to contain images, plot structure, characters and themes we would see further developed in his later works. Being a very early work it is not surprising that the writer simplifies the structure: Sidney's *Arcadia* is complex and the playwright takes one element of that story and develops it, but he does not use the doubling of characters that Sidney uses in *Arcadia* (and of which later the bard would become a master). If *Mucedorus* was written about 1584, this is just when Neville married Anne Killigrew (in December, 1584: James & Rubinstein, 2005, 84). A play about a single couple, with the hero winning the bride from another suitor, fits the chronology of Neville's life.

Orpheus

At the heart of *Mucedorus* is the encounter between the wild (the forest, the bear and Bremo) and the civilised (Mucedorus, Amadine and the court). Mucedorus, in an attempt to civilise the wild man Bremo, speaks of the role of the poet **Orpheus** in bringing men out of wild nature into culture:

> In time of yore, when men like brutish **beasts**
> Did lead their lives in loathsome cells and woods
> And wholly gave themselves to witless will,
> A rude unruly rout, then man to man
> Became a present prey, then might prevailed,
> The weakest went to walls:
> Right was unknown, for wrong was all in all.
> As men thus lived in this great outrage,
> Behold one **Orpheus** came, as poets tell,
> And them from rudeness unto reason brought,
> Who led by reason soon forsook the woods.
> Instead of caves they built them castles strong;
> Cities and towns were founded by them then:
> Glad were they, they found such ease,
> And in the end they grew to perfect amity;
> Weighing their former wickedness,
> They termed the time wherein they lived then
> A golden age, a goodly golden age.
> Now, Bremo, for so I hear thee called,
> If men which lived tofore as thou dost now,
> Wily in wood, addicted all to spoil,
> Returned were by worthy **Orpheus**' means,
> Let me like **Orpheus** cause thee to return
> From murder, bloodshed and like cruelty.
> What, should we fight before we have a cause?
> No, let's live and love together faithfully.

(Q1: 4.3.72)

Sidney wrote his *An Apologie for Poesie* between 1581-3. In it he wrote of poetry having been the original art and a prior source of civilisation, history and science: he named **Orpheus** as the poet who, through his "charming sweetness" drew "the wild untamed wits to an admiration of knowledge. So, as Amphion was said to move stones with his poetry to build Thebes, and Orpheus to be listened to by **beasts**, indeed, stony and **beastly** people..." (Duncan-Jones, 2002, 213). I hypothesise that Neville had access to a manuscript copy of *An Apologie for Poesie* (which was not published until 1595 as *A Defence of Poesie*). In the above passage he uses the words "men like brutish **beasts**". Sidney refers to "**beasts**... and **beastly** people..." An alternative source was Ovid ('Shakespeare's' favourite classical source): Book XI opens with Orpheus, "By such songs

69

as these the Thracian poet was drawing the woods and rocks to follow him, charming the creatures of the wild..." (Innes, 1955, 246). This is echoed by Proteus in *The Two Gentlemen of Verona*:

> For **Orpheus**' lute was strung with poets' sinews,
> Whose golden touch could soften steel and stones,
> Make tigers tame and huge leviathans
> Forsake unsounded deeps to dance on sands.
>
> (3.2.78)

There is a brief mention of **Orpheus** in *The Rape of Lucrece* (553). Lucrece begs Tarquin to spare her: she

> Pleads, in a wilderness where are no laws,
> To the rough **beast** that knows no gentle right,
> Nor aught obeys but his foul appetite.
>
> (544-6)

This sounds very much like Bremo, though the latter does not actually rape Amadine. The poet likens the effect of her words to **Orpheus** charming the god of Hell, "And moody Pluto winks while **Orpheus** plays" (553). In *The Merchant of Venice* Lorenzo speaks of the power of music to tame wild nature:

> the poet
> Did feign that **Orpheus** drew trees, stones and floods;
> Since nought so stockish, hard and full of rage,
> But music for the time doth change his nature.
> The man that hath no music in himself,
> Nor is not moved with concord of sweet sounds,
> Is fit for treasons, stratagems and spoils;
> The motions of his spirit are dull as night
> And his affections dark as Erebus:
> Let no such man be trusted.
>
> (5.1.80)

This again recalls that Bremo is not reformed by Mucedorus: the man who cannot respond to art cannot be civilised. There is a song in *Henry VIII* about the calming effect of music on wild nature and the human heart:

> **Orpheus** with his lute made trees,
> And the mountain tops that freeze,
> Bow themselves when he did sing:
> To his music plants and flowers
> Ever sprung; as sun and showers
> There had made a lasting spring.
>
> Every thing that heard him play,
> Even the billows of the sea,
> Hung their heads, and then lay by.
> In sweet music is such art,
> Killing care and grief of heart
> Fall asleep, or hearing, die.
>
> (3.1.3)

These examples show the **Orpheus** myth appearing at the very start, in the middle and at the end of Shakespeare's career as a writer. Sams (1986, 205) showed how the bard's use of Ovid and an indirect reference to Orpheus, especially as the exemplary poet able to charm wild and dangerous natures with words, was characteristic of Shakespeare and therefore evidence of his authorship of *Edmund Ironside*.

I will now look at four representative plays spanning Shakespeare's works to see how elements already present in *Mucedorus* were later used and developed by the bard. The recurrent themes of lovers in the forest, civilising wild men, travel, banishment, clowns playing with words, assertive women choosing their husband, disguise, bears, Art and Nature show that *Mucedorus* is closely related to the Shakespearean canon.

Mucedorus and *The Two Gentlemen of Verona*

Sidney's *Arcadia* is an acknowledged source for both plays. Both plays begin with two friends parting, as one starts his travels. The friend in both cases tries to dissuade the traveller from leaving. In the first scene, Mucedorus says to his friend, Anselmo, "Desist dissuasion" (Q3: 1.1.27). *The Two Gentlemen of Verona* opens with Valentine saying, "Cease to persuade, my loving Proteus" (1.1.1). Perhaps Neville had had this experience as he set out on his European travels in 1578. The friend in both plays is concerned with the dangers the traveller will face. In *Mucedorus*, Anselmo says:

> Do not, sweet Prince, adventure on that task,
> Since **danger** lurks each where: be won from it.
>
> (Q3: 1.1.25)

In The Two Gentlemen of Verona Proteus says:

> and in thy **danger**
> (If ever **danger** do environ thee)
> Commend thy grievance to my holy prayers...
>
> (1.1.15)

The opening scene of *The Two Gentlemen of Verona* is the mirror image of that of *Mucedorus* in which the hero is leaving because of love; in *The Two Gentlemen of Verona* Valentine is leaving and Proteus is staying for love of Julia. In both plays the lover is banished and the woman follows him into the forest. Indeed in both the lover is banished through the plotting of their rival. Both Julia and Amadine not only follow their true love but flee another, unwanted suitor to whom their fathers have decided to marry them. Segasto gives up his claim to

Amadine's hand: this is echoed by Valentine giving up Silvia to Proteus (5.4.83). Julia disguises herself, Amadine plans to do so:

> I will disguised wander through the world,
> Till I have found him out.
>
> (5.1.81)

In both one of the lovers uses disguise and there is a recognition scene. Indeed the first disguise used by Mucedorus is from a masque: Anselmo says:

> Within my Closet does there hang a Cassock,
> Though base the weed is; twas a Shepherds,
> Which I presented in Lord **Julio**'s Mask.
>
> (Q3: 1.1.49)

In *The Two Gentlemen of Verona* **Julia**, disguised as a boy, Sebastian, replies to Silvia's enquiry as to how tall Julia is by saying he/she wore one of Julia's dresses in a pageant (4.4.157). Neville's father and grandfather took part in court masques, his father used disguise and Neville himself used disguise during his ambassadorship to Paris (James & Rubinstein, 2005, 133).

Mucedorus laments his banishment in the forest:

> Ye goodly groves, partakers of my songs
> In time tofore when fortune did not frown,
> Pour forth your plaints and wail a while with me;
> And thou bright sun, my comfort in the cold,
> Hide, hide thy face and leave me comfortless;
> Ye wholesome herbs, and sweet smelling savours,
> Ye each thing else prolonging life of man,
> Change, change your wonted course, that I,
> Wanting your aide, in woeful sort may die.
>
> (Q1: 3.1.52)

Let us compare this to Valentine's speech in *The Two Gentlemen of Verona*:

> This shadowy desert, unfrequented woods,
> I better brook than flourishing peopled towns:
> Here can I sit alone, unseen by any,
> And to the nightingale's complaining notes
> Tune my distresses, and record my woes.
> O thou that dost inhabit in my breast,
> Leave not the mansion so long tenantless,
> Lest growing ruinous, the building fall,
> And leave no memory of what it was.
>
> (5.4.2)

Both banished men, missing their love, are despairing; both feel at home in the woods; both harmonise their distress with the natural world; both speak of singing. Neville's father, whilst not banished, went into voluntary exile during Mary Tudor's reign, because her Roman Catholicism was not acceptable to him as a Protestant. He was also a forester (see above). Neville himself, as already stated, thought of escaping into the forest from his ambassadorship, and may indeed have done so (James, 2007a).

Mucedorus and Amadine agree to meet in the forest at a well (3.1.107). In *The Two Gentlemen of Verona* Proteus and Thorio agree to meet "at St. Gregory's well" (4.2.81). Mucedorus disguises himself as a friar whilst in the forest. In *The Two Gentlemen of Verona* two friars are mentioned: Friar Patrick (5.1.3) and Friar Laurence, the latter "in penance wander'd through the forest" (5.2.36).

In both plays there are wild men in the forest who are potentially dangerous: the outlaws in *The Two Gentlemen of Verona* however accept Valentine's civilising influence whereas Mucedorus must kill the wild man Bremo.

In both plays the clowns play with words and have an interest in food. Launce puns on Speed's words "a notable lover" making them "a notable lubber". Speed says "thou **mistak'st** me" (2.5.40). Again when they next meet Launce plays with Speed's words and the latter complains, "Well, your old vice yet: **mistake** the word" (3.1.280). In response to Mouse punning on 'hermit' as '**emmet**' (an ant) Mucedorus says, "Thou dost **mistake** me" (Q1: 4.2.33). In *Edward III* Audley speaks of the "French, like **emmets** on a bank..." (3.5.28). *Edward III* dates from 1592-3. I have also found "ants and **emmets**" in Nashe's *The Unfortunate Traveller* (line 1864; printed 1594) but this postdates *Mucedorus*.

Speed, like Mouse, complains about his food: "Ay, but hearken, sir: though the camelion Love can feed on air, I am one that am nourished by my victuals; and would fain have **meat**" (2.1.162). Mouse spends much of Act 3, scene 2 begging his master to come in to dinner. When reminded of his task of searching for Amadine he says, "Faith, I have forgotten it; the very scent of the **meat** hath made me forget it quite" (Q1: 3.2.30). Mouse describes himself as a "rusher of the stable" (Q1: 4.2.65), which Mucedorus interprets as an "usher of the table". Mouse replies, "Nay I say rusher and Ile proove mine office good; for looke, sir, when any coms from under the sea or so, and a dog chance to blow his nose backwards, then with a whip I give him the good time of the day, and strawe rushes presently: therefore I am a rusher..." (Q1: 4.2.67).

We can compare this with Launce speaking of his dog Crab:

> He thrusts me himself into the company of three or four
> gentlemen-like dogs, under the Duke's table; he had not been
> there (bless the mark) a pissing while, but all the chamber smelt
> him. "Out with the dog," says one; "What cur is that?" says
> another; "Whip him out," says a third…
>
> (4.4.16).

Launce offers himself to be whipped to protect the dog.

One mystery about *The Two Gentlemen of Verona* is the confusion about where it takes place (Verona, Milan, Mantua or Padua)! Padua is mentioned 27 times in the canon, including in *The Taming of The Shrew, The Merchant of Venice* and *Much Ado About Nothing*. Henry Neville was in Padua in August, 1581 (Duncan 1974, 62).

Mucedorus and *As You Like It*

Another play that takes place in a forest is *As You Like It*. Just as Mucedorus is banished and enters the forest, so Duke Senior is banished and goes into the forest. Rosalind is also banished and, like Amadine, encounters her lover, Orlando, in the forest. Celia, also like Amadine, defies her father and goes with her banished friend into the forest. Celia and Rosalind in *As You Like It*, Amadine in *Mucedorus*, Julia and Sylvia in *The Two Gentlemen of Verona* are all assertive women who choose their husbands as much as being chosen. (We believe that Anne Killigrew was likewise an assertive woman, we do not know whether Neville's marriage to her was a love match or arranged by their fathers who were friends.)

The theme of the wild and the civilised echoes in both plays. Orlando briefly becomes a wild man in the forest: he threatens violence to get food from, and is re-civilised by, a patient Duke Senior. The bear in *Mucedorus* is echoed by an off stage lion in *As You Like It*. When Mucedorus goes into the forest he disguises himself as a hermit. There is a religious man in the forest in *As You Like It* who plays a crucial off-stage role in disarming the dangerous Duke Frederick to bring the play to a happy ending. Jacques meanwhile is a melancholic secular hermit in the forest. Indeed he goes to join this "old religious man" (5.4.155) at the end. This play was written at the time when Neville himself wanted to withdraw from public life, writing in a letter to Robert Cecil that he would return home from France to "live hermit in Ashridge or the forest and contemplate my time as a bad ambassador" (James & Rubinstein, 2005, 263).

In *Mucedorus* we have already noted the hero's talk with Bremo about Orpheus.

> Behold one Orpheus came, as poets tell...
> They termed the time wherein they lived then
> A **golden age**, a goodly **golden age**.
>
> (Q1: 4.3.89)

The banished Duke and his followers in the woods of *As You Like It* are said to "fleet time carelessly, as they did in the **golden** world." (1.1.112; Lings, 1984, 115). The "**golden age**" is mentioned in *The Rape of Lucrece* (60) and *The Tempest* (2.1.163).

Jaques says of the clown Touchstone that he "hath been a **courtier**" (2.7.36 and 5.4.42). In *Mucedorus* Mouse, puffing his clownish self up with airs, says, "I called for three pots of ale, as tis the manner of us **courtiers**" (Q1: 3.5.4). In *Thomas of Woodstock*, a play now recognised to be by Shakespeare (see chapter 5) Nimble, the clownish servant, dresses himself up in the latest fashions and says he does it to "show myself a **courtier**" (3.1.120). In *The Winter's Tale* the comic Autolycus, having swapped clothes with Prince Florizel, puffs himself up and declares to the old shepherd and his son, "I am a **courtier**" (4.4.725).

Mucedorus and *The Winter's Tale*

There are echoes of Sidney's *Arcadia* in *The Winter's Tale*. This is not surprising because the major source for the play is Greene's *Pandosto*. Greene did take names from the *Arcadia*. Duke Basilius, wanting to know the future, consults the oracle of Delphos (Duncan-Jones, 1999, 5). This is the very oracle that Pandosto and Leontes consult. In *The Winter's Tale* Prince Florizel disguises himself as a shepherd and uses the name Doricles (4.4.146). The original Florizel in Greene's *Pandosto* is called Dorastus. When, in *Arcadia*, he has disguised himself as a shepherd Musidorus calls himself Dorus. A shepherdess in *The Winter's Tale* is called Mopsa, this is also the name of Fawnia's (Perdita's) step-mother in *Pandosto*. Mopsa is the name of Dametas' daughter from the *Arcadia*.

The Winter's Tale is the mirror image of *Mucedorus*: in the former a prince disguised as a shepherd falls in love with a princess; in the latter a princess disguised as a shepherdess falls in love with a prince. In both plays the father opposes the marriage until the secret, royal identity is revealed and there is a happy ending. Disguise is used in both plays. Leontes' jealousy of Polixenes is an echo of Segasto's jealousy of Mucedorus. The continuity of sources and plots here might be regarded as simply the result of a shared literary culture but there are other links that are indicative of Shakespeare-Neville.

Shakespeare's most famous stage direction is "Exit pursued by a bear" in *The Winter's Tale* (3.3.57). In the play *Mucedorus*, written up to 25 years earlier, there is a stage direction: "Enter Segasto running and Amadine after him, being pursued with a bear" (1.3). The bear is the most obvious link between these two plays. It is interesting to note that an edition of *Mucedorus* was brought out in 1610 (the third quarto: Q3). This indeed is the quarto that has revisions by an unidentified writer whom critics have regarded as more "Shakespearean" than the original writer of Q1. I suggest it was Neville who was the reviser and this explains his interest in *Mucedorus* at the time, as he was writing another play with a bear in it. The earliest recorded performance of *The Winter's Tale* was 1611. There is no bear in Greene's *Pandosto* (1588), the source of story for *The Winter's Tale*: its addition therefore is a deliberate creative act. Ted Hughes (1992) showed how the bear fitted into the archetypal scheme of metaphors that underlies the Shakespeare canon so its appearance in the play is not simply a gratuitous theatrical device. The bear is savage, tearing the shoulder bone from the unfortunate Antigonous before devouring him. Wild Nature is further imaged in the storm that wrecks and then drowns the men in the ship that delivered Antigonous and Perdita to the shores of Bohemia. She alone survives. Whilst the storm is in the source *Pandosto*, the shipwreck and drowning are not, so the bard is deliberately making the scene wilder and more terrible. However this exposure of the child to the wilderness is the result of the savage cruelty of Leontes' jealousy: just as Amadine's and Mucedorus' exposure to the forest and the wild cannibal Bremo, is the result of Segasto's jealousy. In *Mucedorus* Segasto and Bremo are far more dangerous than the bear. Indeed Nature seems benign compared to the cruelty of man. As Antigonus takes up the baby Perdita, intending to abandon her in "some remote and desert place" (2.3.175) he prays that:

> Some powerful spirit instruct the kites and ravens
> To be thy nurses. Wolves and bears, they say,
> Casting their savageness aside, have done
> Like offices of pity.
>
> (2.3.185)

It is man, more than wild nature, that is truly dangerous. There are wild men in *The Winter's Tale*: at the sheep sheering festival there are 12 satyrs, "all men of hair", (4.4.321). These wild men, however, are civilised into dancers. Bremo mentions satyrs in *Mucedorus* (Q1: 4.3.44). In *The Winter's* Tale the danger is human, natural and mythic: Perdita refers to the myth of the rape of Proserpina by Dis (Pluto), warning her friends of the danger to their maidenheads (4.4.116). The cycle of nature is uncontrollable. Time will bring "summer's death" and "trembling winter" (4.4.80).

Given Neville's concern with illegitimacy it is interesting to note that Perdita speaks of carnations and streaked gillyvors as "nature's bastards" (4.4.82). She says, "There is an art which in their piedness shares with great creating nature" (4.4.86).

Polixenes replies, using the stock-grafting metaphor which I mentioned above:

> Yet nature is made better by no mean
> But nature makes that mean: so, over that art
> Which you say adds to nature, is an art
> That nature makes. You see, sweet maid, we marry
> A gentler scion to the wildest **stock**,
> And make conceive a bark of baser kind
> By bud of nobler race: this is an art
> Which does mend nature, change it rather, but
> The art itself is nature.
>
> (4.4.89)

This passage reveals the continuing Shakespearean interest in the relationship between Art and Nature, which we also find in *Mucedorus*. That play begins with a son setting out on his travels. In Act 4 his father, the King of Valentia, speaks of how deeply he is missing his son:

> How can a Father that hath lost his Son,
> A Prince both wise, virtuous, and valiant,
> Take pleasure in the idle acts of Time?
> No, no; till Mucedorus I shall see again,
> All joy is comfortless, all pleasure pain.
>
> (Q3: 4.1.12)

This may recall Henry Neville's father's feelings about his oldest son who travelled round Europe for five long years. There is no mother here missing her son: Neville's mother died when he was 10 years old. The joyous reunion of parent and child is a theme especially developed in the late plays including *The Winter's Tale*, but it had been a feature of plots since *The Comedy of Errors*. Here again *Mucedorus* and Neville's life experience match.

Mucedorus and *The Tempest*

Bremo is a cannibal, killing people who wander into the forest for his meat. He is also a figure of rage and lust (Scherer, 1999, 55). It is not difficult to see in him a proto-Caliban (= cannibal). The word 'cannibals' appears in the early play *Henry VI* part 3: "hungry cannibals" (1.4.152) and "bloody cannibals!" (5.5.61); 'cannibal' occurs in *Thomas of Woodstock* (5.1.240: see chapter 5).

One undoubted source for *The Tempest* was Montaigne's Essay *On Cannibals* (Kermode, 1990, xxxiv). It was first published in French in 1580: other editions were printed in 1583, 1588 and 1595 before Florio's English translation in 1603. From 1578-83 Neville was travelling through Europe. From 1580 Montaigne went travelling, to Germany and Italy, passing through Venice. He was at the Villa Pratolino, near Florence, in 1581, when Neville was also in Italy. We do not know whether they ever met. Montaigne's Essay *On Cannibals* does however contain one reference that is echoed in *Mucedorus*: speaking to Bremo, Mucedorus recalls the mythical Golden Age (4.3.89). Gonzalo in *The Tempest* also refers to the Golden Age (2.1.164) and Gonzago's ideal commonwealth is based on Montaigne's Essay *On Cannibals*. It is therefore possible that Neville had come across Montaigne or his *Essays* during his travels. Grady (2002) argued that Montaigne's influence on Shakespeare predated Florio's translation.

Like Prospero does with Caliban, Mucedorus tries in vain to civilise Bremo. Prospero does make some progress: instead of killing Caliban, he has domesticated him so he carries logs. However Prospero knows he can never fully reform him: "This thing of darkness" (5.1.275) remains irredeemable and must be acknowledged, contained, controlled. Like Bremo, he is a sexual threat to the play's heroine. However Caliban is not just a monster. He has a poetic soul, as is evident from his famous speech:

> The isle is full of noises,
> Sounds and sweet airs, that give delight, and hurt not.
> Sometimes a thousand twangling instruments
> Will hum about mine ears, and sometime voices
> That, if I then had waked after long sleep,
> Will make me **sleep** again: and then, in dreaming,
> The clouds methought would open and show riches
> Ready to drop upon me that, when I waked,
> I cried to dream again.
>
> (3.2.132)

Bremo likewise is poetic in *Mucedorus*.

> If thou wilt love me thou shalt be my queen:
> I will crown thee with a chaplet made of Ivy,
> And make the rose and lily wait on thee:
> I'll rend the burley branches from the oak,
> To shadow thee from burning sun.
> The trees shall spread themselves where thou dost go...

Thou shalt be fed with quails and partridges,
With black birds, larks, thrushes and nightingales.
Thy drink shall be goat's milk and crystal water,
Distilled from the fountains & the clearest springs.
And all the dainties that the woods afford.
I'll freely give thee to obtain thy love...
The satyrs & the woodnymphs shall attend on thee
And lull thee **asleep** with music's sound,
And in the morning when thou dost awake,
The lark shall sing good morn to my queen,
And whilst he sings, I'll kiss my Amadine.

(Q1: 4.3.24)

Both Bremo and Caliban have music lulling them to sleep. Jupin (1987, 49, footnote 91) pointed out that just as Bremo offers Amadine birds as food, so Caliban offers to teach Trinculo and Stephano how to find the natural foods on the island, including birds, roots and fruits (2.2.166). As a boy Neville would have wandered through the Windsor forest of which his father was guardian. His love of the forest is shown in his expressed wish to withdraw from his ambassadorship into the peace and refuge of the woods.

In chapters 3 and 7 I show how Shakespeare recapitulates his early plays in his late plays. The play he wrote after *The Tempest* was *Cardenio* (with Fletcher), which, like *Mucedorus*, is set in Spain. In the Epilogue of *The Tempest* Prospero mentions, Naples which was ruled by the Spanish. Interestingly the dates of these plays: 1584-5, 1611 and 1612-3 were periods when Spain was an important factor in British politics. In *Double Falshood* (see chapter 7), which is based on *Cardenio*, there is a mad man (Julio) in the wilderness who seems to combine the roles of the hero searching for his love and the wildman, as if Mucedorus and Bremo (as Ferdinand and Caliban) had fused. All three plays end happily with lovers/families reunited.

Mucedorus and the Phaeton sonnet:

Written between 1578-80 Sidney's *Arcadia* contains two brief references to Phaeton (Duncan-Jones, 1999, 232, 131; Evans, 1987, 718, 299). It was first published in 1590. In *Mucedorus*, which is partly based on *Arcadia*, the hero says:

Ah, luckless fortune, worse than **Phaeton**'s tale,
My former bliss is now become my bale.

(Q1: 3.1.19)

I believe *Mucedorus* was certainly written before the Phaeton sonnet (printed in Florio's *Second Fruits,* 1591), which I have attributed to

Shakespeare-Neville (see chapter 1). One of the first 'clues' that alerted me to the possibility that *Mucedorus* might be by Shakespeare-Neville was the occurrence of this Phaeton image. *Mucedorus* was published in 1598: just one year after the last Shakespeare play (*Richard II*) in which Phaeton is mentioned. I have suggested that Neville used '**Phaeton**' as his nom de plume before he chose 'Shakespeare' so I regard its occurrence in *Mucedorus* as a possible signifier of his secret authorship.

Let us therefore look at the Phaeton sonnet and see how often words used in that poem occur in *Mucedorus* (the number of occurrences in the play are in round brackets). I am ignoring smaller words like "with, fit, and, thy, how" etc. Thus out of 47 longer or more significant words in the Phaeton sonnet, nearly half, 23, occur in *Mucedorus*. I have also put in square brackets the occurrences of these words in the standard Shakespeare canon. Unless otherwise stated all these words are in Q1.

Mucedorus:	Whole Canon:
sweet (x 11; sweetness x 1; used before names x 6)	[765]
friend (x 4, friendship x 1, friends x 2)	[398]
name (x 15)	[615]
increase (Q3) (1)	[31]
spring (1)	[74]
branch (1)	[16]
pleasures (x 3, pleasure x 7)	[39]
cease (x 4)	[46]
peace (1)	[462]
spends (spend x 1)	[5]
living (x 4)	[125]
thing (x 8)	[489]
little (x 5)	[468]
birds (1; bird 1)	[45]
sing (1; sings 1)	[131]
herbs (1)	[10]
plants (plant x 2)	[17]
vaunt (x 2)	[4]
dead (x 6)	[505]
except (1)	[31]
ever (x 15)	[596]
green (1)	[105]
o'er-spread (spread x 5)	[1]

Whilst these words are not especially rare their use together in one play is startling and points to a common author of sonnet and play. Let us compare these for example with other known Shakespeare plays and the plays *Edmund Ironside, Arden in Faversham* and *The Troublesome*

Raigne of John King of England all of which I believe are by Shakespeare-Neville. For comparison I also include Peele's *Edward I*, *Arraignment of Paris, David and Bethsabe, Battle of Alcazar* and his *Old Wives Tale*; Marlowe's *Dr. Faustus, Tamburlaine* parts I and II; Kyd's *The Spanish Tragedy*; Lyly's *Endymion* and *Sappho and Phao* and Sidney's *Astrophil & Stella* (see Appendix 1). For this comparison I am interested in five particular words in the sonnet: (in square brackets after the word, is the number of times the word occurs in the standard Shakespeare canon):

Increase [31]; **branch** [16]; **herbs** [10]; **rival** [6]; **vaunt** [4].

Mucedorus has four of these words: **increase** (Q3), **branch** (Q1), **herbs** (Q1) and **vaunt** (Q1): more than any other play of the period.

In Sidney's *Astrophil and Stella* there are 18 Phaeton words in that sonnet sequence and two of these words: '**increase**' and '**herbs**'. Given that Sidney influenced Shakespeare-Neville from the very start of his writing career these scores are hardly surprising. Marlowe, Kyd, Lyly, Green and Peele also influenced the young bard.

Mucedorus has other words such as '**plant**' [23] twice (Q3: Induction, 8; Q3: 1.1.7) and '**spread**' [30] five times (Q1: Induction, 77; Q1: 1.3.62; Q1: 2.2.74; Q1: 4.3.30 & 31) Whilst *Edmund Ironside* contains none of the above five words it does contain '**plant**' (1.1.29) and '**spread**' (of flowers: 3.5.57). In the Phaeton sonnet we find:

> Thou with thy Frutes our **barrenness o'er-spread**...

In *Mucedorus* the word '**spread**' occurs in a context similar to that of the Phaeton sonnet:

> I'll go **spread** my branch,
> And scattered blossoms from mine envious tree.
>
> (Q1: Induction, 77)

And later:

> The trees shall **spread** themselves where thou dost go,
> And as they **spread**, I'll trace along with thee.
>
> (Q1: 4.3.29)

In Shakespeare '**spread**' is usually used in relation to colours (military banners) but twice it is used of leaves: in Sonnet 25: "their fair leaves **spread**" and in *Romeo and Juliet* old Montague says, "Ere he can **spread** his sweet leaves to the air..." (1.1.150). In *The Comedy of Errors* (1594) the words '**barrenness**' (3.2.118) and '**spread o'er**' are used in the same scene as "flood of tears" (a phrase which also occurs in *Locrine*, see chapter 3).

George Peele's *The Old Wife's Tale*

There are curious echoes of *Mucedorus* in Peele's *The Old Wife's Tale* (1593-5). In that play there is a princess lost in the woods, a man (enchanted by a spell) in the shape of a white bear, lovers who meet at a well, a friar and an old man who gathers "**hips and haws**". This recalls:

> Mucedorus: I tell you, sir, I am an hermit, one that leads a
> Solitary life within these woods.
> Mouse: O, I know thee now, thou art he that eats up all
> The **hips and haws**; we could not have one piece
> Of fat bacon for thee all this year.
>
> (4.2.30)

Peele's play is a melange of genres and he may well have taken these elements from *Mucedorus* to make a popular play. The old man tells us that the sorcerer Sacrapant turned him, "straight into an **ugly bear**" (186). The bear is also described as: "the **White** Bear of England's wood" (167, 170). This recalls Segatso and Mouse talking of **white** bears in *Mucedorus*.

Given that there are bears in *Mucedorus, The Old Wife's Tale,* and *The Winter's Tale* it is a curious coincidence that Madge, who tells the tale in Peele's play, is specifically requested to tell "a merry winter's tale" (79). What a comparison between *Mucedorus* and *The Old Wife's Tale* immediately makes clear is the superior quality of the writing of *Mucedorus*. Given the clear source for *Mucedorus* is *Arcadia* it must be Peele who is the borrower.

The curious case of *The Tragical History, Admirable Atchievements and Various Events of Guy Earl of Warwick*

This play borrows lines, plot ideas and characters from *Mucedorus.* Sparrow is obviously based on Mouse, he makes the same jokes, mishearing things and has the same character, being a glutton, clown and coward. (He repeatedly hides his head in a bush at the first sign of danger, just like Dametas in *Arcadia*, which Mouse does not do, thus demonstrating that the author knew the source of *Mucedorus*.) Sparrow is also sexually promiscuous whereas Mouse is more interested in food. Sparrows were considered proverbial for lechery. What is more remarkable is that scholars have noticed that Sparrow seems to be a "hit" at Shakespeare: the crucial identifying line reads:

> Sparrow: I was born in England at Stratford upon Aven in Warwickshire.
>
> (5.2.29)

This is no respectful reference however but a satirical portrait of a puffed up lecherous buffoon. The date of this play is believed to be 1592-3: what is extraordinary about this is that it is precisely the year that Shakespeare begins to appear: 1592 is the date of Greene's attack on "Shake-scene" and 1593 the date that the name William Shakespeare appeared in *Venus and Adonis*.

At the start of **Guy Earl of Warwick** we meet Sparrow who asks a hermit whether he has not heard of a heroic figure "one squire Sparrow".

> Guy: Away you Hedg-bird.
> Sparrow: Philip is his name,
>   A bird of **Venus**, and a Cock of the Game.

(2.1)

I note the mention of Venus and Sparrow's lecherous nature. Later Sparrow is asked about his name and replies, "I have a fine finical name, I can tell ye, for my name is Sparrow; yet I am not no house Sparrow, nor no hedge Sparrow, nor no peaking Sparrow, nor no sneaking Sparrow, but I am a high mounting lofty minded Sparrow, and that Parnell knows well enough, and a good many more of the pretty wenches of our parish ifaith" (5.2.31).

I note that the idea of a name, of what's in a name, is repeatedly stressed here. (Perhaps Sparrow = **S**(hakes)**p**(ere) + **arrow**: an arrow being a little spear, pointing to his identity.) Is there then any reason to consider that there may be embedded in this play not just a hit at Shakespeare but a hint of Neville?

Neville was related to the Earls of Warwick. Guy of Warwick was a mythical ancestor claimed by the Earls. Guy was one of the Nine Worthies in Richard Lloyd's 1584 *A brief discourse of the most renowned actes and right valiant conquests of those puisant princes, called the nine worthies*. The legend of Guy (for he was not in fact historical, though he was believed to be a real person and Elizabeth I paid for his relics to be guarded at Warwick) dates back to the 13th Century. Historian M. Dominica Legge, suggested that *Gui de Warewic* may have been written sometime between 1232 and 1242 by a canon of Oseney to flatter Thomas, Earl of Warwick.[10] Guy of Warwick is a heroic knight who disguises himself as a hermit and wanders in the woods. He swears to give up his military career after the crusade to the Holy Land and becomes a hermit in the forest, vowing to remain incognito for 26 years. This is startlingly reminiscent of Henry Neville, who ceased any military activity after the Cadiz raid of 1596, had

---

[10] http://www.bbc.co.uk/legacies/myths_legends/england/coventry_warwick/article_3.shtml [Accessed 2008]

sold his cannon foundry by 1598 and who chose lifelong anonymity. He also fantasised about being a hermit in a forest.

We do not know when the present text of the play *Guy Earl of Warwick* was composed but if it dates from 1592 it is remarkably prescient; if the text was revised over the years it may have taken into account Neville's biography. Or of course it may be sheer coincidence. However the coincidences become meaningful synchronicity as they pile up: in *Guy Earl of Warwick* the hero kills a giant Colbrand. This giant is named twice in the canon: first in *King John* (1.1.225) and later in *Henry VIII* (5.4.22) Significantly the reference to Colbrand is NOT in *The Troublesome Raigne*, which was first published in 1591, but is in *King John* (dated about 1596 so written after *Guy Earl of Warwick*, 1592-3) when the Bastard Faulconbridge sarcastically refers to his legitimate brother in:

> My brother Robert? old sir Robert's son?
> **Colbrand** the giant, that same mighty man?
>
> (1.1.224)

Furthermore there is a reference to Philip Sparrow! Just six lines after the mention of Colbrand, the Bastard (now Sir Richard Plantagenet after his knighting) retorts to being called "Philip" by snorting "Philip? - sparrow!" (1.1.231).

If Philip Sparrow in *Guy Earl of Warwick* is Shakespeare (the actor);
As the name 'Faulconbridge' conceals a real historical Neville (see chapter 1);
And the Bastard Faulconbridge is an alter ego of Henry Neville (the bard);
And the Bastard Faulconbridge calls himself Phillip Sparrow;
Then Philip Sparrow is Shakespeare AND Neville
Therefore Henry Neville (the hidden writer) is Shakespeare (the nom de plume).

There is an intriguing loop here back to the source of *Mucedorus* in Sir Philip Sidney's writings, because in *Astrophil and Stella*, (sonnet 83) the poet jealously threatens Stella's pet sparrow, called Philip, suspecting his lecherous nature:

> Leave that, Sir Phip, lest off your neck be wrung.

John Skelton (1460-1529), tutor to the young Henry VIII, wrote a poem on the death of a pet sparrow called Philip. Neville's grandfather was a close friend of Henry VIII and his father was the king's godson. Given that the earliest reference to Shakespeare as "Shake-scene" referred to him in 1592 as "an upstart crow, beautified with our feathers," this bird imagery is perhaps significant.

In *Mucedorus* Mouse is keen on his food: Segasto says, "Your minde is all upon your belly" (Q1: 3.2.23). Mouse has just called him to dinner with, "I tell you all the messes be on the table already. There wants not so much as a mess of **mustard** halfe an hower agoe" (Q1: 3.2.22). Sparrow in *Guy Earl of Warwick* is likewise keen on his food. He also mentions **mustard**, fearing that he might fall into a pot of **mustard** and be swallowed by a giant (2.1). **Mustard** is mentioned 8 times in the Shakespearean canon: 5 times in *The Taming of the Shrew* and three times in *As You Like It*. Touchstone, like Mouse and Sparrow, a fool/clown who goes into the forest, tells a mysterious joke in reply to Rosalind's question: "Where learned you that oath, fool?" Touchstone replies:

> Of a certain knight that swore 'by his honour' they were good pancakes, and swore 'by his honour' the **mustard** was naught. Now I'll stand to it the pancakes were naught and the **mustard** was good, and yet was not the knight forsworn…this knight, swearing by his honour, for he never had any; or if he had, he had sworn it away before ever he saw those pancakes or that **mustard**
>
> (1.2.61-74).

This could be explained as a joke about Sir Henry Neville and the actor Shakespeare. James (2007) has noted another obscure Neville-Shakespeare joke in *As You Like It*. It occurs when Touchstone meets William (5.1.40). Touchstone says, "You are not ipse for I am he." (5.1.43. There may be a pun on 'tipsy' and 'ipse' here as he is talking of drink.) Perhaps this records Neville's actual first meeting with William Shakespeare from Stratford, as William's age is stated as 25: thus the date of that meeting would have been 1589.

As You Like It is believed to have been written 1599-1600. This is just after Jonson's *Every Man Out of His Humour* (1599) in which the rustic clown Sogliardo is mocked for buying a coat of arms (which include a boar's head) and his motto "Not Without **Mustard**". This has been seen as a satire on Shakespeare's attempt to get a coat of arms with a motto "Non sans droit", the **mustard** being the gold colour of the Shakespearean coat of arms (Ackroyd, 2005, 176; Schoenbaum, 1987, 229). The first quarto of *Mucedorus* was printed in 1598 thus the mention of **mustard** may have meaning.

In *Guy Earl of Warwick*, Sparrow says he is "high **mounting** lofty **minded**". This is an interesting phrase and echoes Guy of Warwick's earlier statement that

> These kingly favours…
> Hath plumed my thoughts with Eagle-flighted wings,
> And bears my **mounting mind** as high as heaven.
>
> (1.1.10)

Here Sparrow and Guy are identified (like Caliban and Prospero; Hal and Falstaff, Bremo and Mucedorus, Shakespeare and Neville, sparrow and eagle, bird and Phaeton). Shakespeare-Neville uses the word "mounting" 8 times, (6 of which are in plays from the early 1590s) to refer to birds, ambition, mind/spirit. The word is to be found in *King John* (1596) when the Bastard says, "And fits the **mounting** spirit like myself" (1.1.206). I suggest this is based on the passage in *The Troublesome Raigne* (1591) where the bastard says:

> My brother's **mind** is base, and too too dull,
> To **mount** where Philip lodgeth his affects.

(1.1.362)

In *Love's Labour's Lost* (1594-5): the princess says, "Whoe'er a' was, a' show'd a **mounting** mind" (4.1.4).

The sequence then is:

Mucedorus (1583-7)	princely mind (Q1:1.3.25)
The Troublesome Raigne (1588-91)	mind …mount…
Edward I (Peele: 1593)	mounting mind
Guy Earl of Warwick (1592-3)	high mounting lofty minded
Battle of Alcazar (Peele: 1594)	mounting mind
Love's Labour's Lost (1594-5)	mounting mind.
King John (1596)	mounting spirit

If *Guy Earl of Warwick* is by Ben Jonson then this was his first hint that he knew the secret of the true identity of the writer of Shakespeare's plays. He was later to write poems (Casson, 2007b, 2009) and a play, *The Staple of News* (James 2008b, chapter 13) encoding the secret of Neville's identity as the writer Shakespeare.

Neville's plan to find a substitute front man

The discovery of Henry Neville as the real writer behind the front man, William Shakespeare, implies that Neville actually planned to find such a substitute. He realised he could not simply be anonymous as people would enquire who the writer was and the pseudonym 'Phaeton' (see chapter 1) would not be sufficient in itself as it clearly was a pseudonym and invited speculation. He needed an actual man who would be accepted as the writer. There is in *Mucedorus* a clue to this plan. In the Induction Envy appears. I speculate that this word contains NV (eNVy) and might be **Nev**ille himself, indeed **He**nry. Ben Jonson was to use this word in his introductory verses in the First Folio: "To draw no **envy** (Shakespeare) on thy name…" (see James & Rubinstein, 2005, 256).

Envy threatens Comedy with blood and tragedy. (Why not call this role Tragedy?) But there is more: in the Epilogue (Q3: 29) Envy suggests he has a fiendish plan:

Envy: Comedie, thou art a shallow goose;
    Ile overthrow thee in thine own intent,
    And make thy fall my Comick **merriment**.
Comedie: Thy pollicie wants grauitie; thou art
    Too weake. Speake **Fiend** as how?
Envy: Why, thus:
    From my fowl Studie I will hoyst a Wretch,
    A leane and hungry Meager Cannibal,
    Whose iawes **swell** to his eyes with chawing **Malice**:
    And him Ile make a Poet.
Comedie: What's that to th' purpose?
Envy: This scrambling **Rauen,** with his needie Beard,
    Will I whet on to write a Comedie,
    Wherein shall be compos'd darke sentences,
    Pleasing to factious braines:
    And every other where place me a Iest,
    Whose high abuse shall more torment than blowes:
    Then I myself (quicker then Lightning)
    Will flie me to a puissant Magistrate,
    And waighting with a Trencher at his backe,
    In midst of iolittie, rehearse those gaules,
    (With some additions)
    So lately vented in your Theator.
    He, vpon this, cannot but make complaint,
    To your great danger, or at least restraint.

Comedie laughs off this threat. Is this the setting up the man from Stratford, William Shakespeare, as a poet who would then become embroiled in a battle with Nashe, Greene, Harvey and others? This section of the Epilogue is only in the 1610 quarto (Q3). Envy's speech is echoed in *As You Like It*: (1600) as Jacques plans to become a fool and satirise the world in the words: 'merrily' (2.7.11), 'goose' (2.7.86), 'galled' (2.7.50), 'theatre' (2.7.137) are used. In the previous scene the words 'raven' and 'sparrow' occur (2.3.44-5)! There are 18 ravens in the canon: four occur in the early play *Titus Andronicus*. Given the occurrence of the words 'raven', 'fiend', 'malice' and 'swell' in the above speech it is interesting these recur in the early play *Titus Andronicus*. Tamora says:

Here never shines the sun; here nothing breeds,
Unless the nightly owl or fatal **raven**:
And when they show'd me this abhorred pit,
They told me, here, at dead time of the night,
A thousand **fiends**, a thousand hissing snakes,
Ten thousand **swelling** toads...

                             (2.2.96)

Later Aaron says:

> Some **devil** whisper curses in mine ear,
> And prompt me, that my tongue may utter forth
> The venomous **malice** of my swelling heart!
>
> (5.3.11)

I submit that the same poet wrote these lines as wrote *Mucedorus*. Jupin (1987, 5-7) and others have suggested the above passage about the Poet "with his needie Beard" is an allusion to the War of the Theatres in 1601-2, and that the Poet is Ben Jonson. However Drummond's epitaph and Jonson's portrait show he "had not a beard on his chin" (Jupin, 1987, 6). Again a passage that was mysterious before we knew Neville was the writer is illuminated by James' discovery. Neville used both the words '**malice**' and '**merriment**' in his letters (Winwood, 1725, Vol 1, 26, 55).

The first performance?

I have suggested a date of 1584-5 for the composition and first performance of *Mucedorus*. Neville married Anne Killigrew in December 1584. Philip Sidney was then still alive (he died in 1586). I have already written of the multiple connections between Sidney and Neville (see chapter 1). As the fathers of the bride and groom were friends of the Sidneys they might reasonably be expected to be at Neville's wedding (though Neville had missed Sidney's wedding in 1593 as he was travelling with Walsingham – the bride's father - in Scotland). Perhaps then Sidney saw the first performance of *Mucedorus* at Neville's wedding!

Conclusion

No one has conclusively identified the author of *Mucedorus*. Within 40 years of Shakespeare's and Neville's deaths it was attributed to the bard. The evidence I have provided offers a view that this is the first extant play by Shakespeare-Neville: a window into his early style and, due to its success, a fore-runner of the greater plays to come. Some critics have tended to dismiss *Mucedorus* as trivial and not particularly well written. In fact Jupin (1987, 37-54) has been able to show quite what a sophisticated play it is and how in exploring the relationship between Comedy and Tragedy (Envy) it has an underlying structure that belies its simplicity. Indeed we can now see that the patterning of the play prefigures later plays by Shakespeare-Neville with their intimate interplay of comedy and tragedy.

The very anonymity of the playwright is itself evidence that Neville chose secrecy from the very start of his writing career. However he left enough clues in the vocabulary and themes for us to see his inky, juvenile fingerprints...

At the end of the play Comedy says to Envy (**Henry Neville**)

> How now, Envy? what, blushest thou all ready?
> Peep forth, hide not thy head with shame...

(Q1: Epilogue, 1)

Chapter 3

LOCRINE

In 1595 a play, *The Lamentable Tragedy of Locrine*, was published. It had been registered the year before, on 20th July 1594. The title page stated the text was: "Newly set forth, overseen and corrected by W.S."[11]. If this play is by Shakespeare it was the first to be so identified and just two years after the very first appearance of the name 'William Shakespeare' as the author of *Venus and Adonis* (1593) and one year after *The Rape of Lucrece* in 1594. At the start of his career as a playwright Shakespeare-Neville chose anonymity. For four years, from 1594 – 1598, the early canonical plays were published without any writer on their title pages: the quartos of *Henry VI* parts 2 and 3 (1594), *Titus Andronicus* (1594), *Richard III* (1597), and *Romeo and Juliet* (1597) were printed anonymously. To these we can add *Edward III* (1596), which has recently been accepted into the canon. I believe that *Edmund Ironside* also belongs in the canon (this was never published, surviving in one manuscript copy now in the British Library: it is believed to date from 1588). The other three plays written during this period were not published until the First Folio in 1623 (*Henry VI* part one, *The Taming of the Shrew* and *The Two Gentlemen of Verona*). In 1598, three years after *Locrine* was printed as being by W.S., *Love's Labour's Lost* was first published: it was stated to be by 'W. Shakespere' and the same year the second quartos of *Richard II* and *Richard III* were identified as by 'William Shake-speare'.

The German scholar Tieck insisted that Shakespeare was the youthful author of *Locrine*. It has been ascribed to Marlowe, Greene and Peele; the writing was influenced by Kyd and Spenser; there are also links with a poem by Lodge (see Appendix 7 for an examination of all these writers' contributions). This chapter examines what evidence there is for this being a work by the young Henry Neville. It does so by placing *Locrine* in the context of what other possible juvenilia: *Mucedorus, The Troublesome Raigne of John King of England, Edmund Ironside, Arden of Faversham* and the *Phaeton* sonnet. I also look at the *Henry VI* trilogy and *Cymbeline*. I examine Neville's vocabulary in his diplomatic letters. This intertextual study will focus on the patterning of

---

[11] The 1598 quarto of *Love's Labour's Lost* stated it was "newly corrected and augmented by W. Shakespeare".

words, plots and imagery in these works and look for evidence of Neville's life and experience filtered through the historical tale of *Locrine*. A number of scholars have taken a negative view of *Locrine*, criticising the quality of the writing and the drama. I am withholding any such judgements and looking at what is there in the text.

The name 'Locrine' is derived from the Welsh 'Loegria' (meaning England) so this story can be seen as a national myth. Let us begin with an outline of the play.

The plot of *Locrine*

Brutus, the first mythic King of Britain, on his deathbed, arranges the marriage of his son and heir, Locrine, to Guendoline and then divides up his kingdom between his sons (Locrine, Albanact and Camber), hoping thereby to ensure a tranquil realm. After his death, Humber the Hun, King of the Scithians, invades and there is a battle in which Albanact is killed. The ghost of Albanact haunts Humber and calls for revenge. Locrine defeats Humber, who roams the countryside looking for food. He meets a clownish Cobbler, Strumbo, who earlier had been press-ganged into the army. Humber eventually commits suicide (in the river which ever afterwards bears his name). Strumbo's first wife dies in a fire and he is forced into marrying a second wife. Locrine meets Humber's grieving wife Estrild (she is called his 'spouse' and "the Scithian queen") and is immediately attracted to her. He breaks his oath to his father and his marriage vows to Guendoline - much to his uncle Corineius' disgust - and hides Estrild in a cave below Troynovant (London), visiting her for lovemaking: they eventually have a daughter, Sabren. Guendoline goes to Cornwall for her father's funeral and Locrine takes the opportunity to reject her and live openly with Estrild. Guendoline, unable to put up with this public infidelity, leads an army against Locrine; defeated, he and Estrild commit suicide. Sabren falls into Guendoline's vindictive hands but escapes her clutches by committing suicide, drowning herself in the river Severn (which then is named after her). Guendoline's son Madan inherits the throne. (See Appendix 3 for the structure of the interweaving elements of the plot.)

External evidence

Thomas Creede, the printer of *Locrine*, printed six Shakespeare plays, the first of which, *Henry VI* part 2, he printed without identifying the author, the year before *Locrine*. Maxwell (1969, 5) pointed out that Creede was solely responsible for the publication of ten plays, half of which were anonymous, the others being correctly attributed to their authors, identified either by their full names or by their initials. We have therefore no reason to believe that Creede was dishonest at this time: it was only much later, indeed during the following century, that the initials W.S. were used on the title pages of plays that were definitely not by Shakespeare: Creede printed *The London Prodigal* in 1605 as by William Shakespeare[12]. Philip Chetwinde put *Locrine* in the Third Folio published in 1664, thus attributing it to Shakespeare just 50 years after his death.

On the title page of a quarto of *Locrine*[13] there is some handwriting:

The S of **VV.S.** is underlined.

On the left is a capital N :   on the right is H :

It is impossible to say whether this is evidence for Henry Neville's authorship or the initials of an early owner and so just a coincidence. The fact that the initials are the wrong way round, being N.H. instead of H.N. need not rule out Neville. In the 1609 dedication to Shakespeare's sonnets, the initials of the dedicatee, Mr. W. H., are reversed to protect the identity of Henry Wriothesley, Earl of Southampton. It was Brenda James who alerted me to this title page: she had noticed it in *Ungentle Shakespeare* (Duncan-Jones, 2001, 41) and I inspected the copy in the British Library. There are other initials lower down but these are obscured by an inkblot.

Charles Tilney: the writer who never was

Sir George Buc (also spelt Buck, 1560-1622) annotated his copy of the *Locrine* quarto as follows:

> "Charles Tilney wrot[e a] Tragedy of this mattr [which] hee named Estrild [which] I think is this. it was [lost] by his death. & now s[ome] fellon [or fellou] hath published [it]. I made du[m]be shewes for it w[hi]ch I yet haue. G. B."

What might this tell us?

1) That *Locrine* is Charles Tilney's *Estrild*.
2) OR that there were two plays: Tilney's *Estrild* and a new version: *Locrine* by "some fellow".
3) That Buck did not know who had published the play: even though the initials W.S. were on the title page he did not recognise who the "some fellon/w" was.

---

[12] From: http://en.wikipedia.org/wiki/Thomas_Creede [Accessed 2008]
[13] British Library Shelf marked C 34 b 28, this quarto is part of the 'Garrick Collection of Old Plays' which were bequeathed to the British Museum in 1779.

4) Buck was not entirely sure that "this" (i.e. *Locrine*) is the original *Estrild*: he says "I think" it is.
5) That Buck himself had been involved in the original *Estrild*.
6) The original *Estrild* was extant before Tilney died in 1586 but then lost.
7) That someone preserved the lost play and then possibly used it as a basis for the new *Locrine*.
8) *Estrild* had dumb shows, just as *Locrine* does.
9) That the date of composition of the play, if written by Tilney, would be at least as early as 1585-6.

Griffin (1997, 37 footnote 3) suggested that Buck's hesitancy about whether the play was by Tilney could be explained by the fact that it had been revised. Maxwell (1969, 207) doubted that the dumb shows of *Locrine* were by Buck on the grounds that two of them include extensive quotations from Spenser's *Visions of the World's Vanitie* (which, since it dates from 1591, could not have been known to Tilney).

Who was Tilney? Charles Tilney (1561-86) was one of Her Majesty's Gentlemen Pensioners, in effect her body guard, who had his chambers at the court in Westminster. He was drawn into the 1586 plot to assassinate Elizabeth and bring Mary Queen of Scots to the throne, by Anthony Babington. Tilney was opposed to the proposal to assassinate Elizabeth but suggested surprising and kidnapping her and then persuading her to grant greater toleration of religion and accept a change of ministers. It was Babington who stated in his confession that Tilney had agreed to kill the Queen but this confession was made under torture. Tilney was found guilty of treason and executed. By linking Tilney with *Locrine*, was Buck suggesting a connection between the play and the Babington plot?

Buck names the early play *Estrild*, thus highlighting the queen of the invading army and so pointing to her tragedy: although she becomes the lover of the native reigning King, Locrine, she is held in secret, underground for seven years and then dies. Indeed this is a play about two rival queens! The real queen, Guendoline, survives. Thus it seems this play, with its link to Tilney and therefore the Babington Plot, is about Mary Queen of Scots and the possibility of a Spanish invasion. Mary was held prisoner for 18 years by Elizabeth I. The identification of Estrild with Mary Queen of Scots is arguable because the playwright makes Estrild the queen consort of Humber the invader, whereas in Holinshed she was one of "three yong damsels taken of excellent beautie… daughter to a certain king of Scythia." The play prophecies the doom of the invader and the usurping ('strumpet') queen and of those who are attracted to her (even if, like Locrine, they are the highest in the land). The old, loyal retainers and the true, native Queen, will defeat this unholy alliance. The legitimate heir (Madan) will survive and take over the reign(s). This is emphatically NOT a play a Babington plotter such as Tilney would write: he would choose to show the triumph of an exiled or imprisoned queen, not her humiliation and suicide. At the end of *Locrine* the connection with Mary Queen of Scots and Elizabeh I is made almost explicit: there certainly can be no mistaking the deferential reference to Elizabeth.

> Let them be warned by these premises.
> And as a woman was the only cause
> That civil discord was then stirred up,
> So let us pray for that renowned maid,
> That eight and thirty years the scepter swayed,
> In quiet peace and sweet felicity;
> And every wight that seeks her grace's smart,
> Would that this sword were pierced in his heart!
>
> (5.6.199)

Whilst the woman mentioned here is Estrild we can also presume Mary Queen of Scots is intended as the woman who "stirred up civil discord"; the next person mentioned is Elizabeth I. We are also offered an implicit date: Elizabeth came to the throne in 1558 so the 38th year of her reign would be 1596. (The play was printed in 1595.) Furthermore when we consider the plot of the whole play we see that it opens with the mythical hero-founder of the nation: Brutus. He wishes to settle his kingdom on his son Locrine and binds him in a witnessed oath of loyalty to his future wife Guendoline. Then he can die in peace. There is an implicit anxiety about the monarchical succession, peace and loyalty. It is his oath of loyalty that Locrine breaks in making Estrild his mistress and the consequences are disastrous. In effect the playwright is saying to his audience, "We must keep faith, keep our oaths of loyalty to the Queen and resist any invasion or any other Queen however attractive she may be." Again this is not a message the Catholic Tilney would have offered an audience. However there is another possible view offered by Griffin (1997) who suggested that it is Guendoline who is Mary Queen of Scots come to throw the illegitimate Queen Estrild out. He suggested that Guendoline comes at the head of an invading army; but surely this is not the case: Guendoline is supported by Locrine's uncle Thrasimachus and the army is from Cornwall: hardly a foreign country! It is Estrild who is the foreign consort of the invader and the usurper of the royal bed. In the play she taunts Guendoline as "a vestal Nun" (5.5.45), surely pointing to Elizabeth as the Virgin Queen who is also called "that renowned maid"

(5.6.202) in the final speech of the play. In *A Midsummer Night's Dream* Oberon refers to Elizabeth I as "a vestal throned by the west... chaste... the imperial votaress...maiden" (2.1.158). Yates (1975, 5, 103) wrote of the Tudor propaganda myth of Elizabeth as a just, vestal virgin reforming and purifying church and state, and that this symbolism "incorporated the legend of Trojan descent of the Tudors." (i.e. Brutus in the Locrine legend.) She goes on to link *Cymbeline* with this (see below). Whoever wrote *Locrine* then was a member of the Tudor establishment.

I have found no evidence that Charles Tilney was a writer. Edmund Tilney, Master of Revels from 1578-1610, was a writer: in 1568 he published *The Flower of Friendship*, a humanist dialogue on marriage.[14] Charles was Edmund's cousin. It was Edmund Tilney who refused to license the play of *Sir Thomas More*, (written c 1592-3) and wrote a warning on the manuscript "leave out ye insurrection wholly and the cause thereof at your own perills."[15] Some of that play is believed to be by Shakespeare. Buck was also related to Charles Tilney (Charles' grandmother was Buck's aunt). Buck's note then that Charles Tilney wrote a version of the *Estrild/Locrine* story has some force. We cannot doubt that Buck was politically aware: he was an envoy to France in 1587, just after the Babington plot. He became the censor of plays as Master of the Revels from 1610-1622. He was a careful scholar and historian (ODNB, 2004, Vol 8, 498, Harrison, R.). Buck was also a friend of the Earl of Essex and was on the Cadiz expedition in 1596 during which Henry Neville was knighted. We can therefore presume Buck knew Neville.

If Charles Tilney had written the original play, it would date from before his execution in 1586 for his participation in the Babington Plot. There is no evidence, however, that Charles Tilney did any dramatic writing, other than this alleged connection with *Locrine*.[16]

Some have speculated that the 'W.S.' of the title page is actually intended to represent Wentworth Smith. However Smith is not known to have written any play before 1601. The attribution to 'W.S.' on the title page of 1595 should not be dismissed. In the past such attributions of apocryphal works to Shakespeare were regarded with suspicion because the booksellers later sought to profit from the saleability of the Shakespeare attribution. This however would be the first play attributed to Shakespeare and published after *The Rape of Lucrece* (1594) so it is unlikely the printer was cashing in on the name by only using initials.

---

[14] http://en.wikipedia.org/wiki/Edmund_Tilney [Accessed 2008]
[15] From: http://home.att.net/~mleary/conceal.htm [Accessed 2008]
[16] From: http://en.wikipedia.org/wiki/Locrine [Accessed 2008]

Perhaps the very cautious use of just the initials was aimed to test what reaction this attribution would cause: Neville testing the water. If the original play was by Tilney, Neville would be able to deny authorship. Perhaps when there was little or no reaction he felt confident he could attribute other plays more openly to Shakespeare: he had been using the pseudonym for over 5 years (1593-98) before plays were openly stated to be by William Shakespeare.

What does "Newly set forth, overseen and corrected by W.S." actually mean? It could mean either that W.S. was the only author revising his own work or that he was an editor revising someone else's play. It could mean that W.S. was simply tidying up the text: correcting rather than wholesale re-writing. It does seem to suggest there was an earlier version to that published in 1595. Griffin (1997) suggested that "corrected" means that Tilney's original play had been revised specifically to alter its original pro-Catholic bias in order to make it more politically acceptable. Or did Neville just use the idea of Tilney's play to further hide his own authorship? Surely this was a very high risk strategy given Tilney was a condemned traitor. An alternative is that Neville experimented in attributing a play to a dead man because the playwright could not then be interrrogated. But this is surely too Machiavellian a strategy. In any case *Locrine*'s publisher made no mention of Tilney (probably wise, as to mention an executed traitor as the author would not exactly encourage sales!) Without Buck's note we would never have guessed Charles Tilney was the author because we have no evidence that he wrote anything at all. However another result of Buck's hint is that it has pointed us to look at the links between the play and the Babington Plot. A more fruitful question then is to ask how might W.S./Neville get hold of the manuscript of *Estrild* (if such a play ever existed)?

Henry Neville's connections with the Babington Plot

The period immediately after Neville's return from his European travels in 1583 saw three plots involving Mary Queen of Scots: The Throckmorton Plot (1583), The Parry Plot (1585) and the Babington Plot (1586). There were Neville connections with all three plots.

In 1583 Francis and Thomas Throckmorton were caught up in a plot to murder Elizabeth I and put Mary Queen of Scots on the throne. Francis Throckmorton was interrogated and tortured in the Tower of London by Thomas Norton, co-author of the first English tragedy, *Gorboduc*, and Rackmaster (Hicks, 1964, 31-2). Francis was eventually executed in 1585. (Norton had died the year before.) Thomas escaped abroad. Neville had met up with Arthur Thockmorton (a cousin of

Francis) in Germany and Italy in 1580-1. Arthur's father, Nicholas Throckmorton (brother of Francis' father), had earlier been ambassador to France. Neville's father-in-law, Henry Killigrew, had been Nicholas' secretary in 1559 (Miller, 1963, 49). Arthur was a friend of Anthony Bacon who was operating a spy network on the continent (James & Rubinstein 2005, 76). Arthur had met Anthony in France in January 1582 (Rowse, 1962, 93). The Throckmorton and Neville families were already connnected: Henry Neville's aunt Catherine (Neville) had married Clement Throckmorton of Haseley, Warwickshire in about 1540.

Sir Henry Neville (Neville's father) and Sir Ralph Sadler were given custody of Mary Queen of Scots for a while in 1584-5. Elizabeth I's letter authorising this is dated 1st April 1584 (Hicks, 1964, 149). From 1585 Sir Amias Paulet was appointed Keeper of Mary Queen of Scots until her death in 1587. It is likely that Neville had met Paulet (Ambassador to France, 1576-1579) as he passed through Paris on his European tour (1578-83). There was a further connection between them as Paulet had Francis Bacon (Anthony's brother) with him at that time and the Bacon brothers were closely related to Neville (their half-sister being Neville's step mother).[17] Neville noted the death of Paulet's son Anthony in a letter dated 29/7/1600 (Winwood, 1725, Vol 1, 233).

William Parry was a Member of Parliament and double agent working for Cecil and Walsingham. During The Parry Plot of 1585, Parry attempted to involve his 'cousin' Sir Edmund Neville, in assassinating the Queen. Edmund denounced him and Parry was convicted and executed on 2nd March 1585.[18] Even though Edmund turned Queen's evidence, and was pardoned, he was still imprisoned in the Tower of London for 13 years.[19]

Not all the Nevilles were so loyal: a spy-report sent from Paris to London in August 1585 warned that Charles Neville, the 6th Earl of Westmoreland, might, as part of a Catholic invasion of England, land in N.W. England. In 1588 he was to be one of the leaders of an invasion force at the time of the Spanish Armada.[20] Solomon Aldred, at one time a servant of Charles Neville, was involved in spying under Walsingham's direction in France, reporting to the then British Ambassador, Sir Edward Stafford (Smith, 1936, 57, 118). He was also

---

[17] Some of this material is drawn from: http://en.wikipedia.org/wiki/Amias_Paulet [Accessed 2008]
[18] From: http://www.tudorplace.com.ar/Documents/parry_plot.htm [Accessed 2008]
[19] From: http://www.tudorplace.com.ar/NEVILLE3.htm [Accessed 2008]
[20] From: http://www.tudorplace.com.ar/Bios/CharlesNeville(6EWestmoreland).htm [Accessed 2008]

involved in deceiving Catholics in Rome, with English government propaganda (Hicks, 1964, 137). Aldred continued spying in France until at least 1586 but eventually Catholics realised he was a government agent. Aldred was therefore on the continent during Neville's European travels (1578-83). Aldred was certainly in France in 1582 and in Rome in 1583. We do not know if they ever met.

There are links between Neville and elements of the Babington Plot. Neville had connections with Sir Francis Walsingham, (the head of Elizabeth's secret service and the mastermind manipulating the conspirators of the Babington Plot) from at least 1583 when they went to Scotland together on government business. Neville's father-in-law, Sir Henry Killigrew, had gone on a secret mission to Scotland in 1572 to discuss the elimination of Mary Queen of Scots (Hicks, 1964, 95). Killigrew was a life long friend of Neville's father and a friend of Walsingham (James, 2008b, 99). Neville would probably have met Walsingham before 1583 as Philip Sidney was married to his daughter and Sidney's father was Neville's father's best friend. Robert Poley was a double agent at the heart of the Babington plot. He was also in the service of Sir Philip and Lady Sidney.

James (2007c, 47) has traced the links between Neville and Charles Paget, a double agent (working mainly for Walsingham) who told Mary Queen of Scots that she should contact Babington. He was in Paris at the time of the plot, had probably already met Neville during his first visit to Paris in 1578, and later returned to Paris when Neville was ambassador to meet him on numerous occasions: Neville mentioned Paget often in his letters to Robert Cecil. Paget was involved in the Throckmorton, Parry and Babington Plots (Hicks, 1964).

Neville showed he was aware of the continuing aftermath of the execution of Mary Queen of Scots in a letter to Cecil, dated 27/6/1599 in which he discussed negotiations about the succession to Elizabeth I, using code numbers to conceal the names of James VI of Scotland and the Infanta of Spain (it was treason at the time to publically discuss the succession). He wrote of the dissension amongst the English Catholics abroad and the division between extremists and moderates. Of the latter:

> "Charles Paget hath bin their chiefe; who could not be bought, as they pretend, to consent, or concurre, to the invasion and conquest of our Kingdom by a foraine Prince. This division beganne amongst them, soon after the Death of the Queene of Scotts, upon whom they did all concurre whiles she lived"
>
> (Winwood, 1725, Vol 1, 51).

At the conclusion of the Babington plot Mary Queen of Scots was taken to Fotheringhay Castle in Northamptonshire for trial and execution. Fotheringhay was traditionally the home of the Dukes of York. Richard III was born there in 1452, and his father, Richard Neville, Duke of York, was re-buried at the nearby church in 1476. His wife, Cecily Neville, was interred in a tomb opposite. Henry Neville, the 6th Baron of Abergavenny (Neville's uncle), was one of peers who tried Mary Queen of Scots on 6 Oct 1586 at Fotheringhay.[21] This Henry Neville supported a theatre company (Lord Abergavenny's Men) between 1571-1576 (Cavendish, 1923, Vol 2, 92). Griffin (1997, 39) pointed out that one of Tilney's judges was none other than Thomas Sackville, the first Earl of Dorset and later Baron Buckhurst, author, with Thomas Norton, of *Gorboduc*. Sackville was related to Neville through marriage. (The opening scene of *Locrine* imitates that of *Gorboduc*.) Thus through his father, his uncle, through his connections with Walsingham, Buck and Sackville, Neville was well placed to receive any dubious manuscript for revision or safe keeping. Neither is this the only such doubtful document to come into Neville's hands: the famous Northumberland Manuscript, which originally belonged to Neville, was a bundle of papers which included two banned works: Nashe and Jonson's play *The Isle of Dogs* and *Leicester's Commonwealth* (which James, 2007b believes to have been written by Paget). Thus if Tilney was a writer and had written a first version of a play he called *Estrild* there are possible routes that this manuscript could have filtered through to Neville. However I have come to doubt that any such play ever existed. Either Buck did not know who the author was and guessed it was Tilney, or he had been told the play was by Tilney to deceive him, or his note was conscious or unconscious disinformation, which in effect protected the identity of the real writer. There also remains the possibility that, as some have suggested, Buck's note is an 18th Century forgery.

There were a number of pamphlets written after the Babington plot: one was a doggerel 'Invective' by the clown William Kempe; another was by Bishop George Carleton who later married Neville's widow Anne (ODNB, 2004, Vol 3, 79, Williams, P.).

The date of *Locrine*

Kyd's *Spanish Tragedy* is believed to have been written between 1585-90. It is possible it was written before the Armada (to which it makes no reference), thus we could refine the date to 1585-7 (Cairncross,

---

[21] From: http://www.tudorplace.com.ar/NEVILLE4.htm [Accessed 2008]

1967, xxxi). *Tamburlaine* was probably written 1587-9 (and registered in August 1590, published 1593). The author of *Locrine* was probably influenced by Kyd and Marlowe (see Appendix 7). From these we can suggest that the first version of *Locrine* was written between 1587-9. *Locrine* has what seems to be a reference to the defeat of the Armada (1588): Humber, the leader of an invading army, lamenting his defeat, cries:

> Curst be the sea, that with outrageous waves,
> With surging billows did not rive my ships
> Against the rocks of high Cerannia,
> Or swallow me into her watery gulf!

$$(3.7.28)$$

From this we can suggest that whatever the date of the original composition, *Locrine* was revised from 1588. I therefore suggest a process of writing and revising that stretched from 1585 – 1595 when it was printed with a reference to Elizabeth's 38th year on the throne (which started on November 17th 1595). The early date of 1585 in this scheme allows for the possibility of an early version, *Estrild*, by Tilney. McKerrow and Tucker Brooke (Gooch, 1981, 5, 9) both supported this early dating on grounds of the style of the drama. If Tilney was never involved the date could revert to 1587-9 for the first version. Dickinson (1909, lvii) offered a hypothetical date for *Locrine*, placing it between Greene's *A Looking Glass for London and England* (written 1587-91, printed 1594) and *Orlando Furioso* (1588, printed 1594): this would suggest the play was written 1587-8. Farmer (1910) had also allocated 1587-8 as the date for *Locrine*. Since one possible source for the play is the 1587 edition of Holinshed this would confirm that date but there is a possibility (since his father-in-law was editing it) that Neville had access to this Holinshed edition before it was published. (Tilney however was executed the year before.) It is now accepted that Shakespeare used the 1587 edition of Holinshed, not the first edition of 1577. Bate (1997, 201) and others pointed out that Shakespeare "was the only dramatist of the age who returned frequently to that foundation-text of Tudor ideology, Holinshed's *Chronicles*" (Egan, 2006, 61).

In poenam sectatur et umbra
Whitney's Choice of Emblemes 32[22]

The opening Latin line of *Locrine*, spoken by Ate: "In paenam sectatur & umbra" ('In retribution even a shadow seems to pursue a guilty man.' Or: 'the ghost pursues for punishment') is motto 32 from Whitney's *Choice of Emblemes* [23] which comes complete with woodblock illustrations.

O vita, misero longa
Whitney's Choice of Emblemes 75[24]

Another Latin line "O vita, misero longa" in *Locrine* can be traced to Whitney's motto 75. That Shakespeare knew this volume cannot be doubted for Pericles bears motto 183a on his shield: "Qui me alit me extinguit" (2.2.33).

---

[22] http://www.mun.ca/alciato/whit/w032.html [Accessed 2008]
[23] From: http://www.mun.ca/alciato/wcomm.html [Accessed 2008]
[24] http://www.mun.ca/alciato/whit/w075.html [Accessed 2008]

Qui me alit me extinguit
Whitney's Choice of Emblemes 183a[25]

Whoever wrote *Locrine* had access to a library containing expensive new books! This also possibly throws light on the date of *Locrine*. Whitney's book was published in 1586 in Leiden, Holland, although it was available in manuscript from 1566 and based on Andrea Alciato's *Emblematum liber* or *Book of Emblems* which was first published in 1531.

Sams (1986) convincingly dated *Edmund Ironside* to 1588. I accept his conclusion that *Edmund Ironside* was written by Shakespeare. Therefore if *Locrine* and *Edmund Ironside* are by the same playwright and written about the same time we would expect some links between them and I explore these below.

Gooch (1981, 10) summarises the issues of date and revisions of the text thus: "The available evidence suggests that *Locrine* was first written around 1585 and then went through several stages of revision, perhaps by a number of different hands, until it was completed in its final form in 1594." I will finally suggest that Neville wrote the first version in 1586-7 after he had written *Mucedorus*, thus I will date the play between 1586-89, with revisions until 1595. If Neville was the author of *Locrine* he was aged between 24-28 when he wrote the first version.

Ovid and *Locrine*

Non potuit Juno vincere, vicit amor.
(He whom Juno could not overcome, love overcomes.)

This, the openning line of the Prologue to Act 4, is a quotation from Ovid's *Heroides* (IX Deianira to Hercules).[26] Other lines from the *Heroides* are quoted in two early plays dating from 1589-90, *The Taming*

---

[25] http://www.mun.ca/alciato/whit/w183a.html [Accessed 2008]
[26] From: http://www.theoi.com/Text/OvidHeroides2.html [Accessed 2008]

of The Shrew (3.1.28) and in *Henry VI* part 3 (1.3.48): in both cases Shakespeare-Neville quotes from the Latin as the author does here in *Locrine* (Sams, 1986, 208). There are also quotes from Virgil's *Aeneid* in both *Locrine* and *Henry VI* part 2 (2.1.24) in Latin. The earliest extant letters written by Neville, dating from 1578-9, are in Latin.

Gooch (1981) lists Ovid's *Metamorphoses* as a source for the references to Orpheus, Icarus, Perseus and Sisiphus in *Locrine*. Ovid of course was Shakespeare's favourite poet and *Metamorphoses* his favourite work. I have found Ovid in *Mucedorus, Locrine* and *Arden of Faversham* (see chapter 4). (See Appendix 5 for other classical references in the play.)

Historic sources

The author of *Locrine* drew upon legends of early Britain to be found in Geoffrey of Monmouth's *Historia Regum Britanniae*, (reissued in **1587** by Commeline in the original Latin, in which Neville was fluent), the 1574 edition of *The Mirror for Magistrates* (reissued in **1587**), and Holinshed's *Chronicles* of **1587**. Henry Killigrew, Neville's father-in-law, was involved in editing the **1587** edition of Holinshed[27]. This suggests that *Locrine* was written from about 1587 onwards.

At the start of his *Chronicle*, in the opening dedication, Hall mentions Brutus: he refers back to Geoffrey of Monmouth who "translated a certain Britishe or Welshe boke, contenyning the commyng of Brute with the sequel of his linage..." Amongst the annotations Keen discovered in a copy of Hall's *Chronicle* there is the following note:

> "Brutus Kinge of England devided the kingdom thres"
> (Keen & Lubbock, 1954,137).

Thus we can see that Shakespeare-Neville was noting the myth of Brutus (Locrine's father) in Hall; furthermore he noted that "bellona the goddesse of battayle hath III handmaydes blode, fyre and famyn" (Keen & Lubbock, 1954,145). Bellona is mentioned twice in *Locrine* (3.5.4 and 4.2.1), twice in *Mucedorus* (Induction, 6 and 15), once in *Edward III* (3.3.189) and twice in *The Two Noble Kinsmen* (1.1.75 and 1.2.13).

A section of *The Mirror for Magistrates* was created by Thomas Sackville, author of *Gorboduc*. Indeed *Gorboduc* is a possible influence on *Locrine*. In both a King divides up his kingdom and the result is civil war (this is, of course, also the pattern of *King Lear*). Both may be

---

[27] Howard, (2003, 65), from *Censorship and the Problems with History*; see also
http://www.kcl.ac.uk/depsta/iss/library/speccoll/bomarch/bomfeb05.html [Accessed 2008]

seen as political plays expressing anxiety about the future of the realm after Elizabeth's childless reign. We know Neville was in touch with Sackville and his son Robert as there are extant letters between them concerning Neville's manufacture of cannon, 1595-7. Sackville, Lord Buckhurst, himself was involved in this trade. Tim Cornish (2007), who has studied the trade in cannon, writes:

> "Neville's aim was the same as his father-in-law's (Killigrew's): Protestant leaders on the continent had to be provided with Mayfield guns if they were to sustain their fledgling regimes against the growing threat of a Catholic conspiracy that, if unchecked, would eventually wipe out the results of England's Reformation. The memory of the Armada and its threat was still vivid in the imaginations of the gunfounders of Sussex."

Locrine was also a result of that Protestant imagination. Furthermore *Locrine* fits into Neville's political thinking that above all civil war must be avoided. The nation must be united against any foreign threat. Neville's thinking on this was remembered by his grandson, also a politician and concealed poet, who wrote a dialogue stating that had Neville's advice been followed then the English Civil War could have been avoided. Shakespeare-Neville demonstrated the evils of "civil discord" in his history plays (James, 2008b, 184).

What is new and original

The playwright distorted the main story with a number of additions. Several minor characters, Hubba, Segar, Trussier and Trasimachus, are not found in any of the sources (Gooch, 1981, 1 footnote 1). Strumbo and the comic subplot are further inventions, as are the suicides of Albanact, Locrine, Estrild and Sabren. The playwright especially distorted the story so that he could write a series of laments, delaying Humber's death by seven years and thus giving Humber three laments. The four key changes to the story are:

1) Brutus arranges Locrine's marriage to Guendoline before he dies.
2) Estrild is Humber's queen.
3) Humber survives his defeat and wanders in the wilderness for seven years, starving before committing suicide.
4) Estrild commits suicide on Locrine's sword and Sabren escapes Guendoline's vengeance by drowning herself.

The last of these points can be explained by the identification of Guendoline, the legitimate Queen, with Elizabeth I: it would hardly be appropriate to show her vindictively tying Estrild and Sabren together before drowning them in the river, as is the case in most sources. At the end of *Locrine* Estrild is, like Tamora, another 'strumpet' queen in *Titus Andronicus*, left unburied.

Internal evidence: the language of *Locrine* and Shakespeare
Rather than trace the use of individual words (which could be regarded as in the general vocabulary of the time) I have chosen to focus on pairs or groups of words that are also used by Shakespeare, for example: 'effusion' and 'blood'. In *Locrine* Hubba (Humber's son) brags he will cause a "great **effusion of blood**" (2.2.88). In *Henry VI* part 1 Gloucester speaks of stopping the "**effusion of** our Christian **blood**" (5.1.9); later '**blood**' is '**effus'd**' (5.4.52). In *Henry VI* part 3 Clifford speaks of "much **effuse of blood**" (2.6.28). In *Henry V* Mountjoy refers to "th'**effusion of** our **blood**" (3.6.129). Furthermore, I find "much **effusion** of our English **blood**" in *The Troublesome Raigne of John King of England* (1.2.416), which I consider is another early work by Shakespeare-Neville. The word '**effusion**' occurs in *King John* but it is of tears (5.2.49). (For further links between *Locrine* and *The Troublesome Raigne* see below.) When such pairs/groups of words occur in *Locrine* and in a Shakespeare play I see it as possible evidence that the same writer was the author of both. When I find another contemporary author using such a combination of words I will list the reference: in this case it is Marlowe, who in *Edward II* (acted 1592-3, registered 1593, printed 1594) has a Herald speak of avoiding an "effusion of bloud" (LION: 3.1.162).

'**Depopulate**' is only used by Shakespeare in the period 1585-1610 and, as it occurs in *Locrine* in a cluster of associations that are Shakespearean, it is furthermore suggestive of the bard's authorship. In *Locrine* Albanact says:

> It grieves me, lordings, that my subjects' goods
> Should thus be spoiled by the Scithians,
> Who, as you see, with **lightfoot foragers**
> **Depopulate** the places where they come.
>
> (2.4.94)

The word '**depopulate**' occurs just once in the canon when it is used by Sicinius in *Coriolanus* (3.1.265). According to the OED this word occurs in Hall's Chronicles (1548) and North's Plutarch (1580): both sources used by Shakespeare. The word '**lightfoot**' is used five times in *Locrine*. In *Richard III* the king speaks of: "Some **light-foot** friend" (4.4.439). In 1579 Spencer used '**lightfoot**' in his *Shepheardes Calendar* (OED). '**Foragers**' is used just once in *Troilus and Cressida* (1.3.82). Lodge, in his poem *The Complaint of Elstred*, used the word '**forage**' twice (stanzas 14 and 18). '**Forage**' is used in *Venus and*

Adonis (554), which was printed the same year as Lodge's poem. '**Foraging**' occurs in *Arden of Faversham* (3.3.22). Apart from Shakespeare, I have found no other poet who uses all three words: **lightfoot, foragers, depopulate**.

A rare word, '**invocate**', is used in Shakespeare's Sonnet 38:

> Be thou the tenth **Muse**, ten times more in worth
> Than those old nine which rhymers **invocate**...

The play *Edward III*, which was, until recently, thought of as an apocryphal play of doubtful authorship, has now been accepted into the Shakespeare canon. The word '**invocate**' is used by the King: "Now, Lodowick, **invocate** some golden **Muse**." Not only does he use the word '**Muse**', as in sonnet 38, but other words such as 'paper', 'sweet' and "ten times" in the same passage; in both they are writing love poems. The occurrence of '**invocate**' in sonnet and play suggests a common author. In *Locrine* Estrild says:

> Then lo, brave Locrine, Estrild yields to thee;
> And by the gods, whom thou doest **invocate**,
> By the **dead ghost** of thy deceased sire,
> By thy right hand and by thy burning love,
> Take pity on poor Estrild's **wretched** thrall.
>
>   (4.2.146)

In *Henry VI* part 1 Bedford says, "Henry the Fifth, thy **ghost** I **invocate**" (1.1.52). Within the same passage he uses the words '**wretched**' and '**dead**'. In *Richard III* Anne says, "Be it lawful that I **invocate** thy **ghost**" (1.2.8). What is especially interesting about this echo by Anne is that Locrine's wooing of Estrild in this scene recalls Richard's wooing of Anne. (Note: both Richard and Anne were Nevilles). The word '**invocate**' cannot be considered a commonplace. According to the OED Drayton used this word in 1593: "Some call on Heaven; some invocate on Hell." Bacon used it twice in his *Advancement of Learning*, (1605), once of 'spirits' (1153) and then of 'Neptune' (4715). I have found no other writer of the period who links '**invocate**' and '**ghost**' except the bard. It is also noteworthy that all these uses of '**invocate**' are in early works.

Ate begins *Locrine* with a description of a lion that, "**sparkleth fire** from forth his flaming **eyes**..." (Prologue, 15). Women's **eyes sparkle** with Promethean **fire** in *Love's Labour's Lost* (4.3.324). In *Henry VI* part 2 Suffolk says, "Mine **eyes** should **sparkle** like the beaten flint" (3.2.321). In *Henry VI* part 3 the Queen speaks of "**fiery eyes sparkling** for very **wrath**" (2.5.131). In *Henry VI* part 1 Gloucester says, "His **sparking eyes**, replete with **wrathful fire**, more **dazzled**..." (1.1.12)

'**Dazzled**' is also in *The Two Gentlemen of Verona* (2.4.206). Brutus in *Locrine* speaks of his "**dazzled** eyes" (1.2.10: the word is used twice in the play). 'Wrathful' also is used twice in *Locrine*: once it is '**wrathful eyes**' (4.4.17). Peele used "**dazzled** eye" twice in *The Arraignment of Paris* (4.1.86 and 4.1.109) but in both cases he uses the singular 'eye'. In 1594 two works were published in which the words "sparkling eyes" were used: Greene's *Friar Bacon and Friar Bungay* and Lodge's *The Wounds of Civil War* (LION). If an early dating of *Locrine* is accepted these would both post-date the play.

The words "**bereft of life**" are used 5 times in *Locrine*. For example:

> This heart,   (4 lines cut)
> Is **clove asunder** and **bereft of life**,
> As when the sacred **oak with thunderbolts**...
>
> (1.2.20)

"**Bereft of life**" occurs in *Henry VI* part 2 (3.2.271); in *Henry VI* part 3 (2.5.93); and in *Titus Andronicus* (2.2.282). Furthermore Locrine's use of the words "**clove asunder**" and "**oak with thunderbolts**" are echoed by Lear's "**oak-cleaving thunderbolts**" (3.2.5). (See the section on *Mucedorus* below, for further exploration of the words "bereave of life".)

In *Locrine* the word '**venge**' is used 7 times: for example,

> I offer up to **venge** my brother's **death**.
>
> (3.2.79)

and

> That I may **venge** my noble brother's **death**.
>
> (3.5.28)

Shakespeare used '**venge**' 8 times, 5 of which are in early works and 3 of these are near the word '**death**' (*Henry VI* part 3, 2.1.87; *Richard II* 1.2.36; *Romeo and Juliet* 3.5.86; and in *Cymbeline*, 1.6.92). In *Edmund Ironside* the word '**vengeance**' is used near '**death**' (2.3.140). Greene also used '**venge**' in *Orlando Furioso* (4.1.10), but not near '**death**'.

In *Locrine* Corineius says, "A **grateful gift** given by a gracious King" (1.2.136). A probable source for this is *The Mirror for Magistrates* (The Complaint of Albanact: 436) in which Brutus says, "I spente my **gratefull giftes** in vayne." In *The Taming of The Shrew* Gremio says, "this is a **gift** very **grateful**..." (2.1.76) In a diplomatic letter dated 29/1/1600 Neville used the words: "any **grateful** service" (Winwood, 1725, Vol 1, 291).

The word '**bowels**' is used ten times in Locrine: in four of these they are the bowels of the Earth, for example:

> We'll either rent the **bowels** of the **earth**,
> Searching the **entrails** of the brutish **earth**,
>
> (1.2.78)

> Let me be flung into the Ocean,
> And swallowed in the **bowels** of the **earth**,
>
> (1.2.162)

In *Henry IV* part 1, Hotspur says, "Out of the **bowels** of the harmless **earth**" (1.3.60). In *Titus Andronicus* Martius says, "the ragged **entrails** of the pit..." (2.3.230). In *Orlando Furioso* Greene wrote: "The **earth** within her **bowels** hath enrapt...millions of gold" (1.1.41). In *Locrine* and the canonical works the word 'bowels' comes before 'earth', which is not the case in this last example from Greene. Locrine says:

> Or as the **plough**man with his piercing share
> Renteth the **bowels** of the fertile fields,
> And rippeth **up** the roots with **razours** keen...
>
> (4.2.19)

In *Titus Andronicus* Aaron warns that, "this sword shall **plough** thy **bowels up**" (4.2.89). The word 'razors' is also used in *Titus Andronicus* (1.1.319).

Locrine says, "Thy **trampling coursers** ruled with **foaming** bits..." (4.2.14). In *Venus and Adonis* there is a "**trampling courser**" (261); in *Henry VI* part 3 "our **foaming** steeds" (2.1.182); in *Richard II*, "his **foaming courser's** back" (1.2.51). 'Foaming' occurs just 5 times in the canon: in later plays the word 'foaming' is associated with the sea (*Tempest*, 1.2.211 and *Othello*, 2.1.11) whereas in the earlier works 'foaming' is associated with horses.

Locrine contains water imagery characteristic of Shakespeare:

> **Pour down** some drink, or else I faint and die...
>
> (4.3.74)

> **Pour down your tears**, you watery regions...
>
> (5.6.48)

In *Richard III* the Duchess of York says, "...on me ... **pour** all **your tears**" (2.2.86). In *King John* the King says:

> So foul a sky clears not without a storm:
> **Pour down** thy weather...
>
> (4.2.109)

In *Love's Labour's Lost* Berowne says that, "the stars **pour down** plagues" (5.2.394).

In the Act 2 Prologue of *Locrine* Ate speaks of "**a flood of tears**" (2.1.9). In *Henry VI* part 1, Joan speaks of "**a flood of tears**" (3.3.56).

In *The Comedy of Errors* Antipholus of Syracuse speaks of a "**flood of tears...Spread o'er** the **silver** waves..." (3.2.46-8). In *Locrine* the words '**overspread**' and '**silver**' (streams) are also used. In *Locrine* Strumbo talks of "**shedding salt tears**" (1.3.8); Locrine himself echoes this later with: "And **shed salt tears** for her overthrow..." (4.2.82). Shakespeare uses the words "**salt tears**" 8 times: six of which are in works from the 1590s. Furthermore he uses the words 'shed' [16] and 'shedding' [3] with 'tears': the majority of these usages again are from the 1590s. In *Edmund Ironside* Canutus speaks of "Many a **salt tear** had been now un**shed**..." (5.2.174).

In *Venus and Adonis* Shakespeare wrote:

> ...as the **snail**, whose tender horns being hit,
> Shrinks backward in his shelly cave with pain...
>
> (1033)

In *Edward III* the King threatens the Scottish King David, "I will make you shrink your **snaily** horns!" (1.1.138). In *The Unfortunate Traveller* (1594) Thomas Nashe wrote: "What need the **snail** care for eyes when he feels the way with his two horns as well as if he were as quick-sighted as a decipherer?" (414). In *Locrine* we find:

> **At length** the **snail** doth clime the highest tops,
> Ascending up the stately castle walls;
> **At length** the water with continual drops,
> Doth penetrate the hardest **marble stone**...
>
> (2.2.1)

In *Henry VI* part 3 Richard, Duke of Gloucester, says, "much rain wears the **marble**" (3.2.50). This is echoed in *The Rape of Lucrece*: "Tears harden lust, though **marble** wear with raining" (560). The idea is repeated in *Venus and Adonis*: "**stone** at rain relenteth" (200). The words "**At length**" occur 11 times in canonical works.

Estrild, praising the English countryside, tells how:

> from the **moisture** of the **mountain tops**,
> The silent springs dance down with **murmuring streams**...
>
> (2.2.42)

In *Romeo and Juliet* Romeo says, "jocund day stands tiptoe on the **misty mountain tops**" (3.5.9). This is echoed in Sonnet 33:

> Full many a glorious morning have I seen
> Flatter the **mountain-tops** with sovereign eye,
> Kissing with golden face the meadows green,
> Gilding pale **streams** with heavenly alchemy...

Celia in *As You Like It* speaks of "the **murmuring stream**"(4.3.80). **Murmuring** occurs just 4 times in the canon: 2 of which are connected to water: *King Lear* (4.6.20) and a third, in *Anthony and Cleopatra*, has the Nile in the same line (1.5.25).

Strumbo, in his love letter to Dorothy writes: "the little sparkles of affection kindled in me towards your sweet self hath now increased to a great flame, and will ere it be long consume my poor heart, except you, with the **pleasant** water of your secret **fountain**, quench the furious heat of the same" (1.3.36). This erotic invitation was echoed by Shakespeare in *Venus and Adonis* when Venus invites her lover to:

> Graze on my lips, and if those hills be dry,
> Stray lower, where the **pleasant fountains** lie.
>
> (231)

Published in 1593 this must have been written within 5 years of *Locrine*. The parallel was first noticed by Steevens in 1780 (Gooch, 1981, 59 footnote).

A Shakespearean imagery cluster: a picture of Death

Caroline Spurgeon's classic (1958) examination of Shakespeare's imagery identified the main types and specific, characteristic ways the bard used metaphors. She noted that his main areas of imagery included **nature**, specifically weather, winds, gardens, the sea, rivers, grasses, animals (especially birds) etc: above all **movement**. She also found he used many images concerning the **body**, illness and medicine, and other **domestic** areas such as fire, food and drink. It is not difficult to see that the imagery of *Locrine* fits these categories. Spurgeon sees falconry and snaring birds as especially characteristic of Shakespeare and both of these are used in *Locrine*. Spurgeon (1958, 180) also identified image clusters that she saw as signifiers for Shakespeare's authorship. One is a death image cluster, which includes the words: **hollow**, **vault**, **cave**, **tears**, **sea**, **eye/s**, **mouth/teeth/tongue**, **maw/womb**, **war**. Spurgeon (1958, 192) explained this as a picture of skeletal death including cannon, eye-ball, eye-socket of skull, (a hollow thing), tears, vault, mouth (sometimes teeth). In Brutus' first speech in *Locrine* we find this death cluster: he begins by evoking the death picture:

> Black ugly **death**, with visage pale and wan,
> Presents himself before my dazzled **eyes**…
>
> (1.2.9)

Already we have **death** and **eyes**; within the scene we also find the words: **greedy gulf**, **devoid**, **sea**, **vaults**, **throat**, **bowels**, **entrails**, **grieve**. When Albanact is wounded in Act 2 scene 6 and facing death (he falls on his sword) his speeches contain **paunch** (= maw), **gorge** (= mouth), **sea**, **death**. When Humber is defeated he seeks a **hollow** cave in which to live (3.7.7); in this speech he uses the words **teeth, throats, sea, gulf, jaws**. In Humber's final, suicide speech we see this chain of associations again (in place of **maw** there are again **bowels** and **entrails**, which being famished are empty/hollow).

> **Caves** were my beds, and stones my pillow-bears,
> Fear was my sleep, and horror was my dream,
> For still me thought, at every **boisterous blast**,
> Now Locrine comes, now, Humber, thou must **die**:
> So that for fear and **hunger**, Humber's mind
> Can never rest, but always trembling stands,
> O, what Danubius now may quench my thirst?
> What Euphrates, what lightfoot Euripus,
> May now allay the fury of that heat,
> Which, raging in my **entrails**, eats me up?
> You ghastly devils of the ninefold Styx,
> You damned ghosts of joyless Acheron,
> You mournful souls, vexed in **Abyss' vaults**,
> You coalblack devils of Avernus' pond,
> Come, with your fleshhooks rent my **famished** arms,
> These arms that have sustained their master's life.
> Come, with your razors rip my **bowels** up,
> With your sharp fireforks crack my starved **bones**:
> Use me as you will, so Humber may not live.
> Accursed gods, that rule the starry poles,
> Accursed Jove, king of the cursed gods,
> Cast down your lightning on poor Humber's head,
> That I may leave this **death**like life of mine!
> What, hear you not? and shall not Humber **die**?
> Nay, I will **die**, though all the gods say nay!
> And, gentle Aby, take my troubled **corpse**,
> Take it and keep it from all mortal **eyes**,
> That none may say, when I have lost my breath,
> The very **floods** conspired gainst Humber's **death**.

> (4.4.6)
> (He flings himself into the river.)

Immediately after this suicide the triumphant ghost of Albanact says, "Back will I post to hell **mouth**" with the news. Thus we have the essential ingredients of this death image cluster: **vault, cave, eyes, floods** (=sea/river), **mouth, entrails/bowels** (=maw/womb). We may even detect a hint of the cannon in "**boisterous blast**". The occurrence, in both Brutus' and Humber's speeches of the word 'vaults' is especially significant as the word (or its equivalent in "vaultly/vaultages/vaulted" etc) is used in ten of Spurgeon's key examples of the Shakespeare death image cluster. Let us then compare the above with an example of this cluster in an early Shakespeare play: *Henry VI* part 2. The passage occurs after the murder of Humphrey, Duke of Gloucester in Act 3, scene 2, lines 43 – 121. The cluster includes the words **hollow**, **eyes** and **eyeballs**, **tongue**, **death**, **tears**, **vaulting sea**. It lacks **cave**, **mouth/teeth**, **maw/womb**, **war**. In other words the *Locrine* passages offer more complete examples of this canonical image cluster. I have also found the "blot imagery cluster" in *Locrine* (see chapter 6). For a further examination of the vocabulary used in *Locrine* see Appendix 4.

Is Strumbo young Falstaff?

Strumbo is a happy cobbler whose first speech is a comic tour de force (see Appendix 6). He describes himself as: "a gentleman of good fame and name, majestical, in parrel comely, in gate **portly**... a proper tall, young man of a handsome life..." (1.3.41). This sounds like a self-portrait of Neville, who, in 1587, was aged 25 - 26. The word '**portly**' occurs just 7 times in the canon, two of which are used by Falstaff to describe himself: firstly in *Henry IV* part 1, as "A goodly **portly** man, " (2.4.416); in *The Merry Wives of Windsor* he speaks of "my **portly** belly" (1.3.59). Neville was nicknamed 'Falstaff' by friends (James & Rubinstein, 2005, 54).

As he composes a love letter to Dorothy, Strumbo says, "I will dite an **aliquant** love-pistle" (1.3.28). Gooch (1981, 59) suggested this was a pun on a Spanish wine from Alicante and the word 'eloquent'. This very same pun is used in *The Merry Wives of Windsor* by Mistress Quickly, when she is talking to Falstaff about courtiers sending love letters to Mistress Page: "in such **alligant** terms, and in such wine and sugar..." (2.2.65). The link with wine is made immediately. Strumbo tells his servant Trompart to "carry **this letter to Mistress** Dorothy" (1.3.64). In *Merry Wives* Falstaff also writes love letters. He tells Nim to "bear thou **this letter to Mistress** Page;" and instructs Pistol "and thou **this to Mistress** Ford" (1.3.69). Just as Falstaff here has an interest in two wives, so Strumbo has two wives in *Locrine*. Strumbo speaks of his tears as plenteous as "the water runneth from the **bucking**tubs" (1.3.11). The only time Shakespeare uses the word '**bucking**' (meaning washing) is when Falstaff hides in the laundry basket (*Merry Wives*: 3.3.121). Strumbo speaks of "the little god, nay the desparate god **Cuprit**" (1.3.14), whilst Falstaff evokes "**Cupid** a child" (*Merry Wives*: 5.5.28).

In Strumbo's first speech he uses "**Not only…but also**" twice, once at the beginning and again at the end. This is precisely what Falstaff does in *Henry IV* part 1:

> Harry, I do **not only** marvel where thou spendest thy time,
> **but also** how thou art accompanied…
>
> (2.4.393)

Falstaff ends the speech with a return to this figure of speech:

> for, Harry, now I do not speak to thee in drink but in tears, not in pleasure but in passion, **not** in words **only**, **but** in woes **also**…
>
> (2.4.410)

Bryson (2007, 193) pointed out that the bard rarely used the word 'also' and mostly put this word into the mouths of comic characters. The only other time Shakespeare uses "**not only/but also**" is in *Richard II* (4.1.328). Strumbo also links the words 'may' and 'but': "you **may** laugh, **but** I must weep; you **may** joy, **but** I must sorrow" (1.3.6). Falstaff also follows '**may**' with '**but**' in *Henry IV* part 2: "He **may** keep his own grace, **but** he's almost out of mine…" (1.2.24). Later he says, "You **may**: **but** if he had been a man's tailor, he'ld ha' pricked you" (3.2.151). In *Love's Labour's Lost* Longaville echoes Strumbo: "You **may** look pale, **but** I should blush" (4.3.126). James (2008b, 118) pointed out that the name Longaville not only contained a syllable of Neville's name but also the Longavilles were ancestors of the Nevilles.

Strumbo begins his speech with reference to astrology: "**the seven planets**, and all the particular **stars** of the pole Antastick, are **adversative** against me, or else I was begotten and born in the wane of **the Moon**" (1.3.1). Falstaff's first words in *Henry IV* part 1 include: "we that take purses go by **the moon** and **the seven stars**" (1.2.14). In *Henry VI* part 1 the words "**adverse planets**" are used (1.1.54). Furthermore Strumbo complains the planets are 'adversative' just 27 words before the word 'asward' (= arseward, backwards). In a letter dated 9/5/1600, Neville used the words 'adverse' and 'usward' (= towards us: Winwood, 1725, Vol 1, 184).

In *Henry IV* part 1 Falstaff asks Hal whether there will be "gallows standing in England" when he is King (1.2.57). Falstaff says, "I doubt not but to die a fair death for all this, if I 'scape **hanging** for killing that rogue" (2.2.13). Strumbo speaks of hanging himself and later, addressing the audience, asks, "how have you **scaped hanging** this long time?" (4.3.22). He goes on to say, "I have scaped many a **scouring** this year" (4.3.23). Falstaff says, "I were better to be eaten to death with a rust than to be **scoured** to nothing with perpetual motion" (*Henry IV* part 2, 1.2.218). In *Henry VI* part 2 the word '**scouring**' is used by

Peter (1.3.193: just five lines later Horner says, "**Hang** me") and 'scoured' is used by Suffolk (3.2.199). In *The Two Gentlemen of Verona* '**scour**' and '**scoured**' occur (3.1.305-6) in a comic passage. In another comic passage in *The Comedy of Errors* Dromio of Ephesus says, "She will **scour** your fault upon my **pate**" (1.2.65). Strumbo also uses the word '**pate**' (1.3.27 & 50). In all three comedies the idea of scouring refers to a wife, as in *Locrine*. Furthermore in Shakespeare's very last play (written with John Fletcher) *The Two Noble Kinsmen*, we find the word '**scoured**' just two lines before "I should **drown,** or stab, or **hang myself**" (3.2.30). In *Locrine* Strumbo says to himself, "kill thy self, **drown** thy self, **hang thy self**" (1.3.25).

The Annotator of Hall's *Chronicles* (thought to be Shakespeare) left a note in the margin: "A victorye on the sea at the first **scowrynge**" (Keen and Lubbock, 1954, 143). Neville used this word in a letter, dated 28/12/1600, when writing about the struggle in Ireland, "My Lord is now again in the field to **scowre** and clear the Province of Lemster..." It is especially interesting to note that the Annotator and Neville use the very same spelling: **scowr**.

Whereas Strumbo is pressed into the army, it is Falstaff who presses a motley crew into his regiment. Strumbo is a man in love at the start of the play, he is later seen to be a drinker, a lusty lover, a man who runs away in fear, just like Falstaff. Strumbo and Falstaff are both interested in their food; they both make long comic speeches; they begin in their own comic subplots but then are brought into the main tragic plot and in both cases they escape death by playing dead. In the battle between Humber and Albanact, Strumbo is seen to "**fall down**" and though he rouses himself to speak to the despairing, wounded Albanact before the latter kills himself, he is obviously playing dead when Trompart enters and speaks to his master. Strumbo replies, "Leave me alone, I tell thee, for I am dead" (2.6.95). However when Trompart laments his master's death and warns him of approaching thieves, Strumbo gets up and runs off. This recalls the scene in *Henry IV* part 1 (5.4.75) when Falstaff plays dead. The stage direction states: "Douglas...fighteth with Falstaff, who **falls down** as if he were dead." In *Locrine* the stage direction is: "let Strumbo **fall down**."

Falstaff calls Quickly, "my good **she-Mercury**" (*Merry Wives of Windsor* 2.2.76). Humber calls Strumbo, "**Mercury** in clownish shape" (4.3.75). Another clown who has a connection with **Mercury** is Autolycus in *The Winter's Tale* who introduces himself thus: "My father named me Autolycus; who being, as I am, littered under **Mercury**, was likewise a snapper-up of unconsidered trifles" (4.3.24).

Strumbo uses the rare word '**capcase**' (a travelling bag, see below). '**Capcase**' was used in Thomas Preston's *Cambyses* (Corbin and Sedge, 2002, 172). This was licenced for publication in 1569 so it definitely predates *Locrine*. The bombastic grandiloquence of the piece became proverbial, and Shakespeare is believed to allude to it in *Henry IV* part 1, when he makes Falstaff say, "I must speak in passion, and I will do it in King Cambyses' vein" (2.4.381).[28]

If *Locrine* was written ten years before Falstaff appeared we can see here the younger version of that great mountain of a character! It seems impossible that Shakespeare would copy so many of the words and mannerisms of a minor comic character in an anonymous play: Strumbo is like Falstaff because he is the idea of such a character germinating in the bard's imagination. The latest possible date for *Locrine* is 1594-5, when it was published. The earliest date for the Falstaff plays *Henry IV*. parts 1 & 2 is 1597.

Strumbo, Oliver and William
In *Henry VI* part 1 Alencon says, "England all Olivers and Rolands bred" (1.2.29). Oliver then can be taken to be an archetypal name for an Englishman, noted as such by Shakespeare. Indeed he uses the name in *As You Like It*, in which play there is also a countryman called William. In *Locrine* there are also two countrymen called Oliver and William. Strumbo is forced by Oliver and William into marrying his second wife, Margery. Shakespeare used the name Margery in four plays. This may simply be the result of these names being common but it is interesting to note the coincidence of their joint occurrence in these two plays especially as James (2007b) has elucidated cryptic remarks in *As You Like It* that point to William (the country bumpkin) being a cipher for William Shakespeare and Touchstone a cipher for Neville. William and Touchstone are rivals for Audrey. I have suggested that Strumbo is a cipher for Neville. Both Touchstone and Strumbo use the words 'rhetoric' and 'bastinado'. Thus in both plays the Neville figure is in a struggle with William about a woman... Neville would have been taught rhetoric at Merton College when at Oxford 1574-8 (James, 2008b, 242).

The rhetoric and verse forms in *Locrine*
Strumbo says, "you have your **rhetoric** so ready at your tongue's end..." (3.4.33). *Locrine* has many examples of rhetorical repetition.

---

[28] From: http://en.wikipedia.org/wiki/Thomas_Preston_(writer) [Accessed 2008]

"No other play of the earlier Elizabethan drama contains so many examples, such elaborate ones, and so great a variety of forms" (Hubbard 1905, 374; Gooch 1981, 15). Hubbard suggested that such repetition is in imitation of Seneca. There are many similar examples of such repetition in *Edmund Ironside* and the *Henry VI* trilogy. It seems to me that the young Neville first stuck close to his models and then gradually became more naturalistic in his style: *Locrine* enables us to see his very first tragic style emerging. This repetition is often couched in **rhetorical questions**. The starving Humber cries:

> **Was ever** land **so fruitless** as this land?
> **Was ever** grove **so graceless** as this grove?
> **Was ever** soil **so barren** as this soil?

(4.3.53)

In *Henry VI* part 3 we find:

> Son: **Was ever** son **so rued** a father's death?
> Father: **Was ever** father **so bemoan'd** his son?
> King Henry: **Was ever** king **so grieved** for subjects' woe?

(2.5.109)

These two passages of hopeless grieving, wherein three consecutive lines begin with "**Was ever**" and continue with "**so**" and then three related words, clearly resemble each other: I suggest they are by the same poet.

Warren (2003, 42) pointed out that Margaret's long speech in *Henry VI* part 2 (3.2.72-121) is "constructed out of traditional rhetorical devices" including rhetorical questions. In the *Henry VI* trilogy there is much repetition such as York's speech in *Henry VI* part 2:

> **Nor** shall proud Lancaster usurp my right
> **Nor** hold the sceptre in his childish fist,
> **Nor** wear the diadem upon his head....

(1.1.243)

There are two other passages in which three/four lines begin with 'Nor' in *Henry VI* part 3 (4.3.37) and *Richard II* (2.1.165). These can be compared with the following two instances of *Locrine*:

> **Nor** could the barbarous Dacian sovereign,
> **Nor** yet the ruler of brave Belgia...

(2.2.7)

and

> **Nor** wreak I of thy threat, thou princox boy,
> **Nor** do I fear thy foolish insolency...

(2.5.21)

116

In Henry Neville's defence statement at his trial after the Essex rebellion, when he needed to employ his rhetoric to save his own life, we find Neville using repeated rhetorical questions and repeated '**Nor**'s. Neville protested, "it was not for any malice or discontent against the state, for who had more interest therein than I? **Nor** any desire that the attempt should succeed, for who could more have disliked it than I? **Nor** any personal affection to my Lord, for I never had any particular obligation to him" (Winwood, 1725, Vol 1, 303).

In *Locrine* Corineus says:

> **In vain** you sorrow for the slaughtered prince,
> **In vain** you sorrow for his overthrow...
>
> (3.2.58)

After her rape, Lucrece uses "**in vain**" three times in four lines:

> **In vain** I rail at Opportunity,
> At Time, at Tarquin, and uncheerful Night;
> **In vain** I cavil with mine infamy,
> **In vain** I spurn at my confirm'd despite...
>
> (1023).

In *Locrine* the words "**in vain**" occur five times, three of which are at the start of lines. Shakespeare uses "**in vain**" 52 times, the majority of these uses are in early works. It is used at the beginning of the line only in *Henry VI* part 3, *The Rape of Lucrece* and *Timon of Athens*.

The poet of *Locrine* also uses **rhyme**, not only at the end of lines but internal to lines and also uses half rhymes thus:

> Or, with his Ixion's **overdaring** son,
> Be bound in chains of **everduring** steel.
>
> (1.2.80)

> Take up the corse, and, princes, **hold** him dead,
> Who while he lived, up**held** the Trojan state.
>
> (1.2.261)

> Come, let us in and **muster** up our train,
> And furnish up our **lusty** soldiers,
>
> (2.2.106)

> And kept for treasure mongst his **hell**ish crew,
> I would either **quell** the triple Cerberus
>
> (3.3.47)

An example from *Henry VI* part 3 illustrates both repetition and an internal rhyme: Clifford taunts Richard with:

> **This is the hand that** stabbed thy father York,
> **And this the hand that slew** thy brother Rutland,
> **And** <u>here's</u> the *heart* that triumphs in their death
> **And** *cheers* these **hands that slew** thy sire and brother....
>
> (2.4.6)

We find not only an echo of the words *heart/cheers* in *The Rape of Lucrece* and an internal half rhyme, but also another rhetorical device:

> His drumming *heart cheers* up his burning **eye**,
> His **eye** commends the leading of his **hand**;
> His **hand**, as <u>proud </u>of such a dignity,
> Smoking with <u>pride</u>...
>
> (435)

This patterned rhetoric is **anadiplosis** (when the last word in a line is repeated at the beginning of the next). *The Rape of Lucrece* appeared in 1594, just one year before *Locrine* was printed. Another example is to be found in the early *Comedy of Errors*, which Dorsch (2005, 40) dated "from the mid to late 1580s", and therefore possibly written soon after *Locrine* (the first recorded performance being 1594). Dromio of Ephesus says,

> She is so hot because the meat is cold;
> The meat is cold because **you come not home**;
> **You come not home** because **you have no stomach**;
> **You have no stomach** having broke your fast...
>
> (1.2.47)

This device of anadiplosis occurs in *Locrine* when Thrasimachus is trying to persuade Guendoline to convert her grief into revenge (note also the internal rhyme):

> **This open** wrong must have an **open plague**,
> **This plague** must be repaid with grievous **war**,
> **This war** must <u>finish</u> with Locrine's **death**;
> His **death** will soon <u>extinguish</u> our complaints.
>
> (5.3.26)

Furthermore this passage is echoed by another section of *The Rape of Lucrece* in which Brutus encourages Collatine to convert his grief into revengeful action (lines 1821-1832). The repeated '**This**' at the start of the lines above can be found in *Henry VI* part 1 (4.1.187). Gaunt, in his famous panegyric on England in *Richard II* repeatedly begins lines with '**This**'. In a speech that seems a prototype for Gaunt's, Estrild, describing England, also uses anadiplosis:

> The airy hills enclosed with shady **groves**,
> The **groves** replenished with sweet chirping **birds**,
> The **birds** resounding heavenly melody...

(2.2.36)

I will further examine Estrild's speech below.

Stichomythia[29] is a rhetorical device in which lines, or half-lines, are given to alternating characters. The most extended example of stichomythia in *Locrine* is the when Estrild and Locrine meet and the King, who killed her previous paramour, Humber, falls in love and persuades her to accept him as her new lover. This exactly parallels Gloucester's seduction of Anne Neville (whose husband he had killed) in *Richard III*. Whilst a comparison of the two plays serves to show how vastly superior the canonical play is (it was written about five years later) nevertheless there are not only similarities of situation and technique but also in one significant phrase:

Estrild asks, "How can he favor me **that slew my** spouse?" (4.2.126).

Anne hopes, "To be revenged on him **that slew my** husband" (1.2.135).

There are also other words in this scene in *Richard III* (1.2) that we also find in *Locrine*: 'unworthy', 'untimely', 'pattern', 'invocate', 'homicide', 'basilisks' and "salt tears".

There are a number of **hendiadys** (pairs of words which complement each other: a device used by Shakespeare) in *Locrine*: "rent and cloven"; "honor and prosperity"; "notes and tunes"; "deceits and crafty treacheries"; "guiles and damned stratagems"; "instruments and workers"; "my manhood and my strength"; "downfall and decay". This last is echoed in *Richard III*:

> But we will plant some other in the throne,
> To the **disgrace and downfall** of your house.

(3.7.198)

The *Locrine* passage is:

> Of those that still desire her ruinous **fall**,
> And seek to work her **downfall and decay**?

(5.2.7)

Both passages are concerned with the throne of England. Both use alliteration. Neville often uses hendiadys and alliteration in his letters, for example: "**D**isadvantage and **D**isreputation" (8/9/1599); "**C**ommandment and **C**omfort" (24/9/1599); "thi**s s**ide of the **s**ea with

---

[29] Definition From: http://en.wikipedia.org/wiki/Stichomythia [Accessed 2008]

safety, till he be assured of a safe retreat there" (27/6/1599: Winwood, 1725, Vol 1, 111, 102, 52).

Alliteration was a favourite device of the young bard and there are many examples in *Locrine*, such as:

> And cast away the clods of cursed care…
>
> (2.7.23)

Shakespeare writes a similar line in *Henry VI* part 1: "Care is no cure but rather corrosive" (3.3.3). In *Locrine* we also find:

> Like to a lion mongst a flock of lambs…
>
> (3.2.27)

This recalls the King's speech in *Henry VI* part 3:

> Whiles lions war and battle for their dens,
> Poor harmless lambs abide their enmity.
>
> (2.5.74)

The writer of *Locrine* also peppers his text with **proverbs** such as:

1) The more haste the worst speed.
   (1.3.34)

2) The poorest state is farthest from annoy.
   (2.3.37)

3) Friends in trouble are but few and rare.
   (4.2.66)

4) One dram of joy, must have a pound of care.
   (4.2.102)

5) A barking dog doth seldom strangers bite
   (4.2.120)

At this time Florio was collecting proverbs for his *Second Fruits* for which Shakespeare-Neville wrote the Phaeton sonnet (see chapter 1). Indeed the first of the above is to be found verbatim in *Second Fruits*: "Haste makes waste, and **the more haste the worse speede**" (Simonini, 1977, 11). In *Edmund Ironside* Canutus tells Stitch, "the more you delay the time, the worse you speed" (2.3.124). Shakespeare used many proverbs.

I will now examine the connections between *Locrine* and seven significant plays: *Mucedorus*, *Edmund Ironside*, *The Troublesome Raigne*, the *Henry VI* trilogy and *Cymbeline*.

Locrine and Mucedorus

In chapter 2, I identified *Mucedorus* as an early comedy by Shakespeare-Neville: indeed as his first play, dating it to 1584-5. If *Locrine* then is his second play, and first tragedy, written between 1587-8, are there links between them? Both plays interweave comedy with tragedy: *Mucedorus* begins with an encounter between figures that symbolise Comedy and Tragedy (Envy). The emphasis in *Mucedorus* is comedy, in *Locrine* it is on tragedy. Indeed Envy promises "A double revenge another time" (Epilogue, 14) and *Locrine* is a double revenge play. (See Appendix 3 for the way comedy and tragedy interweave in *Locrine*.) Mehl (1982, 72) stated that, of the plays at the time, *Locrine* is "closest in style and structure to the tradition of classical tragedy." However, like all the other plays, apocryphal or canonical under consideration here, it mixes tragedy and comedy.

Mucedorus is partly based on Sidney's *Arcadia*. The Goddess Ate opens *Locrine*, telling of a lion and an archer: imagery that could have been drawn from the very same passage of the *Arcadia* that was the source of *Mucedorus*, in which an archer kills a lion. In *Locrine* the lion symbolises Brutus and the archer is Death. In *Venus and Adonis* Death is an archer with an "ebon **dart**" (948). In *Mucedorus* Envy speaks of "the very **dart** of **death**" (Induction, 71) and later Segasto says, "each minute of an hour doth pierce my heart with **darts** of thousand **deaths**" (1.4.17). In *Locrine* Brutus says:

> Black **ugly death**, with visage pale and wan,
> Presents himself before my dazzled eyes,
> And with his **dart**...
>
> (1.2.9)

Later I will show there are connections between *Locrine* and *Cymbeline*. In that play Arviragus uses the words, "**death's dart**" (4.2.212).

In *Locrine* the King invokes Mars to kill Corineius: "With murthering blade **bereave** him **of** his **life**..." (4.4.14). Mucedorus says the bear has "**bereaved** thousands **of** their **lives**" (Q1: 1.3.8). '**Bereaved**' occurs twice in the canon: the first in the early play *Henry VI* part 3 echoes these which link the word with '**of**' and '**life/lives**': after killing his father in battle a son says:

> And I, who at his hands received my life, him
> Have by my hands **of life bereaved** him.
>
> (2.5.67)

Shakespeare uses the word '**bereave**' five times, always with the word '**of**' (*Henry VI* part 1: 5.3.195; *Troilus and Cressida*: 3.2.56; *Pericles*:

4.1.29; *Antony and Cleopatra*: 5.2.130; *The Two Noble Kinsmen*: 2.2.225). The word 'bereaved' is used in *Gorboduc* (4.1.4); by Sidney ('of' his tongue) in his *An Apology for Poesie* (2163); by Shakespeare in *Edward III* (4.9.24) and *King Lear* (4.4.9); Greene used 'bereaved' in *Alphonsus King of Arragon* (with 'of', 2.2.49) and 'bereav'd' in *A Looking Glass* (2.1.112): I believe both of these were written after *Mucedorus*. Shakespeare then is the only writer who uses 'bereave/d' with 'of' and 'life', as in *Mucedorus* and *Locrine*. In a letter dated 27/6/1599 Neville wrote that Charles Paget was "very wary not to bereave himself of all the means of living..." (Winwood, 1725, Vol 1, 52). In *Leicester's Commonwealth* (1584) I have found the phrase: "bereave him of all his living" (Peck, 2006, 83). Neville owned two copies of this and I suggested in chapter 2 that it was a source for *Mucedorus*. Furthermore James (2007b, 33) suggested Paget was one of the authors of *Leicester's Commonwealth*.

In *Mucedorus* the cannibal Bremo gleefully spies Amadine as a possible meal with: "Dainties, Bremo, dainties, thy hungry panch to fill!" (3.3.17). 'Paunch' and 'dainty' are both used in *Locrine*. The words 'paunch' and 'dainty' occur together in *Love's Labour's Lost* when Longaville says:

> Fat paunches have lean pates, and dainty bits
> Make rich the ribs, but bankrupt quite the wits.
>
> (1.1.26)

In *Locrine* Albanact imagines how the "Chimaera in her triple shape rolleth hot flames from out her monstrous paunch" (2.6.54). 'Paunch' occurs in Greene's *Alphonsus, King of Arragon*: "the roaring cannon shot spit forth the venom of their firèd paunch..." (Prologue to Act 5.3). 'Paunche' was used by Alexander Neville (1544-1614) in his 1581 translation of Seneca's *Oedipus* (2.1.87). Alexander was related to Henry Neville and *Locrine* is influenced by Seneca. Furthermore in the 1587 edition of Holinshed (1976, 437) at the start of the section which is a source of *Locrine*, namely the history of King Brutus (with which the play opens), there is a marginal note naming "*Alex. Neuil*" as a reference.

The defeated, starving Humber, living in the wilderness, complains:

> Long have I lived in this desert cave,
> With eating haws and miserable roots...
>
> (4.5.4)

Like Humber in *Locrine*, Mucedorus laments his banishment in the wilderness. He meets the comic Mouse, just as Humber meets the comic Strumbo. Mucedorus says, "I tell you, sir, I am an hermit, one that leads a solitary life within these woods" (4.2.27). Mouse replies, "O, I know thee now, thou art he that eats up all the hips and **haws**." **Haws** are hawthorn berries. These two anonymous plays refer to 'haws' in similar circumstances. Bremo, a wild man of the woods who lives in a **cave** in *Mucedorus*, is able to rely on the bounty of nature to survive, indeed he promises Amadine a positive banquet of quail, partridge and other wild birds, **goats' milk**, crystal water and "all the dainties the woods afford" (4.3.32). In *Titus Andronicus* Aaron, seeking a way to save his new born son's life, speaks of bringing him up in a **cave**, feeding him on berries, roots and **goat's milk**. (4.2.179). I believe these three plays were written by Neville, whose father was a forester, and so he had grown up knowing about the woods, trees and their berries.

Mucedorus enjoys his time in the forest, optimistically waiting for re-union with Amadine. Humber in *Locrine* starves slowly and miserably, cursing the barren wilderness. Mucedorus speaks of "holsome hearbes" (3.1.57) whilst Humber complains of "withered herbes" (4.2.8). Mucedorus enjoys "goodly groves" (3.1.52) whilst Humber laments "cursed groves" (4.2.3). The difference between them being that Mucedorus is in a comedy and Humber in a tragedy: in the first, the world, however dangerous, is ultimately benign whereas the world of *Locrine* is tragic. Bremo and Humber (who, having been in the wilderness for seven years, has grown long hair and become a wild man) both live in caves. Both Bremo and Humber die.

Luckless occurs three times in *Mucedorus*, one of which is:

> **Luckless** his **lot** and **caytiffe** like acourste,
> At whose proceedings **fortune** ever **frowns**.
>
> (1.4.5)

Luckless occurs five times in *Locrine*, one of which seems to echo the above:

> By **luckless lot** and froward **frowning fate**.
>
> (5.6.110)

The word '**cative**' also occurs in *Locrine* (4.2.117).

"I'll dash **thy** cursed **brains**," Humber threatens (4.3.81). Strumbo protests, "Dash **out** my **brains**? **O horrible! terrible!**"(4.3.86). In *Mucedorus* Bremo threatens Amadine that, "With this my bat will I beat **out thy brains**" (3.3.32). Chased by the bear Mouse cries, "**O horrible, terrible!**" (1.2.1).

There are bears in *Locrine*: in the Prologue dumb show a lion is seen running after a bear. Later Sabren speaks of, "You savage **bears** in caves and darkened dens." (5.6.141.) I pointed to the significance of the bear as a symbol of the Earls of Warwick and the Nevilles in chapter 2.

The words "**lukewarm blood**" occur twice in *Locrine*:

> Were bathed in our enemies' **lukewarm blood**...
>
> (2.4.4)

and:

> That I may **glut** my mind **with lukewarm blood**...
>
> (5.6.100)

Similarly, the words "**lukewarm blood**" occur twice in *Mucedorus*! Bremo greedily anticipating his cannibal feast of the heroine, also uses the word '**glut**':

> Now **glut** thy greedy guts **with luke warm blood**!
>
> (3.3.18)

In *Henry VI* part 3, Richard declares:

> I cannot rest
> Until the white rose that I wear be dyed
> Even in the **lukewarm blood** of Henry's heart.
>
> (1.2.32)

"**Lukewarm blood**" is to be found in Marlowe's *Dr. Faustus* (617) but that post dates both *Mucedorus* and *Locrine*. "**Lukewarm blood**y streams" occurs in Peele's *Edward I* (Scene XXIV line 206: Bullen, 1888, 212).

This bloody theme continues with **blood-sucking**: in *Locrine* we find: "these **blood-sucking** masty curs..." (5.6.170). In *Henry VI* part 3 Lady Elizabeth Grey laments:

> Ay, ay, for this I draw in many a tear
> And stop the rising of **blood-sucking** sighs...
>
> (4.4.22)

In *The Troublesome Raigne* King John laments that he is seen as a "Butcher, **bloodsucker** and murtherer" (1.8.252). In *Richard III* Grey refers to '**bloodsuckers**' (3.3.6). In *Thomas of Woodstock* the phrase "**sucked their blood**" occurs (4.2.36: see chapter 5). In *Mucedorus* Bremo warns Amadine that he thirsts "to **suck** thy **blood**" (3.3.23). Furthermore, Segasto calls Mucedorus a "**Bloodthirsty** villain," for killing Tremelio (2.2.102). In *Locrine* we also find "**blood-thirsty** Mars" (1.2.253). In *Edmund Ironside* Alfric speaks of "**bloodthirsty** Danes" (5.1.10). Indeed there are three references to drinking blood in *Ironside*. In *Henry VI* part 1 the Countess of Auvergne calls Talbot a "**blood-thirsty** lord" (2.3.33). In *Edward III* Charles, the French King's son, says that England harbours '**bloodthirsty**' men (3.1.14). Holinshed used the word.

I noted the importance of the **Orpheus** myth in *Mucedorus* in chapter 2. It also occurs in *Locrine*. In the very first scene Corineus says:

> Playedst thou as sweet, on the sweet sounding lute,
> As did the **spouse of fair Eurydice**,
> That did enchant the waters with his noise,
> And made stones, birds, and beasts, to lead a dance,
> Constrained the hilly trees to follow him...

(1.2.239)

Later Locrine, lamenting Albanact's death, curses Humber with:

> O that I had the Thracian **Orpheus**' harp,
> For to awake out of the infernal shade
> Those ugly devils of black Erebus,
> That might torment the damned traitor's soul!

(3.2.5)

Thus we can see that in words, images and plot devices there are links between the *Mucedorus* and *Locrine* which I thus suggest are the first and second plays by the young bard, Shakespeare-Neville.

Locrine and *Edmund Ironside*

These two plays were written at virtually the same time: we can therefore expect to find links. Indeed they are very strong. For those readers who do not know *Edmund Ironside* I warmly recommend Eric Sams' (1986) comprehensive study of the play, which is so thorough as to leave no possible doubt that the play is by Shakespeare. Both plays deal with the threat of foreign invasion: from at least 1585, this was a distinct possibility as Spain planned its Armada, which eventually set sail in 1588. Both plays show rulers dividing the kingdom. If *Locrine* was written 1587-8 it may have been the play Neville wrote just before *Ironside*.

Strumbo, in his letter writing scene suggests to the audience that they use "new coined words" (1.3.96) if they want to seduce a woman. In *Edmund Ironside* Edricus, in his letter writing scene, also seeks "some never-heard-of words" (3.5.140).

Sams (1986, 316) pointed out that the bard uses inappropriate laughter as a response to torture/cruelty/tragedy in *Edmund Ironside*, *Titus Andronicus* and *Henry VI* parts 1 and 2. In each of these plays a character responds with "Ha ha ha". In *Locrine* Strumbo's house is burned down in the war and his much loved wife 'roasted'. He responds to Albanact's question, "Where are your houses, where's your dwelling place?" with a pun on place/palace (possibly due to the way Alba pronounces the word 'place'):

> Place? **Ha, ha, ha!** laugh a month and a day at him.
> Place! I cry God mercy: why, do you think that such
> poor honest men as we be, hold our habitacles in kings'
> palaces? **Ha, ha, ha!**
>
> (2.4.49)

Greene, in *Orlando Furioso* (3.1.40) has the mad Orlando insist that his page, Orgalio, must laugh at Angelica's death but this is forced on the boy, and is not a spontaneous reaction; furthermore the text has four 'ha's not the three as in all the above examples.

In *Edmund Ironside* Edrick says: "Nay, Stitch, and you once see my son you'll swear he is a bouncer, all in silks and gold, **vengeable** rich" (2.2.1). Sams (1986, 348) thought '**vengeable**' was unique.[30] In fact the word, spelt differently, is in *Locrine*: Strumbo complains he is wounded by "the little god, nay the desparate god **Cuprit**, with one of **his vengible birdbolts...**" (1.3.13). It is noteworthy that the speaker here is Strumbo, a clown who I will later link with Stitch in *Edmund Ironside* to whom Edrick's remark above is directed. The words "**vengible birdbolts**" take us however to the bard, who in *Love's Labour's Lost*, has Berowne say, "Proceed, sweet **Cupid**: thou hast thumped him with thy **bird-bolt**" (4.3.20). Just as above, in *Locrine*, in *Much Ado About Nothing* Beatrice also couples '**bird-bolt**' with **Cupid**: "He set up his bills here in Messina and challenged **Cupid** at the flight; and my uncle's fool, reading the challenge, subscribed for **Cupid**, and challenged him at the **bird-bolt**" (1.1.35).

In *Twelfth Night* Olivia uses the word '**bird-bolts**' (1.5.92). The OED has a 1440 usage of 'burdebolt' and notes that 'burbolt' is used in Nicholas Udall's 1553 play *Roister Doister*. Lyly also used it in his *Endimion* (1591, line 486): "Here is the **bird-bolt** for the ugly beast, the blackbird," but this usage would probably post-date *Locrine* and is not linked with Cupid. Lyly also complained of "**vengible** long sentences" in *Mother Bombie* (1594). I take the occurrence of these two very rare words '**vengible**' and '**birdbolt**' together with **Cupid** as evidence of Shakespeare-Neville's hand in *Locrine*. There is other bird/falconry imagery in *Locrine*, which is typical of Shakespeare. Neville knew about falconry and hunting/birds from his father who

---

[30] George Gascoigne had used the word to describe beer in Antwerp as "**vengeable** bitter" in *The Glass of Government* (1575) and William Stevenson described a "**vengeable** knave" in *Gammer Gurton's Needle* the same year (LION).

specifically left his favourite bird to a friend in his will (James & Rubinstein, 2005, 116).

Stitch in *Ironside* and Strumbo in *Locrine* are both clownish cobblers. They begin as comic turns but get caught up in the tragic action. It is therefore startling to find they share vocabulary: scour/scouring, vengeable/vengible, hang/hanging, sauciness/saucebox and slopsauce, tongue, stomach. They are both also concerned with letter writing, ink and paper.

A '**guerdon**' is a reward. In *Locrine* Corineus, confronting the King for his infidelity to Guendoline with Estrild, asks:

> Is this the **guerdon** for my grievous wounds,
> Is this the **honour** for my labours past?

(4.2.158)

This is the fifth of five rhetorical questions from an outraged man. In *Edmund Ironside* Edricus asks, as the first of another set of four rhetorical questions:

> Is this a **guerdon** for my scars and hurts,
> For all my bruises and my broken joints?

(5.1.40)

The similarity of the passages is startling. The word is also used four times in *The Troublesome Raigne* (7.111; 8. 109; 11.231; 11.251). More startling still is the following passage in *Henry VI* part 3 in which Warwick asks five rhetorical questions:

> Did I forget that by the house of York
> My father came untimely to his death?
> Did I let pass the abuse done to my niece?
> Did I impale him with the regal crown?
> Did I put Henry from his native right?
> And am I **guerdon'd** at the last with shame?

(3.3.187)

Warwick's very next line includes the word '**honour**', just as in Corineus speech above in *Locrine*. The Warwick who asks these rhetorical questions is none other than Richard Neville. Furthermore he is speaking about the treachery of an English king who, like Locrine, has two Queens: a Queen to whom he is betrothed, Bona of France, and a Queen he has chosen for lust, Lady Elizabeth Grey: in other words the use of this rare word is in exactly the same place and context in *Locrine* and *Henry VI* part 3. This further illuminates the hidden links between the plays, which are concerned with the dangers of royal marriages to foreign partners. Elizabeth I spent years teasing England and Europe with the question of whether and whom she would marry, causing anxiety in her subjects about the succession. She also forbade discussion of the subject so using old tales of royal marriages was the only way to broach the issue. '**Guerdon**' is used four times in *Love's Labour's Lost* (3.1.164) and is in *Much Ado About Nothing* (5.3.5). Greene used '**guerdon**' in *A Looking Glass for London* as the third of three outraged rhetorical questions:

> And is the **guerdon** of my chivalry
> Ended in this abusing of my wife?
>
> (2.3.114)

This differs from the *Edmund Ironside* and *Locrine* usages which both start: "Is this a/the **guerdon** for my" and follows on with a wound/scar/hurt. **Guerdon** is used by Alexander Neville in his 1581 translation of Seneca's *Oedipus*; twice by Peele in his 1584 *The Arraingment of Paris* (2.1.121 and 157); 4 times in Kyd's *Spanish Tragedy*, twice in Marlowe's *The Massacre at Paris*, once in Nashe's *Summer's Last Will and Testament*, once in Spenser's *Shepheardes Calendar* and 18 times in his *Faerie Queen* **but none of these are in a rhetorical question**. In Shakespeare's late play *Henry VIII* Queen Katherine asks four rhetorical questions, the last of which is, "And am I thus **rewarded**?" (3.1.132).

In *Locrine* Strumbo complains, "How fine you can **nickname** me" (3.4.32). In *Edmund Ironside* Edmund confronts the villainous Edricus with "thou cam'st to gain with cursed treachery the surname of vild **nickname** - 'Policy'" (4.1.93). In *Love's Labour's Lost* the Princess says, "You **nickname** virtue" (5.2.349). Mercutio, in *Romeo and Juliet*, says:

> Speak to my gossip Venus one fair word,
> One **nickname** for her purblind son and heir...
>
> (2.1.11)

Hamlet accuses Ophelia: "you lisp, and **nick-name** God's creatures," (3.1.146). I have found no other writer before 1599 that used '**nickname**': Nashe used it in 1599 in his *Summer's Last Will and Testament* (OED) but this is a decade after *Locrine* and *Edmund Ironside* were written.

In *Locrine* Humber invites his men to "Carouse whole cups of Amazonian wine, **Sweeter** than **nectar** or **Ambrosia**..." (2.7.21). In *Edmund Ironside* Canutus celebrates with "**Ambrosian** dainties...**sweet**-passing **Nectar**..." (5.2.255).

Both *Locrine* and *Edmund Ironside* are plays in which battles are important: they share a number of military images/phrases. In *Locrine*

Camber promises "**twenty thousand** brave courageous knights" (3.2.74) and Thrasimachus tells how:

> Hubba, with **twenty thousand** soldiers,
> Cowardly came upon our weakened backs,
> And **murthered** all with **fatal massacre**.
>
> (3.2.32)

In *Edmund Ironside* Canutus asks, "what, **twenty thousand slain** of common soldiers?" (2.3.168). Shakespeare uses the words "**twenty thousand**" 21 times in 12 plays. Nine of these 12 plays date from the early 1590s. These uses include a messenger in *Henry VI* part 3 reporting that the Queen is approaching with "**twenty thousand** men" (1.2.51); Richard II saying, "now the **blood** of **twenty thousand** men" (3.2.76) and Hamlet's "The imminent **death** of **twenty thousand** men" (4.4.60). We can see that in *Locrine*, *Edmund Ironside*, *Richard II* and *Hamlet* the reference to "**twenty thousand**" is concerned with **deaths**. Coriolanus adds to these numbers:

> Within thine eyes sat **twenty thousand deaths**,
> In thy hand clutch'd as many **millions**
>
> (3.3.70)

In *Locrine* the word '**millions**' also appears four times, three of which are of troops: "**millions** of men" (1.2.64), "**millions** of hosts" (1.2.67), "Beating down **millions** with his furious mood" (2.6.3). The word is used four times in *Edward III*: two of these usages refer to troops. In *Edmund Ironside* the word is used twice, once for money, the second time for troops (2.1.69 and 5.2.27). In Neville's diplomatic letters (of 12/3/1599 and 9/5/1600) the word '**millions**' refers to money (Winwood, 1725, Vol 1, 158, 180).

In battles men sometimes **fly** in panic as in *Locrine*, when Thrasimachus advises:

> **Fly**, noble Albanact, and save thy self.
> The Scithians follow with great celeritie,
> And there's no way but **flight**, or speedy **death**;
> Fly, noble Albanact, and save thy self.
>
> (2.6.73)

Albanact replies:

> Nay, let them **fly** that fear to die the **death**,
> That tremble at the name of **fatal mors**.
> Never shall proud Humber boast or brag himself
> That he hath put young Albanact to **flight**…
>
> (2.6.77)

Flight is here associated not with survival but **death**. The word 'fly' is used nine times in *Edmund Ironside* and is associated with death as, for example, when Southampton warns:

> He that gives back, let him be **slain**
> by his next fellow that doth second him.
> If Englishmen at first begin to **fly**,
> Southampton willingly for them will **die**.
>
> (3.2.61)

The word '**fly**' is used 14 times in *Edward III*, for example when Charles advises:

> **Fly**, father, **fly**! the French do kill the French,
> Some that would stand let drive at some that **fly**;
> Our drums strike nothing but discouragement,
> Our trumpets sound dishonor and retire;
> The spirit of fear, that feareth nought but **death**,
> Cowardly works confusion on it self.
>
> (4.6.28)

The association of '**death**' and '**fly**' is seen in *Henry VI* part 1 when Talbot asks his son:

> Wilt thou yet leave the battle, boy, and **fly**,
> Now thou art seal'd the son of chivalry?
> **Fly**, to revenge my **death** when I am **dead**:
>
> (4.6.28)

And in *The Two Gentlemen of Verona* when Valentine says:

> I **fly** not **death**, to **fly** his deadly doom:
> Tarry I here, I but attend on **death**:
> But, **fly** I hence, I **fly** away from life.
>
> (3.1.185)

Furthermore, in *Edmund Ironside* the Chorus explains how the villain Edricus deceived the army by:

> Telling the soldiers Edmund Ironside
> Was **slain**, bidding the soldiers yield
> Or **fly** the field and trust unto their heels.
> The soldiers in amaze began to **fly**;
> Then Edmund, hearing of this stratagem,
> **Amongst the thickest** of his enemies,
> Gave notice that he lived a conqueror.
>
> (3.3.31)

Sams (1986, 259) noted that Richard in *Henry VI* part 3 says, "Methought he bore him in **the thickest** troop as doth a **lion** in a herd of neat..." (2.1.13). In *The True Tragedy of Richard Duke of York*

(1595: a 'bad' quarto of *Henry VI* part 3) the words "in the **thickest throngs**" occur twice (2.3.15 and 5.4.46). In *Locrine* Alba says:

> I, that ere while did scare mine enemies,
> And drove them almost to a shameful **flight**,
> I, that ere while full **lion-like** did fare
> Amongst the dangers of the **thick thronged** pikes,
> Must now depart most lamentably **slain**.
>
> (2.5.36)

In *Richard III* Queen Margaret asks, "Where be the **thronging** troops that follow'd thee?" (4.4.91). In *Locrine* Old Corineius is willing to "**lose my life** amongst the **thickest prease**" (3.5.48) in the battle. This recalls Prince Henry in *King John* who speaks of:

> **Death**, having prey'd upon the outward parts,
> Leaves them invisible, and his siege is now
> Against the mind, the which he pricks and wounds
> With many legions of strange fantasies,
> Which, in their **throng** and **press** to that last hold,
> Confound themselves.
>
> (5.7.15)

In *Locrine* Humber asserts that: "Yet would we **not** start back **one foot** from them" (2.2.76). Sams (1986, 261) pointed out the similarities between the following passages in *Edmund Ironside* when Edricus says, "Yet fled I **not** a **foot**" (5.1.93) and in *Henry VI* part 1 when the Dauphin says he will not "go back **one foot**" (1.2.21) and in *Henry VI* part 3 when Richard cried, "Charge! And give no **foot** of ground" (1.4.15). In a letter dated 15/5/1599 Neville wrote that the King of France "had **not** styrred **one foote**" to greet the Spanish Ambassador (Winwood, 1725, Vol 1, 20).

In *Locrine* Thrasimachus speaks of Albanact "**Hewing a passage through** them with his sword" (3.2.29). In *Edmund Ironside* Canutus says, "valor **hewed** him **through** our troops" (2.3.189) and "Edmund likewise is invincible, for force and valor **hews** him **through** his foes" (5.2.132). In *Henry VI* part 3 Richard, Duke of Gloucester says he will "**hew** my way out with a bloody axe" (3.2.181). In *Thomas of Woodstock* (see chapter 5) Lapoole orders, "**Hew** them straight to pieces" (5.1.267). Whilst Neville may not have seen such ferocity in battle he would have been familiar with the hewing of trees in the forest.

Spurgeon (1958) noticed the frequency of tree images in the early plays. In *Henry VI* part 3 George Duke of Clarence (son of Cecily Neville, married to Isabella Neville) uses this tree imagery: "We set the **axe** to thy usurping **root**...We'll never leave till we have **hewn** thee down" (2.2.165). Later Richard, his brother, (who was to marry Anne Neville) speaking of the murder of Rutland says:

> 'tis Clifford
> Who not contented that he **lopped** the **branch**
> In **hewing** Rutland when his leaves put forth,
> But set his murd'ring knife unto the **root**...

(2.6.46)

King Edward describes his enemies as a "thorny wood which... must by the **roots** be **hewn** up" (5.4.69) The word '**hewing**' is used in *Locrine* (3.2.29).

At the start of *Locrine* Brutus speaks of himself as a tree:

> clove asunder and bereft of life,
> As when the sacred **oak** with thunderbolts,
> Sent from the fiery circuit of the heavens,
> Sliding along the air's celestial vaults,
> Is rent and cloven to the very **roots**.

(1.2.24)

Later Locrine says:

> Or as the ploughman with his piercing share
> Renteth the bowels of the fertile fields,
> And rippeth up the **roots** with razours keen:
> So Locrine with his mighty curtle**axe**
> Hath **cropped off the heads** of all thy Huns;

(4.2.23)

This imagery of rooting up a tree, coupled with chopping off heads recurs in *Edmund Ironside* when Canutus says:

> A traitor may be likened to a **tree**,
> Which being shred and **topped** when it is green,
> Doth for one twig which from the same was cut
> Yield twenty arms, yea twenty arms for one,
> But being hacked and mangled with an **axe**,
> The **root** dies and piecemeal rots away.

(2.3.41)

There are other tree images in the play, including the cedar, which is used as an image of royalty in *Henry VI* parts 2 and 3 (2: 5.1.205; 3: 5.2.11). The cedar is also mentioned in *Cymbeline* (5.6.454), which I will connect with *Locrine* (see below). In the latter Brutus refers to "the lusty cedar worn with years..." (1.2.17).

This combination of imagery of murder/execution, the regeneration of a traitor's family and forestry, points to the Neville family who survived and prospered despite Neville's grandfather's execution. Neville's father was a forester, custodian of the Windsor royal forest and Neville himself wrote a tract on English forests at the request of the crown. He grew up knowing about trees.

The two plays also share a number of animals: horses, fox, lion, tiger: these are commonplace enough but in both plays bees are referred to in a similar context: in *Edmund Ironside* a messenger warns that the Danes are invading the land:

> They swarm along thy coasts like little gnats
> over a river in a summer's night,
> or like to **bees** when they begin to flight...
>
> (4.1.61)

In *Locrine* it is Hubba, one of the invaders, who uses this bee imagery:

> He is not worthy of the honey comb,
> That shuns the **hives** because the **bees** have **stings**...
>
> (3.3.39)

In *Henry VI* part 1 troops are likened to **bees** driven from the **hives** (1.5.23). In *Titus Andronicus* the army of the Goths is described as "**stinging bees**" (5.1.14). In *Henry VI* part 2 the people, angered by the murder of Humphrey Duke of Gloucester, are described as "an angry **hive** of **bees**... who ...**sting** " (3.2.125). It is especially interesting to note that the *Locrine* word order of 'hives', 'bees', 'sting/s', is identical to the canonical play.

A similar pattern of rhetoric is found in both plays about defeat, using the words '**shall**' and '**ne'er/never**' and '**curtleaxe**'. Defeated Locrine laments:

> **Shall** Locrine then be taken prisoner
> By such a youngling as Thrasimachus?
> **Shall** Gwendoline captivate my love?
> **Ne'er shall** mine eyes behold that dismal hour;
> **Ne'er** will I view that ruthful spectacle,
> For with my sword, this sharp **curtleaxe**,
> I'll cut in sunder my accursed heart.
>
> (5.6.17)

In *Edmund Ironside*, reacting to news of a defeat, Canutus says:

> **Shall** it be said hereafter when report
> **Shall** celebrate my noble father's acts
> That Canutus did lose what noble Sveynus got?
> **Shall** it be said that Edmund Ironside,
> Unfriended, poor, forsaken, desolate,
> Did overthrow the power of mighty Canutus,
> Whose wealth was great, friends more, but forces most?
> **Never** since Edmund was of force to bear
> A massy helmet and a **curtle-axe**...
>
> (2.3.177)

There are a number of other words in both plays: 'corsive', 'sugarded', 'distilled/distilling', 'pate', "whirling wheel", 'Ethiopian's/Aethiopians', 'clubs/club', "too too" and 'fickle'.

Fortune is mentioned 12 times in *Locrine*. Albanact speaks of:

> Humber's treacheries and **fortune's spites**.
> Cursed be her charms, damned be her cursed charms
> That doth delude the wayward hearts of men,
> Of men that trust unto her **fickle wheel**,
> Which never leaveth turning upside down.
>
> (2.6.41)

In *Edmund Ironside* Emma speaks of "the chance of **fickle fortune**" (5.2.186); Edricus refers to "**fickle** Chance... her whirling **wheel**" (2.3.196). In *Henry VI* part 3 we have "**fortune's spite**" (4.6.19). In *Henry V* Pistol speaks of "giddy **Fortune's** furious **fickle wheel**..." (3.6.26). In sonnet 90 we find "the **spite** of **fortune**."

In *Edmund Ironside* there are 23 classical references listed by Sams (207) as typical of Shakespeare: 15 of these occur in *Locrine*. (For classical references in *Locrine* see Appendix 5 below.) Sams' analysis of *Edmund Ironside* convincingly ties it into the early works of Shakespeare: the evidence for *Locrine* is weaker but there are clearly links between these two plays and if *Locrine* is earlier then it is not surprising that it is, as an immature work, less like the recognisable Shakespeare plays: *Edmund Ironside* is still not universally accepted but my guess is that this is because people have not read Sams' masterful book.

Locrine and *The Troublesome Raigne of John King of England*
The first of Shakespeare's plays ever to be printed, *The Troublesome Raigne* appeared in 1591. It was anonymous; the second quarto was published in 1611 "by W. Sh."; the third in 1622 "by W. Shakespeare"; finally the fully revised version of *King John* appeared in the First Folio of 1623. *The Troublesome Raigne* therefore first appeared two years before *Venus and Adonis* and so before the name 'Shakespeare' was used. I suggest a date for the writing of *The Troublesome Raigne* of between 1588-89. I am sure from the style that *Locrine* is the earlier play yet there is a relationship between them, of themes, images and vocabulary. They are both concerned with invasions, with oath breaking by monarchs, with legitimate succession and both seem to refer to the Armada. Both end with the deaths of disgraced kings and the succession of their young sons.

Having seen links between *Locrine* and *Mucedorus* it is interesting to find a word that is found in those plays and in *The Troublesome Raigne*. *Locrine* says of Guendoline:

Ne'er shall she come within our palace gate,
To **countercheck** brave Locrine in his love.

(5.2.27)

Envy calls Comedy "thou **counter-checking** trull" in the Prologue of
Mucedorus (18). The word '**counterchecks**' is used by Hubert in *The
Troublesome Raigne* (part 1, 7.125). In *King John* the King says he has
brought "a **countercheck**" before the gates of Angiers (2.1.224). In *As
You Like It* Touchstone, listing various reposts that might be given at
court, names "the **Counter-cheque** Quarrelsome" (5.4.90). It also
occurs in Greene's *A Looking Glass For London*: "but thou of Crete,
that **countercheck'st** thy king Pack hence in exile" (1.1.123).
'**Counter-check**' occurs in *Soliman and Perseda* (3.6.11) which is
believed to be by Kyd (c1592).

Ate's speech at the start of *Locrine* has the line: "With hideous
noise scaring **the trembling trees**..." (1.1.4). In *The Troublesome
Raigne* the Bastard says, "The whistling leaves upon **the trembling
trees**" (1.1.251). Both lines are about sounds, both end with identical
words. Both are onomatopoetic.

In *Locrine* Thrasimachus says, "Their **uncontented** corps were yet
content" (5.6.116). In *The Troublesome Raigne* King John says he is
"**contented uncontent**," (1.1.12). Shakespeare echoed this in *Henry VI
Part 1* when the King asks, "My lord, how say you, are you **not
content**?" Talbot replies, "**Content**, my liege!" (4.1.70).

In *Locrine* Humber says:

The slaughtered Troyans, squeltring in their blood,
Infect the air with their carcasses,
And are a **prey for every ravenous bird**.

(2.7.4)

In *The Troublesome Raigne* the Bastard says to the dead body of the
Duke of Austria, "Lie there **a pray to every ravening fowle**" (part 2,
9.36). When the prophet of Pomfret is hung John says, "There let him
hang, and be the **Ravens** food" (part 2, 10.57).

Trasimachus calls Locrine a '**Losell**' (5.2.71) referring to his loose
morals. '**Lozell**' is used by the Bastard in *The Troublesome Raigne*
about a philandering Friar (6.30). In *The Winter's Tale* Leontes calls
Paulina a '**lozel**' (2.3.108). This change from s – z occurs in another
rare word the plays share: in *Locrine* Humber speaks of a 'corsive':

why comes Albanact's bloody ghost,
To bring a **corsive** to our miseries?

(3.7.36)

In *The Troublesome Raigne* King John says, "Arthur is dead, I there the **corzie** growes" (8.235). In *Edmund Ironside* Canutus says, "This punishment is worse than loss of life, for it is a stinging **corsive** to their souls" (2.3.31). The word 'corrosive' is also used in *Henry VI* part 1 (3.3.3) and in *Henry VI* part 2 (3.2.407). 'Corsive' is used in *The Spanish Tragedy* (1.2.143) and in *Selimus* (1594). In all these uses this is a medical term referring to a physically irritating remedy. Warren (2003, 222) pointed out that this word was used in the same way in Holinshed. Furthermore he stated that the stress falls on the first syllable, unlike in the modern pronunciation, so the *Locrine* 'corsive' corresponds to the use of the word 'corrosive' in Shakespeare's plays.

Shakespeare was interested in poisons (see chapter 4). In *Locrine* Humber speaks of "**Aconitum** mongst these withered herbs" (4.3.8). '**Aconitum**' also occurs in *Henry IV* part 2 (4.4.48). In *Locrine* Ate, in the Act 3 Prologue, speaks of "**poison**...which made him swell, that there his **bowels burst**..." (3.1.12). In *The Troublesome Raigne* King John's '**bowels**' are said to be "devided in themselves" (15.112). In *King John* Hubert tells of a '**poisoned**' monk "Whose **bowels** suddenly **burst** out" (5.6.30). Thus we can see that Shakespeare reverts to the *Locrine* wordage in his revised *King John*. In *The Troublesome Raigne* Margaret says:

> Let not these ears receive the hissing sound
> Of such a viper, who with **poisoned** words
> Doth **masserate** the **bowels** of **my soule**.

(part 1, 1.141)

Locrine uses this rare word, saying, "to **macerate my mind**" (5.2.32).

Both *The Troublesome Raigne* and *Locrine* end in Epilogues, which invite the audience, as England, to stay loyal and join together as a nation, avoiding treachery, civil war and so defeat invasion.

Locrine and the *Henry VI* trilogy

Hattaway (1993, 4) pointed out that the *Henry VI* plays "are best regarded not simply as 'adapted history' or as vehicles for dramatic biography but as a set of complex essays on the politics of the mid-fifteenth century – essays which, of course, also offer reflections on Shakespeare's own times." We have already seen how *Locrine* likewise uses history to reflect on the politics that endangered the realm through a foreign marriage, invasion, civil strife and the imprisoned Mary Queen of Scots. The same intelligence is at work in these plays. At the heart of both *Locrine* and the *Henry VI* trilogy is an unhappy royal marriage. "The vital importance of this unhappy marriage made it, for

Shakespeare, both a natural centre from which to radiate (2H6 1.1) the various strands of 2 Henry VI and the natural climax to the misfortunes of 1 Henry VI" (Cairncross, 1965, 1). The whole political question of Elizabeth I's marriage had bedevilled the age and this is reflected in *Locrine*.

An example of this historical patterning is the opening scene of *Locrine* when Brutus is on his deathbed (where he anxiously arranges his son's marriage). This is echoed by the deathbed scene of Mortimer in *Henry VI* part 1. To clarify these echoes I edit the text to highlight similarities. In both scenes a dying man hands over to his heir, summarises his life and history, stating how he claimed the throne, complains of his physical condition and uses a tree metaphor before dying on stage. Brutus says:

> **These arms** my Lords, **these** never daunted **arms**...
> Now yield to **death**, o'erlaid with crooked **age**,
> **Devoid of strength** and of their proper force,
> Even as the lusty **cedar** worn with years...
> This heart, my Lords, this ne'er appalled heart...
> Is clove asunder and bereft of life,
> As when the sacred **oak** with thunderbolts...
> Is rent and cloven to the very roots...
> **Mine eyes wax dim**, overcast with clouds of **age**...
>
> (1.2.12)

Mortimer speaks of:

> ...**these** grey locks, the pursuivants of **Death**,
> Nestor-like aged in an **age** of care...
> **These eyes... wax dim**...
> And **pithless arms**, like to a wither'd **vine**
> That droops his **sapless branches** to the ground...
>
> (2.5.5 onwards)

Both passages use the rhetorical repetition of '**these**' and body parts to delineate the dying body. Mortimer complains that he was the rightful heir and was (like Mary Queen of Scots) imprisoned for many years. We have already seen how the imprisonment, trial and death of Mary form the backdrop to *Locrine*. Peele used the phrase, "Cupid's eyesight wexen dim" (5.1.103) in *The Arraignment of Paris*: it is notable that the phrase in *Locrine* matches the Shakespeare usage, not Peele's.

Earlier in this dying speech Brutus had said, "My sinews shrunk..." (1.1.7). The Quarto of *Henry VI* part 2 has York say: "thy sinews shrink" (2163).

In *Locrine* the word 'pattern' is used twice: "A perfect **pattern of** all chivalry..." (1.2.206) and "Estrild, the perfect **pattern of**

137

renown…" (5.6.75). Shakespeare uses the word 'pattern', meaning 'example', 15 times across the canon, 8 of which are "**pattern of**". In *Henry VI* part 1, Suffolk speaks of "a **pattern of** celestial peace" (5.5.65). Confronting Richard III, Anne says, "Behold this **pattern of** thy butcheries" (1.2.52). The word 'pattern' is used three times by Sidney in his *Apologie for Poesie* (twice as "pattern of") but I have not found it in any other writer of the time before *Locrine* was printed.

In *Henry VI* part 2, Jack Cade, like Humber in *Locrine*, starves after his defeat; they both encounter a humble man (Iden/Strumbo) and threaten him. They both use the word '**hungry**'. Cade uses the word '**famish**'; Humber says his arms are '**famished**'; Iden speaks of "**famished** men" (4.10.43). Cade talks of '**famine**', Humber evokes "dreadful **Fames**" (4.3.9). Humber repeatedly uses the word '**meat**' and demands from Strumbo, "Give me some **meat, villain**; give me some **meat**" (4.3.80). Likewise Cade calls Iden a '**villain**'. Cade then says, "I have eat no **meat** these five days" (4.10.37). Both Humber and Cade mention devils and both die. Speaking to Cade's dead body, Iden wishes he "might thrust **thy soul to** hell" (4.10.78). Locrine says to Tharimachus, "I would send **thy soul to** Puriflegiton (i.e. Hell)" (5.2.48). Hubba says to Corineus, "I'll send **thy soul unto** the Stigian lake" (3.6.5).

Strumbo tells us he feared that his wife, "would **set** her **ten commandments in** my **face**" (4.3.41). In *Henry VI* part 2 Eleanor says, "I'll **set** my **ten commandments in** your **face**" (1.3.143).

In *Locrine* we have:

> A subtle **Adder**, creeping closely near,
> Thrusting his **forked sting** into his claws…
>
> (3.1.9)

In *Henry VI* part 2 York introduces the snake imagery, "the…**snake**… will **sting** your hearts." (3.1.343-4). Salisbury then speaks of a serpent "with **forked** tongue…and fatal **sting**"(3.2.261, 269). In the same scene Margaret refers to an **adder** (3.2.76). This imagery continues in *Henry VI* part 3: York describes Margaret's tongue as more poisonous "than the **adder**'s tooth" (1.4.112); later in that play Clifford speaks of "the lurking serpent's mortal **sting**" (2.2.15). Richard II talks about "a lurking **adder** whose double tongue may with a mortal touch" (3.2.20).

In *Henry VI* part 1: "All the figures and devices of classical rhetoric, the Senecan stichomythia, the soliloquy, classical similes and allusions, appear in profusion…" (Cairncross, 1965, lv). *Richard III* contains direct borrowings from Seneca. Jowett (2000, 49) singled out Clarence's dream and noted that it had "echoes in its phrasing of journeys to the underworld in Virgil, Seneca, the Englished Seneca of Thomas Sackville, in his allusions to *Mirror for Magistrates*, and

Thomas Kyd, in *The Spanish Tragedy*. These are interwoven with recollections of drownings at sea in Ovid and the Cave of Mammon in Spenser's *Faerie Queene*. There are also Biblical allusions and echoes of Marlowe." These are the very same influences on the writer of *Locrine*.

Echoes of *Locrine* in *Cymbeline*
Previous scholars have noticed that Shakespeare tended to recapitulate his early writings in his late works: so for example I have linked *Mucedorus* with *The Winter's Tale* and *The Tempest* in chapter 2; *Double Falshood* with *The Two Gentlemen of Verona* and *The Two Noble Kinsmen* in chapter 7; I can also see links between *Titus Andronicus* and *Coriolanus*; *Henry VIII* obviously recapitulates the early history plays, including as we shall see in chapter 5, *Thomas of Woodstock*. What late play then might recall *Locrine*? Almost as soon as I started examining this early play I encountered reminders of *Cymbeline* (which also has echoes of the early poem, *The Rape of Lucrece*). Brutus names his wife as Imogen (1.2.199). Strumbo's first wife is called Dorothy, as is Imogen's maid in *Cymbeline*. Both plays tell of ancient Britain, marital conflict, invasion and have ghosts (in *Locrine* vindictive, in *Cymbeline* supportive). Humber refers to "Postumius' son" (meaning Brutus, 2.2.10) whom Holinshed names as Posthumus. Posthumus Leonatus is the name of Imogen's husband-to-be in *Cymbeline*. Thus three names from *Locrine* are taken up by the bard for characters in his late play. These names are not in Holinshed's section on Kymbeline (Third Book, Chapter XVIII, 479). Neville's aunt, Elizabeth Hoby, had a son called Posthumous (James, 2008b, 69).

Given the connections between *Locrine* and the Babington plot I note that Milford Haven, which is mentioned in *Cymbeline* as a port to be used by the invading Roman army, was a possible harbour for the Spanish invading fleet (Smith, 1936, 43). It was also the harbour used by Henry Earl of Richmond (later Henry VII) when he invaded to confront Richard III (4.4.533). Furthermore there is a hint of the Babington plot in *Cymbeline*: when Cloten tries to enlist Pisanio into betraying Imogen, he says he would think of him as "an honest man." (3.5.113). "The Honest Man" is the only name by which we know the brewer who delivered the fatal, secret letters, hidden in beer barrels, to Mary Queen of Scots at Walsingham's behest.

Cymbeline is a play about the relationship between Britain and Rome, with the King finally agreeing, voluntarily, to pay tribute to the Roman Emperor. Does this reflect the relationship between the

Protestant and Catholic faiths? The last plays are about reconciliation, forgiveness and split families being re-united. Whilst it may revisit the themes of *Locrine,* which emerged from the Babington plot, *Cymbeline* moves forward in a visionary way towards healing and concord: the doctor in the play is called Philharmonus. *Locrine* is a play about discord and there is no healing, just the repeated statement "all our life is but a Tragedy" (3.1.17). Yates (1975, 49) pointed to *Cymbeline* being written to celebrate the revival of chivalric Britain under James I's eldest son Henry and his sister Elizabeth's wedding to the Elector Palatine.

Neville knew Henry but he sadly died, aged just 18. Thus we can see that *Cymbeline*, like *Locrine*, has a political aspect linking the mythic Trojan Brutus with the contemporary monarchy.

Did Neville re-read his early works towards the end of his life and so was reminded of images and vocabulary? This would explain the strange reoccurrence of rare vocabulary in the two plays.

In response to Albanact's invitation to Strumbo to rebuild his house by the palace gate Strumbo replies, "Gate! O petty treason to my person! Nowhere else but by your **backside**?" (2.4.82). The word '**backside**' occurs in *Cymbeline* when a Lord says in an aside, "His steel was in debt; it went o' the **backside** the town" (1.2.10). This may seem a strange coincidence but it is the only time the bard uses the word '**backside**'! The only other writer of the period I have found to use this word is Nashe in his *Pierce Penilesse* (1592) when he writes: "on the **backside** of a dore in a Chandlers shop" (346). What this use by Nashe highlights is that in both *Locrine* and *Cymbeline* the '**backside**' is a part of town.

In *Locrine* Strumbo, the Cobbler, asks, "Will you have your **shoes clouted**?" (2.3.44). Clouted means patched. These words are used in *Henry VI* part 2 when Jack Cade says, "Spare none but such as go in **clouted shoon**" (4.2.175). In *Cymbeline* Arviragus says:

> I thought he slept, and put
> My **clouted** brogues from off my feet, whose rudeness
> Answer'd my steps too loud.
>
> (4.2.215)

In *Cymbeline* Posthumus says, "It is a **basilisk** unto mine eye, kills me to look on't" (2.4.107). The **basilisk** was fabulous creature, part bird, part snake, whose breath and look were fatal. In *Locrine* the defeated Humber, starving, alone in a forest, asks, "What **basilisk** was hatched in this place?" (4.3.1). We find this also in *Edmund Ironside*:

His sight, his breath, his fell infectious tongue
Is venomer than is the **basilisk**'s.

(5.1.36)

and in *Arden of Faversham* when Alice says, "So looks the traveller to
the **basilisk**" (1.1.215). In *Henry VI* part 2, the King says, "Come,
basilisk, and kill the innocent gazer with thy sight" (3.2.52). Suffolk
curses:

Poison be their drink!
Gall, worse than gall, the daintiest that they taste!
Their sweetest shade a grove of cypress trees!
Their chiefest prospect murdering **basilisks**!

(3.2.328)

In *Henry VI* part 3: Gloucester declares, "I'll slay more gazers than the
basilisk" (3.2.187). Anne in *Richard III*, in a scene we have already
seen to have associations with Locrine, curses Richard, wishing there
were **basilisks** to strike him dead (1.2.148). Hotspur dreams of
basilisks in *Henry IV* part 1 (2.3.54). Queen Isabel speaks of
"murdering **basilisks**" in *Henry V* (5.2.17). Thus we can see that the use
of the **basilisk** myth in the early plays of *Locrine*, *Edmund Ironside*,
Arden of Faversham and the history plays, is echoed in the late plays,
Cymbeline and *The Winter's Tale* where Polixines says, "Make me not
sighted like the **basilisk**" (1.2.383).

In both *Cymbeline* and *Locrine* the king is likened to a cedar tree. I
have already noted Neville's use of tree images and his ancestral role as
a forester.

Locrine and the Phaeton sonnet

I explored the Phaeton sonnet in chapter 1 and further examined it in
relation to *Mucedorus* in chapter 2. The number of Phaeton sonnet
words used in *Locrine* is quite extraordinary. The column on the right is
the incidence of five particular words: **increase, branch, herbs, vaunt**
and **rival**.

Play	Total number of words:	Rare words:
Richard II	27	rival, branch, herbs
Henry VI part 2	23	increase, herbs
Locrine	**22**	**increase, branch, herbs**
Henry VI part 3	22	increase, branch
Edward I (Peele)	22	vaunt
Richard III	21	increase, herbs

(See Appendix 1 for a fuller list.)

This alone might be taken as evidence of Shakespeare-Neville's authorship, if the Phaeton sonnet is accepted as being by him. Whilst Peele's *Edward I* has the same number of Phaeton words as occur in *Locrine*, the fact is that the word '**vaunt**' in *Edward I* is not in the four canonical plays listed here; however they share with *Locrine* the other rare words: **increase**, **branch**, **herbs**, which are the more characteristic of Shakespeare's ('**vaunt**' and '**rival**' being rarer).

In the sonnet there is a line, "Thou with thy **Frutes** our **barrenness** o'er-spread..." The Phaeton sonnet is a dedicatory poem to **Florio**'s *Second Fruits* so there is an implicit pun on Florio/Flora and flowers/fruits. In *Locrine* Estrild praises the English countryside:

> The plains, my Lord, garnished with **Flora**'s wealth,
> And **overspread** with party colored **flowers**...
>
> (2.2.33)

'**Overspread**' occurs in *Henry IV* part 2 (4.4.56). Spenser uses '**overspread**' twice in his *Faerie Queene*: in Book 1, Canto XI, stanza XI it is spelt '**overspred**'; in Book 5 Canto IX, stanza 14 spelt '**oversprad**'. Marlowe used '**overspread**' in his 1592 play *The Jew of Malta* (line 2695). In 1594 Nashe used it in *The Unfortunate Traveller* (line 685). '**Overspread**' is also to be found in Greene's *Orlando Furioso* (1.1.204). I have examined Greene's vocabulary and noted that he does not use many of the Phaeton words at all (see Appendix 2).

In *Locrine* Humber complains that:

> Hath triple Cerberus, with contagious foam,
> Sowed **Aconitum** mongst these withered **herbs**?
> Hath dreadful Fames with her charming rods
> Brought **barrenness** on every **fruit**ful tree?
>
> (4.3.7)

The Phaeton sonnet line we are examining is: "Thou with thy **Frutes** our **barrenness** o'er-spread..." It is therefore startling to find in *Henry IV* part 2 that the word '**overspread**' occurs just 8 lines after the word '**Aconitum**' (4.4.48-56). Humber's lament also contains another Phaeton word: '**herbs**'(4.3.8). '**Barrenness**' is to be found in only one Shakespeare play, *The Comedy of Errors* (3.2.118) but twice in Nashe's *The Unfortunate Traveller* (lines 1504 and 2665), both of which postdate *Locrine*. The vocabulary of *Locrine* includes not only 22 words from the Phaeton sonnet but also ten near misses, showing that this vocabulary was in the writer's usage.

Word↓	*Locrine*
sweet	√
friend	√
name	√
agrees	agree/d
increase	√
rival	
spring	√
branch	√
flourishing	
Summers/'s	summer
shady	√
pleasures	√
cease	√
Winters/'s	
storms	√
repose	
peace	√
spends	spend
franchise	
living	live/s/d
thing	√
daisies	
sprout	
little	√
birds	√
sing	√
herbs	√
plants	
vaunt	avaunt
release	
English	
wits	
dead	√
laurel	√
except	√
green	√
fruits	fruit/ful/less
barrenness	√
o'erspread	overspread
flowery	flowering
pleasance	pleasant
flowerets	flowers
morality	
Italy	√
Total:	22

Flora and the prototype for John of Gaunt's speech

On arrival in England Humber asks Estrild what she makes of the country. She delivers a rhapsodical speech on the beauty of the land:

> The plains, my Lord, garnished with **Flora**'s wealth,
> And **overspread** with party colored flowers,
> Do yield sweet **contentation** to my mind.
> The airy hills enclosed with **shady** groves,
> The groves replenished with sweet chirping **birds**,
> The **birds** resounding heavenly melody,
> Are equal to the groves of Thessaly,
> Where Phoebus with the learned Ladies nine,
> Delight themselves with music harmony,
> And from the moisture of the mountain tops,
> The silent springs dance down with murmuring streams,
> And water all the ground with crystal waves.
> The gentle blasts of Eurus, modest wind,
> Moving the pittering leaves of Silvan's woods,
> Do equal it with Temp's **paradise**;
> And thus consorted all to one effect,
> Do make me think these are the **happy** Isles...

> (2.2.33)

In John of Gaunt's famous speech in *Richard II* he speaks of England as another 'Eden', a 'demi-**paradise**', and uses the word '**happy**' (2.1.42-45). Is this *Locrine* speech an early attempt at such a lyrical evocation of England by the young poet? The above passage is remarkable for several reasons, apart from its beauty. I have highlighted words that occur in the Phaeton sonnet (see Chapter 1). '**Shady**' is a rare word: Shakespeare using it in *Romeo and Juliet* (1.1.134), *A Midsummer Night's Dream* (1.1.71), *The Rape of Lucrece* (881) and sonnet 77; it is used by Marlowe in *Tamburlaine II* (line 806) and by Greene in *Orlando Furioso*. Furthermore there is a passage in *Orlando Furioso* which echoes Estrild's speech:

> Sweet solitary **groves**, whereas the nymphs
> With **pleasance** laugh to see the satyrs play,
> Witness Orlando's faith unto his love.
> Tread she these lawnds, fair **Flora**, boast thy pride.
> Seek she for **shade**, **spread**, cedars, for her sake.
> Fair **Flora**, make her couch amidst thy **flowers**.
> Sweet **crystal** springs,
> Wash ye with roses when she longs to drink...
> Smile, joy in her that my **content** hath wrought.

> (2.1.137)

The similarities between these passages and the Phaeton sonnet may be simply the result of conventional language. It may offer further evidence of Greene's hand in *Locrine* or suggest that Greene was a plagiarist! Greene uses the word '**content**' whereas the author of *Locrine* uses '**contentation**'. Neville uses the word '**contentation**' four times in his diplomatic letters between April and October 1599: in each case it is her majesty's '**contentation**' and I note that Estrild, who uses this word, is Humber's queen (Winwood, 1725, Vol 1, 18, 79, 80, 84). The OED states it is found in Holinshed. I have also found it in Sir Philip Sidney's *Lady of May* (1578) and other works of the 1540-80s (LION).

Neville's vocabulary in his letters

Brenda James (2008b, 246-252) presents a list of characteristic words and phrases found in Neville's letters and in Shakespeare. Neville's letters were written some years after *Locrine* so the occurrence of any words in both suggest either coincidence or that these were so habitual for the writer that they were deeply embedded in his subconscious. Three such occur in *Locrine*: '**clean**', "**with a pretence**" and '**celerity**'. Clearly there are two possible meanings of '**clean**', one being washed clean and the rarer meaning of clean = absolutely (e.g.: I clean forgot). It is this latter sense that is particular to Neville's usage in his letters and of the 23 times '**clean**' is used in canonical works it is startling to find that these two different senses are used an equal number of times. In *Locrine* a furious Guendoline cries, "Banish remorse **clean** from my brazen heart" (5.6.105). This is also to be found in *Edmund Ironside* when a messenger says, "thy forces in the north, which thou did'st send 'gainst Edmund Ironside, are **clean** dispersed and piecemeal **overthrown**" (2.3.166). In *Cymbeline* Imogen, fainting with hunger (recalling Humber in the wilderness, outside his cave) stumbles towards the cave of Belarius with the words, "I dare not call: yet famine, Ere **clean** it **o'erthrow** nature, makes it valiant" (3.6.19).

Guendoline says, when confronting Locrine that she comes "**With full pretence** to seek thine **overthrow**" (5.5.39). Continuing the above links with *Cymbeline* Imogen uses the phrase "**with a pretence**": (3.4.103). Both Guendoline's and Imogen's speeches in which these words occur are the complaints of abused, angry women.

'**Celerity**' occurs in *Locrine* when Thrasimachus says, "The Scithians follow **with great celerity**" (2.6.74). Shakespeare echoes this use in *Troilus and Cressida* when Nestor says:

> **with great** speed of judgment,
> Ay, **with celerity**, find Hector's purpose

> (1.3.329)

Neville likewise uses the words "**with vehemency and celerity**" (a hendiadys!) in a letter dated 28/8/1600 (James, 2008b, 252; Winwood, 1725, Vol 1, 248). '**Celerity**' also occurs in *Henry V* (Prologue, Act 3, 2); twice in *Measure for Measure* (4.2.93 and 5.1.390); twice in *Antony and Cleopatra* (1.2.143 and 3.7.24) and once in *The Two Noble Kinsmen* (1.1.202). (See Appendix 8 for further exploration of this word.)

Neville used many words beginning with dis- in his letters. In *Locrine* we have: **dispossess**, **disanull/s**, **displeasure**, **dishonoured**, all of which can be found in Shakespeare's plays. Three of these usages in *Locrine* are echoed in the plays:

Assarachus, speaking to his brother, the dying King Brutus, says, "what so ere the fates determined have, it lieth **not** in us to **disannul**" (1.1.33). This word is used in two early plays. In *The Comedy of Errors* the Duke says:

> Now, trust me, were it not against our laws,
> Against my crown, my oath, my dignity,
> Which princes, would they, may **not disannul**,
> My soul would sue as advocate for thee.
>
> (1.1.144)

In *Henry VI* part 3 Oxford, referring to two of Neville's ancestors, says, "Then Warwick **disannuls** great John of Gaunt" (3.3.81). **Disannul** is also in *The Troublesome Raigne* (part 1.3.70).

Locrine accuses Thrasimachus: "thou didst our **high displeasure** scorn" (5.2.67). The words "**high displeasure**" are used by Benvolio in *Romeo and Juliet* (3.1.157).

Guendoline protests, "Have I **dishonoured** thy **marriage** bed?" (5.5.44). In *Henry VI* part 3, Gloucester accuses, "Warwick, doing what you gave in charge, is now **dishonoured** by this new **marriage**"(4.1.32).

Neville used the word '**massacre**' in his letter to Cecil, 26/5/1599, referring to the St. Bartholomew's Day Massacre in Paris, 1572 (Winwood, 1725, Vol 1, 34). The word is used 6 times in *Locrine*. It occurs in three early Shakespeare plays: three times in *Henry VI* part 1 (1.1.135; 2.2.18; 5.4.160); once in *Titus Andronicus* (1.1.455) and twice in *Richard III* (2.4.56; 4.3.2). The fact that the word is most in the writer's mind nearest to the date of the fatal events in Paris is no surprise.

'**Argentine**' (meaning silvery) occurs in the 1577 edition of Holinshed (OED); '**Argentine**' appears in Neville's Tower note book (1602-3), on the right hand page of sheet 50, in notes about a royal ritual procession which included the Earls of Somerset, Northumberland, Westmoreland, Oxford and Tho Bellocampo (Beauchamp):

> "with **Argentynd** Knight to carry the first cup of silver for the K. (King's) drink…"

(and again, four lines further on:)

> "Jno (John) **argentyn** knight deserved with **argentyn** dye with servis (one word undeciphered) and Hertfordshire Tho **Nevell** Lo(rd) Furnivall to carry…."

This rare word, repeated three times, obviously impressed itself on Neville's mind and he used it seven years later in *Pericles* (1609): "Celestial Dian, goddess **argentine**" (5.1.254). The word '**argent**' occurs in *Locrine* (3.5.14). 'Argent' is in Marlowe's *Massacre at Paris* (1590: 6.23). The OED states it was first used in the heraldic colour sense (as it is in *Locrine*) in 1562.

Neville uses the rare *Locrine* word '**enthronized**' (2.2.24) in a letter (2/11/1600: spelling it '**inthronize**': James, 2008b, 158). Whilst the word is not used in any canonical work it is echoed in *Thomas of Woodstock* (see chapter 5) when Richard II says, "this day we will be new **enthronished**" (2.2.114).

Hints of Neville's life in the text of *Locrine*

Strumbo says, "I was begotten and born in the wane of the Moon, when every thing as **Lactantius** in his fourth book of Consultations doth say, goeth asward" (1.3.4).

Who was Lactantius? Lucius Caelius Firmianus Lactantius (c 250 – 325 AD) was born a 'pagan' in Africa. The Emperor Diocletian made him professor of Rhetoric in Nicomedia. He became a Christian and went to Constantinople. He became tutor to the Emperor Constantine's son (c 311 AD). He wrote a poem about the Phoenix (*De Ave Phoenice*). "He was called the Christian Cicero by the humanists." [31] Copernicus however mocked Lactantius in his *De Revolutionibus Orbium Coelestium* of 1543:

> "…babblers who claim to be judges of astronomy although completely ignorant of the subject… will dare to find fault with my undertaking and censure it. I disregard them even to the extent of despising their criticism as unfounded. For it is not unknown that Lactantius, otherwise an illustrious writer but hardly an astronomer, speaks quite childishly about the earth's shape, when he mocks those who declared that the earth has the form of a globe… Astronomy is written for astronomers." [32]

[31] http://www.newadvent.org/cathen/08736a.htm [Accessed 2008]
[32] http://en.wikipedia.org/wiki/Lactantius [Accessed 2008]

Henry Neville studied astronomy at Oxford University. Neville could have learned of Lactantius through Henry Savile, his tutor, with whom he travelled through Europe when the latter was reseaching the early Christian writers, especially St. John Chrysostom (349 - 407 AD) Archbishop of Constantinople. Savile established a professorship in astronomy at Oxford.

Lactantius' writings were admired in the Rennaissance as much for the quality of his Latin. Neville wrote in Latin. What is apparent is that the writer of *Locrine* is poking fun at Lactantius: the reference to him is in the mouth of a comic character. In a very real sense we are hearing the author's own voice here: a cobbler is hardly likely to have sprinkled his talk with reference to a 4th Century Christain professor of Rhetoric! In fact given the historical period of *Locrine*, the earliest days of Britain, sometime before Christ's birth, the reference is an anachronism that speaks more about the interest of a 16th Century man who had researched Lactantius and astronomy!

Although Shakespeare never refers directly to Lactantius there is a near miss in *Henry VI* part 1: describing Joan of Arc, the Bastard of Orleans says:

> The **spirit of** deepe **Prophecie** she hath,
> Exceeding the nine **Sibyls** of old Rome...
>
> (1.2.55)

Cairncross (1965, xxxv) pointed out that the source of this was Cooper's *Thesaurus* (1565) where the Glossary gives, under **Sybilla**, "A generall name of all women which had the **spirite of prophecie**: of them (as Varro and **Lactantius** doe write) were tenne... every one of these (as **Lactantius** sayth) prophecied of the incarnation of Christ." Cooper's *Thesaurus* is one of Shakespeare's recognised sources.

Furthermore in his *Institutes* Lactantius wrote about Hermes Trimegistus, a central figure in the Occult Neoplatonism of the Renaissance. Yates (2002) explored the connections between this movement, Giordano Bruno and Shakespeare (see chapter 1). Hermes Trimegistus is identified with Mercury, the messenger and the Egyptian god of writing, **Thoth**. Hall opened his *Chronicle* (1548) with a dedicatory address to Edward VI, in which he refers to "Mercurie in Egipte inuented letters and writing." In *Edmund Ironside* Edricus refers indirectly to Mercury's connection with writing when he aspires to "pluck Cyllen's feathers and make pens with them." (3.5.137) Cyllen is Mercury: he was born on Mount Cyllene in Arcadia. Mercury is mentioned in *Locrine*: indeed Strumbo, who refers to Lactantius and who states that his house is near the temple of Mercury (2.4.60), is mistaken for Mercury by Humber (4.3.75). In *Titus Andronicus*, the distressed Titus mistakes a clown for Jupiter's messenger (i.e. Mercury: 4.3.78-90). As James (2008b) decoded the dedication to the sonnets the words, **"The Wise Thoth"** were the first to emerge, before Henry Neville's name was revealed. Far from being a throwaway reference then, this mention of Lactantius in *Locrine* opens a door on the influences which the young Neville absorbed during his studies with his Oxford tutor Savile.

Strumbo uses Italian, promising success to lovers who use new coined words, "succado de labres", (1.3.97: meaning the "sweetness of lips" but with a possible double entendre). Neville, having spent time in Italy during his European tour, knew Italian; his father had also spent time in Italy. Italy is mentioned twice in *Locrine*: both times are about leaving Italy with a hint of regret (perhaps this echoes Neville's own feelings).

Locrine has a number of descriptions of battlefields, including of:

> The slaughtered Troyans, squeltring in their blood,
> Infect the air with their carcasses,
> And are a prey for every ravenous bird.
>
> (2.7.4)

Neville may well have seen battlefields. Robert Sidney accompanied Neville on his European tour, and his brother, the poet Philip, was fighting in the Netherlands with Leicester and Henry Killigrew (Neville's future father-in-law). It is possible that the group paid them a visit, especially as Neville was a relative of the Digges. One of the Digges had written a book about military tactics, and as Neville knew he was going to be producing cannons he may have wanted to see some military action. Neville took on his iron foundry business in 1583 (he sold it in 1598). The words 'iron' (4.3.66), 'steel' (1.2.81; 2.2.91; 5.6.88) and 'brass' (3.1.7) occur in *Locrine*. Thrasimachus says:

> We did behold the **straggling** Scithians' camp,
> Replete with men, stored with **munition**...
>
> (2.4.25)

In *Henry VI* part 1 Gloucester says:

> I'll to the Tower with all the haste I can,
> To view the artillery and **munition**...
>
> (1.1.167)

Lewis the Dauphin also uses this word in *King John* (5.2.98). I have only found one other writer who uses this word in this period: Marlowe in *Tamburlaine 1* referred to "warlike engines and **munition**" (1876). Neville as a cannon manufacturer knew about munitions. Indeed in a letter dated 26/5/1599 Neville wrote of "Armes, Munitions, or Materials for Warre..."(Winwood, 1725, Vol. 1, 29-35). Furthermore Neville used the words "**straggling** rebels" in a letter dated 28/12/1600 (Winwood, 1725, Vol. 1, 287).

At the start of the play Brutus, the patriarch, speaks of, "Th' unhappy slaughter of my luckless sire..." when he was young. Neville's father was just 9 when his father, Sir Edward Neville, was executed. Furthermore Brutus says they were:

> As exiles from the bounds of Italy:
> So that perforce we were constrained to fly...
>
> (1.2.89)

Neville's father went to Italy as a voluntary exile during Mary Tudor's reign.

Guendoline in reply to the invitation to marry Locrine replies, "I will not stand aloof from off the **lure**..." (1.2.184). In *Taming of The Shrew* Petruchio says,

> My **falcon** now is sharp and passing empty;
> And till she stoop she must not be full-gorged,
> For then she never looks upon her **lure**.
>
> (4.1.177)

Juliet calls Romeo from her balcony: "Hist! Romeo, hist! O, for a **falconer**'s voice, To **lure** this tassel-gentle back again!" (2.2.158). In *Venus and Adonis* we find: "As **falcon** to the **lure**, away she flies..." (1027). This is falconry imagery: the word '**lure**' is used just three times in the canon: all are related to the connection between lovers. As already stated, Neville would have known about falconry because his father was a keen falconer.

Finally Queen Guendoline comes from Cornwall to reclaim the kingdom: Anne Killigrew was from a Cornish family so perhaps this detail of the story appealed to Neville. This further points us to Jonson's play *The Staple of News* which James has shown contains hidden references to Henry Neville and the First Folio, including a Cornish lady whom she idenifies as Anne Killigrew. "Jonson peppered his drama with passing echoes from the Shakespeare plays" (James, 2008b, 301). It is startling then to find him using a number of very rare words that occur in *Locrine* in this play: 'lickfinger', 'ophir', 'argent'. Lickfinger is the name of the artistic cook in *The Staple of News* whom James identifies as the Spirit of Poetry. Indeed, the word is only used by Jonson and the author of *Locrine* (according to LION).

Conclusion

If Buck had not written the note about Tilney's *Estrild* in his copy of *Locrine* we would never have guessed that Charles Tilney had anything whatsoever to do with this play: there is no other evidence pointing to him as a writer. There is on the contrary, plenty of evidence pointing to the play being Shakespearean and some evidence pointing to Neville. For this, his first tragedy Shakespeare-Neville took a high sounding heroic tone from previous academic Inns of Court tragedies like *Gorboduc*. He was later to make his style more naturalistic. He was able however at times to write in "old fashioned" styles. It is therefore possible Neville chose to disguise his hand by writing in anachronistic ways and, after all, the play was set 2000 years before his time. The influence and quotations from Marlowe, Kyd, Peele, Greene and Spenser (see Appendix 7) can either be viewed as a young writer learning his craft or a man intent on hiding his identity by literally disguising himself within other writers' styles. Indeed given that the play refers even obliquely to the very recent trial and death of Mary Queen of Scots such disguising would have been very wise. The play is a labyrinth and we may get lost, wondering who wrote which bits and what belongs to any mythic, original text. Despite the smoke and mirrors however, we can still discern Neville's youthful hand.

Chapter 4

ARDEN OF FAVERSHAM

The Tragedy of Master Arden of Faversham was published anonymously in 1592 (being entered on the Stationer's register on 3 April, 1592): this was before the name 'Shakespeare' was **ever** used in print (even Greene's *Groatsworth of Wit,* in which he refers to 'Shake-scene', was only registered in December 1592). Scholars have variously attributed it to Kyd, Marlowe, Peele, Greene, Munday, Rowley, Yarrington, Heywood, Oxford, Wilkins and Shakespeare. It seems that no consensus has been reached. Recent computer analysis suggests Kyd had a hand in the play (Vickers, 2008, 13). With the hidden figure of Henry Neville now emerging from the shadow of his front man, William Shakespeare, this chapter examines what new light this throws on the play.

The plot of *Arden of Faversham*

Arden is an ambitious man in an unhappy marriage. In the first scene he is told he has been granted the titles to the Abbey of Faversham lands. However this brings him no joy, as he knows his wife, Alice, is having an affair with Mosby, a tailor who has risen to the rank of steward. Alice and Mosby plot Arden's murder, eventually employing Black Will and George Shakebag as assassins. These two prove, in a series of missed opportunities, to be incompetent, so eventually the murder happens in Arden's own house, thus leaving a trail of evidence that damns them all. Caught up in this tragedy are Michael (Arden's servant) and Clarke (a painter) who are rivals in love with Susan (Mosby's sister and Alice's servant).

The sources of *Arden of Faversham*

The play is based on a real murder. Arden was killed on February 15th 1551 and the story is told in Holinshed. In 1571/2 a theatre company, Lord Abergavenny's Men, performed in Faversham (Chambers, 1923, Vol 2, 92). Although twenty years had elapsed since the murder it would still have been remembered in the town: indeed it is to this day, as the house still stands. Lord Abergavenny was Henry Neville's uncle.

John Stow, one of the editors of the 1587 edition of Holinshed's chronicles, had a manuscript, (now in the British Museum, Harley MSS. 542, ff. 34-37B) that is an account of Arden's murder (Wine, 1973, xlii). There is one incident in this manuscript which is **not** in Holinshed which **is** in the play, suggesting that the playwright had access to the manuscript. Arden becomes enraged enough to fight after Mosby calls him a "horned beast" (i.e. a cuckold: 4.4.82). Only the manuscript contains this information: "for he [Mosby] had piked a qwarrell wt hym [Arden] ...calling hym Knave, vyllane & cokeolde" (Wine, 1973, xlii). Neville could have had access to this manuscript because he knew Holinshed's publisher and printer – Newbury (James, 2005, 99, 320). Newbury and Neville were neighbours, and Newbury's son Ralph was a 'feofee' of Neville's will. His accounts show that at one time he paid Newbury, the publisher and printer, £106, which was a huge sum in those days. It is highly likely that Neville's father knew Holinshed, because Holinshed dedicated his work to Burghley, and Neville's father was a friend of his. Added to this, Neville's father-in-law, Sir Henry Killigrew, was an editor of the 1587 edition of Holinshed, and therefore would have seen various source materials, which he would have decided either to include or omit. Neville and his wife and family lived part of the year at Killigrew's house in Lothbury, even while he was overseeing his business in Mayfield, so he was in a unique position to see the revisions of Holinshed and the original sources. Neville, uniquely, was therefore surrounded by both Holinshed and the Kent/East Sussex landscape, which formed the background to *Arden of Faversham* (James, 2008b).

The date of *Arden of Faversham*

Published in 1592 the play must have been written before then: a play was only published after a series of successful performances. It is believed that Shakespeare's *Henry VI* parts 2 & 3, which were published in 1594, were performed from 1590. *Arden of Faversham* is based on the second edition of Holinshed's *Chronicles*, which was published in 1587. *Edmund Ironside* is believed to date from 1588. The plot includes dismembering (cutting off hands, noses) and oaths, both of which occur in *Arden of Faversham*, *Henry VI*, *Titus Andronicus* and *Edward III*. In the last of these, Warwick links both themes: "What if I swear by this right hand of mine, to cut this right hand off?" (1.3.351). So *Arden of Faversham* fits the themes of this early period. However the writing in *Edmund Ironside* seems earlier than that of the more sophisticated *Arden of Faversham*, therefore I suggest that the latter was written between 1589-90. As such it was probably written about the same time as *Henry VI* and before *Edward III* and *Titus Andronicus*. However there is some evidence that it may have been written earlier, indeed in the gap between *Mucedorus* and *Locrine* (1585-7): the low number of words beginning with 'un' (see Appendix 4) and the low number of Phaeton sonnet words (see Appendix 1) suggest it could predate *Edmund Ironside*. As the *Arden of Faversham* story had been told in the first edition of Holinshed (1577) and Neville could have had access to the second edition of Holinshed whilst his father-in-law, Henry Killigrew, was editing it between 1585-7, it is not impossible that the date could be as early as 1586. This early date would explain what Wiggins (2008, 285) criticised as the lack of the playwright's experience of the practical aspects of stagecraft. He pointed out that the unknown author was influenced by Kyd and Marlowe. *The Spanish Tragedie* was probably written between 1585-7. Therefore the date for *Arden of Faversham* must lie between 1586-1590.

Evidence for 'Shakespeare' in *Arden of Faversham*

Before we look at the question of evidence for Neville in the play I will present a review of the evidence for the play being a genuine part of the 'Shakespeare' canon, including new discoveries I have made.

The play was published by Edward White who also brought out *Titus Andronicus*. White also published Kyd's *Spanish Tragedy*: both being typeset by the printer Edward Allde. In 1599 White brought out a second edition of *Arden of Faversham*, this time printed by 'I. Roberts' (James Roberts) who was the printer for several 'Shakespeare' quartos.

Whilst scholars have found parallels in *Arden of Faversham* with Kyd's and Marlowe's plays and language, there are more than twice as many parallels with Shakespeare's writings. The source for the play is principally Holinshed's *Chronicles*, which, together with Hall's *Chronicles*, was also a source for the tetralogy of *Henry VI* Parts 1, 2 & 3 and *Richard III*. The playwright used the second edition of Holinshed, published in 1587. In this edition the text is complemented by marginal glosses that comment on the story: one such is a reference to Alice as a "bloodie minded strumpet". In the play Mosby finally calls Alice "that strumpet" (5.5.13).

Ovid is recognised as a favourite source for 'Shakespeare'. Ovid is referred to by name in *The Taming of the Shrew* and *As You Like It* and he is a source referred to in other plays, such as *Titus Andronicus*, *A Midsummer Night's Dream* and *Cymbeline*. Arden, speaking to his wife, in the opening scene of *Arden of Faversham* says, "Sweet love, thou know'st that we two, Ovid-like..." (1.1.60).

Arden uses the word 'rival' (1.1.37). It is in fact a very rare word for the bard, only occurring six times in Shakespeare's works: in *The Two Gentlemen of Verona*, *The Taming of the Shrew*, *Richard II*, *A Midsummer Night's Dream* and *The Merchant of Venice*; **note**, all of these are from the 1590s. Marlowe used the word once (*Tamburlaine II*, 1587); Thomas Nashe used it once (*The Unfortunate Traveller*, 1594); Ben Jonson used it four times in the plays (*Everyman in his Humour,* 1598; *Sejanus*, 1603;

Volpone, 1606); Bacon only used the word once (in the *Advancement of Learning*, 1605). Thus at this time (1589-90) Marlowe is the only playwright to have used the word and Shakespeare the writer who used it most during the 1590s. It is also in the Phaeton sonnet (see chapter 1).

Another rare word, 'intergatories', occurs in *Arden of Faversham* (3.6.6). It is a syncopated form of 'interrogatories' which Shakespeare used in *King John* (3.1.147). He also used a shortened form (inter'gatories) in *All's Well That Ends Well* (4. 3.184) and in *Cymbeline* (5. 4. 393) and used the singular 'inter'gatory' in *The Merchant of Venice* (5.1.300). This is a legal term for questions answerable under oath (Wine, 1973, 82). Shakespeare used many legal terms.

Oaths being made and broken is a recurring theme in Shakespeare's plays (the word 'oath' is used 133 times in the canon). Mosby makes an oath to Arden, which Alice prevails on him to break (1.1.434). Black Will brags he has broken five hundred oaths (2.2.94). Alice makes and breaks promises. Michael breaks his oath to the killers in order to keep his oath of loyalty to Arden but only to save his own skin. The preoccupation with oaths is especially strong in the early plays of *Edmund Ironside*, *Titus Andronicus*, *Henry VI*, *Edward III*, *The Two Gentlemen of Verona*, *Love's Labours Lost* and *King John*. In *Love's Labour's Lost*, Longaville reads his sonnet which includes the line:

> Vows are but breath, and breath a vapour is.

> (4.3.65)

The poet here uses a similar line of argument as Alice does in *Arden*: she says, "Oaths are words, and words is wind, And wind is mutable" (1.1.436). In *The Comedy of Errors* Dromio of Ephesus, speaking of a man breaking his word, says, "Words are but wind" (3.1.75). If we judge by its preoccupation with oaths, Sonnet 152 may also have been written in this early period:

> In loving thee thou know'st I am forsworn,
> But thou art twice forsworn to me love swearing,
> In act thy bed-vow broke and new faith torn,
> In vowing new hate after new love bearing:
> But why of two **oaths**' breach do I accuse thee,
> When I break twenty? I am perjured most,
> For all my vows are **oaths** but to misuse thee:
> And all my honest faith in thee is lost.
> For I have sworn deep **oaths** of thy deep kindness:
> **Oaths** of thy love, thy truth, thy constancy,
> And to enlighten thee gave eyes to blindness,
> Or made them swear against the thing they see.
> For I have sworn thee **fair**: more perjured I,
> To swear against the truth so **foul** a lie.

The word 'oaths' appears in no other sonnet: 'oaths' occurs six times in *Arden of Faversham*. This sonnet may have been written around the same time as *Love's Labour's Lost*, which includes sonneteering, oathbreaking and a dark lady. Alice is certainly a dark lady: Mosby calls her a raven during one argument and, echoing sonnet 152 above, then says, "thou art not **fair**...how **foul** thou art..." (3.5.97-103). This reminds us of *Macbeth* ("Fair is foul and foul is fair": 1.1.11) and some scholars have seen Alice as a prototype Lady Macbeth. Mosby sees her as a witch: "thou unhallowed hast enchanted me. But I will break thy spells..." (3.5.94). It is Alice who uses the words 'witchcraft' (1.1.201), 'bewitched' (3.5.78) and 'witched' (4.4.203). Since *Arden of Faversham* predates these sonnets and these other plays, we can see themes and images emerging which later are fully developed.

In *The Comedy of Errors*, (written between 1589-94, and so most probably after *Arden of Faversham*), Dr Pinch is described as "**lean-faced**" and "**hollow-eyed**" (5.1.238, 241: Foakes, xix) just as Bradshaw describes Jack Fitton in *Arden of Faversham*:

> A **lean-faced** writhen knave,
> Hawk-nos'd and very **hollow-eyed**.
>
> (2.1.51)

Shakespeare showed very considerable medical knowledge, and an interest in poisons (Bucknill, 1860; Kail, 1986). The *Arden of Faversham* playwright demonstrates some medical knowledge and an interest in poisons. Arden uses '**mithridate**' as an antidote to poison (so called because Mithidates VI, king of Persia [died c 63 BC] rendered himself proof against poisons by constant use of antidotes, Wine, 1973, 26). '**Mithridate**' is mentioned by Marlowe in *Tamburlaine I* (5.1.133). Clarke, the painter, asked how he can avoid the effects of poison, says, "I put a leaf within my nose, So I put **rhubarb** to avoid the smell" (1.1.632). These antidotes are not in Holinshed. In 1606 Shakespeare again referred to **rhubarb** as a purgative in *Macbeth*:

> What **rhubarb**, senna, or what purgative drug,
> Would scour these English hence?
>
> (5.3.54)

One other interesting echo in *Arden of Faversham* is the mention by Michael of a painted cloth (1.1.153). Lucrece "calls to mind where hangs a piece of skilful painting..." (1366). In *Henry IV* part 1, Falstaff refers to "Lazarus in the painted cloth" (4.2.23).

Apart from these echoes and many parallels how close is the play to the spirit of Shakespeare's worldview? From the start the play is psychological: a study of characters and motives. It opens with Franklyn saying: "Arden, cheer up thy spirits and droop no more…leave this melancholy mood." This recalls the opening lines of *The Merchant of Venice* when Antonio says, "In sooth I know not why I am so sad, It wearies me…" The author of *Arden of Faversham* studies how people feel, think, suffer doubts, change their minds, lie, manipulate, dream, struggle with their consciences, grieve. Black regarded the play as "the best psychological drama of the period." Craig considered it "a masterpiece of psychological interpretation, which foreshadows *Macbeth*" (Wine, 1973, lxvi & lxxxiii). Most characters have soliloquies in which they explore their motivations and emotions: Mosby talks of his "disturbed thoughts…moody brain…troubled mind" (3.5.1,3,10). Furthermore the individuals are set in their historical, cultural, social and economic environment. All this then seems to point to the bard.

The seed images of Shakespeare's archetypal schema

Ted Hughes' (1992) monumental study of the canon: *Shakespeare and The Goddess of Complete Being* offers another perspective. Hughes traced a complex of myth and imagery throughout the plays and poems. He showed how the narrative poems of *Venus and Adonis* and *The Rape of Lucrece* are the underlying myths of the whole canon. He traced the themes of the rejection of the feminine (Venus/love/nature) by the rational male (Adonis/Puritan), the resultant eruption of the dangerous, irrational female (queen of hell/witch/boar/storm/madness), the death of Adonis or his transformation into a Tarquin/tyrant/usurper/irrational brother and subsequent attack on the feminine (Lucrece/Desdemona/Ophelia/Hermione et al). Hughes called this the tragic equation and showed its operation through the plays. He also noted related themes such as the rival brothers (representing the poles of Adonis/Tarquin such as Hamlet/Leartes) and the redemption in the purple/red/white flower: the violet. This archetypal underpinning of the plays is Hughes' discovery: is it to be found in *Arden of Faversham*? The answer is yes and no: after all the play was probably written several years before the narrative poems so we might only expect to find traces of this mythic underpinning, like seed images buried in the soil, waiting to germinate. Hughes himself said that the myth only really began to develop in the plays from *As You Like It* (1599), though he could see it beginning to operate in *The Merchant of Venice* (1596).

157

However in *Arden of Faversham* I have found images reminiscent of *The Rape of Lucrece*, as if before that poem was born the images were incubating in the poet's mind. The theme is lost chastity in marriage and the foolish trust of Arden (in this he is like Collatine). In a sense Alice is the polar opposite of Lucrece as a woman who betrays. True, Mosby "usurps" Arden (3.1.29). He has the "opportunity", just as Black Will and Shakebag seek an "opportunity" (2.2.114) to kill. Lucrece laments the Time and Opportunity that Tarquin took to rape her (876). She calls Time the "**copesmate** of ugly night" (925). Mosby uses this rare word to dismiss Alice during an argument: "Go, get thee gone, a **copesmate** for thy hinds!" (3.5.104). The word '**copesmate**' occurs in Peele's *Edward I* (printed in 1593, a year after *Arden of Faversham* was published).

Had Mosby been able to assert his rational conscience he might have rejected Alice (as he twice tries to do) as Adonis rejected Venus, but both men die, after struggling with the persistent attentions of the lustful woman.

Certainly there are rival lovers: Arden and Mosby for Alice, Clark and Michael for Susan. This in itself is evidence for Shakespearean authorship as the doubling of roles and themes is typical of the bard. Arden abandons Alice to Mosby and she becomes a veritable Queen of Hell (in Hughes' terms). Mosby in the end asks to be taken from "this hell of grief" away from Alice (5.5.12). Black Will and Shakebag play the role of the boar and at the scene of the murder Alice tries to pass off her husband's blood as "the pig's blood we had to supper" (5.1.400). In *Titus Andronicus* (probably written during 1593 about the same time as *Venus and Adonis*), we find this same image of murder, developing into the boar. As Aaron kills the nurse he says:

> if you brave the **Moor**,
> The chafed **boar**, the mountain **lioness**,
> The **ocean** swells not so as Aaron **storms**...
> Weke, weke! so cries a **pig** prepared to the spit....
>
> (4.2.139)

Aaron links pig, **Moor**, boar, lioness and ocean storm here. In *Arden of Faversham* we also have pig, **Black** Will, lioness (2.2.115), and sea storm (4.4.43, between two occurrences of the word "mad" in lines 38 & 55). The boar image, linked with rage, violence and madness, continues then to develop through the plays: it occurs 30 times, over half of which are in *Venus and Adonis* (16) and significantly 10 times in *Richard III* (which was first performed in 1592). It also occurs in *The Taming of the Shrew,* (1593), where the image is also linked with sea storm and rage:

Petruchio: Have I not heard the sea puff'd up with winds
　　　　　Rage like an angry **boar** chafed with sweat?

(1.2.200)

Thus it can be seen that *Arden of Faversham,* written between 1586-1590, fits into the emerging pattern of imagery in plays and poems written by Shakespeare between 1590-1595. That the images are hardly developed, indeed are in embryo, fits their early position in the canon. "Again and again," wrote M.B. Smith of *Arden of Faversham*, "an image calls to mind his (Shakespeare's) early work, especially in the Histories" (Wine, 1973, lxxxv).

The curious coincidence of the Shakebag

One reason for the play having been thought to be by Shakespeare is the mysterious coincidence that the villains of the play are Black **Will** and George **Shake**bag: the names seem to recall 'William Shakespeare'. That the victim is called Arden, Shakespeare's mother's maiden name, would seem confirmation that Shakespeare was drawn to this story by these names. However the names were not invented but were a matter of historical record, being in Holinshed (though the historical victim's name could also be spelt 'Ardern' and in one record the villain is called 'Loosebag'). Yet there may be a grain of truth here. If Neville is the real author then he may have enjoyed the joke that his factotum-to-be was presented to the audience as a despicable villain. The play was published in 1592, the very year Greene satirised 'Shake-scene' and just before the first use of the name 'Shakespeare' with the publication of *Venus and Adonis* in 1593. I am inclined however to think this is all simply a strange coincidence. Yet Neville was always attracted by coincidences of name and situation. For instance, 'Arden' and 'Ardennes' are confused in *As You Like It.* What's more, it is - as in *Arden of Faversham* - a confusion that encompasses the lives of both Shakespeare and Neville. Shakespeare's mother was an Arden, and the Forest of Arden was the place where he and all his family were born. The Ardennes was most likely the place to which Neville disappeared during a three-week period before he was finally allowed to come home for a break in his Ambassadorship (James, 2007a).

New evidence for Neville in *Arden of Faversham*

Arden, speaking to his wife, in the opening scene says:

Sweet love, thou know'st that we two, Ovid-like,
Have often chid the morning when it 'gan to **peep**…

(1.1.60)

'Peep' is an interesting word: it occurs 22 times in the canon, from the earliest (*Henry VI* part 2) to the last (*Henry VIII*). Most significantly for this *Arden* use are the early occurrences in *Venus and Adonis* and *The Rape of Lucrece*. These both are about light peeping out.

> And therefore would he put his bonnet on,
> Under whose brim the gaudy sun would **peep**...
> > (*Venus and Adonis,* 1087)

The sun also peeps out in Sonnet 24:

> Mine eyes have drawn thy shape, and thine for me
> Are windows to my breast, where-through the sun
> Delights to **peep**, to gaze therein on thee...

The word occurs twice in *Rape of Lucrece* (1594), again concerned with light, but perhaps more significant for this chapter is the quotation from *Lucrece* in the Northumberland Manuscript (c1597) that links the name of Henry Neville with that of Shakespeare (James & Rubinstein, 2005, 237-243 & Cockburn, 1998, 170). This is a version of line 1086:

> Revealing day through every cranny **peepes**

Here the word 'spies' (in *Lucrece*) has been changed to 'peepes'. The word 'peeps' occurs only twice in the canon: in *Henry V* (4.2.43) and *As You Like It* (2.1.31: both c 1599). Its appearance in the Northumberland Manuscript suggests that Neville feared the truth of his authorship would peep out: indeed the Northumberland Manuscript is the only contemporary document in which his name is visibly associated with that of Shakespeare. Probably written in 1597, it dates from just before the name Shakespeare was printed as author of the two plays mentioned in the manuscript, *Richard III* and *Richard II*. There is also a one word reference to *Love's Labour's Lost* (honorificabilitudini): all three plays were published the next year under the name Shakespeare (1598).

Beheading, dismemberment and Neville

What further evidence peeps out from the text of *Arden of Faversham*, revealing Neville as the hidden author? Wine (1973, lxv) pointed out that, "One of the play's most recurrent images is that of the maiming and destroying of the human body ('dissevered joints and sinews torn', 'eat the heart', 'make thee crawl on stumps', 'Till Arden's heart be panting in my hand', 'lop...away his leg, his arm, or both', 'Cut the nose from the coward's face', 'there be butchered by thy dearest friends'). My dating of this play places it close to *Edmund Ironside* (in which noses and hands are severed) and *Titus Andronicus* (in which heads, hands and tongue are cut off). In these and the early histories there are many murders and executions. In *Henry VI* part 2 we see four severed heads on stage. *Arden of Faversham* ends with Franklyn reporting the multiple executions of the murderers.

Shakespeare's strange, early preoccupation with the cutting off of various parts of the body, murder and execution can be understood when Neville is placed in the picture. Neville was his father's oldest son, so presumably would have been the first of the children to be told about his grandfather's execution (in 1539 for conspiring to overthrow the Tudor dynasty, James & Rubinstein, 2005, 61; see chapter 5). However, Neville's father was a man of humour and peace. Rather than get into conflict with the Catholic Queen Mary he had exiled himself during her reign, spending his time mainly in Italy, especially in Venice. With such a personality, he must have found it extremely difficult to tell his son Henry the awful story of the decapitation of his grandfather. When younger children were born to him, Sir Henry Neville senior may have put off telling the boy about the family tragedy, expecting that, whenever he told his eldest son, it would not be long before the rest of the children also discovered the dreadful truth. We can only guess at the effect such a gruesome revelation must have had on such a sensitive, imaginative youngster as Henry Neville - or perhaps we may do better than mere guessing, for if Neville wrote the Shakespeare plays, then we are in the privileged position of being able to see exactly what effect the re-telling of this terrible story had on the young man. He worked through the trauma by re-telling it again and again in the early plays until he had freed himself from its terrible fascination.

Barbaric punishments were not however simply a matter of history but of contemporary life: hanging, drawing (disembowelling whilst the victim was often still conscious) and quartering, burning and maiming were normal punishments. One example that Neville would have known about was the fate of John Stubbe, a religious writer. In 1579 Stubbe wrote *The Discoverie of a Gaping Gulf*, objecting to Elizabeth's proposed marriage with the Duke of Anjou. Elizabeth was incensed: Stubbe had no claim to offer counsel, his criticism of Anjou was vituperative, and he openly questioned her commitment to Protestantism. On 27 September 1579 a royal proclamation was issued prohibiting the circulation of the book. Stubbe was arrested. Elizabeth wanted to hang him by royal prerogative. He was eventually sentenced to have his right hand cut off and be imprisoned. The sentence was carried out in the market place at Westminster, with surgeons present to prevent him bleeding to death. Camden's eyewitness account records Stubbe's speech on the scaffold: he asserted his loyalty and asked the silent, horrified crowd to pray that God would give him strength to endure the punishment. After his hand was chopped off (it took three blows) he managed to cry out, "God save the Queen!" before he fainted. Stubbe remained in the Tower until 1581. In 1589 he became MP for Great Yarmouth (Mears, 2004). Neville had become an M.P. in 1584, so they probably met in Parliament. Stubbe died in 1590: it was about this time that *Arden of Faversham* was written. In *Edmund Ironside* (dated 1588) two men have their hands cut off on stage as punishment by the pitiless tyrant, Canutus. This of course is echoed by the cutting off of hands in *Titus Andronicus*.

Thus we can see that Neville might well feel vulnerable as a writer of history plays which were commenting on political matters, even indirectly, to such summary punishment. After all, Kyd was tortured and Marlowe eliminated. '**Hand writing**' was a dangerous business! Neville could only be an anonymous writer. Keeping his identity secret would have been a matter of self-preservation.

Hidden connections and protecting powerful people

In 1539, Henry VIII, having ordered the principal part of the monastic buildings at Faversham, in Kent, to be pulled down, granted the site of the abbey, with some adjoining lands, to Sir Thomas Cheyney, who alienated them five years afterwards to Mr. Thomas Arden, or Ardern, a gentleman of Faversham[33] (Wine, 1973, 87). Thomas Cheney is listed, with Edward Neville (Neville's grandfather), as challengers at jousting held in Paris in October 1515 (Hall, 1965, 571). Holinshed, in the account of Arden's murder reported that "Sir Thomas Cheinie" was Lord Warden of the Cinque Ports. Henry Neville was a Baron of the Cinque Ports (James & Rubinstein, 2005, 47). Henry Wriothesley, Earl of Southampton (Shakespeare's early patron and Neville's best friend with whom he spent two years in the Tower of London) was related to the Cheyney family (Jane Cheyney was the Earl's paternal grandmother). In the play Bradshaw, a Faversham goldsmith, states that a thief who had stolen some plate from Lord Cheyne sold it to Bradshaw, saying he had served Sir Anthony Cooke (2.1.40). This detail is not in Holinshed. Sir Anthony Cooke was Neville's mother-in-law's father. He was tutor to Edward VI. Furthermore Sir Thomas Cheyne leased property in the Blackfriars complex where Sir Henry Neville (Neville's father) also had rooms (Chambers, 1923, Vol 2, 499).

---

[33] From: http://www.thebookofdays.com/months/nov/23.htm [Accessed 2008]

Neville is adding local touches of colour that offer us evidence of his authorship.

One interesting piece of continuity between the play and the Holinshed source is the attempt to protect Lord North's family from embarrassment. In this the playwright goes further than the Chronicle, which does reveal that Mosby was Lord North's servant whereas the playwright invents a 'Lord Clifford' to replace the real Lord North. (A Clifford also appears in *Henry VI* parts 2 & 3.) Holinshed had already begun this censorship by not revealing that Alice was Lord North's stepdaughter, a fact that is in the manuscript that was his source (Wine, 1973, xlii, footnote 1). The Lord Clifford is mentioned just once in the first scene so Alice's and Mosby's connections with the North family are neatly airbrushed out. In fact Arden himself had served Sir Edward North in the Court of Augmentations created by Henry VIII to arrange for the dispersal of church property after the dissolution of the monasteries in 1538. He had married Sir Edward's stepdaughter, Alice Mirfyn, and was commissioned thereafter as the King's Controller of the Customs of the port of Faversham. So all three main protagonists in the play were connected with North (Wine, 1973, xxxv).

Sir Edward North, M.P. for Cambridgeshire, 1st Baron North of Kirtling, had had charge of Princess Elizabeth, afterwards Queen, as a state prisoner at Kirtling Hall during Mary's reign[34]. His second son, Sir Thomas North, was the translator of Plutarch's *Lives*. Thomas North's vigorous English influenced contemporary writers, and some critics have called him the first master of English prose. The book was a major source for *Julius Caesar, Coriolanus* and *Antony and Cleopatra*.[35] In the latter play whole speeches are taken from North. 'Shakespeare' therefore had reason to protect the North family. They were powerful, well placed and Thomas was at this time a J.P. in Cambridge.

James also discovered a reason why Neville might use the name 'Clifford' in a negative context: he probably disapproved of the behaviour of George Clifford third Earl of Cumberland (1558–1605), towards his wife Margaret (nee Russell, married 1577) and daughter Anne. In 1586 Clifford sat on the commission which tried Mary, Queen of Scots, and attended her execution. He was made Elizabeth I's champion in 1590, being given the nickname 'Rogue'. Clifford entered enthusiastically into the rich life of a courtier. It was partly to recoup

[34] From: http://hipweb.cambridgeshire.gov.uk/cgi-bin/cambscoll/history.pl?term=Kirtling&category=village&exact=exact [Accessed 2008]
[35] From: http://www.1911encyclopedia.org/Sir_Thomas_North [Accessed 2008]

his losses as a gambler and a courtier that in 1586 Clifford began his career as a privateer. He had at least two illegitimate children with different mistresses. Two centuries ago the antiquary William Whitaker acknowledged the Earl's military prowess but condemned him as an unkind father, a faithless husband, and a poor manager of his estates (Holmes, 2007). In offending his in-laws, the Russells, by his behaviour towards his wife, George alienated their allies the Hobys of Bisham who were Neville's wife's relatives. Anne Clifford's diary for the years 1603 - 1619 is extant and in it she mentioned the many Nevilles she knew, including the 9th Baron, Lord Bergavenny, Sir Henry Neville (who was her uncle and Henry Neville's cousin). She was a friend of Moll (Mary) Neville (see chapter 1; Sackville-West, 1923).

Wiggins (2008, 290) suggested the Lord Clifford in the play was Henry Clifford, second Earl of Cumberland. Henry married twice: both wives had Neville family connections, the second being Katherine Neville, daughter of Richard Neville, 5th Earl of Salisbury.[36]

Historical, legal, political and social perspectives

The *Arden of Faversham* playwright does not follow Holinshed entirely. He minimises the source's suggestion that Arden knowingly colluded with his wife's infidelity. Holinshed clearly states he did this in the hope of further favours from her friends. The play gives an altogether different picture of Arden as a naive, trusting man who vacillates between outraged knowledge of the infidelity and loving denial, depressive foreboding and jealous rumination about his reputation. Wine (1973, lxix) saw him as "one who is so altogether ambivalent that probably no other character in the early English drama – at least not before *Julius Caesar* – presents such a crucial problem; almost any statement about him can be contradicted." The playwright retains Arden's avariciousness but gives the grant of church lands a legal basis not in the source, "through letters patent from his majesty" and by "Chancery seal". Clearly the playwright knew his law, which having become a J.P. in 1583, Neville did. Also this legal title to the lands is granted by "My gracious Lord the Duke of Somerset": this is Edward Seymour, Lord Protector to Edward VI. Somerset profited from the sale of church lands during the dissolution of the monasteries (Wine, 1973, 4). In other words the playwright, unlike Holinshed, is setting the tragedy in its political and historical context.

"…the unknown author of *Arden* was acutely aware of the social upheavals which had taken place in his own and his father's lifetime.

---

[36] From: http://en.wikipedia.org/wiki/Henry_Clifford,_2nd_Earl_of_Cumberland [Accessed 2008]

The play takes into account, **as the source does not**, the widespread dislocation resulting from the dispersal of church property, from the enclosure of small farms by large landowners, and, above all, from the slow disintegration of a rural economy and its values before the new agrarianism of middle-class entrepreneurs intent on amassing property while disregarding the social obligations that ownership of property entails. Tawney has described the medieval village as 'a fellowship of mutual aid, a partnership of service and protection, "a little commonwealth"'; but the playwright, attuned to the social reality of his day, depicts a community where rampant individualism is destroying that ideal." (Wine, 1973, lxii, emphasis added.) Judge Whitlock's assessment of Neville after his death included the words, "he was the most sufficient man for understanding of the State" so linking Sir Henry with the concerns embodied in *Arden of Faversham*.[37]

The playwright is especially interested in the land rights of ordinary people. In the play two minor characters (Master Greene and Dick Reede) bitterly lament the loss of their lands to Arden and this impels Greene to become involved in the murder. The impoverished Reede curses Arden and the murder seems the fulfilment of that curse. Michael, Arden's servant, is also avaricious: having become involved in the murder plot for his own benefit he thinks of murdering his brother to get the farm at "Bolton" (1.1.173). This is actually Boughton under Blean, a village just three miles east of Haversham. This vivid little detail (also not in Holinshed) reveals a Neville connection: Sugden (1925) quotes a letter of Cranmer to Cromwell written in 1558, in which he speaks "of a farm at Bowghton-under-Blayne which his servant **Nevell** had of the Abbot and Convent of Faversham" (Wine, 1073, 15). Thomas Neville (1484 - 1542) had dealings with Cranmer including estates resulting from the dissolution of the monasteries. Neville's uncles, cousins and ancestors all owned a great deal of land and property in Kent and East Sussex, so it is indeed probable that the Nevell in question was a relative of the Earls of Abergavenny.[38]

The Neville family knew this area. Sir Henry Neville's grandfather, Sir Edward Neville, lived at Addington Park, Kent, which is equidistant between Mayfield and Faversham, being approximately 30 miles from both. Henry Neville later lived in Mayfield where Archbishop Cranmer's Palace stood (it had been confiscated and sold by Henry VIII in 1545). The Parish was nevertheless still under the authority of the Archbishop. Cranmer was burnt at the stake in Oxford on 21 March

[37] Duncan, (1974, 275) quoting Judge James Whitelock,'s *Liber Familicus,* ed. John Bruce for the Camden Society, London, 1858.
[38] See numerous catalogues in http://www.a2a.org.uk [Accessed 2008]

1556. In the same year, Sir John Gresham died. He had been the asset-stripping, absentee landlord of the Mayfield Palace estate and had cut down all the trees, given the land over to sheep and had turfed the smallholders off their common grazing.[39] Neville's father inherited these lands through his second wife, Elizabeth Gresham. In Mayfield and the Faversham area the Nevilles had benefited from the sale of church lands, just as Arden of Faversham. Why then should our Henry have such empathy with poorer people stripped of their land? Was this simply guilt at the asset stripping from which he had benefited? James (2008b) has uncovered a deeper anxiety: Henry Neville was in fact illegitimate. This was kept secret and so he was able to inherit his ancestral lands. Had it been discovered he would have been impoverished, the ownership of these lands becoming open to legal challenge. His empathy therefore came from personal vulnerability and was another deep reason for his life long shame and secrecy about his true identity. Had his illegitimacy been discovered he may well have lost his lands to a legitimate sibling (as occurs at the beginning of *The Troublesome Raigne* and *King John*).

Class-consciousness is a theme in *Arden of Faversham*. Confronting Mosby, Arden contemptuously stands on his class status and humiliates him, referring to his earlier work as a tailor. Mosby replies, "**Measure me what I am, not what I was**" (1.1.322). In *Richard III* there are two examples of this figure of speech: in asking Queen Elizabeth to persuade her daughter to accept his proposal of marriage, Richard says, "**Plead what I will be, not what I have been**" (4.4.414). Earlier Richard had said:

> Let me put in your minds, if yours forget,
> **What you have been ere now, and what you are;**
> Withal what I have been, and what I am.

(1.3.132)

Richard III is believed to have been written in 1591 - 3, so such parallels coming after the writing/publication of *Arden of Faversham* (1589 – 90/1592) might be evidence of Shakespeare picking up on another writer's language but the many textual parallels between *Arden of Faversham* and Shakespeare's early plays suggest the writer was the same person. In *Henry VI* part 1 the King says:

> If you do censure me **by what you were,**
> **Not what you are...**

(5.5.97)

---

[39] From: http://www.mayfieldvillage.info/history/martyrs.htm   [Accessed 2008]

This passage, probably written between 1589-90 is much closer in date to the *Arden of Faversham*. Henry Neville also used this phrase in his defence statement at his trial for involvement in the Essex rebellion. Of the Earl he said, "I desire (he) may be considered, **not as he hath been found since, but as he was reputed**" (Winwood, 1725, Vol 1, 304).

Nightmares and hunting in the forest: bird imagery

In Act 3, scene 3, Arden describes a nightmare he has had of being hunted and killed in a forest (see chapter 5). M. B. Smith saw this nightmare as further evidence tying the play into the Shakespeare canon and found echoes of Clarence's nightmare in *Richard III* (1.4.21: Wine 1973, lxxxv). Neville and his father were wardens of **Windsor** Park forest and Neville's ironworking business in Mayfield was near to Ashridge Forest, which his ancestors had owned. Neville actually mentions this forest in a letter to Robert Cecil.[40] In the *Merry Wives of Windsor* Mistress Page says:

> There is an old tale goes that Herne the hunter,
> Sometime a keeper here in **Windsor** forest.
>
> (4.4.26)

Elsewhere in *Arden of Faversham* there are other hunting images such as when Greene says, "**Lime** well your **twigs** to catch this wary **bird**" (3.4.38). This is a very characteristic Shakespearean image and is comparable to the Duke of Suffolk's plan to trap the Duchess of Gloucester in *Henry VI* part 2. Speaking to the Queen he says:

> Madam, myself have **lim'd** a bush for her,
> And placed a quire of such enticing **birds**
> That she will light to listen to their lays...
>
> (1.3.88)

In the same play the Cardinal uses this image: "Like **lime-twigs** set to catch my winged soul" (3.3.16) and again the Duchess of Gloucester complains that her enemies have "...all **lim'd** bushes to betray thy wings..." (2.4.54).

In *Henry VI*, part 3, the king says:

> The **bird** that hath been **limed** in a bush,
> With trembling wings **misdoubteth** every bush...
>
> (5.6.13)

These images, in the *Arden* and *Henry VI* plays were composed about the same time, the late 1580s, by the same writer: Neville. He went on

---

[40] See Hasler (1981) notes for Sir Henry Neville

to use this imagery in *Hamlet* and *Macbeth*. Kyd used the same image in his *Spanish Tragedy* when Lorenzo says:

> I set the trap; he breaks the worthless **twigs**,
> And sees not that wherewith the **bird** was lim'd.
>
> (3.4.41)

I note however that it is in the Shakespeare that the bird '**misdoubteth**' - which matches the '**wary**' in the *Arden of Faversham* passage. Furthermore Kyd's word order, **twigs-bird-lim'd**, is different to the word order in *Arden* and Shakespeare, which is generally **limed-twig/bush-bird**: whilst the word order varies in the canonical examples, the word '**limed**' is never last as it is in Kyd's metaphor.

Iron and cannon imagery

In Act 2, scene 1, Bradshaw tells of his experience as a soldier at Boulogne. The Treaty of Burlogne (1550) was signed the year before Arden was murdered. In 1599 Neville went to France as British Ambassador and visited Boulogne for talks with the Spanish. His father had also undertaken secret diplomatic missions abroad, including to France: he had once been considered for the Ambassadorship that his son was later given. Neville therefore would have known about Boulogne. Indeed in 1578 Neville, aged about 16, left England for a five year European tour: he probably travelled through Faversham on the way to Dover and through Boulogne on the way to Paris. On his return in 1583 he went to Mayfield to take over the family iron foundry business, including the manufacture of cannon. Earlier I quoted two lines from *The Taming of the Shrew* which continue:

> Petruchio: Have I not heard the sea puff'd up with winds
> Rage like an angry boar chafed with sweat?
> Have I not heard great ordnance in the field,
> And heaven's artillery thunder in the skies?
>
> (1.2.200)

This linkage with ordnance is significant for us because it points to Neville's authorship: he was a manufacturer of cannon. There are images of gunpowder and cannon in *Arden of Faversham*, including Mosby's response to a passionate outburst by Alice, which he describes as, "like to a cannon's burst discharged against a ruinated wall..." (3.5.51). What links these two examples of Shakespeare-Neville's cannon imagery is that they are both concerned with the sound of the cannon's blast (see also: 3.6.2, 8 & 29). The *Arden* playwright also uses other images of iron and steel such as "steel soft-mettled cowardice" (2.2.103). The word 'steel' occurs 72 times in the canon. In *Henry VI* part 2, York says, "steel thy fearful thoughts" (3.1.331). In *Henry VI* part 3, Clifford says, "steel thy melting heart" (2.2.41). Whilst the other uses of the word are concerned with hard hearts, sharpness and strength it is noticeable how these two uses in the first history plays match the *Arden*.

Speculative reflections

Neville may have realised that there were too many references in *Arden of Faversham* that would betray his authorship and so decided that this play should remain outside his work acknowledged even under the pseudonym of 'Shakespeare'. Perhaps he realised that it was literally too close to home and so his next play *Titus Andronicus,* was set at a greater dramatic distance, in ancient times and a distant place. *Arden of Faversham* was written before Neville's father's death in 1593: and it is only after that death that the author abandons anonymity and adopts the name 'Shakespeare'. *Richard II* is one of the first plays to be identified as by him. Given the political dangers attendant on that play, being identified as the writer would put him at risk.

Conclusion

Within the text of *Arden of Faversham* there is not only plentiful evidence of 'Shakespeare' but also clear evidence for Neville. This early play ties the author and his eventual pseudonym together even before the name Shakespeare first appears. Perhaps, at last, the paternity of this orphan play can be identified from the scraps of genetic code hidden in the text

Chapter 5

THOMAS OF WOODSTOCK

Thomas of Woodstock survived in just one manuscript, bound together with other plays including *Edmund Ironside*, in the British Library (MS Egerton 1994). It is anonymous, has no title and is incomplete, lacking the final page/s. Thomas of Woodstock, Duke of Gloucester, was the uncle of Richard II and in the play he is Lord Protector of England during Richard's minority. A number of scholars have seen it as part one of a two-part play, of which Shakespeare's *Richard II* is the second part. The quarrel in the opening scene of *Richard II* is explained by the events in *Thomas of Woodstock*. Thomas Mowbray, who is confronted by Bolingbroke at the start of *Richard II*, was governor of Calais at the time of Woodstock's murder there. Bolingbroke asserts that, "he did plot the Duke of Gloucester's death" (1.1.100). The two plays fit together: indeed *Woodstock* follows *Edward III*, thus completing the entire sequence of Shakespeare-Neville's history plays spanning the period 1327-1485. Over the last 100 years several scholars have made the case for its attribution to Shakespeare, others have denied it. Lake (1983) proposed that Samuel Rowley was the 17th Century reviser of this late 16th Century play. In 2006 Michael Egan published a major study of the play, showing that whoever the reviser might have been, the original was undoubtedly by Shakespeare. In this chapter I reveal new evidence for Neville's authorship. (Because of the link with *Richard II* an alternative title is *Richard II* part 1 or 1 *Richard II*: to avoid confusion between these two plays I prefer to use the title *Thomas of Woodstock*.)

The plot of *Thomas of Woodstock*

The play erupts onto the stage with an assassination attempt against the King Richard II's uncles, the Dukes of Lancaster (John of Gaunt), York (Edmund Langley) and Gloucester (Thomas of Woodstock). The abortive plot to poison these grandees is revealed by the Carmelite friar who was to be the assassin. All suspect however that the young King's flattering friends, Greene, Bagot and Tresilian were behind it. Rather than react precipitously, the Lords agree to wait and attend the wedding of the King to Anne of Beame (Bohemia). Thomas of Woodstock, the Protector, who prides himself on his plain clothes and plain speaking, is persuaded by his colleagues to dress up for the wedding.

The three upstarts, Greene, Bagot and Tresilian, plot their take over of the kingdom. Tresilian is to be made Lord Chief Justice and as he puffs himself up we meet Nimble, his comic servant, who debunks him by reminding him of his school boy and junior lawyer days, revealing his humble origins and dishonesty. Ominously and ironically (given what will happen later) Tresilian promises to make Nimble his executioner.

The wedding between Richard and Anne takes place but the ceremony is disturbed by an outbreak of hostility between the older Lords and the younger courtiers. News arrives of civil dissension and the Lords leave to calm the rebellious commons. Thomas of Woodstock agrees to call a Parliament to address their grievances.

Reading the chronicled history of the realm, Richard discovers his birthday and finds he has already passed the age of majority: at the Parliament he takes over the kingdom and dismisses Thomas and his fellow peers from their offices, awarding them to his friends. The upstart clique takes over the kingdom in a series of political moves, graduating from the ridiculous to the terrifying. They design new fashions. They send out blank charters for citizens to sign, which, when filled in, oblige them to pay the King sums of money. They instigate a reign of terror with agents spying and arresting people who complain, imprisoning and executing them. They draw up a scheme to rent the kingdom from the King and pay him sums of money whilst enriching themselves. They plot the arrest and death of Thomas of Woodstock. In the face of all these difficulties Richard plans feasts whilst his queen engages in charitable work to relieve the poor.

Having broken his staff of office Thomas has gone home. His wife has a terrifying dream but he dismisses it, not realising its prophetic truth. His wife leaves to visit the Queen who is ill. Thomas welcomes a group of masquers into his house. Unbeknown to him, the group have come to arrest him and Richard is in disguise as a masquer. Thomas recognises his voice and confronts the King. He is arrested and sent to Calais. In the night he is woken by the ghosts of the Black Prince (his brother) and Edward III (his father) who come to warn him of assassination. Again Thomas does not heed the warnings and is killed by the hired murderers, who are themselves killed to cover up the crime. The Queen dies. Richard, grieving, too late tries to prevent the murder of Thomas. The surviving dukes raise arms against the flattering courtiers and defeat them. Greene is killed and Nimble, to escape retribution himself, hands over Tresilian to be executed. Here the play ends abruptly as the last page is missing.

The date of *Thomas of Woodstock*

Many scholars date the play between 1590-4 and the manuscript about 1604-10,[41] "a Jacobean transcription of an earlier 1590s text, copied for a revival of the play" (Corbin & Sedge, 2002, 3). As the earliest date for *Richard II* is 1594 and *Thomas of Woodstock* predates that play, the date must be before 1594. Egan's analysis led him to conclude that Shakespeare wrote it in 1592-3, after the *Henry VI* trilogy and before *Richard II*. Egan showed that the masque, during which Woodstock is arrested, is Elizabethan, not Jacobean. The play was revived and revised for performances in the 17th Century.

A political play

The play begins and ends with assassinations. It is about political power, right governance, law, oppression and corruption. Neville was a politician, a Member of Parliament, son, son-in-law and grandson to political figures, who thought deeply about the governance of England. Egan (2006, Vol 1, 168) pointed out that one of the sources used by the author of *Thomas of Woodstock* was Parliamentary records: as an M.P. Neville would have had access to these.[42] The play explores fundamental issues of statecraft, "defines the criteria of good government... the responsibilities of 'Kingship', the proper administration of the law, the appropriate role of the King's council and the destructive attractions of pride and will" (Corbin & Sedge, 2002, 9-10, 14). The playwright "plainly recommends some form of constitutional monarchy as best for England... the proposal is ...politically progressive" (Egan, 2006, Vol 1, 477).

Later Neville was to attempt to negotiate such a balance between monarch and Parliament with James I. "Neville's efforts in this direction formed the basic ideas of Constitutional Monarchy" (James, 2008b, 53). Henry Neville's grandson was to write about his grandfather's role in attempting to establish a constitutional settlement which could have prevented the Civil War of 1642-51 (James, 2008b, 370).

Thomas of Woodstock is a mouthpiece for the playwright in fearlessly speaking Truth to Power. In this he is in a line of figures which starts with the Bastard Falconbridge in *The Troublesome Raigne/King John* and continues with John of Gaunt in *Richard II*.

---

[41] From: http://en.wikipedia.org/wiki/Richard_II,_Part_I [Accessed 2008]
[42] In his 'Tower Notebook', Neville refers to these 'Parliamentary Records' which were then kept as 'Ancient Records' in the Tower of London. Neville remarks in his annotations within the Tower Notebook that Richard II was deposed for his 'misgovernance'. (Brenda James, personal communication 8/8/08)

Furthermore Neville spoke Truth to Power in the person of James I: indeed the King invited Neville to do so, preferring his plain speaking to Francis Bacon's "extravagant stile" (James, 2008b, 369, note 209; see Winwood, 1725, Vol 3, 235).

The Earl of Essex was a descendant of Thomas of Woodstock. Neville was a supporter of Essex. The play, "using a famous historical example to sanction 'loyal rebellion' and even suggest that its leadership might be supplied by a small group of nobles critical of the Crown, could hardly fail to attract attention and stir powerful emotions. Here was the Essex uprising in embryo" (Egan, 2006, Vol 1, 130). Scholars have noted the unorthodox political thinking behind the play, one calling it "the boldest and most subversive of all Elizabethan historical plays" (Corbin & Sedge, 2002, 37). Neville, as politician and political thinker, was such a writer and became involved in the Essex Rebellion (see James, 2008b, 60).

In *Thomas of Woodstock* Tresilian is called "that sly machiavel" (1.1.66). In *Henry VI* part 1, York calls Alencon, "that notorious machiavel!" (5.4.74). Gloucester refers to 'Machiavel' in *Henry VI* part 3 (3.2.193). The Host asks, "Am I a Machiavel?" in *The Merry Wives of Windsor* (3.1.91). Neville's grandson, another Henry Neville, published translations of Machiavelli's works in 1674/5. Some of these may originally have been translated by Neville's father who spent time in Italy. Egan (2006, Vol 3, 294) pointed out that the references to Machiavel in both *Thomas of Woodstock* and *Henry VI* part 3 occur near the name of John of Gaunt. Thus we can see that the writer is coupling the Italian political thinker with an ancestor of the Nevilles.

In the play there are scenes in which people are accused of treason for whispering, singing satirical verses and whistling. The Tudor laws of treason allowed for a prosecution based on spoken words alone (Egan, 2006, Vol 1, 481). It is no wonder that the author felt he must keep his authorship of such a political play secret.

There are notes, believed to be by Buck, on the manuscript. Buck only became Master of the Revels from 1609. By this date the play could be seen as dangerously topical, given that James I was being criticised for his expenditure and his male favourites: in *Thomas of Woodstock* there is a suggestion of a homosexual relationship between Richard II and Robert Vere, Duke of Ireland (2.3.12). Indeed a reference in the text to England's monarch being "Superior Lord of Scotland" was marked for cutting possibly by Buck (Egan, 2006, Vol. I, 141). Perhaps this is why, like *Edmund Ironside*, the play was never printed: it was censored or considered too dangerous to publish.

Thomas of Woodstock, Shakespeare and Neville

The principal source for *Thomas of Woodstock* was Holinshed: this was also a source for *Arden of Faversham, Locrine* and other history plays by Shakespeare. I have already noted that Neville's father-in-law was an editor of the 1587 edition of Holinshed. In *Henry VI* part 2, the Duke of York, speaking to the Earls of Warwick and Salisbury, (both of whom are Nevilles, and who indeed are named as such twice in the scene) lists "Thomas of Woodstock, Duke of Gloucester" as the sixth son of *Edward III* (2.2.16). In *Henry VI* part 3 Richard (who is later to become Richard III) is offered the Dukedom of Gloucester (2.6.107). He complains it is ominous, remembering by implication, amongst others, the fate of Thomas of Woodstock. There is external evidence of these three figures being linked: Ben Jonson, in his *The Devil is an Ass* (1616) wrote:

> But Thomas of Woodstock,
> I'm sure, was Duke, and he was made away
> At Calais; as Duke Humphrey was at Bury;
> And Richard the third, you know what end he came to.
>
> (2.4.8)

Furthermore the speaker here, Fitzdottrel, states he learned this "from the play-books" (2.4.14). Jonson knew the secret of Neville's authorship and so to find him linking two known Shakespeare plays, *Henry VI* part 2 and *Richard III* with a play on *Thomas of Woodstock* is suggestive of Shakespeare-Neville's authorship of the latter.

Furthermore the annotator of Hall's *Chronicle* left the following note in the margin: "The murther of brother Thomas Woodstocke duk of Gloster" (Keen & Lubbock, 1954, 128). In his Tower Notebook, under the heading "The Coronation of King Richard II", Neville twice notes in the margin, "Tho: de Wodstok" and "Tho: Wodstok".

Henry Neville was related to Richard II (1377-1399) and also to Henry Bolingbroke - Richard II's usurping successor. Neville was therefore also related to Thomas of Woodstock through his brother, John of Gaunt's descendants. John of Gaunt was the fourth son of Edward III, the younger brother of the Black Prince and so was an uncle of Richard II. Gaunt's legitimate male heirs included the Kings Henry IV, Henry V and Henry VI. Gaunt's illegitimate descendants ultimately were legitimised by his marriage to his third wife, Katherine Swynford, in 1396. Katherine's daughter, Joan Beaufort, married Ralph Neville, 1st Earl of Westmoreland. Neville was descended from this line. Furthermore Katherine Swynford's third child, Thomas Beaufort,

1377-1427, married Margaret Neville.[43] King Richard II's uncle, the Duke of York, who appears in the play, was Edmund Langley: his grandson married into the Neville family.

Woodstock, in one of his plain speaking confrontations with the King, complains that, "A hundred oaks" and "ten acres of good land" (1.3.95,98) were needed to pay for the expensive clothes he is wearing. Neville was a forester and would know the value of oak trees. Indeed in a letter dated 13/7/1599 Neville wrote that a forest fire had "burned...about 40,000 Acres of Wood, to the loss of at the least of 200 thousand Crownes..." (Winwood, 1725, Vol 1, 66). There are, as in Shakespeare's canonical works, many tree images in *Thomas of Woodstock*.

The Masque: *Thomas of Woodstock* and *Henry VIII*

In the play Thomas of Woodstock is arrested by courtiers and the King, disguised as masquers. This incident is not based on historical fact but is an invention of the playwright. Corbin & Sedge (2002, 45, note 76) indeed noticed that the masque in *Thomas of Woodstock* resembled that in Shakespeare's *Henry VIII*: "The masque performed for Woodstock does not follow the elaborate patterning of the Jacobean masque but is closer to the 'disguising' in which Henry VIII courts Anne Boleyn in *Henry VIII (All is True)*". Both masques originate from a Neville family story.

Neville's grandfather was Sir Edward Neville of Addington Park, Kent. He was born in about 1482 and was executed in 1538, having been implicated in the Courtenay conspiracy. He was a younger son of George Neville, the second Baron Bergavenny. Hall (1965, 517) in his *Chronicle* tells of Edward's part as the knight *Valiaunt Desire* in a theatrical pageant at the end of the Christmas period in the second year of Henry VIII's reign (1510). Later, for May Day, he took part in another theatrical celebration (Hall, 1965, 520). "Neville was not only a notable masquer. He was also an accomplished singer with a liking for 'merry songs'. He possessed a talent for extemporary verses, often of current topicality" (ODNB, 2004, Vol 40, 489, Hawkyard, A.). We can see verbal creativity and theatricality were hereditary traits in the Neville family! Edward was a close friend of the King and took part in embassies to France (in 1518 and 1532) and the famous Field of the Cloth of Gold (1520). However because of his brother's closeness to the Duke of Buckingham he became entangled in the Courtenay conspiracy and, despite maintaining his innocence, was beheaded in the

---

[43] From: http://www.answers.com/topic/john-of-gaunt-1st-duke-of-lancaster [Accessed 2008]

Tower of London. Whilst Sir Edward Neville does not appear in *Henry VIII*, Lord Abergavenny (his brother) and the Duke of Buckingham do. Indeed it is remarkable that given the enormous number of incidents Shakespeare could have chosen to dramatise from the reign of Henry VIII, he focuses on incidents that relate to the fortunes of members of the Neville family.

At a banquet given by Cardinal Wolsey in 1527 Edward appeared disguised in a masque and "the cardinal was deceived, or pretended to be, in identifying Neville in his vizard as the King..." (ODNB, 2004, Vol 40, 489, Hawkyard, A.). Edward physically resembled Henry VIII so Wolsey's misidentification is understandable. A version of this incident occurs in Shakespeare's *Henry VIII*. In Act 1 scene 4 masquers enter a banquet at Cardinal Wolsey's house. One of them is the King himself, disguised. The Cardinal guesses the royal person is present: he asks the Lord Chamberlain,

> **Wolsey:** <u>Pray</u>, tell 'em thus much from me:
> <u>There should be</u> one <u>amongst</u> 'em, by his person,
> <u>More worthy this place than</u> myself; <u>to whom</u>,
> <u>If I</u> but <u>knew him</u>, with my love and duty
> <u>I would surrender</u> it.
> **Chamberlain:** I will my Lord. (*He whispers with the masquers.*)
> **Wolsey:** What say they?
> **Chamberlain:** <u>Such a</u> one, <u>they</u> all <u>confess</u>,
> <u>There is</u> indeed; which they would have <u>your grace</u>
> Find out, and he will take it.
> **King Henry VIII** (*Unmasking*) Ye have found him, cardinal.

Halio in his edition of *Henry VIII* (1999, 106, footnote) identified this incident as the occasion involving Edward Neville. The words <u>underlined</u> in the above speeches are taken directly from George Cavendish's *Life of Cardinal Wolsey* (composed between 1554-8 and only available in manuscript during Shakespeare's lifetime). Whereas the play has Henry VIII unmasking in response to the Cardinal, Cavendish's account continues with Wolsey saying, "Me semys the gentilman w^t the blake beard shold be even he/ And w^t that he arrose out of hys chayer and offered the same to the gentilman in the blake beard (w^t his Cappe in his hand) The person to whom he offered than his Chayer/ was **sir Edward Neveyll** A comely knight of a goodly personage that myche more resembled the kynges person in the Maske than any other/ The kyng heryng & perceyvyng the Cardynall so disseyved in his estymacion and choys cowld not forbear lawyng/ but plucked down his visare & **mr Neveylles** & dasht owt..." (Sylvester, 1959, 27).

When Shakespeare distorts history it is sometimes done to protect a Neville; for example in *Henry VI* part 2 the King's son, Prince John of Lancaster, tricks the rebels into disbanding their army and then arrests their leaders, Hastings, Mowbray and the Archbishop of York (4.2.107). Whilst the Earl of Westmoreland is present in this scene, the play does not reveal that it was in fact Westmoreland who perpetrated this treachery. Westmoreland was actually Ralph Neville, 6th Baron of Raby, (who had married Joan Beaufort, daughter of John of Gaunt).

Thus we can detect in this *Henry VIII* masque scene a hidden Neville and see that this theatrical device was not only one which the playwright Shakespeare might want to use in his play of pageantry but that Neville had reason to remember and had indeed, I propose, already used in *Thomas of Woodstock* years before.

Furthermore Neville had a personal connection to Wolsey. The palace in Mayfield, where Neville lived when he was in charge of the iron works, was an old monastic property, which had once housed Wolsey. It came to the Nevilles on the death of Sir Thomas Gresham, who was Elizabeth Gresham's uncle. Elizabeth Gresham was Neville's mother. According to Duncan (1974, 66) it was a favourite residence of the Archbishops of Canterbury, until turned over to Henry VIII by Cranmer in 1545. It was then that John Gresham purchased it.

The masque in *Thomas of Woodstock* replays this incident when a King is disguised in a masque but was written before *Henry VIII*. I have already noted a tendency in late plays to recapitulate material in earlier plays: see chapters 2, 3 and 7. Just as Shakespeare remembers and uses the story of Neville's father teaching Elizabeth I to hunt deer in *Mucedorus* and *Love's Labour's Lost* (see chapter 2) so the author of *Thomas of Woodstock* and *Henry VIII* seems to be recalling a story about Sir Edward Neville, masquing, disguise and a King. It is perhaps also significant that this masque leads to the death of the protagonist. If the incident in the play is based on the old family story of Sir Edward Neville at the Wolsey banquet masque, then it would be coupled with the knowledge of Edward's execution. Egan (2006, Vol 1, 399) made a comparison between the masque scenes in *Thomas of Woodstock* and *Henry VIII* finding many parallels between them. These can be summarised as:

1) Both masques share rural themes (hunters in *Woodstock*; shepherds in *Henry VIII*).
2) Both troupes of masquers arrive suddenly and unexpectedly.
3) The masquers are welcomed in similar ways: a banquet is prepared.
4) The moon is mentioned, with symbolism that points to Elizabeth I.

5) Kings are present, disguised as masquers.
6) There is whispering between the masquers.
7) A powerful figure in his home at night is solicited by masquers, among whom his sovereign is disguised. Woodstock and Wolsey both guess the identity of this disguised King. In both cases they fall from grace and ultimately die after this scene.

Thomas of Woodstock, the Nevilles and their enemies

Thomas of Woodstock was murdered in Calais: this much is accurate. The play however casts 'Lapoole' as the governor of Calais: indeed Edmund, the brother of Michael de la Pole, the first Earl of Suffolk, was governor of Calais early in Richard's reign (Corbin & Sedge, 2002, 50). However at the time of the murder the governor was Thomas Mowbray: in *Richard II* Shakespeare corrects this historical error. However when the writer distorts history we have come to suspect there is a hidden Neville. Sir Edward Neville, Neville's grandfather, was related to the Pole and Courtenay families and became entangled in the Pole/Courtenay conspiracy. It was Sir Geoffrey Pole who, under torture in 1538, accused Neville of high treason. Neville was executed; Pole was pardoned (Hall, 1965, 827). Thus the writer is further identifying these two men: Sir Edward Neville and Thomas of Woodstock (in the play), both of whom are betrayed by a member of the de la Pole family. In fact the historical Thomas of Woodstock was an enemy of Michael de la Pole, the first Earl of Suffolk, forcing Richard II to dismiss him as Chancellor in 1386. He was impeached and imprisoned. Richard soon released and reinstated him, but when the baronial opposition again demanded his arrest, de la Pole fled to France. Accused of treason and sentenced to death in the Merciless Parliament of 1388, he died in exile.[44]

This identification is further strengthened by recalling that William de la Pole, Duke of Suffolk, grandson of Michael de la Pole, is the Nevilles' adversary in *Henry VI* part 2 and arranges the murder of Humphrey, Duke of Gloucester, who like Woodstock, was Lord Protector of the Realm. Sir Edward Neville was accused by the Marchioness of Exeter of dabbling in prophecy (ODNB, 2004, Vol 40, 490, Hawkyard, A.), just as Humphrey's wife was similarly accused in *Henry VI* part 2.

There are further connections: the Duke of Buckingham in *Henry VIII* was a descendant of Thomas of Woodstock, one of whose titles was Earl of Buckingham. This is made explicit in the play when Bagot arrests him:

---

[44] From: http://www.encyclopedia.com/doc/1E1-Pole.html [Accessed 2008]

> Thomas of Woodstock: Duke of Gloucester,
> **Earl** of Cambridge and **of Buckingham**,
> I here arrest thee…

(4.2.175)

Indeed Egan (2006, Vol 1, 92) noted that a play called *Buckingham* was performed in December 1593: this might have been *Thomas of Woodstock* (the surviving manuscript has no title). Thomas of Woodstock's eldest daughter, Anne of Gloucester, married into the powerful Stafford family, who became Dukes of Buckingham. Four generations after Thomas, the disposition of the de Bohun estates may have been a motivating factor in the involvement of Henry Stafford, 2nd Duke of Buckingham in plots against the crown during the period of Richard III.[45] Buckingham's fall is shown in Shakespeare's *Richard III*. Another Duke of Buckingham falls in *Henry VIII* and in this case he dragged Edward Neville, Neville's grandfather, down with him (though this is not shown in the play). Thus we can see a line of descent between these three plays, with three Dukes going to execution: in each case there is a Neville connection.

Another trace of Sir Edward Neville is to be found in the play. Lancaster (John of Gaunt, and therefore a Neville ancestor) having been dismissed from the court by the King, says, "For me, I lived with care at court, I am now free" (3.2.5). Sir Edward Neville, alienated from life at court, was reported as saying, "The King keepeth a sort of knaves here that we dare not speak; and if I were able to live, I would rather live any life in the world than tarry in the privy chamber" (ODNB, 2004, Vol 40, 490, Hawkyard, A.). Later Henry Neville himself was to wish to escape to the forest from his frustrating life as an ambassador.

Furthermore there is another connection between the masque and the Nevilles. The masque involves the deliberate use of disguise: not only do the kidnappers disguise themselves and their intentions but they also disguise Woodstock in order to spirit him away to Calais. We have seen that Sir Edward Neville enjoyed masquing and disguise at the court of Henry VIII. Sir Henry Neville (Neville's father) used disguise on diplomatic missions abroad and Neville himself went in disguise to the King of Spain's memorial service in Paris when he was ambassador (James & Rubinstein, 2005, 64, 133) and of course, as the writer of the Shakespeare canon, he used disguise all his life and repeatedly in his plays. As already stated, given the dangerous politics of *Thomas of Woodstock* Neville had good reasons for disguising his authorship.

---

[45]From: http://en.wikipedia.org/wiki/Thomas_of_Woodstock,_1st_Duke_of_Gloucester [Accessed 2008]

Egan (2006, Vol 1, 100) stated that the author of *Thomas of Woodstock* "was on intimate terms with Elizabethan masque conventions, suggesting some familiarity with the court. He seems to have had access to the Revels office." Neville's father took part in and devised such court entertainments. Neville himself was born and lived in the building that later became the Blackfriars Theatre which was next to the Revels Office (James, 2008b, 209-10).

The language of *Thomas of Woodstock*, Shakespeare and Neville

I will not closely examine the language of *Thomas of Woodstock* as that has already been done by Egan (2006) who convincingly, indeed overwhelmingly, shows the play to be by Shakespeare. In this section I focus on the relationship between the language in the play and its relationship with three of the other texts studied in this volume, also pointing to evidence for Henry Neville's authorship as it arises.

Thomas of Woodstock and *Arden of Faversham*

I have suggested a date of 1586-90 for *Arden of Faversham*; Egan suggested 1592-3 for *Thomas of Woodstock*. We can therefore expect some relationship between the vocabulary and incidents in the plays, and indeed they are there.

Sir Thomas Cheney appears in *Thomas of Woodstock*. The name Thomas is unhistorical as the Cheney who was allied to Woodstock was Sir John Cheyne of Beckford, Gloucestershire, who was proceeded against by Richard II after Woodstock's death (Corbin & Sedge, 2002, 49). As we have already seen in chapter 4, a Lord Cheney appears in *Arden of Faversham* and I noted there that Thomas Cheney was a friend of Sir Edward Neville, the grandfather of Henry Neville (Hall, 1965, 571). Sir Thomas Cheyne's eldest son's widow, Margaret, married Henry Pole. Pole and Cheyne got into a legal dispute about property on the site of the first Blackfriars Theatre where Henry Neville's father had leased rooms (Chambers, 1923, Vol 2, 499). Perhaps casting Lapoole as one of the villains of *Thomas of Woodstock* had a contemporary, family resonance. I have already traced the historic reasons for antipathy between the Nevilles and the de la Pole family.

Woodstock's wife, the Duchess, complains that she has been "troubled with sad dreams... never so fearful were my dreams till now... I beheld you murdered cruelly" (4.2.11). Woodstock complacently replies, "take comfort, then, all dreams are contrary." The Duchess of Gloucester describes her dream:

you were ranging through the woods
An angry lion with a herd of wolves
Had in an instant round encompassed you;
When to your rescue, against the course of kind,
A flock of silly sheep made head against them,
Bleating for help, against whom the forest King
Roused up his strength, and slew both you and them.

(4.2.20)

Woodstock laughs this off and suggests what prompted the dream:

Afore my god thou art foolish, I will tell thee all
Thy dream. Thou knowest last night we had some private
Talk about the blanks the country is taxed withal,
Where I compared the state (as now it stands,
Meaning King Richard and his harmful flatterers)
Unto a savage herd of ravening wolves,
The commons to a flock of silly sheep
Who, whilst their slothful shepherd careless stood,
Those forest thieves broke in, and sucked their blood.
And this thy apprehension took so deep
The form was portrayed lively in thy sleep.

(4.2.28)

When the disguised King and courtiers come to arrest him, the masque begins with the moon, Cynthia, who picks up this hunting imagery:

The groves of Calydon and Arden woods
Of untamed monsters, wild and savage herds,
We and our knights have freed, and hither come
To hunt these forests, where we hear there lies
A cruel tusked **boar**, whose terror flies
Through this large Kingdom, and with fear and dread
Strikes her amassed greatness pale and dead.

The stage direction states: "Music. Enter King, Greene, Bushy, Bagot, like Diana's knights, led in by four other knights, in green, with horns about their necks and **boarspears** in their hands." Thomas greets them with:

Ye come like knights to hunt the **boar** indeed;
And heaven he knows we had need of helping hands,
So many wild **boars** roots and spoil our lands
That England almost is destroyed by them.
I care not if King Richard heard me speak it...

(4.2.138)

The irony is of course that Richard does hear it and Thomas is the boar that is hunted. Indeed as Richard orders Thomas' arrest he says:

> This is the cave that keeps the tusked **boar**
> That roots up England's vineyard uncontrolled.
>
> (4.2.168)

This **boar** metaphor ties the play into Shakespeare's archetypal imagery, expounded by Ted Hughes, and to the Neville family, as the boar was the symbol of Richard III (a Plantagenet-Neville who married a Neville: see chapters 2, 4 and 7). In chapter 4 I pointed to the emergence of this imagery: it is not surprising that it is further developed in *Thomas of Woodstock*, which is later than *Arden of Faversham*.

As he arrests him, Bagot warns Thomas, "Ye cannot 'scape, my lord, the **toils are pitched**." (4.2.173). In *Love's Labour's Lost* Berowne says, "The King he is hunting the **deer**; I am coursing myself: they have **pitched a toil**..." (4.3.1). No other writer of the period uses the words '**pitched**' and '**toil/s**' together, except the author of *Arden of Faversham* who uses this phrase twice in describing a nightmare about being hunted, which precedes a murder. Arden tells Franklin:

> This night I dream'd that, being in a park,
> **A toil was pitched** to overthrow the **deer**,
> And I upon a little rising hill
> Stood whistly watching for the herd's approach.
> Even there, methoughts, a gentle slumber took me,
> And summoned all my parts to sweet repose;
> But in the pleasure of this golden rest
> An ill thewed foster[46] had removed the **toil**
> Which late, methought, was **pitched** to cast the **deer**.
> With that he blew an evil sounding horn,
> And at the noise another herdman came,
> With falchion drawn, and bent it at my breast,
> Crying aloud, 'thou art the game we seek!'
> With this I wak'd and trembled every joint...
>
> (3.3.6)

Just as Thomas explained away his wife's dream by what had occurred the previous evening, Franklin rationalises Arden's nightmare:

> This fantasy doth rise from Michael's fear,
> Who being awaked with the noise he made,
> His troubled senses yet could take no rest;
> And this, I warrant you, procured your dream.
>
> (3.3.32)

---

[46] Foster = forester. Neville and his father were foresters.

In *Henry VI* part 2 another Duke of Gloucester, Humfrey, has an ominous dream which his wife dismisses (1.2.25). Like Thomas of Woodstock, Humfrey is murdered in his bed by two murderers. In *Richard III*, on the orders of another Duke of Gloucester, Clarence is murdered. He too has a nightmare (1.4.9) and he also has two murderers whose dialogue recalls that of Woodstock's killers: when one of them has pangs of conscience the other reminds him of "the **gold** we shall have for doing it." (5.1.235), just as the first of Clarence's executioners reminds his colleague of their reward. In *Arden of Faversham* the murderers talk of the **gold** they will be paid. In both *Thomas of Woodstock* and *Arden of Faversham* the method of killing involves the murderers creeping up from behind and using a towel to disable the victim.

Thomas of Woodstock begins with an attempted poisoning. Lancaster asks:

> Has no man here some helping **antidote**
> For fear already we have taken some dram?
>
> (1.1.10)

In *Arden of Faversham* poison is frequently explored as a method of killing and after a suspected poisoning incident Arden asks his friend Franklin for the antidote '**mithridate**' (1.1.383).

In *Thomas of Woodstock*, King Richard reassures his friends:

> Fear not my uncles, nor their proudest strength
> For I will **buckler** ye against them all.
>
> (2.1.6)

And again Richard promises, "Do what ye will, we will shield and **buckler** ye" (2.2.181). In *Arden of Faversham* Michael says:

> I that should take the weapon in my hand
> And **buckler** thee from ill intending foes...
>
> (2.2.205)

In *The Taming of The Shrew* Petruchio reassures Kate, "I'll **buckler** thee against a million." (3.2.237) Edricus in *Edmund Ironside* says: "I shall... be esteemed my country's **buckler**" (5.2.106). The word occurs within one line of the name Neville in *Henry VI* part 2:

> Suffolk: And never of the **Neville**'s noble race.
> Warwick: But that guilt of murder **bucklers** thee...
>
> (3.2.215)

In a letter dated 29/6/1599, Neville wrote of Elizabeth I: "she alone had bin a **buckler** of Christianity against" the King of Spain (Winwood,

1725, Vol. 1, 53). It is noticeable that the form of language in *Woodstock*, *Faversham* and *The Taming of The Shrew* is very close: "I'll (will) **buckler** thee/ye." All three are future oriented, as is the example from *Edmund Ironside*. This word is used by Marlowe, Nashe and Spenser. Marlowe in *Edward II* writes: "'Tis not the King can **buckler** Gaveston" (1.4.288); Nashe in *The Unfortunate Traveller* (1594): "make his withered body a **buckler** to bear off any blow advanced against him" (297) and "stead than a sword and **buckler**" (413); Spenser in his *Faerie Queene* "her body, as a **buckler** broke the puissance of his intended stroke" (21320). None of these is in the form of "**I'll buckler thee**..." as in *Woodstock*, *Faversham* and *The Taming of The Shrew*.

Both *Thomas of Woodstock* and *Arden of Faversham* are plays which climax in the murder of an innocent man who is over-trusting. Whilst the former is a political history play and the latter is a domestic tragedy they both show the developing conspiracy that leads to the murder; in both the plotters use a stratagem to draw their victim into the trap: in *Thomas of Woodstock* a masque, in *Arden of Faversham* a game of backgammon. Both plays also show the injustice done to poorer people by those in power, with the misappropriation of lands.

Thomas of Woodstock and *Edmund Ironside*
In *Edmund Ironside* Uskataulf says, "**degenerate** bastard, falsely bred, foul mother-killing **Viper**..." (1.1.158). This is echoed in *Edward III*:

> **Degenerate** Traitor, **viper** to the place
> Where thou was fostered in thine infancy...
>
> (1.1.105)

In *Thomas of Woodstock* (see chapter 5) York says:

> Never such **vipers** were endured so long
> To grip and eat the hearts of all the kingdom.
>
> (5.2.30)

The viper was believed at this time to kill and eat its mother after birth. It was therefore used as a symbol of ultimate treachery to the motherland. In *Henry VI* part 1 this image is made explicit:

> Civil **dis**sension is a **viperous worm**,
> That gnaws the **bowels** of the commonwealth.
>
> (3.1.72)

This recalls the epilogue of *Locrine* where Ate speaks of "**civil dis**cord". This snake imagery had a contemporary political instance. In

Oct 1583, a young Warwickshire man, John Somerville, fell into a "frantic humor" and started off, glassy-eyed, for the court where he meant to shoot the queen. Elizabeth was a "serpent and **viper**" and he wanted "to see her head set upon a pole", he told to anyone who would hear him.[47] All these plays are intended to warn their audiences against civil strife with the ever-present threat of foreign invasion.

Thomas of Woodstock and *Locrine*

There are great differences between these plays: *Thomas of Woodstock* is immediately recognisable as Shakespearean whereas I had to examine the text of *Locrine* very carefully to appreciate it was an early work. This is not surprising when we consider that *Locrine* may predate *Thomas of Woodstock* by as much as six years. Eventually I realised the political similarities: in both plays the King divides up the kingdom; in both there is a foreign queen; in both a young King behaves in a dissolute manner, bringing disaster on the realm. Janet Clare suggested that there were references to the death of Mary Queen of Scots in *Thomas of Woodstock* (Egan, 2006, Vol 1, 145). Egan agreed and suggested that Richard's behaviour in ordering that Woodstock be killed and then regretting it, mirrored Elizabeth I's ambivalence about Mary's trial and death. Elizabeth went so far as to suggest to Sir Amias Paulet that he might kill his prisoner. Such a monarch's request to a servant to assassinate a rival claimant to the throne troubles the consciences of Lapoole in *Thomas of Woodstock* and Hubert in *The Troublesome Raigne/King John*. Paulet had sufficient conscience to refuse to gratify his sovereign. Neville and his father both knew Paulet so they may have been privy to this secret. I have already explored the idea that *Locrine* was concerned partly with Mary Queen of Scots (see chapter 3).

There are also recognisable echoes in the poetry of these two plays. In *Thomas of Woodstock* Richard II says:

> If men might **die** when they would 'point the time,
> The time is now King Richard would be gone,
> For as a fearful **thunder**clap doth strike
> The soundest body of the tallest **oak**
> Yet leaves the outward **bark** untouched,
> So is King Richard struck. Come, come, let's go.
> My wounds are inward; inwards **burns** my woe.

(4.3.178)

---

[47] From: http://www.tudorplace.com.ar/Documents/parry_plot.htm [Accessed 2008]

The dying Brutus at the start of *Locrine* speaks of:

> This heart, my Lords, this near appalled heart...
>   (2 lines cut)
> Now by the weapons of unpartial **death**,
> Is clove asunder and bereft of life,
> As when the sacred **oak** with **thunder**bolts,
> Sent from **the fiery circuit** of the **heavens**,
> Sliding along the air's celestial vaults,
> Is rent and cloven to the very **roots**...(1 line cut)
> Then **welcome death**, since God will have it so.
>
>   (1.2.20)

Both men are welcoming death, both using a lightning struck oak tree image, which shows close observation of nature. Brutus uses the words, "**the** fiery **circuit** of the **heavens**" (1.2.26). Later in *Locrine* Corineus' ghost says, "Behold, **the circuit** of the azure **sky**..." (5.5.1) and Guendoline speaks of: "**the circuit** of the **heaven**ly vault..." (5.3.2). These are echoed by Thomas of Woodstock's "**the** vast **circuit** of this empty room" (5.1.113). Thomas uses the word '**heaven**' three lines before and again, ten lines after '**circuit**'. Both men are about to die. In *Tamburlaine I* Marlowe used the phrase, "measured **heaven** with triple **circuit**" (3.1.36) and again the word '**circuit**' in relation to Death's scythe (5.1.112) but neither of his '**circuit**'s are prefaced by '**the**', as they are in *Locrine*, *Thomas of Woodstock* and the bard. Shakespeare only uses the word '**circuit**' in early works: *Henry VI* parts 2 and 3, *Venus and Adonis* ("**the circuit**" 230). In *Henry VI* part 2 York threatens:

> I will stir up in England some black storm
> Shall blow ten thousand souls to **heaven** or hell;
> And this fell tempest shall not cease to rage
> Until **the** golden **circuit** on my head,
> Like to the glorious sun's transparent beams,
> Do calm the fury of this mad-bred flaw.
>
>   (3.1.349)

In *Henry VI* part 3 Richard says:

> How sweet a thing it is to wear a crown;
> Within whose **circuit** is **Elysium**.
>
>   (1.2.29)

Elysium was the classical heaven. Thus whilst Marlowe may be an influence we can see Shakespeare is the writer who uses the words '**the circuit**' in relation to '**heaven**'.

In *Locrine* Hubba says:

> ...valiantness is **like** unto **a rock**
> That **stand**eth in the waves of **Ocean**,
> Which though the billows beat on ever side,
> And Boreas fell with his tempestuous storms

> Bloweth upon it with a hideous clamour,
> Yet it remaineth still **unmoveable**.

(1.2.54)

In *Thomas of Woodstock* Greene says:

> Thanks, dearest lord, let me have Richard's love
> And **like a rock unmoved** my state shall **stand**...

(2.1.8)

'Chuffs' is used three times in *Woodstock*: punning this word for a rude boor, a miser, with the black bird, a chough. Falstaff uses this word in *Henry IV* part 1, calling the rich travellers he is about to rob, "ye fat **chuffs**." (2.2.84) It also appears in *Locrine* (5.4.1). All three plays use the plural '**chuffs**'.

In *Locrine* Strumbo tells us that: "my great learning is an **inconvenience** unto me." In *Thomas of Woodstock* this word is used by Woodstock, who speaking of the oppressive taxation of the commons, says, "To salve which **inconvenience**..." (1.3.148). In canonical Shakespeare '**inconvenience**' occurs just once, in *Henry VI* part 1 (1.4.14). Florio had used the word in 1591 in his *Second Fruits*: "Povertie is no vice, though it be an **inconvenience**" (Simonini, 1977, 105). In a diplomatic letter dated 26/5/1599, Neville urged that the King of France was bound in honour to satisfy Elizabeth I for money she had lent him, "rather than drive her for want of it, unto any extremity or **inconvenience**". Neville also used it in another letter dated 7/8/1599 (Winwood, 1725, Vol 1, 85). It is noticeable that the *Woodstock* and Neville usages are both about money.

Woodstock says, "These cuts the **columns** that should prop thy house" (1.3.121). The word '**column**' occurs in *Locrine* but not in the Shakespeare canon. Brutus calls Locrine:

> the **column** of my family,
> And only **pillar** of my weakened age...

(1.2.145)

Shakespeare does use the word '**pillar**' in this sense of a prop for a kingdom/family in three plays: *Merchant of Venice* (4.1.235); *Troilus and Cressida* (4.5.211); *Anthony and Cleopatra* (1.1.12). '**Pillars**' as supports occur in *Edward III* (5.1.170). In *Thomas of Woodstock* we also have:

> If once the **pillars** and supporters quail
> How can the strongest castle choose but fail?

(2.2.167)

In *Locrine* the word '**pillar**' is used twice with the meaning of supporting the state. Assarachus says, "That as a **pillar** might uphold our **state**..." (5.2.3). In *Henry VI* part 2, Duke Humphrey uses these words: "Brave peers of England, **pillars** of the **state**..." (1.1.74). In *Henry VI* part 3 troops who support their commanders are called '**pillars**' (2.3.51). '**Pillar**' is used in *Arden of*

Faversham (4.1.98). Neville, in a letter dated 24/4/1600, described an emblem of "a Globe **supported** by fower **pillers**" (Winwood, 1725, Vol 1, 176).

An important source for Shakespeare and one of the sources of *Thomas of Woodstock* is *The Mirror for Magistrates* (reissued in 1587): in the fourth line of the speech of Thomas of Woodstock, the word 'pillar' is used. Just two lines later there is: "**Froward Fortune** lyst for to **frowne**" (Campbell, 1960, 91). In *Mucedorus* we find that "**fortune** ever **frowns**" (1.4.5). In *Locrine* we have "**froward frowning** fate" (5.6.110). The words 'forwardness', 'fortune' and 'frown' also occur in *Thomas of Woodstock*.

In *Locrine* Strumbo asks for help after the destruction of his house in the war:

> Except you seek a remedy
> Our **houses** to **reedify**
> Which now are **burnt** to dust.

(2.4.72)

In *Thomas of Woodstock* Lancaster, also speaking of rebuilding after war, says:

> You peers of England, raised in righteous arms
> Here to **re-edify** our country's ruin,
> Join all your hearts and hands never to **cease**
> Till with our swords we work fair England's **peace**.

(5.3.22)

Shakespeare used 're-edified' in *Richard III* (of the Tower of London: 3.1.71) and in *Titus Andronicus* (of the family tomb: 1.1.356). Marlowe used 're-edified' in *Tamburlaine II* (3.5.37) but does not mention any war or houses, referring instead to a metropolis. Jasper Heywood had used the word in 1581 in a translation of Seneca's Troas: significantly of the **burnt** ruins of Troy (LION). Neville used the words "**houses re-edifyed**" in a letter dated 11/10/1599 and 're-edifie' in another of 3/1/1600 (Winwood, 1725, Vol 1, 121, 142). In both cases the reference is to property demolished in conflicts. Neville is the only writer of the period I have been able to find who uses the word 're-edify' in the same context as in *Locrine* and *Thomas of Woodstock*.

Furthermore Locrine says, "**Peace**, uncle, **peace**, and **cease** to talk hereof" (5.2.86). In *Henry VI* part 1, Bedford says, "**Cease, cease** these jars and rest your minds in **peace**." (1.1.44) The rhyming of 'cease' and 'peace' occurs, in the same order as in *Thomas of Woodstock* (see above) and *Henry VI*, in adjacent lines, in the Phaeton sonnet:

> And green-lockt Sommers shadie pleasures **cease**:
> She makes the Winters stormes repose in **peace**…

Phaeton sonnet words in *Thomas of Woodstock*

Of all the words in the Phaeton sonnet one of the rarest is 'o'er-spread'. Shakespeare used it just once in *Pericles* (without a hyphen: 1.2.24). This very rare word occurs twice in *Thomas of Woodstock*: 'o'erspread' (2.3.18) and 'o'erspreads' (5.1.224). 'Overspread' occurs in *Locrine* (see chapter 3). Thus the only writer to use the form of this word with the apostrophe is Shakespeare-Neville.

Word↓	*Thomas Woodstock*
Sweet	√
friend	√
name	√
agrees	Agree
increase	
rival	
spring	
branch	
flourishing	√
Summers/'s	Summer
shady	
pleasures	√
cease	√
Winters/'s	Winter
storms	√
repose	
peace	√
spends	Spend
franchise	
living	Livings
thing	√
daisies	
sprout	
little	√
birds	√
sing	√
herbs	
plants	Plant
vaunt	
release	
English	√
wits	Wit
dead	√
laurel	
except	√
green	√
fruits	Fruit/ful
barrenness	Barren
o'erspread	√
flowery	Flowering
pleasance	Pleasant
flowerets	Flowering
morality	
Italy	
Total:	**17**

Whilst the count of Phaeton words at first seems relatively low there are a high number of near misses. Adding the near misses to the actual total gives us $12 + 17 = 29$. Even taking into account the near misses in the plays of Greene and Peele this is a higher total than for either of those playwrights. (See Appendices 1 & 2.)

The last words

The final scene of the play breaks off in the middle of Nimble's reply to **Arundel**'s question, "What moved thee, being his man, to apprehend him?" Nimble answers, "partly for these causes: first, the fear of the proclamation, for I have plodded in **plowden** and can find no law..." (5.56.33). **Plowden** was a famous lawyer who wrote a Treatise on the Succession. In *Leicester's Commonwealth*, there is a discussion about the rightful succession to the throne and Henry VIII's will, of which Sir Henry Neville (Neville's father) was a signatory. One particular incident shows Plowden knew Sir Henry. A foot note (Peck, 2006, 245) reports:

> "...the great lawyer **Plowden**, however, claimed to have been present and said that Sir Henry Neville could prove that it had occurred"
>
> (Jordan, 1968, 55n)

Furthermore I note Nimble is replying to **Arundel**. Charles **Arundell** is considered one of the possible authors of *Leicester's Commonwealth*. I have previously noted that Neville owned two copies of this work. In the Cornwall Record Office there is a document concerning gifts of land from the Arundell Barons of Wardour to the Nevylls in the 15th Century.

Conclusion

Thomas of Woodstock may well have been too politically sensitive even in 1623 to include in the First Folio. I have shown that Neville's political thinking runs through this play which at last is moving towards recognition as belonging to the canon of Shakespeare's works.

Chapter 6

A YORKSHIRE TRAGEDY

This short play is based on a real murder case: the killer is not named in the play but he was Walter Calverley. The play was registered on 2nd May 1608 as by "Wylliam Shakespere" and the 1608 quarto states it was written by "W. Shakspeare". It was added to the Third Folio of Shakespeare's plays, along with *Pericles* and *Locrine*, in 1664. Duncan-Jones (2001, 210) believes *A Yorkshire Tragedy* is by Shakespeare, as have a number of previous scholars: others have doubted the attribution. Some scholars have suggested it is by Thomas Middleton or George Wilkins. My focus here will be on the evidence for Neville's involvement. I will not exhaustively try to prove authorship, as this play may be the result of collaboration.

The Plot of *A Yorkshire Tragedy*
The play opens with servants (Oliver, Ralph and Sam - the only named characters in the play) who talk about their master's imminent return from London and his marriage. It is revealed that another woman, who has eagerly been awaiting his return, is in love with him (this jilted lover is not mentioned again). The wife is then seen complaining about her husband's spending, his gambling, dissolute behaviour and sullen melancholy. She speaks to him but he reviles her, accusing her of being a harlot and her children being bastards. He demands money and sends her off to sell her dowry. Three gentlemen enter and remonstrate with him for his disgraceful behaviour. When he insults one, he is challenged and wounded in the subsequent fight. He determines to revenge himself for this upon his wife. She visits her uncle who offers to arrange a court appointment for her husband, thus saving her dowry. She returns to her husband hoping this will solve their problems but he again demands money: she is only saved from imminent assault when a Master from the University arrives to plead for the husband's brother, who has been imprisoned for the non-payment of a debt owed by the husband. The latter promises to pay the debt and invites the Master to view his estate whilst he gets the money. He then takes the opportunity to murder his two sons, attacking his wife and two servants as he does so. He rides off to kill his third baby son who is at another house. He is chased and caught when his horse throws him and is brought to face justice. The final scene is a tearful farewell between husband and wife.

191

Though we do not hear of his fate, the Master speaks of him facing "a deadlier execution" (10.75).

In *A Yorkshire Tragedy* there are no names after the first scene: just roles, Husband, Wife, Knight, Master, etc.

The Date of *A Yorkshire Tragedy*

Walter Calverley murdered his sons on 23rd April 1605. The pamphlet, *"Two Most Unnatural and Bloodie Murthers"*, on which the tragedy is based, was registered on 12th June 1605 and must have been published soon after. Thus the play must have been written between 1605-8, when it was printed. Maxwell (1969, 175) suggested that *A Yorkshire Tragedy* was written in the latter part of 1605. During this period the bard was writing *King Lear* (1605, registered in November 1607 and printed in 1608), *Timon of Athens* (1604-6, first published in 1623) and *Macbeth* (1606, first quarto published in 1608). It is immediately apparent that *A Yorkshire Tragedy* matches the themes of these three dark tragedies.

There are echoes of *King Lear* in *A Yorkshire Tragedy*. The Master confronts the Husband after he has killed his sons with:

> Unnatural, flinty, **more** than **barbarous:**
> **The Scythians** in their **marble-hearted** feats
> Could not have acted more remorseless deeds
> In their relentless natures than **these of thine!**
>
> (8.18)

Lear speaks of "**The barbarous Scythian**" (1.1.115) and "Ingratitude, thou **marble-hearted** fiend **more** hideous..." (1.4.259). Cornwall later uses the words "**these** eyes **of thine**..." (3.7.66). Lear himself warns Kent, "**Come** not **between** the dragon and his wrath" (1.1.121). The Husband in *A Yorkshire Tragedy* rages at a servant who is trying to stop him killing, "**Comest** thou **between** my fury..."(5.34). Indeed in both plays a compassionate servant tries to stop evil deeds and is attacked.

Jowett (2004, 6) suggested that the Husband's profligacy might have influenced the creation of Timon. They both end up financially ruined, blaming others in their rage. During this period Neville also had financial difficulties: the aftermath of the expenses of his ambassadorship and the heavy fines Elizabeth imposed following the Essex rebellion. He had reasons to be bitter. There may also be a subtext concerning James I's money worries at this time. Jowett (2004, 7) writing about *Timon of Athens* stated that, "King James's Timonesque generosity in gift-giving had been especially evident in the celebrations of the marriage of the Earl of Essex... on 5th January 1606. James's reliance for financial relief on the Members of

Parliament, an equivalent of the play's senators, was a matter of public comment in the months that followed. In early 1606 Parliament voted to grant funds to the King and then debated whether to increase its subsidy. It is at this time, according to the *OED*, that the noun *supply* began to be used in this context, and the sense is used in *Timon of Athens*." Indeed the word '**supply**' is used six times in *Timon of Athens* (twice as many times as in any other Shakespeare play) including Timon's "**supply** of **money**" (2.2.196). In *A Yorkshire Tragedy* the Husband shouts at his wife, "**Money, money, money**, and thou must **supply** me!" (2.57). Neville was a Member of Parliament at this time and involved in delicate negotiations about money with James I. He wrote about this in a letter dated 11/3/1606 (Winwood, 1725, Vol 2, 197).

James I visited Oxford in August 1605. Matthew Gwynne presented his *Tres Sibyllae*, a Latin poem which referred to the prophecy that Banquo's descendants would inherit an endless empire (a possible source for the three witches of *Macbeth*). This was the occasion when Neville was awarded his M.A. This event ties together Neville, James I, *Macbeth* and *A Yorkshire Tragedy*. In the latter play a Master from the university comes to plead with the Husband for his brother who is in prison due to being bonded for the Husband's debt. In response to his eloquence the Husband says, "You are your **arts' master**" (4.33). Neville was awarded his **Master of Arts** degree just before *A Yorkshire Tragedy* was written.

Macduff's children are murdered in *Macbeth* and Lady Macbeth talks of killing a suckling babe. Children are murdered in *A Yorkshire Tragedy* and the Husband talks of killing his third son, a suckling child: "my brat at nurse, my sucking beggar" (5.45). In *A Yorkshire Tragedy* and *Macbeth* people are possessed by the forces of evil: this was an interest shared by James I who wrote books on demonology and witchcraft. The writer of *A Yorkshire Tragedy* may have read James' (1597) *Daemonologie* (Cawley & Gaines, 1986, 81 footnote 40). James went to visit Neville to discuss his writing in 1608 (James & Rubinstein, 2005, 328). It is unlikely that these were the first such discussions.

The Calverley Family, their Friends and Connections
Walter Calverley, the murderer on whom the play is based, was of an ancient family, based in Yorkshire. From the mid 14th century Calverleys married into and were related to the Neville family. Walter's father, William, went to All Souls College Oxford in December 1576 (Maxwell, 1969, 158). From 1574-8 Neville was at Merton College,

Oxford, so it is possible he met William Calverley. Walter was born in 1579. William died in 1596 when Walter was 17. Being underage he was made a ward, his guardians being Anne, Lady Gargrave and her son Richard. Anne was widow of Sir Cotton Gargrave (whom Neville may well have known as they were fellow M.P.s in the 1580s). Lady Gargrave attempted to marry her daughter to Walter. She was unsuccessful so the reference to a jilted woman in the first scene of the play is based on fact.

Anne, Lady Cobham, wife of Sir Henry Cobham, wrote to Sir Robert Cecil on May 30th 1599 asking him to support a marriage between her daughter Philippa and Walter Calverley. (Cecil was responsible for nonage wards.) Lady Cobham was related to Sir Robert and her letters to him about this marriage proposal survive to this day. Cecil was also related to both Henry Neville and Anne Killigrew. On April 26th 1599, (just a month before Lady Cobham's letter to Sir Robert) Cecil had written to Neville in France, telling him that Lord Cobham had been "chosen knight of the garter" (Winwood, 1725, Vol 1, 95). The Cobhams had also intermarried with the Nevilles. They objected to the portrait of Sir John Oldcastle (who became Lord Cobham in 1409) in the *Henry IV* plays so that the bard changed the character's name to Falstaff.

The judge before whom Walter Calverley was tried for the murder of his sons was in fact Sir John Savile. He was none other than the brother of Sir Henry Savile, Neville's Oxford tutor and life long friend. Sir John Savile was a Barrister and a Judge. He was knighted in 1603 just two years before the murders. In the play he is identified only as the 'Knight'. In the play the Knight says of Walter, "I am sorry I e'er knew him." Savile did know Calverley because in 1601, when the latter was in debt, Savile bought property from him. Indeed they were related: the Saviles had intermarried with the Calverleys in 1480 (Garnett, 1991).

Thus we can see that there are multiple Neville connections that would motivate his interest in Walter Calverley.

A Yorkshire Tragedy and *The Miseries of Enforced Marriage*
There is another play, George Wilkins' *The Miseries of Enforced Marriage* that is partly based on this case and on *A Yorkshire Tragedy* but which has a happy ending. It was written "not later than the first five months of 1606" (Maxwell, 1969, 175), registered in July 1607 and printed the same year. Maxwell argued that *A Yorkshire Tragedy* was written first because it is extremely faithful to the pamphlet about the murders, whereas Wilkins' play takes greater creative liberties with the story. Scholars studying this pair of plays have suggested varying

degrees of connection between them. It has been suggested that the text of *The Miseries of Enforced Marriage* shows evidence of earlier versions within itself and attention has been drawn to names used to identify the character of the protagonist's guardian in the printed text which are not used in the spoken text: i.e. these names would only be apparent to a reader, not to a spectator of the drama. This is intriguing indeed when we realise the names are 'Hunsd' (or 'Huns', thought to be an abbreviation of Hunsdon) and 'Faulconbridge'. We can see immediately a Neville connection in the name 'Faulconbridge': the barony which had been in abeyance since the death of William Neville in 1463 and which is repeatedly used, as I have shown in Chapter 1, for characters in Shakespeare's plays. In the play as spoken on stage, this character is only referred to as 'Lord'. During Walter Calverley's minority the title of Lord Hunsdon was held by George Carey, "cousin and Lord Chamberlain to Queen Elizabeth and patron of the company who acted the play. Although by the time the play was written the title had passed to his brother John and the company had been accepted as the King's Men, it seems unlikely that the company would within three years of his death have presented their former patron in so unkind a manner" (Maxwell, 1969, 174). Furthermore Lord Hunsdon took over the Blackfriars theatre, including the rooms covered by Sir Henry Neville's 1560 lease so there is a connection between Neville's father, Hunsdon and the theatre (Chambers, 1923, Vol 2, 497). Hunsdon's successor as Lord Chamberlain (in 1597) was none other than William Brooke, 7th Lord Cobham, Walter Calverley's wife's (Philippa's) uncle. Indeed he may even feature as the uncle in the play whom the Wife goes to for help and who promises to find her husband a court appointment.

The name 'Hunsd' is then changed to 'Faulconbridge'. What is perhaps a significant indicator here is that Hunsdon was a real person known to the company: was then 'Faulconbridge' a real person known to them as well? The role of 'Faulconbridge' is that of William Scarborrow's guardian. Is it merely a coincidence that a Neville is the guardian of a man whose initials are W.S.?

Wilkins also mentions the Mitre in Bread Street (lines 1175 and 1523) which is where Neville and others met for the Mitre Club, a literary symposium at which John Donne and Inigo Jones amongst others shared drinks and jokes, discussed life and literature. What is startling about the reference to the Mitre is that Ilford talks of being taken from the Mitre to prison and then Wentworth says, "this is *Mellis Flora*, the sweetest of the **honey**, he that was not made to fat **cattle** but to feed gentlemen"(Wilkins, 1963, 1181). This cryptic remark reminds us of the **Bull** in Neville's family coat of arms and the rhyme about 'Nevill' on the Northumberland Manuscript, which includes the words "**Mell** in ore" (**Honey** in mouth). Francis Meres described Shakespeare as "**mellifluous** and **honey** tongued."

Wilkins has long been believed to have co-authored Shakespeare's *Pericles*. The play was entered into the Stationer's Register in 1607, and was followed in the next year by George Wilkins' 1608 novel, *The Painful Adventures of Pericles, Prynce of Tyre*: again he had pre-empted the publication of Shakespeare's play by a year (the first quarto of *Pericles* appeared in 1609) just as he pre-empted the publication of *A Yorkshire Tragedy* with his *The Miseries of Enforced Marriage*.

Shame

What might attract Neville to this murder story? At this time Shakespeare was exploring evil: in *King Lear* and *Macbeth* he went down, like Dante, into the darkest depths of hell. *A Yorkshire Tragedy* fits into this period, indeed between these two plays. Furthermore it is a story of a gambler who gambles and loses everything, bringing shame on his family and harming his wife and children. This is exactly what Neville may have felt he had done during the Essex rebellion and his imprisonment in the Tower: gambled and lost. Having had to pay the considerable expenses for his ambassadorship without reimbursement and been heavily fined by Elizabeth I after his imprisonment following the Essex debacle, Neville was also aware of the threat of financial ruin faced by Walter Calverley, who killed his children to save them from beggary. Cawley and Gaines (1986, 20) pointed out that the play focuses on the psychology of the husband and that the source pamphlet "gives no hint of the Husband's hopelessness and boundless despair." The playwright is empathising with his central character, as Shakespeare did with Macbeth the following year. Neville knew what it was like to face imprisonment, loss of his family and execution.

The murders come from the Husband's despair and his distorted idea of saving his sons from beggary whilst also disowning them as bastards. One of the gentlemen who upbraid the Husband says:

> Yourself to **stain** the honour of your wife,
> Nobly descended. Those whom men call mad
> Endanger others, but he's more than mad
> That wounds himself, whose own words do proclaim
> Scandals unjust, to soil his better **name**…

(2.106)

The last line here could indeed apply to Neville. In *Edward III* we find the word '**stain**' used five times about adultery and '**blot**' also occurs five times, as when Warwick warns his daughter he would curse her:

> When thou convertest from honor's golden **name**
> To the black faction of bed **blotting shame**.

(2.2.457)

The same rhyme is used twice in *A Yorkshire Tragedy* as when the Knight speaks of:

> The desolation of his house, the **blot**
> Upon his predecessors' honour'd **name**:
> That man is nearest shame that is past **shame**.

(9.33)

A gentleman says to the Husband:

> I am sorry for thee: that man spends with **shame**
> That with his riches does consume his **name**...

(2.132)

In sonnets 36, 95 and 127 the bard rhymes '**shame**' and '**name**'. Furthermore in sonnet 36 we find '**blots**' and in 95 '**spot**' and '**blot**'. This '**shame**' and '**name**' rhyme is used in *Henry VI* part 1 (4.4.9); *Henry VI* part 2 (2.1.193); *Richard II* (1.1.166); *Comedy of Errors* (2.1.112); *Troilus and Cressida* (5.10.33); *All's Well That Ends Well* (2.1.169); and four times in *The Rape of Lucrece* (597, 618, 814, 890).

The gentlemen stress the shame the Husband has brought on generations of a noble family.

> You have a wife
> Kind and obedient: heap not wrongful **shame**
> On her, your posterity.

(2.173)

This theme of shame echoes through Shakespeare's works: indeed the word 'shame' is used 346 times in the canon. This is much higher than the usage of the emotion words grief, anger, guilt, jealousy, envy, hurt or hate: only love has a higher occurrence. The highest number of uses of the word 'shame', in a single work for obvious reasons, is 31 in the *Rape of Lucrece*. The highest number in any play is *King John*: 18. Many of these are to do with the illegitimacy of the Bastard Philip Falconbridge (a Neville name) but they are spread across the play and are evidence of the shameful conduct of King John, of political betrayal, of the plan to kill the innocent Arthur. In other words shame is connected to illegitimacy, political betrayal and Kings killing innocents: a constellation of factors which match the history of Henry Neville, his illegitimacy and his grandfather's execution (it was of course written before the shame of his imprisonment in the Tower). 'Shame' occurs five times in *A Yorkshire Tragedy*: a high number given how short the play is. Shakespeare uses the word 'shame' more in early works than later, though three connected plays are a sudden upward spike in the graph: *Hamlet*, *Troilus and Cressida* and *Measure for Measure*, namely the plays probably written in the Tower of London when Neville had been shamed by his trial and imprisonment.

There are of course many bastards in the plays. They are often angry characters, powerful and dangerous. In *The Comedy of Errors* Luciana says, "**Shame** hath **a bastard** fame" (3.2.19). In sonnet 127 we find "**a bastard shame**". In *Pericles* the Bawd in the brothel has brought up eleven bastards (4.2.13). Henry Neville mentioned in a letter that he had 11 male siblings (James & Rubinstein, 2005, 64). Furthermore Neville had 11 children (James, 2008, 49). From 1604-1606, precisely the period when *A Yorkshire Tragedy* was written Neville served on a Parliamentary committee concerned with illegitimate children (James, 2008b, 347).

The blot image cluster

This Shakespearean image cluster places the word '**blot**' in relation to 'heaven/sky', 'night', 'moon', 'constancy/inconstant', 'disguise' (mask), 'winter/coldness', 'sovereign/king*'*, 'eye', 'sun' and 'cheeks' (face/complexion), (Muir, 1960, 22: in Egan, 2006, Vol 3, 284). The word '**stain**' is also used with these images. The imagery contrasts the wish to hide the shame of a blot/stain/disgrace (by disguising, darkness, night, cloud) and the revealing of a blushing shamed face to the eye of day (= sun = sovereign). A canonical example can be found in *Venus and Adonis*:

> And now Adonis, with a lazy spright,
> And with a heavy, **dark**, disliking **eye**,
> His louring brows o'erwhelming his fair sight,
> Like **misty vapours** when they **blot the sky**,
> Souring his **cheeks** cries "Fie, no more of love!
> The **sun doth burn my face**: I must remove."
>
> (186)

Other examples can be found in Sonnet 28 and *Love's Labour's Lost* (4.3.237). Muir identified this blot cluster in *Edward III*; Sams (1986, 249) found it in *Edmund Ironside*; Egan (2006, Vol 3, 271, 284) found it in *Thomas of Woodstock* and I have found it in *Double Falshood* (see chapter 7).

In *Locrine*, whilst there is no 'blot', there are "**ugly spots** of monstrous infamy," (5.2.63). (In Sonnet 95 we have the words '**spot**' and '**blot**'.) Assarachus uses the word '**inconstant**'. Thrasimachus talks about the '**stain**' of his '**sovereign**' Locrine's adultery. Sonnet 33 shows the word '**stain**' is an alternative to '**blot**' in the blot cluster: it includes the words '**ugly**', "sovereign eye", 'cloud', 'face', "visage hide", 'mask'd', 'sun' and 'heaven'. The word '**stain**' is used twice in *A Yorkshire Tragedy*, the first time in relation to the dishonouring of the Wife, just as in *Locrine*. In the latter play we find Gwendoline speaking of the '**sky**' and shame:

> **Blush heavens, blush sun**, and **hide** thy shining beams;
> Shadow thy radiant locks in gloomy **clouds**;
> Deny thy cheerful light unto the world,
> Where nothing reigns but **falsehood** and **deceit**.
> What said I? **falsehood**? Aye, that filthy crime,
> For Locrine hath forsaken Gwendoline.
> Behold the **heavens** do wail for Gwendoline.
> The shining **sun** doth **blush** for Gwendoline.
>
> (5.3.13)

In hiding/disguising/masking the sun's face/beams behind clouds the associations point towards coldness and darkness: light and warmth are withdrawn, as in the *Richard II* blot cluster (1.3.201 onwards). Egan found the blot cluster in *Thomas of Woodstock* included the words '**stain**', '**heaven**', '**sun**' and '**false**'. Sams (1986, 250) further pointed out that the poet mentioned Ethiopians in relation to this blot cluster in *Edmund Ironside, Love's Labour's Lost* and *The Two Gentlemen of Verona* (all early plays). Locrine's adultery is introduced by Ate in the prologue to Act 2 when she mentions "**sun-burnt** Aethiopians". This chain of associations ending in sun-burn is visible in the blot cluster in *Venus and Adonis* quoted above. The links seem to be between burning shame = blush = sun burn = Ethiopian/black face. There may also be a link back to Phaeton as his fall resulted in the Ethiopians being burned black by the sun (see chapter 1); indeed some accounts say Phaeton was from Ethiopia. It is very unlikely that this particular set of vocabulary and train of thought could issue from more than one pen: what we can detect here are the associations of one mind, of Henry Neville.

Within a few lines of the blot cluster, Locrine's illegitimate child, Sabren, walks onto the stage. The Husband in *A Yorkshire Tragedy* is obsessed with his sons being bastards. This reveals then the underlying meaning of the blot cluster - as in *The Rape of Lucrece*, who kills herself in order not to bequeath to future generations:

> The **shame** that from them no device can take,
> The blemish that will never be forgot;
> Worse than a slavish wipe or **birth-hour's blot**:
> For marks descried in men's nativity
> Are nature's faults, not their own infamy.
>
> (535)

In *A Yorkshire Tragedy* within the next 30 lines after the word '**blot**' the Husband speaks of **eyes, dark** and **heaven** and continues:

> Oh, were it lawful that your pretty souls
> Might look from **Heaven** into your father's **eyes**,
> Then should you see the penitent glasses melt,
> And both your murthers shoot upon my **cheeks**!
> Oh, 'twas the enemy my **eyes** so blear'd!
> Oh, would you could pray **Heaven** me to forgive...
>
> (10.36)

In these examples of the '**blot**' cluster there is shame and grief for the damage done to the family name by the Husband's behaviour. Neville, emerging from the Tower in 1603, had to come to terms with the damage done to his reputation, family and career: he had survived and could grieve for those who did not. It may be that this blot cluster is associated in Neville's mind with the blot on the Nevilles' name due to his grandfather's execution, his own illegitimacy and his shame at being sent to the Tower. In Sonnet 95 we have the words '**shame**', '**name**', '**spot**' and '**blot**'. If this sonnet is addressed to Southampton (and it includes the word 'rose' above 'name' (= Wriothesley/**Rose**ly) then it may date from their period together in the Tower.

The play ends before the Husband's execution: that at least Neville, having faced the threat, did not have to undergo. Indeed he gradually rebuilt his parliamentary career but never rose to the height he had aspired to: Winwood became secretary of state instead. In *Henry VIII*, the research for which, as James (2008b) has shown, dates back to Neville's time in the Tower, he writes of the rise and fall of politicians. Speaking of which, Cardinal Wolsey says:

> when he **falls**, he **falls** like **Lucifer**,
> **Never to** hope again.
>
> (3.2.372)

One of the gentlemen who confronts the Husband in *A Yorkshire Tragedy* says:

> Let only sin be sore,
> And by this **fall**, rise **never to fall** more.
>
> (2.176)

Neville knew what it was to fall and despair. Neville's wife, Anne Killigrew, had pleaded with the Queen and Cecil for his life and release. The Wife in *A Yorkshire Tragedy* likewise pleads:

> I will kneel,
> Sue for his life, number up all my friends
> To plead for pardon my dear husband's life.
>
> (10.67)

Neville survived and the last plays show deeply grieving and repentant men (Pericles, Posthumus, Leontes) being reunited with their families and forgiven. They are also plays of resurrection (for further exploration of this theme see chapter 7).

A Yorkshire Tragedy and *Mucedorus*

We might not expect to find any links between these plays written up to 18 years apart so it is startling to find even small echoes.

In *A Yorkshire Tragedy* the Wife says, "his deserts are in form **uglier** than an **unshap'd bear**..." (3.18). This detail is not in the original pamphlet about the murders so it is the playwright's image. Whilst the mere mention of a bear hardly merits a link with *Mucedorus*, the coupling of the words 'ugly/uglier' and 'bear' does recall the source of Sidney's *Old Arcadia* (see chapter 2). The word 'unshaped' is used in *Hamlet* (4.5.8). In *Henry VI* part 3 Gloucester described Richard as "Like to a **chaos**, or an **unlick'd bear-whelp**" (3.2.161). Mother bears were believed to lick their newborn cubs into shape.

It is however intriguing that we found a link between the bear, Neville, and *Leicester's Commonwealth* in *Mucedorus* (see chapter 2): these three elements then occur together in *A Yorkshire Tragedy* which will become evident when we consider its links with *Arden of Faversham* below.

A Yorkshire Tragedy and *Locrine*

I have, above, shown the occurrence of the blot cluster in *Locrine* and in *A Yorkshire Tragedy*. We have already seen an echo of *King Lear* when, in *A Yorkshire Tragedy*, the Master speaks of "The **Scythians** in their **marble-hearted feats**..." (1.4.259). In *Locrine* we find '**Scithians**' mentioned 18 times; 'marble' 3 times; 'Hard-**hearted**' twice, "iron **hearted**" and "brazen heart". In *Edward III* we find "A flint-heart **Scythian**" (2.1.72).

In *Locrine* Strumbo says, "oh **fine phrase**"; "**a capcase**"; "hang thy self" and "how have you scaped hanging?" In *A Yorkshire Tragedy* Sam says, "There's a **fine phrase**"; "**a cap-case**"; "You see I am **hanged**." Both are comic characters.

A Yorkshire Tragedy and *Arden of Faversham*

There is an intriguing link between these two plays, which are both tales of domestic murder. In *Arden of Faversham* Shakebag brags of killing "the widow Chambly":

> ...I spurned her **down the stairs**,
> And **broke her neck**, and cut her tapster's throat.
>
> (5.2.8)

In *A Yorkshire Tragedy* the Husband says to the nursing maid who tries to protect his son,

> Are you gossiping, prating, sturdy quean?
> I'll **break** your clamour with **your neck downstairs**:
> Tumble, tumble, headlong!   (Throws her down.)
> So, the surest way to charm a woman's tongue
> Is **break her neck**: a politician did it.
>
> (5.10)

This last line is a direct reference to Robert Dudley, The Earl of Leicester, who was believed to have killed his wife, Amy Robsart, in this way. In *Leicester's Commonwealth* one section tells of this 'crime', which the author suggests was intended to free the Earl to marry Elizabeth I:

> "when his Lordship was in full hope to marry her Majesty and his own wife stood in his light, as he supposed, he did but send her aside to the house of his servant Forster of Cumnor by Oxford, where shortly after she had the chance to fall from a pair of **stairs** and so to **break her neck**, but yet without hurting of her hood that stood upon her head"
>
> (Peck, 2006, 58).

Leicester's Commonwealth specifically mentions Neville's father's warnings about Robert Dudley, Earl of Leicester's intentions (James, 2008, 128). In 1583 Elizabeth I had sent Ambrose, the brother of Robert Dudley, down to Mayfield to discipline Neville for his export of ordnance. Neville argued with Ambrose, thus incurring Elizabeth I's displeasure (James & Rubinstein, 2005, 90). Neville had reasons to dislike the Dudleys.

Conclusion

A Yorkshire Tragedy contains evidence for Shakespeare-Neville. Whilst I doubt that Wilkins was the co-author, the case for Middleton is stronger (Cawley & Gaines, 1986, 5). He is also believed to have had a hand in revising *Macbeth* (Brooke, 1990, 57) and writing *Timon of Athens* (Jowett, 2004, 2) but this does not alter the evidence I offer here in support of Neville's authorship. I think the play was written rapidly and not re-worked so that we have a simpler, rougher text than the canonical plays which show evidence of being re-worked over years.

Chapter 7

DOUBLE FALSHOOD: THE 'LOST' CARDENIO

Time's glory is...
To unmask **falsehood** and bring truth to light.
The Rape of Lucrece (939)

In 1612 the first English translation, by Thomas Shelton, of *Don Quixote* was published. A section of Cervantes' masterpiece tells the story of Cardenio. For Christmas 1612 a play listed as *Cardenno*, was performed at court (hereafter I shall refer to this as *Cardenio*). It was performed again on June 8th 1613 for the Ambassador of Savoy. In 1653 Humphrey Moseley, a collector of play-manuscripts (who died in 1661) registered it as *The History of Cardenio* by Shakespeare and Fletcher (Salerno, 2000, 16). This title was used by Shelton when he translated the story (Freehafer, 1969, 502). 115 years later, in 1728, a play, *Double Falshood*, was performed and published by Lewis Theobald. He claimed it was a version, based on three manuscript copies, of a play by Shakespeare. Theobald stated that one copy of the script was given to him by an unknown 'Noble Person': I shall speculate that this was a member of the Neville family as Theobald had connections with the Nevilles (see below). Because none of these manuscripts has survived (possibly due to being lost in a fire at the Covent Garden Theatre Library) Theobald's claims have been treated with suspicion, some accusing him of perpetrating a forgery. Some of the play undoubtedly is by Theobald: he admitted that he had "revised and adapted" the text. This chapter reveals new evidence that the surviving *Double Falshood* is the lost play, *Cardenio*, and also that Henry Neville was one of the authors.

Lewis Theobald (1688 - 1744)

Theobald was a diligent editor of Shakespeare's works. He trained as a legal executive and thus learned the Court Hand and Secretary Script still used in legal documents of his day. It was through this that he became interested in literature of the Elizabethan and Jacobean era, when these styles of handwriting were used by every educated man. Thus, reading through Shakespeare, Theobald became convinced that Shakespeare's publishers and printers had been working from manuscripts written in the somewhat ambiguous Secretary Script, and had thus confused some of the author's writing. Theobald was therefore able to edit Shakespeare's First Folio with this problem in mind. Many of his revisions and interpretations are accepted as standard to this day.

Theobald claimed to have a manuscript of *Double Falshood* dating from about 1661-7, copied down by the prompter, Mr. Downes, who retired in 1706. Theobald reported that it had been prepared for performance by Betterton, who died in 1710, but not actually staged. Downes, Betterton and Sir William Davenant had radically revised *The Two Noble Kinsmen* (changing its title to *The Rivals)*. In doing so they "left not a line of the passages most confidently ascribed to Shakespeare intact, although several of Fletcher's passages survive with only minor alterations" (Kukowski, 1991, 81). They also changed the plot and the names of the main characters. This same team of revisers may have cut *Cardenio* and may also have changed its title and the names of the characters. There is internal evidence that the play has been cut: it "is shorter than any First Folio play and little more than half the length of most of them. Its nearest counterparts, *Henry VIII* and *The Two Noble Kinsmen*, are nearly twice as long as *Double Falshood*" (Freehafer, 1969, 505).

The plot of *Double Falshood*

Julio is in love with Leonora. He hopes to get their respective fathers' permissions to marry but just at this point he is summoned to court. He does not know that this has been engineered by Henriquez, the Duke's younger son, who has his eye on the beautiful Leonora. Henriquez meanwhile has been wooing Violante but she, suspecting his intentions are not entirely honourable, rebuffs him. He then rapes her. With Julio out of the way, Henriquez proposes to Don Bernard, Leonora's father, that he marry Leonora. She sends a letter to Julio and he rushes home. They meet and she manages to hide him behind a curtain just before the ceremony. At the climactic moment he can bear it no longer and emerges to challenge Henriquez. He is overpowered in a fight. He escapes into the wilderness where he rages in a madness that is observed by the local shepherds. Violante has also gone into the wilderness where, disguised as a boy (Florio), she laments her situation. She attracts the attention of the Master of the Flocks who guesses Florio is a woman and attempts a rape. He is interrupted by Roderick, Henriquez's elder brother, who has come to investigate Henriquez's behaviour. Leonora meanwhile has entered a nunnery. Eventually Roderick helps Henriquez to abduct Leonora from the nunnery by pretending to be in a funeral cortege. Roderick's intentions however are honourable and the cortege meets up with Julio, Florio/Violante and the two fathers in a re-union of lovers and families that is both comic and moving. Henriquez is forced to confess and is forgiven. Violante accepts him as her husband and Julio is reunited with Leonora.

Double Falshood, Cardenio, Cervantes and Shakespeare

The play *Double Falshood* is a radical re-telling of the story, in which the Cervantes' plot is re-structured, episodes subtly changed and details altered. The play begins not in the wilds with the distressed Cardenio (as in Cervantes' original), but in the court with the Duke talking with his eldest son about his wayward brother (neither the Duke not the elder brother appear in Cervantes' story). We see scenes in the present which, in *Don Quixote*, are narrated in retrospect. Some characters are entirely removed and actions displaced from one to another (songs are sung by Cardenio in the Cervantes whereas in the play they are sung by Violante). The denouement is entirely re-structured in the manner of Shakespeare's late plays so that parents are reunited with lost children, thought to be dead, (the parents are absent from the final scene in Cervantes). Indeed the resurrection theme is reinforced by the presence of a hearse that is not in Cervantes' original text. Shakespeare and Fletcher filter and restructure the story for their own purposes. Perhaps this explains why they changed the names of the characters: to differentiate their version from the original (though not that of the 'Master of the Flocks' who is called the 'Master' in the Shelton translation). One name is especially significant: Henriquez (see below). As these name changes may cause some confusion I provide this comparison:

Don Quixote:	Double Falshood:
Cardenio	Julio
Lucinda	Leonora
Dorothea	Violante
Don Fernando	Henriquez
Duke Ricardo	Duke Angelo

Some of the names used in *Double Falshood* had already been used elsewhere in the canon:

Fabian (a clown): *Twelfth Night*
Camillo: *The Winters Tale*
Julio: (a sculptor) *The Winter's Tale*
Angelo: *Comedy of Errors, Othello* and *Measure for Measure*

When writing *All's Well That Ends Well* Shakespeare changed the name of the Florentine Widow's daughter from Violenta to Diana (the name Violenta was accidentally retained in the First Folio by the type setters at the start of Act 3, Scene 5, possibly because the manuscript they were working with had not been corrected). Diana is a more appropriate name for a woman who retains her chastity in the play. In *Double Falshood*, the woman who is raped is called Violante (a name that is a pun on 'violated').

It is also interesting that the historical personage whom young Henry Neville and his father knew as 'Henri of Navarre' becomes 'Ferdinand of Navarre' in *Love's Labour's Lost*. This parallels the reversed change from Fernando to Henriquez in *Double Falshood*.

Textual evidence for Shakespeare

Before we consider evidence for Neville as the co-author (with Fletcher) we must first consider what evidence there is for *Double Falshood* belonging within the Shakespearean canon. Many scholars now consider there is sufficient evidence to support Theobald's claim that the play was (at least in part) written by Shakespeare. The evidence for his authorship is to be found in words, phrases (including 12 hendiadys, more than in other late plays, Salerno, 2000, 134-144), images, rhymes and rhythms in the poetry (including light/weak line endings, Muir, 1960, 153; and rhymes internal to the line, Muir, 1970), spellings, and plot lines, including doubling of characters, scenes and themes characteristic of Shakespeare (Salerno, 2000, 78, 134).

In chapter 6 I introduced the **blot** image cluster. This occurs four times in *Double Falshood*. Professing his loyalty to Leonora, Julio says he "will not **blot** me with a change, for all that sea and land inherit" (1.2.124). Within ten lines we have 'blush', then 'sun', "shade to darkness" and 'constancy'. Earlier in the scene there are the words 'constant', "Hyperion's eye burns" (= the sun); 'frosty', 'coldness', 'frozen'; 'eyes' and 'face'. There is also a reference to 'shame'. Later just before her forced marriage to Henriquez, Leonora hides Julio behind an arras. She speaks of 'night' and wears black. Henriquez says, "dearest Love I **blot** the low-born Julio from thy fair mind" (3.2.84). He refers to her gloom that darkens his triumph and her cheek. Julio emerges from his hiding place, asks Henriquez if he has any sense of 'shame' and confronts him with:

> You have wrong'd me;
> Wrong'd me so basely, in so dear a Point,
> As **stains** the **Cheek** of Honour with a **Blush**.

(3.2.135)

This imagery continues when Julio meets the disguised Violante in the wilderness and speaks of her 'complexion', the "hot sun" and "vermilion cheek" (4.1.66, 68, 72). In the next scene we find 'soul-spotted', 'blush', 'heav'nly' and 'clouds' (4.2.51, 57, 66). The only absent elements of this cluster then are 'moon' and 'sovereign/king'. As the play has a Duke as the senior royal the latter missing element is understandable. The word 'shame' occurs 6 times. The average for canonical plays is 8.5 (as *Double Falshood* has been shortened we can see it has a normal frequency).

I will now turn again to Ted Hughes' (1992) study of the archetypal scheme underlying the canon. Hughes traced a complex of myth and imagery throughout the plays and poems which he called "the tragic equation" (see chapters 2 and 4). He was not aware of *Double Falshood*. Is this archetypal scheme to be found in *Double Falshood*? The answer is an emphatic yes! Obviously the rival brothers are Henriquez and Julio. (There is also a pair of fathers who are rivals: Don Bernard and Camillo.) The myths/images of Venus, Adonis, Tarquin the rapist, the boar, the usurper, the storm and the flower/violet are there in the plot and the text.

First to appear is Venus: Julio is speaking to Leonora, promising fidelity whilst he is away at court (in effect like Adonis/Collatine he is abandoning Venus/Lucrece/Leonora; note also elements of the 'blot' cluster here):

> Oh! do not rack me with these ill-placed doubts;
> Nor think, tho' age has in my father's breast
> Put out love's flame, he therefore has not **eyes**
> Or is in judgment blind. You wrong your beauties,
> **Venus** will frown if you disprize her gifts,
> That have a **face** would make a **frozen** hermit
> Leap from his cell, and **burn** his beads to kiss it.
>
> (1.2.75)

Unfortunately, Julio praises his love's beauty to Henriquez (just as Collatine does to Tarquin in *The Rape of Lucrece* and as Posthumus Leonatus does to Iachimo in *Cymbeline*). Julio later acknowledges his error in language that recalls *The Rape of Lucrece*:

> ...like a credulous fool,
> I shew'd the treasure to a friend in trust,
> And he hath robb'd me of her – trust no friend:
> Keep thy heart's counsels close. Hast thou a mistress?
> Give her not out in words; nor let thy pride
> Be wanton to display her charms to view;
> Love is contagious: and a breath of praise,
> Or a slight glance, has kindled up its flame,
> And turned a friend a traitor.
>
> (4.1.45)

Henriquez, a Tarquin-like usurper, hot foots it to Leonora's house and persuades her father to give his daughter in marriage to him. Henriquez is already known to the audience as a possible rapist following his seduction/assault on Violante, which even he considers as rape. (The idea of rape is not in Cervantes' tale.) In reflecting on the rape Henriquez uses language directly reminiscent of *The Rape of Lucrece*:

> By force alone I snatch'd th' imperfect joy, which now torments my memory. Not love, but brutal violence prevail'd; to which the **time**, and place, and **opportunity**, were accessaries most dishonourable. Shame, shame upon it!
>
> (2.1.19)

After her rape by Tarquin, Lucrece has a long tirade against **Time** and **Opportunity** (874-1024). Henriquez then transfers his attention to Leonora. He succeeds in taking her to the altar where there is a dramatic, violent confrontation with Julio. Leonora has a plan: rather than be disloyal to Julio she will (Lucrece-like, with a dagger) kill herself. She speaks of her impending action using the storm metaphor of the tragic equation:

> ...an everlasting **Storm**
> Is come upon me, which I can't bear out.
>
> (3.2.36)

Later, having survived the worst, re-united with Julio in Act 5 scene 1, she is able to say that the storm is "now o'erblown". We see this storm in *Macbeth, King Lear, Pericles* and of course, *The Tempest*: Hughes shows how it is implicit in many other plays in the poetry, as it is here in *Double Falshood*. The storm is also related to madness: Julio is driven insane and escapes into the wilderness where, Lear-like, he rages. Madness is a descent into the irrational. In *Double Falshood* reason is contrasted with love and madness. Henriquez (the irrational brother/usurper, using a military/ordnance metaphor) says, "No shot of reason can come near the place where my love's fortified" (3.2.108).

Henriquez's attempt at seduction is the first location of the flower motif. Violante's very name contains the image of the purple flower, the viola/violet. Violante rejects Henriquez's advances with:

> Nay, your perfume,
> Which I **smell** hither, cheers not my sense
> **Like** our field-**violet's breath**.
>
> (1.3.54)

We can compare this to the text of *Venus and Adonis*: a purple flower (violet) springs from Adonis' spilt blood after the boar has gored him.

> "She (Venus) bows her head the new-sprung flower to **smell**,
> Comparing it to Adonis' **breath**"
>
> (1168-1172)

In *Cymbeline*, in a passage that echoes *Venus and Adonis,* Iachimo says of Imogen (calling her a fresh lily): "'Tis her breathing that perfumes the chamber thus" (2.2.18).

Later in *Double Falshood*, Violante takes the name **Florio** (Flower) to redeem Henriquez, prompting his confession and atonement through a falsehood/disguise (she confronts him as a boy, pretending to be his page). Hughes has traced this flower motif as transforming death/tragedy into life/redemption: Perdita (who was, as a baby, abandoned in a storm in *The Winter's Tale*) is first called 'Blossom' by the shepherd who discovers her (after the bear [= boar motif] has savaged Antigonus and his ship is sunk in the storm). Later she calls herself **Flora** when she celebrates the spring with her lover **Florizel**.

In *Double Falshood* all ends happily with reconciliation, the humbling of Henriquez, the restoration of lovers and re-uniting of children and fathers. This is a late romance not a tragedy. Interestingly at the end of the play there is what at first appears an entirely gratuitous anecdote when the Duke says to Violante:

> I have a debt to pay: your good old father,
> Once, when I chas'd the **boar,** preserv'd my life:
> For that good deed, and for your virtue's sake,
> Tho' your descent be low, call me your father.
>
> (5.2.262)

Here the encounter with the boar (which killed Adonis), so disastrous in other plays, is survived. The storm and the boar are related images and are playfully twinned by Camillo (Julio's father) when, speaking of young people, he says, "they're young and wanton; the next **storm** we shall have them gallop homeward, whining as **pigs** do in the wind" (5.2.14). Hughes pointed out that in the final plays both hero and heroine survive the (metaphoric) charge of the boar, whereas in the tragedies it is fatal.

Thus it can be seen that the essential features of the tragic equation traced by Hughes as a skeleton key to Shakespeare's plays, are to be found in the structure and imagery of *Double Falshood* (the rival brothers, Venus, the usurper, rape, flower, storm and boar). Hughes (1992, 505), in an appendix, also showed how this equation operates even in the plays co-written with John Fletcher: *Henry VIII* and *The Two Noble Kinsmen*. *Cardenio* (which I assert is, in essence, *Double Falshood*) was the first play Shakespeare and Fletcher wrote together so it is not surprising that we can now see the equation operating in this play.

Furthermore *Double Falshood* fits into the sequence of the last plays. At the end of the magical *Tempest* Prospero forswears magic and this next play then is entirely realist, domestic, naturalistic. There follows a history play and the last play is mythic and romantic. This further fits into a recapitulation of the beginning of 'Shakespeare's' career. *The Two Gentlemen of Verona* has a startling similarity of plot to *Double Falshood*. In both plays two men who are friends become rivals in love, with one deceiving the other. Leech (2001, xxxvi) noticed this recapitulation of themes between early and late plays, linking *The Two Gentlemen of Verona* with *The Two Noble Kinsmen* as examples of 'friendship literature'.

The Phoenix

There is a further image that occurs in the last ten plays that ties them together: *Anthony and Cleopatra, Coriolanus, Timon of Athens, Pericles, Cymbeline, Winter's Tale, Tempest, Cardenio (Double Falshood), Henry VIII* and *The Two Noble Kinsmen*. This is the mythical bird, the phoenix. There are references to the phoenix throughout the canon: from the earliest play to the last: *Henry VI* (parts 1 & 3), *Comedy of Errors* (A house/pub), *Twelfth Night* (a ship), *As You Like it, All's Well That Ends Well*, Sonnet 19, *A Lover's Complaint*, and of course the poem *The Phoenix and the Turtle*. This alerts us to the fact that Shakespeare valued this metaphor of rarity/renewal/resurrection. Yates (1975, 32) saw this image as one of a revival of the mythic spirit of Elizabeth I in the person of James I's daughter Elizabeth. Wilson (2004, 231) suggested that *Cardenio* was written to be performed at the celebration of Elizabeth's betrothal to the Elector of Palatine. Donne celebrated her marriage with a poem in which he eulogised her as a "fair phoenix bride". What we see in these last plays is the image emerging and gradually developing a deeper significance. Rather than the deaths of the tragedies the last romance plays show again and again the survival, indeed the physical/spiritual resurrection, of the protagonists.

Before the phoenix itself emerges in the final sequence of plays, Lady Macbeth laments that, "All the perfumes of **Arabia** will not sweeten this little hand" (5.1.49). For her there is no resurrection, she commits suicide. After the death and mayhem of *Macbeth*, the phoenix appears in the very next play, *Anthony and Cleopatra,* when Agrippa calls Anthony, "O thou **Arabian** bird!" (3.2.12). The phoenix here is the epitome of extreme rarity, indeed is unique. In the final scene Cleopatra herself is the phoenix:

> I shall show the cinders of my spirits
> Through the ashes of my chance...

> (5.2.173)

By cinders she means live coals. The metaphor is of her smouldering anger. Hughes (1992, 302, 313-320) showed how Anthony and Cleopatra enter a transcendent (spiritual/mythic) plane that redeems their folly on the tragic (realist) plane. However they do not survive. *Coriolanus* is also a tragedy that ends in death: there is no phoenix. The tragic hero himself is likened to a bird of prey, an osprey, an eagle and a dragon. His wings enable him to kill and there is no resurrection, only death. But in the following play, *Timon of Athens*, the phoenix reappears amidst bird imagery:

> ...I do fear,
> When every feather sticks in his own wing,
> Lord Timon will be left a naked gull,
> Which flashes now a **phoenix**.

> (2.1.29)

Again here the image is of Timon's unique earlier glory, but he does not survive. Though he sees the endless creativity of Nature ("whose womb unmeasurable and infinite breast teems and feeds all": 4.3.180) renewing herself, he cannot. "But then renew I could not like the moon..." (4.3.69). Timon spends the last section of the play planning his grave and epitaph.

Pericles, the next play, begins with the resurrection of the poet Gower who appears, phoenix-like:

> To sing a song that old was sung,
> From ashes ancient Gower is come...

Whilst the phoenix is not specifically mentioned the image begins to emerge: Pericles feels the "fire of love" (1.1.53). In *Double Falshood* Julio refers to "Love's flame" (1.2) and when Thaisa is revived by Cerimon (who twice calls for fire to aid his medical intervention) he says, "Death may usurp on nature many hours and yet the fire of life kindle again" (3.2.88). He then links this with a flower image: "see how she 'gins to blow into life's flower again!" (3.2.100). Thus we have a new emergent cluster of images of death-resurrection-birth-baby-(phoenix)-flower which will recur in the *Winter's Tale, Henry VIII* and *The Two Noble Kinsmen* (see below). Marina (Thaisa's baby) later wishes the gods to turn her into a bird to escape the brothel (4.6.102).

In the next play, *Cymbeline,* Iachimo compares Imogen to "the arabian bird" (1.6.17) meaning the phoenix. Again here the image is of rarity but now applied to a woman. Iachimo explicitly connects his own invasion of Imogen's bedroom to Tarquin's rape of Lucrece and further connects her with Venus, the flower in the breast (2.2.37-9) and the lily (2.2.12-15; see below).

Imogen then literally becomes the phoenix: drugged, she seems to die and Arviragus says of her: "The bird is dead" (4.2.198). Guiderius immediately links this with a flower image: "O sweetest, fairest lily!" (4.2.202) and they perform a funeral filled with flower imagery. Imogen however revives. Just fifty lines later, within the same scene, a phoenix-type image appears in the soothsayer's dream: of an eagle vanishing into the sun. The scene ends with words that recall the phoenix: "Some falls are means the happier to arise" (4.2.403). The play is much concerned with death and the final scene sees no less than four (apparent) resurrections: those of Imogen, Posthumus, Guiderius and Arviragus, all of whom are reborn and reunited until Cymbeline's joy overflows in a festival of forgiveness and reconciliation.

In *The Winter's Tale* the phoenix is not specifically mentioned but the underlying image continues to develop. Leontes orders Antigonous to burn his new born daughter: "...take it hence And see it instantly consumed with fire" (2.3.133). He relents, but insists that Antigonous expose the child in a remote desert place outside his kingdom (Antigonous prays that the birds will nurse her). Perdita survives and as if to underline the inherent phoenix image there is the famous line:

> thou metst with things dying, I with things newborn...
>
> (3.3.109)

What dies is Antigonous, savaged by the bear. His wife, Paulina, later describes herself as "an old turtle" (5:3:132) meaning a mourning turtle dove. This brings an echo of the poem *The Phoenix and the Turtle* but instead of being left solitary and sad, no sooner has she said this than Leontes brings her back into life by marrying her to Camillo (so the role of husband is resurrected for her).

In all the remaining plays the phoenix is explicitly mentioned.

In *The Tempest* Sebastian says:

> Now I will believe
> That there are unicorns, that in Arabia
> There is one tree, the **phoenix'** throne, one **phoenix**
> At this hour reigning there.
>
> (3.3.21)

Again the image is of uniqueness, 'oneness'; the feeling is wonder. Miranda (meaning 'to be wondered at') is the unique woman of the island who, who having survived the usurpation of her father's dukedom and the threat of rape by Caliban, will marry Ferdinand and become a queen: a wonderful outcome for Prospero after his sufferings.

In the last plays, from *Pericles* onwards, the emotion of wonder is evoked by marvellous denouements. In *Henry VIII* the phoenix is called "the bird of wonder". There is also joy and atonement, reconciliation and 'oneness' at the conclusion of these plays: the phoenix is emblematic of this constellation of feelings and ideas.

The next play in the sequence is *Cardenio/Double Falshood.* Julio, during his madness in the wilderness, asks a shepherd:

> Julio: Have you e'er seen the **phoenix** of the Earth,
>   The bird of Paradise?
> 2 Shepherd: In troth, not I, Sir.
> Julio: I have; and known her haunts, and where she built
>   Her spicy nest: 'till, like a credulous fool,
>   I shew'd the treasure to a friend in trust,
>   And he hath robb'd me of her.
>
> (4.1.42)

The image now has definitely shifted from simply that of unique rarity to a woman who will survive. Immediately after Julio has mentioned the phoenix, Violante (who was raped by Henriquez) appears and Julio uses a flower image to describe her ("the bloom of that vermilion cheek" 4.1.68). Whilst there is no baby in the play, Violante is repeatedly referred to as a child when she is disguised as a boy. We have already noted that Violante takes the name Florio (Flower) during this time of disguise. The 'children' (Julio, Henriquez and Leonora) are reunited with their fathers, (Camillo, Angelo and Don Bernard respectively), just as 'children' are reunited with fathers in *Pericles, Cymbeline, The Winter's Tale* and *The Tempest. Cardenio/Double Falshood* is the very next play in this sequence. Leonora uses an image that equates her to a phoenix: "I'm circled round with fire, no way for my escape, but through the flames" (2.3.122). She is feared dead by her father. She briefly enters a nunnery and Roderick speaks of her giving her "after-life" to this seat of contemplation. Pretending they are a funeral cortege (complete with a hearse) Roderick and Henriquez take her from the nunnery: the coffin on stage symbolising death. The phoenix then is an image of resurrection. In these last plays the women survive the threat of rape and death, and are re-united with those whom they love. When in the last scene her father, Don Bernard, greets Leonora he says, "Thou bring'st new Life" (5.2.52).

When, in the next play, *Henry VIII,* Cranmer speaks of the phoenix (Elizabeth I) the image is again connected with a baby (her heir, James I):

> When
> The bird of wonder dies, the maiden **phoenix**,
> Her ashes new create another heir...
>
> (5.5.39)

Later in the same speech he uses a flower image for Elizabeth, calling her "a most unspotted lily" (5.5.61). The phoenix image now has shifted decisively from rarity through survival to new life.

In the very last play, *The Two Noble Kinsmen*, this image of the phoenix-baby-flower is fully connected with the complex of imagery which Hughes named the Tragic Equation:

> Emilia: ...the flower that I would pluck
> And put between my breasts – O then but beginning
> To swell about the blossom – she would long
> Till she had such another, and commit it
> To the like innocent **cradle,** where, **phoenix**-like,
> They died in perfume;...
>
> (1.3.66)

Emilia is in effect the Venus who placed the flower of Adonis between her breasts at the end of the long poem published twenty years earlier, in 1593. There the image of the cradle first appears:

> Here in my breast;...
> Lo, in this hollow **cradle** take thy rest...
>
> (1183-1185)

This further connects the phoenix (death-rebirth) – flower – baby. Hughes (1992, 509) pointed out that this sequence of images runs through the transcendental development of the Tragic Equation from *Macbeth*, through *Lear* to the last romances. From this exploration we can see that *Double Falshood* fits precisely into the development of the imagery of the last plays. This is not at all the case in *The Second Maiden's Tragedy* which Hamilton (1994) claimed was the lost *Cardenio*. It has none of this imagery and the only conceivable 'phoenix' moment is in fact the very opposite: a statement of the impossibility of resurrection:

> 'Tis as unpossible for living fire
> To take hold there as for dead ashes to burn back again.
>
> (2116)

The title: *Double Falshood*

The word 'falsehood' occurs 33 times in the canon: in 2 sonnets and 21 plays. It is necessarily coupled with 'truth' and 'trust'. The word 'false' occurs in every play in the canon and in 19 sonnets! The word 'false' is almost as common as the word 'truth' and half as common as the word 'true'.

In *Locrine* the word 'falsehood' is repeated in adjacent lines, in effect doubled:

> Deny thy cheerful light unto the world,
> Where nothing reigns but **falsehood** and deceit.
> What said I? **falsehood**?

(5.3.15)

In two canonical plays the word 'falsehood' is likewise doubled. In *King John*, Cardinal Pandulph says:

> The truth is then most done not doing it:
> The better act of purposes mistook
> Is to mistake again; though indirect,
> Yet indirection thereby grows direct,
> And **falsehood falsehood** cures...

(3.1.273)

He could be describing Violante's stratagem at the end of *Double Falshood* whereby she confronts and reclaims Henriquez. Even more relevant to the themes of *Double Falshood* is the following speech of Iachimo's from *Cymbeline* in which he gazes on Imogen like a Tarquin, who does not proceed to rape, but imagines it.

> Had I this cheek
> To bathe my lips upon; this hand, whose touch,
> Whose every touch, would force the feeler's soul
> To the oath of loyalty; this object, which
> Takes prisoner the wild motion of mine eye,
> Fixing it only here; should I, damn'd then,
> Slaver with lips as common as the stairs
> That mount the Capitol; join gripes with hands
> Made hard with hourly **falsehood - falsehood**, as
> With labour; then **by - peeping in an eye**
> Base and unlustrous as the smoky light
> That's fed with stinking tallow; it were fit
> That all the plagues of hell should at one time
> Encounter such revolt.

(1.6.99)

The words peep/spy/spies, eye/eyes and light/night occur in *The Rape of Lucrece* and are repeated in the Northumberland Manuscript. Neville wrote fiction (falsehood) to tell the truth and disguised his identity (another falsehood). He and his father had used disguise during their diplomatic careers and disguise is used throughout the canon – including in *Double Falshood* - as a dramatic device. In the Northumberland manuscript Henry Neville's name is followed by a motto which includes the word 'ffraus' = false, (James & Rubinstein, 2005, 240-242).

215

The word '**falshood**' is used twice in the text of *Double Falshood*:

Julio says to Leonora:
And when I swerve, let Wretchedness o'ertake me,
Great as e'er **Falshood** met, or Change can merit.

(1.2.145)

Roderick says to Henriquez, "O Brother! We shall sound the Depths of **Falshood**" (5.1.74). The word 'false' occurs 8 times in the play: this is actually about the average, which is 7.35 times (272 divided by 37 plays). *Cymbeline*, a play written just three years before *Double Falshood*, has the word 'false' 26 times: more than any other play in the canon. There are some significant lines concerning falsehood: Cymbeline wishes to "winnow the truth from falsehood" (5.4.134). Pisano says: "Wherein I am false I am honest: not true to be true" (4.3.42). This last line might indeed be spoken by Neville himself who, through the fictions he created in his plays, told the greater truth of the human condition. Yet he could not do so directly in his own person but disguised (like so many of his characters). *Double Falshood* was followed by *Henry VIII*: a play subtitled, ***All is True***. In fact as we saw in chapter 5 all is not true in the play *Henry VIII*: Edward Neville is airbrushed out of the masque scene: another falsehood!

The next and last play was *The Two Noble Kinsmen* in which a doctor treating a mad woman says, "It is a falsehood she is in, which is with falsehoods to be combatted" (4.3.88). In *Double Falshood*, Henriquez's initial double falsehood in betraying Julio and raping Violante, is repaired by the double falsehood of the funeral cortege and Violante's disguise as Florio. Neville used the word 'falshood' in his statement when on trial for his life after the Essex rebellion (Winwood, 1725, Vol 1, 302).

The word 'double' does not occur in *Double Falshood*, though it is to be found in all except six of the plays in the canon. However the play has plenty of the doubling of themes, characters and plot so familiar in Shakespeare's plays: there are two pairs of lovers, two rival, grieving elderly fathers, two disguises (Julio and Violante, both of whom escape to the wilderness), two letters crucial to the plot. Interestingly this pattern of doubling is further developed into triads: there are three fathers seeking lost children, (the Duke Angelo, Camillo and Don Bernard) and three sons (Julio, Henriquez and Roderick). As Hughes pointed out (1992, 113) this doubling developing further into a triadic structure occurs in *As You Like It*: two Dukes and Jaques and three sons (one of whom is also a Jaques). Furthermore Yates (1975, 12) noted that one characteristic of Shakespeare's late plays is the "double plot", which includes two generations, indeed whole families, especially fathers and daughters. In this *Double Falshood* is entirely consistent with the other late plays.

Theobald's 1728 edition has a subtitle: *The Distrest Lovers*. My guess is that this is Theobald's invention: it has an 18th Century ring. The word 'distrest' does not occur in the canon. The word 'distressed' occurs ten times but never in connection with lovers. The word 'distress'd' occurs seven times and just once of a lover: Venus when abandoned by Adonis (814).

Evidence for Sir Henry Neville

Neville must have been good at Spanish. Not only did he take part in negotiations with the Spanish whilst ambassador to France but also James I wanted him to become the British Ambassador to Spain. There were there books in Spanish in his library. In the Epilogue to *The Tempest* Prospero states, "I must be here confined by you or sent to Naples." Naples was ruled by the Spanish. Phillip II had ruled it for some time, so to be sent to Naples was tantamount to being sent to Spain. *Cardenio/Double Falshood*, the very next play, is set in Spain. It is possible Shakespeare-Neville wrote a lost play, *The Spanish Maze,* which was performed in 1605, at about the time he was being considered for the post of Ambassador to Spain (James & Rubinstein, 2005, 329). I have argued that *Mucedorus*, which is set in Spain, is an early work by Neville (see chapter 2).

In 1606 two of Neville's friends, Dudley Carleton and John Chamberlain, shared a manuscript copy of an English translation of *Don Quixote*. In December 21st 1611 Arthur Throckmorton recorded in his diary that he had purchased "a book of Don Quixote". *Don Quixote* was published in 1612 so Arthur must have got hold of a pre-publication copy! Arthur had travelled through Europe with Neville in 1580-81. In November 1616 he recorded having dinner with Neville and Sir Henry Savile at Sir Ralph Winwood's house. When *Don Quixote* was published in 1612, Shelton wrote in the dedication that he had translated it five or six years earlier. In a letter believed to date from 1607, Walter Burre wrote that *The Knight of the Burning Pestle* "perhaps... will be thought to bee of the race of *Don Quixote*: we may confidently sweare it is his elder above a yeare" (Chambers, 1923, Vol 3, 220). Burre may have had sight of Shelton's manuscript or the 1607 Brussels edition of *Don Quixote*.

In this period playwrights began to refer to *Don Quixote* (Wilkins in 1607; Middleton in 1608; Jonson in 1610) so it is possible that Neville knew of the book long before he and Fletcher wrote *Cardenio/Double Falshood* (Carr, 2004, 24, 26-7). In the very first of these, George Wilkin's play *The Miseries of Enforced Marriage* Scarborrow says, "Now am I arm'd to fight with a Wind-mill…" (line 1469). This play was related to *The Yorkshire Tragedy* (see chapter 6) and included a character named Falconbridge (a Neville family name) so there is a tantalising link between Neville and the very first reference to *Don Quixote* in English Literature.

Fletcher may already have known *Don Quixote*: evidence for this comes from Ben Jonson's *Alchemist* (1610) "You are … a Don Quixote. Or a Knight o'the **curious coxcombe**" (4.7.39; Bowers, 1966, 264). Indeed by 1609, Fletcher had written (with Beaumont) *The **Coxcomb***, a play which some scholars believe, takes one of its plots from *El **Curioso** Impertinente*: the same *Don Quixote* subplot that was used by Middleton in 1611 in *The Second Maiden's Tragedy*. Fletcher and Massinger went on to write another play based on a Cervantes source: *The Custom of the Country* (1620)[48].

If Fletcher and Neville's friends knew Cervantes' writings, it seems highly likely that Neville also knew of *Don Quixote*. James & Rubinstein (2005, 79) have already pointed out that *The Two Gentlemen of Verona* (1594) was influenced by a Spanish work *Diana Enemorada*, which was not published in English until 1598, after that play was written. Furthermore James (2008a) has discovered that Shakespeare used the same name, Sylvia, in *The Two Gentlemen of Verona*, as Cervantes used in *Galatea*, his version of *Diana Enemorada* published in 1585; so quite possibly Neville had been reading Cervantes in Spanish many years before he read *Don Quixote*!

Neville, Prince Henry and the marriage of Princess Elizabeth
Neville was close to James I's eldest son, Prince Henry, the Prince of Wales, who was the focus of hopes for a revival of chivalric and Elizabethan values. Henry died suddenly, probably of typhoid, on November 6th, 1612, aged just 18.[49] There was a national outpouring of grief. His funeral was on December 7th and his coffin stood in Westminster Abbey throughout the Christmas celebrations, when *Cardenio* was first performed. Wilson (2004, 242) suggested that the presence of a coffin on stage in the play is a reminder to the audience of the recent death of the prince. There is much talk of death and despair in the play. The coffin is not to be found in the Cervantes source so it is an interpolation by the authors. Henry's death resulted in the wedding

---

[48] From: http://www.luminarium.org/sevenlit/massinger/massbio.htm [Accessed 2008]
[49] From:
http://en.wikipedia.org/wiki/Henry_Frederick%2C_Prince_of_Wales [Accessed 2008]

of his sister Elizabeth to Frederick, the Elector Palatine, being postponed until February 14th. That Christmas at court mourning mingled with laughter, mirroring the ambivalence of James I who, strange as it may seem, had reasons to be glad he was rid of his popular son. Wilson (2004, 232) furthermore suggested this tragic-comic play caught the mood and was topical, with apparent references to Prince Henry (Henriquez), King James' favourite Carr (**Car**denio/Julio) and the divorce of Frances Howard and Robert Devereux the 3rd Earl of Essex, which Neville mentioned in a letter dated 18/6/1613 (Winwood, 1725, Vol 3, 463). Furthermore in a Neville notebook we found that he had recorded the Archbishop George Abbott's report to James I on the Earl's divorce and his Majesty's response (15th July 1613: Worsley MSS 47).

The newly wed Elizabeth and Frederick "left England on 25th April 1613, when they sailed from Margate for the Hague, there to be welcomed by the Palsgrave's maternal uncle, Maurice of Nassau..." (Yates, 2004, 9). In a letter dated 25th June 1613 Turnbull wrote to Winwood that Frederick and his pregnant wife had safely arrived in 'Heydelbergh'. On 6th July Turnbull wrote that Neville was in Brussels to see "the Procession of the Sacrament of Miracles, the Princes and this Court in its Glory" (Winwood, 1725, Vol 3, 467). It is not clear whether Neville's visit to the continent at this time was as part of the royal party.

Neville in the text of *Double Falshood*
In the very first scene there is mention of France, spies, and being owed money. Roderick says, "He doth sollicit the return of gold" (1.1.37). Neville was owed £ 4000 by Elizabeth I for when he was ambassador in Paris: a fortune in those days. He went to France to ask for the return of a loan that Elizabeth had made to Henry IV. In one of his diplomatic letters (26.5.1599) he used the word "sollicit" concerning the return of this loan, using the same spelling as in *Double Falshood* (Winwood, 1725, Vol I, 32). There is no mention of France in *Don Quixote*. Neville and his sons had all spent time in France. Furthermore, note the word "doth": "He doth sollicit..." Kukowski (1991, 88) pointed out that Fletcher used "does", whereas Shakespeare used "doth". He concluded that scene 1 of *Double Falshood* is most likely of all the scenes to be by Shakespeare.

Double Falshood starts with a Duke preparing for death and ends with an old man complaining of gout, which we know Neville suffered from: in a letter dated 1/11/1604 he wrote that he was "in mych paine of the gout" (Winwood, 1725, Vol 2, 35). Then there are anxieties about a younger son: indeed the young man is called Henriquez: Spanish for "son of Henry". In 1609 Neville's son Henry was arrested for piracy and only got off the charge because of Francis Bacon's help. It is little wonder then that in the first scene of this play the father should be anxious about a wayward son. Roderick speaks of his brother's "hot escapes of youth". By this we might presume he means exciting/dangerous escapades. In fact we should take the word literally: Neville's son had escaped not only from violence but also from a very serious (indeed capital) charge. Henry had been studying in France; he was accused of theft by a French merchant naval captain, Jean Gandon, and received a serious head injury during a violent arrest (James & Rubinstein, 2005, 249). There is a sad note written by Neville on the outside of the Court report: "My son still continueth in France." This incident, just three years before *Cardenio* was performed, would have been in Neville's consciousness as he wrote a play about a wayward son. In Cervantes' text there are no trips to France: but that is where Julio has been just before the play starts. Neville sent a friend to accompany his son in France and keep an eye on his activities. This friend reported that young Harry was spending too much and cared too much about his clothes. In *Double Falshood* Duke Angelo (speaking to Roderick) hopes Julio will be, "An honest Spy upon thy Brother's Riots" (1.1.44). It seems in his own life Neville followed the path taken by Polonius, who sent Reynaldo to spy on his son Leartes in Paris (Hamlet, 2.1.3). Perhaps Neville's own father had sought reports of his behaviour during his travels (1578-83) on the continent (including a period in France).

Neville had an iron foundry and was a manufacturer of cannon. *Henriquez* (the 'irrational brother', using a military ordinance metaphor) says, "No shot of reason can come near the place where my love's fortified" (3.2.108). There is another metalurgic metaphor in the play: speaking of his son, Julio, who is summoned to the Duke's court, Camillo says, "Those scatter'd pieces of virtue, which are in him, the court will **solder** together, varnish, and rectify" (1.2.29). This image further ties the play into the canon: it is used in *Anthony and Cleopatra* when Octavia says:

> Wars 'twix you twain would be
> As if the world should cleave, and that slain men
> Should **solder** up the rift.
>
> (3.4.30)

Camillo, grieving his apparently lost son (Julio) says, "I've wept so long, I'm blind as Justice. When I come to see my hawks (which I held a toy next to my son) if they be but house-high, I must stand aiming at them like a gunner" (5.2.6). As I have already stated, Shakespeare often uses hawking/falconry imagery and Neville's father left his favourite bird to a friend in his will so we know Neville knew about falconry.

As the play moves towards its denouement, Camillo, who can be seen as an alter-ego for the aging Neville, says:

> Come what can come, I'll live a Month or two
> If the Gout please; curse my Physician once more,
> And then, —— —
> > *Under this Stone*
> > *Lies Sev'nty One.*

(5.2.34)

Neville died partly due to Gout. This gravestone is cryptic: yes, on the surface it seems to state Camillo's age at the time he expects to die. But there is something playful about Camillo's headstone and it is intriguing that he does not suggest it would have a name on it. Why 71? Brenda James suggested I look at Sonnet 71, which is about the poet's death and burial:

> O if (I say) you look upon this verse,
> When I, perhaps, compounded am with clay,
> Do not so much as my poor name rehearse...

In both play and sonnet the name of the deceased is obscured. Likewise there is no name on Shakespeare's gravestone. Furthermore the space intended for Henry Neville's inscription on the Neville monument in St. Lawrence's Church, Waltham St. Lawrence, is left blank. In sonnet 71 the poet repeats the word 'vile' in the fourth line. This points us to sonnet 121 in which the word 'vile' occurs in a poem about the poet's own self esteem versus others' negative views of him. I propose this is a pun on **Neville** and the family motto: "Ne vile velis". Indeed, as James has pointed out, when sonnet 121 is written out, the word 'Neville' (variously spelt, just as the Nevilles, father and son, were wont to do) can be easily perceived.

Friendship, trust, betrayal and forgiveness

Twenty years of trauma studies have led to a greater appreciation of the impact of trauma and the lasting effects of sudden loss. Neville was at the height of his career when he was implicated in the Essex rebellion. He was not suspected until betrayed by a friend: Henry Wriothesley, Earl of Southampton. This nearly cost him his life. It did cost him two years in prison, a huge fine, the loss of his diplomatic career and his chances of high office. The plays written from 1601 onwards portray tragedy, grief and suicidal madness. If some of the sonnets addressed to Southampton, with whom he shared his imprisonment in the Tower, were written during this time their themes of betrayal and shame especially make sense. The final romances show people surviving tragedy and the reconciliation/redemption of humbled and chastened figures (Pericles, Leontes) who, after years, are joyously re-united with their families. This parallels Neville's experience of the Tower of London and his failure to win high office. In the text of *Double Falshood* we find echoes of Neville's betrayal and imprisonment. Julio says:

> What a venomous World is this,
> When Commendations are the Baits to Ruin!
> All these good Words were Gyves and Fetters, Sir,
> To keep me bolted there: while the false Sender
> Play'd out the Game of Treach'ry.

(4.1.35)

This speech recalls Neville's experience of the promises (commendations) Essex made to him that he would become secretary of state, which led him to prison (gyves, fetters, bolted). There is much in the play about friendship, trust and betrayal. The word 'friend' (or friendship) occurs 30 times in the play. The word 'trust' (or related words like 'distrust') occurs 18 times. 'Betray' occurs 7 times. The treachery of a friend is at the centre of the play. Julio complains of Henriquez:

> Is there a treachery, like this in baseness
> Recorded anywhere? It is the deepest:
> None but itself can be its parallel
> And from a friend, professed! Friendship? Why 'tis
> A word for ever maimed; in human nature
> It was a thing the noblest.

(3.1.15)

In this speech we find an echo of Neville's experience of his betrayal by Southampton at the time of the Essex rebellion. The friendship with the latter however survived: in 1611 (just a year before *Cardenio/Double Falshood* was written) Southampton advocated to James I that Neville become Secretary of State. Referring to Southampton's failure to win his friend high office, Henry Howard wrote in a letter of Neville as the Earl's 'Dear Damon', thus linking them as an archetypal pair of friends in the 'friendship literature' (James & Rubinstein, 2005, 246, 341). The friendship of Julio and Henriquez also survives. However the betrayal may have made Neville extremely cautious: in Julio says, "Trust no Friend: Keep thy Heart's Counsels close" (4.1.47).

The debacle of the Essex rebellion did enormous damage to Neville's life and career. Violante, after the rape, laments:

> I am now become
> The Tomb of my own Honour: a dark Mansion,
> For Death alone to dwell in. I invite thee,
> Consuming Desolation, to this Temple,
> Now fit to be thy Spoil: the ruin'd Fabrick,
> Which cannot be repair'd, at once o'er-throw.

(2.2.29)

This speech that could have been spoken by the ruined Neville. Furthermore Henriquez says:

> My Heart grows sick of Birth and empty Rank,
> And I become a Villager in Wish.

(1.3.23)

Eight years before he wrote *Double Falshood*, in 1604, Neville wrote in a letter to Winwood: "I am out of my proper Orb when I enter into State Matters, I will therefore leave these considerations to those to whom they appertain, and think of my husbandry in the Country..." (James & Rubinstein, 2005, 164).

The play however ends with the joy of reunion: Neville and his family must have felt such joy after his release on James I's accession to the throne in 1603.

Fletcher and Neville

John Fletcher worked with Shakespeare-Neville on the last plays. Just as Sussmayer worked for Mozart and Fenwick supported Delius in their last periods so Fletcher made it possible for the playwright to complete three further works.

John Fletcher was born in 1579 in Sussex - the very area where Neville began working on his inherited iron foundry when he returned from his European travels in 1583. John Fletcher's mother was a relative of Neville. It is therefore probable that he knew Richard Fletcher, the father, and may well have watched John grow up. John Fletcher's father was a bishop who was put into debt merely by Queen Elizabeth's manipulations of the system by which she received from a freshly appointed bishop one whole year's income and one tenth of the income ever afterwards. Elizabeth moved Bishop Fletcher around. She also disapproved of his marriage and court gossip reflected the Queen's jealousy: "We divide the name Fletcher: He my Lord F...; and she my Lady Letcher." Another reason for Neville to sympathise with Fletcher was their mutual connection with the Earl of Essex. Fletcher's uncle

Giles (his guardian after his father's death in 1596) was, like Neville, caught up in the Essex rebellion and thus the family were impoverished. Neville was always fond of, and kind to, his own and other people's children (witness his care of his sister-in-law's children after their father died). When *A King and No King* (by Beaumont and Fletcher) was first printed in 1619, Walkley's dedicatory epistle to Sir Henry Neville introduced the play. In it he said that Neville had encouraged the writers (Bliss, 2004). Whether this epistle was addressed to Sir Henry (who died in 1615) or his son (who shared his name and lived 1588-1629) it is independent documentary proof of a relationship between Fletcher and the Nevilles. I hypothesise that the elder Neville (the playwright) had originally received the play from Fletcher, and his son later offered it for publication. *A King and No King* was first performed in 1611 in the same season as *The Tempest*. That year Fletcher had also written *The Tamer Tamed*: the only sequel to a Shakespeare play (*The Taming of The Shrew*). Perhaps he was demonstrating his ability to the bard. It was following this that Fletcher began to co-operate with Shakespeare-Neville: all the plays they co-authored, *Cardenio, Henry VIII, Two Noble Kinsmen*, follow on. Indeed there are some textual echoes of *A King and No King* in *Double Falshood*. *A King and No King* may have been offered to Neville by Fletcher, who was in effect saying, "Look what I can write: now can we co-write, can I help you?" Or Neville saw the quality of the work and said, "You can help me..." If Neville was ill he perhaps needed help, or the ambitious younger playwright persuaded Neville to work with him (perhaps at the behest of the King's Men theatre company). Interestingly the first scene of *Double Falshood* begins with an older man handing on to a younger man as he prepares for death. Duke Angelo uses a metaphor of a laurel wreath and this speech could easily be spoken by an older poet to a younger artistic heir:

> I've worn the garland of my honours long,
> And would not leave it wither'd to thy brow,
> But flourishing and green; worthy the man,
> Who ... heirs my better glories

(1.1.5)

The sequence then is: (earliest known performance or publication dates in brackets)

1611 *The Tempest* (1611, published 1623), *A King and No King* (1619)
1612 *Cardenio/Double Falshood* (Christmas 1612, May 20th and June 8th 1613)
1613 *Henry VIII* (29th June 1613)
1613 -14 *Two Noble Kinsmen* (1634)

Also relevant to this sequence of dates is the fact that Fletcher's collaborator Beaumont retired in 1612-13 to Kent: at precisely the time Fletcher starts to work with Shakespeare-Neville.

Kukowski (1991, 85) noticed that words and phrases typically used by Fletcher recur in *Double Falshood* and *A Very Woman* (such as "loth to say"). He also noted Fletcher's predeliction for the words 'fling/flung'. Sure enough this occurs in *Double Falshood* when Julio says:

> If the curst Henriquez
> Had pow'r to change you to a boy, why, Lady,
> Should not that mischief make me any thing,
> That have an equal share in all the miseries
> His crimes have **flung** upon us?

(4.2.94)

I note it also occurs in *A Very Woman* where John says:

> Why should you, being innocent, **fling** your life
> Into the furnace of your father's anger
> For my offence?

(1.2.19)

This evidence of Fletcher's hand in *A Very Woman* is significant because it further links *Double Falshood* with *Cardenio*: scholars agree that Fletcher wrote parts of *A Very Woman* (which Massinger co-wrote and later revised). In the play two characters are called Cardenes and Leonora. This is significant evidence for Fletcher's involvement in *Cardenio/Double Falshood* as the first of these names is clearly derived from Cardenio and the second, Leonora, is in *Double Falshood*. This is therefore further evidence that *Double Falshood* is the genuine remnant of the play *Cardenio* by Shakespeare-Neville and Fletcher. Specific themes (such as friendship, forgiveness and reconciliation), plot lines (rival lovers, madness) and language also recur in both plays. Of special interest are the words: '**strong imagination**'. These had been used by Shakespeare-Neville first in *A Midsummer Night's Dream* when Theseus says, "Such tricks hath **strong imagination**..." (5.1.18). Later in *The Tempest* Antonio says, "My **strong imagination** sees a crown dropping upon thy head" (2.1.202). In *Double Falshood* (1.3) Henriquez says, "...mended with **strong imagination**." (1.3.7) In *A Very Woman* a Doctor states:

> ...you shall here
> Be witness to his fancies, melancholy,
> And his **strong imagination** of his wrongs.

(4.2.1)

The continuity between these is provided by Fletcher.

Neville and Cervantes

James (2008a) has discovered evidence of connections between Neville and Cervantes. Neville had direct contact with significant Spanish grandees during the negotiations for the treaty of Boulogne in 1600. The chief Spanish delegate was Baltazar de Zuniga who looked down on Neville as he regarded him as not sufficiently ennobled to negotiate with him. The resultant hostility between them led to Baltazar suggesting that Neville was arranging for him to be assassinated. This hostility between Neville and the Zunigas continued and years later Pedro de Zuniga, the Spanish Ambassador to England, suggested to James I that the Virginian group (which included Neville as a founder member of the Virginia Company) was a subversive organisation and therefore a danger to the King. Baltazar's brother was Alonso Diego Lopez de Zuniga to whom Cervantes dedicated his *Don Quixote*. James (2008a) provided evidence that the character and themes of ridiculous knight errantry were based on the Spanish view of Neville and the English negotiations for the treaty of Boulogne.

The Neville-Theobald connection

Lewis Theobald said that he had received one copy of the *Double Falshood* manuscript from a 'Noble Person' whom he did not identify. I hypothesise that this was a Neville because James has discovered that Lewis Theobald had business and property connections with the Nevilles. Documents relating to business between him and a branch of the Neville family still exist[2], and date from 1726 – 27 (the same period that runs up to the performances of *Double Falshood* in 1728). Theobald took a lease on a property owned by the Nevilles in Yorkshire; he also seems to have been carrying out some research for them. Perhaps they gave him the manuscript of *Cardenio/Double Falshood* in return for his services.

James has done further research into Neville-Theobald connections (see Casson, 2007a). She discovered quite extraordinary intergenerational links between Theobald, 'Shakespeare', the Nevilles and their Killigrew relatives through succeeding generations right down to H.P. Lovecraft, the 20th Century writer of horror stories.

---

[2] East Riding of Yorkshire Archives and Records Service: EASTOFT FAMILY OF EASTOFT Catalogue Ref. ref. DDBE/20/25 - date: 8 Mar 1726, Reference: DBE/21/3 - Account of debts of Francis Estofte, esquire Creation dates: 18 Jun 1726 Sent by Lewis Theobald to Madam Neville at 29 Gloucester Street (All this number relates to the list at DDBE/27/37) Also ref. DDBE/20/25 - ref. DDBE/20/28 - date: 29 Apr 1727

In my end is my beginning: *Mucedorus* **and** *Double Falshood*
We might not expect there to be any links between two plays written nearly 40 years apart but if they are by the same writer there might indeed be traces, just as I had used a Punch and Judy metaphor in plays I had written over a 30 year period. The plots of the plays are similar (fathers and sons, disguising as shepherds, going into the forest wilderness, lovers separated, rivals humiliated). These might be regarded as commonplace conventional devices. It is therefore to the metaphors we must turn to see the hidden links. Shakespeare used tree and grafting metaphors. Mucedorus says, "My mind is **grafted** on an humbler **stock**" (Q3: 1.1.48). In *Double Falshood* Camillo says, "You must be **grafted** into noble **stocks**" (3.3.93). I noted the rarity of 'haws' in *Mucedorus*: in *Double Falshood* I found 'hawthorn'. Henriquez says:

> Who ne'er beheld
> More than a **Hawthorne**, shall have Cause to say
> The Cedar's a tall Tree; and scorn the **Shade**,
> The lov'd **Bush** once had lent him.

(2.3.5)

In *Henry VI* part 3 the King speaks of "the **hawthorn-bush** a sweeter **shade**" (2.5.42). The oak tree is also mentioned in both plays, reminding us that these were written by Neville, the forester. The forest is the place of wildmen. I have traced the links between Bremo and Caliban (in chapter 2). In *Mucedorus* Bremo says to Amadine, "I thirst to **suck thy blood**" (3.3.23). In *Double Falshood* the mad Julio says to Violante, "I'll **suck thy** Life-**blood**" (4.1.99). In both cases a wild man is speaking to a vulnerable woman in a forest wilderness. Julio in his madness also has lines that remind us of Caliban's "**Sounds** and **sweet airs**": hearing Violante singing in the wilderness, Julio thinks it is a spirit and says he is "visited with these **sweet airs**" (4.2.13). Like Caliban and Bremo the music calms him: "The heav'nly **sound** diffuses a sweet peace thro' all my soul" (4.2.34). These two 'lost' plays have multiple links with canonical works and reveal the continuity of Shakespeare-Neville's imaginative world.

Conclusion
There is clear evidence in the text for *Double Falshood* being a genuine remnant, even if drastically cut, of the original *Cardenio*. There is also evidence of Neville in the text and the circumstances of its creation.

Chapter 8

REFLECTIONS

If there were no links between these plays then the hypothesis of a common author could be dismissed as fanciful, but the manifest, complex and continuing connections between them and other canonical works are persuasive. Many pieces of evidence point to the author being Henry Neville.

From this work I am now able trace a line of development from the first play *Mucedorus* and to offer the following sequence of Shakespeare-Neville's earliest works:

Mucedorus 1584-5 (published anonymously 1598, revised 1610)

Locrine 1586-89 (revised 1594, published as by W.S. in 1595)

Arden of Faversham 1586-90, (published anonymously 1592)

Edmund Ironside 1587-8 (never published, one manuscript in the British Library)

Hardicanute 1588-? (the lost second part of *Edmund Ironside*, see Sams, 1986, 19)

The Troublesome Raigne of John 1588-9 (published anonymously 1591 in two parts)

The Taming of The Shrew 1589 (*The Taming of A Shrew* published anonymously 1594, *The Taming of* **The** *Shrew* published in First Folio 1623)

Henry VI part 1 1589-1590 (published in the First Folio in 1623)

Henry VI part 3, 1589-91, performed from 1590 (published anonymously 1595 as *The True Tragedy of Richard Duke of York* and in the First Folio in 1623)

Henry VI part 2 1590-91 (published anonymously 1594 as *The First Part of the Contention betwixt the two Famous Houses of York and Lancaster* and in the First Folio in 1623)

Titus Andronicus 1592 (published anonymously 1594)

The Two Gentlemen of Verona 1592 (published in the First Folio in 1623)

Edward III 1592-3 (published anonymously 1596)

Thomas of Woodstock 1592-3 (never published, one manuscript in the British Library)

Richard III 1592-3 (published anonymously Q1, 1597, then again Q2, 1598 as by William Shake-speare)

This sequence then has the bard writing a single comedy and two single tragedies before he takes on the more ambitious two part plays (probably stimulated by *Tamburlaine*) thus enabling him to build up to the massive tetralogy of *Henry VI* (parts 1, 2, 3) and *Richard III*. It also reveals that *The Troublesome Raigne of John* was his first play to be published (in 1591), with *Arden of Faversham* the second (in 1592). In between these Florio published the *Phaeton* sonnet (in 1591). All these were before the name 'Shakespeare' was ever used. 'Phaeton' then was Neville's first nom-de-plume but he must have realised such a mythical name would not serve his purposes because it would only stimulate curiosity about the identity of the person behind such an obvious pseudonym. It is only in 1593 that the name 'William Shakespeare' was first used at the end of the dedication to Henry Wriothesley, Earl of Southampton in *Venus and Adonis*. By 1592 W. Shakespeare from Stratford was in place and ready to take on the role of factotum, which he has continued to play, to great acclaim, ever since.

Neville chose to hide his identity from the very start of his career. It is possible that he used co-writers not merely for their assistance but to further disguise his authorship. These writers may never have known the identity of the original author: they may have been presented with a developing script and asked for their in-put. In Fletcher's case however there is evidence that he knew Neville. The reference to Faulconbridge and the Mitre Inn in George Wilkins' *The Miseries of Enforced Marriage* suggest that he too knew Neville's hidden identity. Greene may have had a hand in *Locrine*. Kyd may have contributed to *Arden of Faversham* and Nashe to *Henry VI*. Later Neville was not well due to gout and may have wanted to develop the emerging talent of younger writers. He may have invited several writers to contribute to scripts such as:

Middleton: *A Yorkshire Tragedy* (1605) and *Timon of Athens* (1605-6). Middleton is believed to have revised *Macbeth* and *Measure for Measure*.
Wilkins: *Pericles* (1607-8)
Fletcher: *Cardenio* (1612), *Henry VIII* (1612) and *The Two Noble Kinsmen* (1613-14)

Certainly the disguising effect of these partnerships worked, obscuring the authorship of *A Yorkshire Tragedy*, *Pericles*, *Henry VIII* and *The Two Noble Kinsmen*. *Cardenio* vanished altogether and the damaged remnant *Double Falshood* is still not widely recognised. This book will, I hope, be a stimulus to others to look again at the authorship of these plays.

I have been able to demonstrate the continuity of Neville's development as a writer and how the late plays mirror the earlier plays. *The Two Noble Kinsmen* was the very last play Shakespeare-Neville co-wrote with Fletcher. It is based on Chaucer's *The Knight's Tale*. Chaucer married Philippa de Roet, the sister of John of Gaunt's third wife, Katherine Swynford. Katherine's daughter Joan married Ralph Neville. Thus Henry Neville was related to Chaucer. In choosing to dramatise Chaucer, I believe Shakespeare-Neville was placing himself in relation to the continuing development of English writing, as he had done by bringing Gower on stage in *Pericles*. *The Two Noble Kinsmen* is a story of two men imprisoned together: there are speeches that seem to recall Neville's friendship with Southampton and their mutual support during their period in the Tower (1601-3). There are other elements which recall earlier works and a half hidden fragment of the Phaeton myth:

> Phoebus, when
> He broke his whipstock and exclaimed against
> The horses of the sun...

(1.2.85)

Waith (1998, 96) provided a footnote explaining that this is the god of the sun in a rage of grief for his son, Phaeton, from Ovid's *Metamorphosis*. We can now realise the full significance of this cryptic reference to the myth of a fallen hero who had dared to ascend the brightest heaven of invention.

Conclusion

I have tested Brenda James' historic discovery, that Henry Neville was the author we know as William Shakespeare, by applying it to anonymous or apocryphal works. If I had found no evidence for Neville this would have been a useful result: showing that these works at least were not by him. However discovery after discovery has shown that these works do have Neville connections. I conclude therefore that James' revelation that Henry Neville was the author of Shakespeare's works is a testable hypothesis that produces unexpected results, revealing new works by the bard, and helping to illuminate his artistic development in the 1580s.

Appendix 1:

With special reference to the incidence of the following five particular words:

rival, branch, herbs, increase, vaunt

Play/Poem	Total number of words:	Rare words:
Richard II	27	rival, branch, herbs
Henry VI part 2	23	increase, herbs
Locrine	22	increase, branch, herbs
Henry VI part 3	22	increase, branch
Edward I (Peele)	22	vaunt
Richard III	21	increase, herbs
Dr. Faustus (Marlowe)	21	branch, herbs, vaunt
The Spanish Tragedy (Kyd)	21	increase, branch
Tamburlaine II (Marlowe)	21	rival, herbs
Titus Andronicus:	20	increase, herbs
The Troublesome Raigne	20	branch, vaunt
James IV (Greene)	20	increase, herbs
The Rape of Lucrece	20	vaunt
Mucedorus	19	increase, branch, herbs, vaunt
Astrophil & Stella (Sidney)	18	increase, herbs
David and Bethsabe (Peele)	18	increase, branch
Two Gentlemen of Verona	18	rival
Love's Labour's Lost	18	branch
Venus & Adonis	17	increase, herbs
Jew of Malta (Marlowe)	17	increase
Edmund Ironside	17	
Thomas of Woodstock	17	
Taming of the Shrew	16	rival
Henry VI part 1	16	branch
Tamburlaine I (Marlowe)	15	vaunt
Arden in Faversham	14	rival
Friar Bacon & Friar Bungay (Greene)	13	vaunt
A Looking Glass for London (Greene)	13	increase, herbs
Orlando Furiouso (Greene)	13	
Alphonsus King of Arragon (Greene)	12	vaunt
Endymion (Lyly)	11	increase, herbs
Arraignment of Paris (Peele)	11	
Battle of Alcazar (Peele)	10	
Sappho and Phao (Lyly)	7	
Old Wives Tale (Peele)	6	

Appendix 2:

Phaeton sonnet words in Marlowe, Sidney, Kyd and Lyly

Word↓	Jew of Malta	Tambur I	Tambur II	Faustus	Astrophil & Stella	Spanish Tragedy	Sappho &Phao	Endy- mion
Sweet	√	√	√	√	√	√	√	√
Friend	√	√	√	√	√	√		√
name	√	√	√	√	√	√		√
agrees								
increase	√				√	√		√
rival			√					
Spring		√	√		√	√		
branch				√		√		
flourishing				√				
Summers/'s			√			√		√
shady			√					
pleasures	√	√				√		
cease			√	√	√	√	√	√
Winters/'s	√					√		√
storms					√			
repose		√	√					
peace	√	√	√		√	√	√	
spends								
franchise								
living		√	√	√				
thing	√		√	√	√	√	√	√
daisies								
sprout								
little	√	√	√	√	√	√	√	√
birds	√				√	√		√
sing			√	√	√	√	√	
herbs			√	√	√			√
plants				√		√		
vaunt		√	√	√				
release			√	√	√			
English				√	√	√		
wits	√	√		√	√	√	√	
dead	√	√	√	√	√	√		
laurel		√	√	√				
except	√	√		√		√		
green	√		√	√				
fruits	√			√	√	√		
barrenness	√							
o'erspread								
flowery		√						
pleasance								
flowerets								
morality								
Italy	√		√					
Total:	17	15	21	21	18	21	7	11

Phaeton sonnet words in Shakespeare's works 1590-95:

Word↓	HVI 1	HVI 2	HVI 3	Titus Andron	LLL	R III	R II	Taming of Shrew	Two Gent Verona	Venus & Adonis	Rape Lucr
sweet	√	√	√	√	√	√	√	√	√	√	√
friend	√	√	√	√	√	√	√	√	√	√	√
name	√	√	√	√	√	√	√	√	√	√	√
agrees		√								√	√
increase		√	√	√		√				√	
rival						√	√	√			
Spring	√	√	√	√	√	√	√	√	√	√	
branch	√		√			√	√				
flourishing		√		√			√		√		
Summers/'s		√	√	√		√	√			√	
shady											√
pleasures					√	√					
cease	√	√	√	√				√	√		√
Winters/'s		√	√		√		√				
storms		√	√			√	√	√			√
repose		√	√	√		√	√	√	√		√
peace	√	√	√	√	√	√	√	√	√		√
spends									√		√
franchise											
living	√	√	√	√	√	√	√			√	√
thing	√	√	√	√	√	√	√	√	√	√	√
daisies					√						
sprout											
little	√	√	√	√	√	√	√	√	√	√	√
birds		√	√	√			√			√	√
sing	√	√	√	√	√		√	√	√	√	
herbs		√		√		√	√			√	
plants					√	√	√			√	
vaunt											√
release							√				
English	√	√	√			√	√				
wits	√	√		√	√	√	√	√	√	√	√
dead	√	√	√	√	√	√	√	√	√	√	√
laurel			√								
except	√	√	√			√	√		√		
green	√	√		√	√	√	√	√		√	√
fruits		√					√				
barrenness											
o'erspread											
flowery											
pleasance											
flowerets											
morality											
Italy							√	√			√
Total:	16	23	22	20	18	21	27	16	18	17	20

Phaeton sonnet words in Robert Greene:

Word↓	Alphonsus	Looking Glass	Orlando Furioso	James IV	Friar B & B
sweet	√	√	√	√	√
friend	√	√	√	√	√
name	√	√	√	√	√
agrees					
increase		√		√	
rival					
Spring	√	√	√	√	√
branch					
flourishing					
Summers/'s		√			
shady			√		
pleasures	√	√		√	
cease				√	√
Winters/'s	√				
storms	√	√		√	
repose				√	
peace		√	√	√	√
spends					
franchise					
living			√	√	√
thing	√			√	
daisies					
sprout				√	√
little					
birds					
sing		√	√	√	
herbs		√		√	
plants				√	
vaunt	√				√
release					
English				√	√
wits	√			√	√
dead	√	√	√	√	√
laurel			√		
except					
green	√				√
fruits		√	√	√	
barrenness					
o'erspread					
flowery					
pleasance			√		
flowerets					
morality					
Italy					
Total:	12	13	13	20	13

Phaeton sonnet words in George Peele:

Word↓	Edward I	David & Bethsabe	Arraign of Paris	Battle Alcazar	Old Wives Tale
sweet	√	√	√	√	√
friend	√	√			√
name	√	√		√	√
agrees	√				
increase		√			
rival					
Spring	√	√	√		√
branch		√			
flourishing					
Summers/'s	√			√	
shady		√			
pleasures	√	√	√		
cease	√	√	√	√	
Winters/'s	√	√		√	
storms	√	√		√	
repose	√	√		√	
peace	√	√	√		
spends					
franchise					
living	√				
thing	√				
daisies					
sprout					
little		√			
birds			√		
sing	√	√	√		
herbs					
plants		√			
vaunt	√				
release					
English	√			√	
wits	√		√		
dead	√	√		√	√
laurel			√		
except	√				
green	√		√		√
fruits	√	√	√		
barrenness					
o'erspread					
flowery					
pleasance					
flowerets					
morality					
Italy				√	
Total:	22	18	11	10	6

Phaeton sonnet words in Apocryphal Plays:

Word↓	Muce-dorus	Locrine	Edmund Ironside	Arden Faversh	Trouble-some Raigne	Thomas Wood-stock	Yorks. Tragedy
sweet	√	√	√	√	√	√	√
friend	√	√	√	√	√	√	
name	√	√	√	√	√	√	√
agrees							
increase	√	√					
rival				√			
Spring	√	√	√	√	√		
branch	√	√			√		
flourishing						√	
Summers/'s			√				
shady		√					
pleasures	√	√	√	√		√	√
cease	√	√		√	√	√	
Winters/'s					√		
storms		√	√			√	
repose				√			
peace	√	√	√	√	√	√	√
spends							
franchise							
living	√		√	√	√		
thing	√	√	√	√	√	√	
daisies							
sprout			√				
little	√	√	√	√	√	√	
birds	√	√			√	√	
sing	√	√			√	√	
herbs	√	√					
plants							
vaunt	√				√		
release							
English			√		√	√	
wits			√		√		
dead	√	√	√	√	√	√	
laurel		√			√		
except	√	√	√			√	
green	√	√	√		√	√	
fruits							
barrenness		√					
o'erspread						√	
flowery							
pleasance							
flowerets							
morality							
Italy		√		√	√		
Total:	19	22	17	14	20	17	4

Appendix 3:

THE PLOT STRUCTURE OF LOCRINE

Previous critics have suggested the comic scenes are interpolations. I consider them integral to the design. They follow on from the author's interest, already apparent in *Mucedorus*, in the relationship between comedy and tragedy, an interest that Shakespeare followed up throughout his career. The comedic betrothal of Strumbo and Dorothy follows the betrothal of Locrine and Guendoline and anticipates their marriage. Strumbo, like Locrine, has two wives in the play. To clarify the structure of the play I suggest there are three inter-weaving plots or storylines introduced by prologues, which use mythic symbolism to draw on archetypal meanings.

Plot 1: centred on Locrine and Guendoline
Plot 2: centred on Strumbo (the comic subplot)
Plot 3: centred on Humber & Estrild

Act 1: Scene 1, Prologue, Ate: mythic symbolism
Scene 2: Tragedy: The dying king; a betrothal (plot 1: Locrine and Guendoline)
Scene 3: Comedy: courting leading to a betrothal (plot 2: Strumbo and Dorothy)
Scene 4: A Royal Marriage (plot 1: Locrine and Guendoline)
Act 2: Scene 1, Prologue, Ate: mythic symbolism
Scene 2: Tragedy: Invasion threatens War (plot 3: Humber & Estrild)
Scene 3: Comedy interrupted by War (plot 2 interrupted by plot 1)
Scene 4: Tragedy: War (plot 1 entangles plot 2)
Scene 5: Tragedy: War (plot 3 meets plots 1 & 2)
Scene 6: Tragedy: War (plot 3 entangles plots 1 & 2, death of Albanact)
Scene 7: Tragedy: War (plot 3 triumph of Humber)
Act 3: Scene 1, Prologue, Ate: mythic symbolism
Scene 2: Tragedy: (plot 1)
Scene 3: Tragedy: War and ghost of Albanact (plot 3)
Scene 4: Comedy: (plot 2: Strumbo and Margery)
Scene 5: Tragedy: War (plot 1)
Scene 6: Tragedy: War (plot 1 fights back against plot 3)
Scene 7: Tragedy: War (plot 3's disaster + ghost of Albanact)

Act 4: Scene 1, **Prologue**, Ate: mythic symbolism
Scene 2: Tragedy: (plot 1 meets plot 3 as Locrine falls in love with Estrild)
Scene 3: Tragedy and Comedy: (plot 3 meets plot 2: Humber and Strumbo)
Scene 4: Tragedy: (plot 1: love frustrated)
Scene 5: Tragedy: (plot 3: Humber's death)
Act 5: Scene 1, **Prologue**, Ate: mythic symbolism
Scene 2: Tragedy: (plot 1: Locrine and Estrild in conflict with Guendoline)
Scene 3: Tragedy: Civil War (plot 1, Guendoline's camp)
Scene 4: Tragedy: Civil War (plot 1, Locrine camp)
Scene 5: Tragedy: Civil War (plot 1: ghost of Corineius, deaths of Locrine, Estrild, Sabren; the triumph of Guendoline and Madan)
Epilogue: Ate links the play with contemporary politics.

Appendix 4:

THE VOCABULARY OF LOCRINE

Compound/Hyphenated words

Sams (1986, 353) has provided convincing evidence that the rich number of compound words in *Edmund Ironside* is an indicator of the bard's verbal creativity. In *Locrine* there are the following compound words:

battle-axe (x2), hard-hearted, blood-thirsty, love-pistle, sun-burnt, town-house, weather-beaten, foe-men's, lion-like, arm-strong, cods-head, Limbo-lake, scotch-cap, hunger-bitten (x2), sun-bright, water-flowing, pillow-bears, widow-hood, ferry-boat, blood-sucking: 20 words in total, half of which were later used by the bard. It is especially notable how many of these usages are in early plays.

battle-axe: *Titus Andronicus* (3.1.169)
hard-hearted: seven times in canonical plays, all before 1600: *Henry VI Part 3* (1.4.167); *Richard II* (5.3.85, 119); *A Midsummer Night's Dream* (2.1.195); *Much Ado About Nothing* (5.1.305); *Twelfth Night* (1.5.247); *Romeo and Juliet* (2.4.4); *Thomas of Woodstock* (5.4.39)
blood-thirsty: *Henry VI part 1* (2.3.33)
weather-beaten: *Henry IV part 1* (3.1.63)
sun-bright: *The Two Gentlemen of Verona*: (3.1. 88)
water-flowing: *Henry VI part 3* (4.8.43)
blood-sucking: *Henry VI part 3* (4.4.22)
widow-hood: appears without a hyphen in *The Taming of The Shrew* (2.1.124)
lion-like: appears without a hyphen in *Edward III* (3.5.29)
foe-men's: the singular 'foeman' without a hyphen is in *Henry VI part 3* (2.5.82)

I have also found the following words in *Locrine* which are not hyphenated but which later appear in Shakespeare's words with a hyphen: '**everduring**', '**lovesick**', '**deathlike**', '**overdaring**' and "**party colored**". The word '**everduring**' is used twice in *Locrine*, once of 'steel' and the second time of 'shame': both these words have special resonance for Neville, the ironworks owner who struggled with the shame of illegitimacy. In *The Rape of Lucrece* we find, rhyming with 'shame':

> Whose crime will bear an **ever-during** blame?
>
> (224)

Love-sick is used twice in *Venus and Adonis* (174; 328); in *Titus Andronicus* (5.3.81); and in *Anthony and Cleopatra* (2.2.201). Without a hyphen it is in *Arden of Faversham* (5.1.157), another play I suggest is an early work by Neville (see chapter 4).

In *Pericles* Antiochus says, "For **death-like** dragons here affright thee hard" (1.1.29).

In *The Troublesome Raigne* King Philip describes John as having "an **over-daring** spirit" (1.2.75). Later in the same text the word appears without a hyphen (1.8.5). In *Henry VI* part 1 Talbot is called 'over-daring' (4.4.5). '**Over-daring**' is in Marlowe's *Edward II* (1.4.47).

"**Parti-colour'd**" is used by Shylock in *The Merchant of Venice* (1.3.83).

'**Hunger-bitten**' occurs in *Arden of Faversham* (2.2.199). '**Hunger-starved**' occurs in *Henry VI* part 3 (1.4.5).

Neville used the words "**weather beaten**" (without a hyphen) in a diplomatic letter dated 1/12/1599 (Winwood, 1725, Vol 1, 135).

"A capcase full of new coined words" (1.3.96)

Strumbo uses a very rare word '**capcase**' in this phrase. The OED dates '**capcase**' to 1577 and defines it as a travelling bag or wallet. However the word was used in Thomas Preston's *Cambyses* (1569). '**Cap-case**' (hyphenated) is also used in *A Yorkshire Tragedy* (written 1606-8, the 1608 quarto identifies the author as W. Shakespeare: see chapter 6). Nashe used it in his 1592 *Pierce Penilesse* (961). Middleton used '**capcase**' in his 1622 play *The Changeling* (3.4.44).

There are 76 rare words in *Locrine* that are NOT in Shakespeare:

o'erlaid; annihilate; eame (= uncle); contributories; transfretting; laborious; column; sempiternal; inheritage; devolted; untamed; concordance; adversative; Antastick (=*Antartic*); **Constultations**; asward; love-pistle; fecundity; *enthronized*; topaz; **temperature**; contentation; pittering; burganet; nappy; buskins; capontail; pasteboard; cavalries; habitacles; overflowing; superbious; squadrants; checquered; brickbats; squeltring (in their blood; Greene has "weltering in their bloods" in *Orlando Furioso*); mungrel; weakened; agnominated; virent; saucebox; lobcock; slopsauce; lickfingers[51]; lackhonesty; nicebice; cods-head; drigle dragle; repercussion; furty; equalize; Troglodites; mavortial;

---

[51] In *Romeo and Juliet* two servants discuss cooks licking their fingers (4.2.4).

roseall; wily; ungratitude; unpunished; couragio; beknight; trumps; **inclos**ures; *brackish*; ophirs; pillow-bears; ninefold; fireforks; fleshhooks; hunger-bitten; macerate; prejudicating; arcane; frumps; overhastened; staileess; amours; overburthened.

Underlined words are used by Greene [9]. *Italic* words are used by Marlowe [2]. **Bold** words are used by Neville [5] in his letters. (Neville used '**inclosed**'. See below for another three rare words used by Neville. The OED lists 1588 as the date of the first usage of two of these words: 'saucebox' and 'drigle dragle'. (OED takes 1595, the publication date, as the date of *Locrine*.)

'Antastick' is obviously a pun on Antartic and fantastic. 'Antartic' is in *Dr. Faustus* (and also in Chaucer, OED); 'brackish' is in Marlowe's *Dido Queen of Carthage* and Peele's *Edward I*. Marlowe may have influenced the writer/s of *Locrine*: see Appendix 7. Indeed his use of these words may post-date *Locrine* if that play was written 1587-9. Greene used nine these rare words (OED), which argues further for his possible involvement in *Locrine*.

'Masserate' occurs in *The Troublesome Raigne* (1.143); the word is spelt 'macerate' in *Locrine*. 'Constultations' is obviously a joke word: bringing together 'consultations' and 'stultify', suggesting perhaps that Lactantius' writings were stultifying. Neville used the word 'consultation' in five diplomatic letters written in 1599, in his defence statement at his trial and again in a letter of 18/6/1613 (Winwood, 1725, Vol 1, 124, 302). 'Unpunished' was used by Alexander Neville in his translation of Seneca's *Oedipus* (Seneca, 11887, 77).

The annotator of Hall's *Chronicles* whom Keen & Lubbock (1954, 140) identified as Shakespeare, and James & Rubinstein (2005, 51) have shown was Neville, used the word 'coragiose'.

The OED lists *Locrine* as the first ever use of a number of these rare words: they are as Strumbo says, "new coined words": 'mavortial', 'squadrants', 'squeltering', 'agnominated', 'virent', 'slopsauce', 'nicebice'. The first OED listed use of 'venerian' is 1590: if the writing of *Locrine* (as opposed to its publication) predates this then this too is a word possibly coined by the author.

The following are not listed in the OED at all: 'strons', 'love-pistle' and 'capontail'. If 'strons' is a printer's misreading of 'strands' (= beaches), which the context suggests, then this word was used by Shakespeare in *The Taming of the Shrew* ('strand': 1.1.170).

'Transfretting', 'fecundity' and 'ungratitude' occur in Hall's Chronicles (1548); 'sempiternal' and 'overburthened' are used in North's *Plutarch* (1579). We have already seen that the word 'depopulate' is to be found in both these sources. 'Burgonet' and 'frumping' are used by Holinshed. 'Prejudicating' is used by Sidney in his *Apologie for Poesie* and *Arcadia* (OED). 'Asward', believed by Gooch (1981, 58) to be 'arseward' (= backwards), occurs in Golding's 1565 translation of Ovid's *Metamorphoses* (see OED, where it is spelt 'arsward'). North, Hall, Sidney and Golding were all sources for Shakespeare.

The following words do not occur in Shakespeare but the word in brackets is used in the canon, the number of times is in square brackets. Words used by Neville in his letters and Tower notebook are in bold.

> strons (strond/strand [5]); *argent* (**argentine** [1]); yelled (yell [1]); quelled (quell [6]); clove (cloven [6]); spoused (espoused [4]); constraining (constrain [1]); cobblers (cobbler [2]); resolutions (resolution [31]); buckingtubs (bucking [1]); **imboldened** (emboldens[1]); **insolency** (insolent [9]); shriking (shrikes [1]); thronged (throng [16]); scorching (scorched [1], scorch [3]); treacheries (treachery [24]); humid (humidity [2]); blissful (bliss [22]); furiously (furious [15]); glistereth (glisters [2]), *overmatched* (o'ermatch'd [2]; over-matching [1]; matched [3]); venerian (venereal [1]); interlast (interlaces [1]); *adamantine* (adamant [3]).

'Overmatched' occurs in *Tamburlaine* II (3.5.76); 'o'ermatch' is in *Edmund Ironside* (944); 'o'ermatch'd' is in *Henry VI part 1* (4.4.11) and in *Henry VI part 3* (1.4.64). 'Overmatch' is to be found in *The Troublesome Raigne* (part 1, 8.6). 'Venerian' is not in the canon but 'venery' is in *The Troublesome Raigne* (part 1, 6.55). 'Venereal' occurs in *Titus Andronicus* (2.2.37).

'Un'- words used in *Locrine*

A number of scholars have noted that Shakespeare uses a high number of word beginning with 'un'. Indeed this has come to be regarded as evidence of his authorship (Sams. 1985, 350). 'Un'- words do not include "unto, unless, undermine": 'un'- words are negatives and the 'un' could be substituted by a 'not' such as ungrateful = not grateful or undone = not done. The number of such words in *Locrine* is almost exactly on the average for early plays (see below) and many of these words are used in plays I have come to regard as early works by Shakespeare-Neville. As *Edward III* has recently been admitted to the canon I have also noted the incidence of such words in that play. When a word has been used more than once I have listed the number in round brackets (x2). The number in square brackets [4] is the number of times the word is used in the established Shakespearean canon. I have stipulated the occurrence of these words in the early plays by Shakespeare.

Unworthy [36] used in *Mucedorus*; *Troublesome Raigne*; *Henry VI* parts1 and 2 and *Richard III*; *The Two Gentlemen of Verona*; *Taming of The Shrew*

Unpartial [1]   *Henry VIII*

Unfold (x2) [33] in *Mucedorus*; *Edmund Ironside*

Unhappy [41] in *Edmund Ironside*; *Troublesome Raigne*; *Arden of Faversham*; *Edward III*; *Thomas of Woodstock*; *Richard III*; *The Two Gentlemen of Verona*; *Taming of The Shrew*

Untamed [0] in *Edward III*

Untimely (x2) [24] in *Troublesome Raigne*; *Edward III*; *Henry VI* part 3; *Richard III*

Unmoveable [0] (immovable used in *Edmund Ironside*; unmoved in *Thomas of Woodstock* and *Richard III*; unmov'd in *The Comedy of Errors*)

Uncouth (x2) [3] *Titus Andronicus*

Unexpected [2] in *Troublesome Raigne*

Unsheath (x3) [3] in *The Troublesome Raigne*; *Henry VI* part 3

Unstable (x2) [1] *Coriolanus*

Unwieldy [3] in *Edmund Ironside*

Undone [51] in *The Troublesome Raigne*; *Edward III*; *Arden of Faversham*; *Henry VI* part 3; *Thomas of Woodstock*; *The Two Gentlemen of Verona*; *Taming of The Shrew*

Unreverent [3] in *The Troublesome Raigne*; *Henry VI* part 1; *Taming of The Shrew*

Ungratitude [0] (ungrateful used in *Edmund Ironside* and 7 times in the canon)

Unpunished (x2) [0] in *Edmund Ironside*

Unbind [2] *Taming of The Shrew*

Uncivil [8] in *Edmund Ironside*; *Edward III*; *The Two Gentlemen of Verona*

Unwonted [2] in *Arden of Faversham*

Unkind (x3) [29] in *Edmund Ironside*; *Arden of Faversham*, *Henry VI* parts1 and 2; *The Two Gentlemen of Verona*; *Taming of The Shrew*

Uncalled [0]

Uncontented [0] (uncontent used in *The Troublesome Raigne*)

Thus 22 words beginning with 'un' are used 30 times in *Locrine*. Sams (1986, 351) stated that the average was 40 occurrences in each

Shakespeare play. In this inter-textual study it is very interesting to note that *The Troublesome Raigne* has the highest score of these *Locrine* words: 9 are used and, if we count 'uncontent' for 'uncontented', and were to add 'unkindly' for 'unkind' this score would be 11. I am convinced that *The Troublesome Raigne* is an early work by Shakespeare-Neville. I believe *Edward III* and *Edmund Ironside* are also by him and these both score 6 on the above list but in fact their total scores for 'un' words are remarkably similar and may even provide evidence of the order in which these plays were written. For example, I may have been wrong in originally dating *Arden of Faversham* to 1589-90: looking at the scores of 'un' words it may have been written earlier, even before *Locrine*.

Play:	Number of 'un' words:	Number of times used:	Date:
Mucedorus	15	22	1585
Arden of Faversham	18	23	1586-90
Locrine	22	30	1587-8
Edmund Ironside	37	40	1588
Troublesome Raigne	33	38	1588-89
Edward III	34	40	1589-90
Average:	22.8	26.5	

Startlingly *Locrine* is closest to the average (-0.8 and +3.5), with *Arden of Faversham* next (-4.8 and −3.5). Let us compare these scores of words beginning with 'un' in the earliest plays traditionally accepted as by Shakespeare:

Taming of The Shrew	28	30	1589-91
Henry VI part 1	26	30	1590
Henry VI part 2	33	41	1591-2?
Henry VI part 3	35	44	1591-2?
Titus Andronicus	30	36	1592
Two Gent of Verona	35	43	1592-3
Total Average:	31.1	37.3	

Adding both sets of averages together to get an overall total, we get:
Total Average:　　　**26.9**　　　　**31.9**

Thus it appears that *Henry VI* part 1 is closest to the overall average (+0.9 and -1.9); *The Taming of The Shrew* second (+1.1 and −1.9); *Locrine* is third (-4.9 and − 1.9); *Titus Andronicus* fourth (+ 3.1 and + 4.1). If we add these scores together we get *Locrine* (- 6.8) and *Titus Andronicus* (+ 7.2) thus showing *Locrine* is nearer the average. We can note furthermore that *Locrine* shares with *Henry VI* part 1 and *The Taming of The Shrew* the same total score of the number of words beginning with 'un': 30, and so this play reveals a finger print of Shakespeare's authorship on this measure alone.

'Unpunished' occurs in *Edmund Ironside* which Sams dates to 1588; it also is in *Locrine* which I have dated to 1587; Greene used 'unpunished' in *Alphonsus of Arragon* (3.2.134) which has been dated 1587-8. 'Unmovable' was used in Hall's *Chronicles* (OED) one of Shakespeare's sources; it was used by John Lyly in his 1591 play *Endimion* and by Francis Bacon's in his 1605 *Advancement of Learning*. Taking the rarest of the above 'un' words in *Locrine* we can see that they occur in:

Unpartial *Henry VIII* (2.2.105)
Uncouth *Titus Andronicus* (2.2.211); *Rape of Lucrece* (1598); *As You Like It* (2.6.6)
Unexpected *King John* (2.1.80; 5.7.64)
Unsheath *Henry VI* part 3, as unsheathe, (2.2.29, 80, 123)
Unstable *Coriolanus* (3.1.130)
Unwieldy *Romeo & Juliet* (2.5. 17); *Richard II* (3.2.115; 4.1.205)
Unreverent *Henry VI* part 1 (3.1.49); *Taming of the Shrew* (3.2.110); *Richard II* (2.1.123); unreverend occurs in *The Two Gentlemen of Verona* (2.6.14)
Unbind *Titus Andronicus* (3.1.24); *Taming of the Shrew* (2.1.4);
Unwonted *Measure for Measure* (4.2.99); *Tempest* (1.2.500)

From this distribution it can be seen that, whilst some words are used across the whole canon the majority of these words are in early works from the period 1590-96. However we should not take this as proof of authorship alone without other evidence, because the play *The Misfortunes of Arthur* by Thomas Hughes (et al. including the young Francis Bacon) which dates from exactly the same time, 1587, has 38 'un' words used 58 times (including 6 of the 'un' words that occur in *Locrine*): more than any of the above plays from the early period by Shakespeare! Did Neville contribute to that play whilst keeping his collaboration secret?

Appendix 5:

CLASSICAL REFERENCES IN *LOCRINE*

Locrine is packed with numerous references to classical mythology. In the following lists those in bold occur in Shakespeare's writings; those underlined are mentioned by Greene. When used by Peele I have put the deity in italics, such as *Ate*. I have used the following notations to denote other occasions when a deity is referred to: * in *Edmund Ironside*; # in *Edward III*; + in *The Troublesome Raigne*; (all of these texts I accept are by Shakespeare-Neville); ^ in Kyd's *Spanish Tragedy*.

In both Shakespeare and Greene:
<u>*Ate*</u>, <u>**Jove**</u>, **Cerberus***^, **Hercules**, *Pluto*^, **Jupiter**, *Mars**^, **Titan**, **Hector**^, **Mercury**, **Olympus**, **Minerva**, *Flora*^, *Phoebus*^, **Orpheus**^, **Troy***, **Hecuba***, ***Thetis***^, **Anthrophagie**, **Limbo**, *Cupid*^, *Venus*^, **Ceres**, *Styx*^, <u>**Medea**</u>, **Hecate**, *<u>Nemesis</u>*^, *<u>Achilles</u>*^, **Pallas**^, **Charon**^, <u>**Satyrs**</u>, <u>**Semiramis**</u>, *Aurora**, *Cyclops**, **Bellona**#^.

In Shakespeare and Peele:
Icarus, *Erebus*^, **Tantalus**, *Minos*^, **Perseus**, **Amazon**, **Troilus**, **Priam**, **Briareus**, **Hydra**, ***The Mermidons***^, **Ilium**, **Pirrhus**, **Niobe**, **Furies**^, **Acheron**^, **Diomedes**, **Simois**, *Alecto*+, **Mors**+, *Elysian* **fields**^ .

In Greene and Peele:
<u>Demagorgon</u>, *Phlegethon*^ (spelt Puryflegiton in *Locrine*), *<u>Ixion</u>*^, <u>Dryads</u>, <u>Atropos</u>. *<u>Tisiphone</u>*, <u>Avernus</u>^.

Tisiphone is mentioned by Alice in *Arden of Faversham* (5.1.151): a play I have suggested is an early work by Neville (see chapter 4).

In neither canonical Shakespeare nor Greene:
Bellerophon, Hebe, *Aeacus*^, Rhodomanth/*Radamanth*^, Eurydice, Pelops, Tithonus, Lacantius, Andromeda, Cepheus, Phineus, Rhamnis, Penthisilea, Policrates, Monichus, Eurus, Chimera^, Amphion, Pergamus^, Cocitus, Errinis Polyphemus, Omphale, Fames, Triptolemus, *Sisiphus*^, Taenarus, Jason, Creon, *Titius*^.

Whilst Tartarus is not canonical, "deepe Tartary" is mentioned in *The Troublesome Raigne*; and 'Tartar' is in *The Comedy of Errors* (4.2.32). Rhadamanth is mentioned in *Thomas of Woodstock* (see chapter 5: 1.2.33). Thus of the classical references in *Locrine*, 31 occur in *The Spanish Tragedie*; 42 in Greene's plays; 57 in canonical works by Shakespeare.

These latter references are mostly obscure to us now. We might wonder if they come from Tilney's hypothetical original play, or alternatively the young Neville perhaps wanted to show off his classical learning in this, his first tragedy. In 1583 Richard Eedes described Neville, aged about 21, as "distinguished for his book-learning" (James & Rubinstein, 2005, 83). Amongst the classical references in *Locrine* are elements of a mythic complex which did interest the young Shakespeare-Neville: a trio of myths of Icarus-Bellerophon/Pegasus-Phaeton. All three are about ambitious young men (with wings/horses) flying into the sky. I have already written about the Phaeton myth in chapter 1. In *Locrine* Assarachus, speaking to the dying Brutus in the first scene says:

> Alas, my Lord, we sorrow at your case,
> And grieve to see your person vexed thus;
> But what so ere the fates determined have,
> It lieth not in us to disannul,
> And he that would annihilate his mind,
> Soaring with **Icarus** too near the sun,
> May catch a fall with young **Bellerophon**.
>
> (1.2.31)

In his early play *Henry VI*, part 1, Talbot twice refers to his doomed son as **Icarus** (4.6.55; 4.7.16). Cairncross (1965, 103) names Ovid's *Metamorphoses* as Shakespeare's source. In *Henry VI*, part 3 (in which the Phaeton myth is also used), King Henry says:

> I, Daedalus; my poor boy, **Icarus**;
> Thy father, **Minos**, that denied our course;
> The sun that sear'd the wings of my sweet boy
> Thy brother Edward, and thyself the **sea**
> Whose **envious gulf** did swallow up his life.
>
> (5.6.21)

In *Locrine* Brutus speaks of, "the **greedy gulf** of **Ocean**" (1.1.3) and **Minos** is mentioned (1.2.251). Thus we can see that similar mythic ideas, images and words are used by the playwright of *Henry VI*, part 3 and *Locrine*. In *The Troublesome Raigne of John King of England* (written before 1591, in which the Phaeton image is used) we have: " thy mother makes thee wings to soar with peril after **Icarus**…" (part 1, 2.8). Whilst Shakespeare does not mention Bellerophon he does refer to Pegasus and a proud young man: in *Henry IV* part 1, Vernon says:

> I saw young Harry…
> Rise from the ground like feather'd Mercury,
> And vaulted with such ease into his seat,
> As if an angel dropp'd down from the clouds,
> To turn and wind a fiery **Pegasus**
> And witch the world with noble horsemanship.
>
> (4.1.104)

Another proud young man, the Dauphin, uses the **Pegasus** myth in reference to his own horse in *Henry V* (3.7.14).

Furthermore another mythic figure appears in *Locrine* connected, like Phaeton, with the chariot of the sun:

> When as the morning shows his cheerful face,
> And **Lucifer**, mounted upon his steed,
> Brings in the chariot of the golden sun...

> (2.2.81)

Greene in *Friar Bacon and Friar Bungay* wrote: "For when proud Lucifer fell from the heavens..." (3.2.58). In *Henry VIII* Wolsey reveals the political meaning of this mythic Phaeton-Icarus-Lucifer image:

> O, how wretched
> Is that poor man that hangs on princes' favours!
> There is, betwixt that smile we would aspire to,
> That sweet aspect of princes, and their ruin,
> More pangs and fears than wars or women have:
> And when he falls, he falls like **Lucifer**,
> Never to hope again.

> (3.2.367)

Neville lived in Wolsey's palace at Ashurst so he had reason to contemplate that proud man's downfall. Neville himself fell at the height of his own political career. (See chapter 6 for further reflections on the above passage.)

(In the following paragraph I have put in bold the mythic figures mentioned in *Locrine*.)

Bellerophon was the grandson of **Sisiphus**, (who for his crimes had been sent to **Tartarus**). **Bellerophon** was sent on a mission to kill the fire-breathing **Chimera**. He flew to confront this monster on the winged horse Pegasus. He lodged a lump of lead in the Chimera's throat and when it melted in the flames the monster suffocated. **Bellerophon** returned in triumph, but his hubris led him to fly up to **Olympus**, the home of the gods. Zeus (**Jupiter**) sent a fly to bite Pegasus: the horse shied and **Bellerophon** fell back to earth. The **Chimera** had a sister, **Hydra** and a brother, **Cerberus**, the three headed dog guarding hell. In *Titus Andronicus* Marcus refers to **Cerberus** being charmed into sleep by **Orpheus** who is called "the **Thracian** poet" (2.3.51). Locrine evokes "**Thracian Orpheus**" (3.2.5). Hubba brags:

> Were they **enchanted** in grim Pluto's court,
> And kept for treasure mongst his hellish crew,
> I would either quell the triple **Cerberus**

(3.3.43)

In composing a flattering letter Edricus, in *Edmund Ironside*, wishes his "pen would have distilled golden drops and varied terms **enchanting Cerberus**" (3.5.151). Sams (1986, 205) pointed out that the source for this myth is Ovid's *Metamorphoses*. "Triple **Cerberus**" is mentioned three times in *Locrine*. **Cerberus** is referred to by Holofernes as "that three headed canis" in *Love's Labour's Lost* (5.2.583).

Appendix 6:

LOCRINE ACT 1, SCENE 3: STRUMBO'S SPEECH

The house of Strumbo.
Enter Strumbo above in a gown, with ink and paper in his hand, saying:

Either the four elements, the seven planets, and all the particular stars of the pole Antastick, are adversative against me, or else I was begotten and born in the wane of the Moon, when every thing as Lactantius in his fourth book of Constultations doth say, goeth asward. Aye, masters, aye, you may laugh, but I must weep; you may joy, but I must sorrow; shedding salt tears from the watery fountains of my most dainty fair eyes, along my comely and smooth cheeks, in as great plenty as the water runneth from the buckingtubs, or red wine out of the hogs heads: for trust me, gentlemen and my very good friends, and so forth, the little god, nay the desparate god Cuprit, with one of his vengible birdbolts, hath shot me unto the heel: so not only, but also, oh fine phrase, I burn, I burn, and I burn a, in love, in love, and in love a. Ah, Strumbo, what hast thou seen? Not Dina with the Ass Tom? Yea, with these eyes thou hast seen her, and therefore pull them out, for they will work thy bale. Ah, Strumbo, hast thou heard? not the voice of the Nightingale, but a voice sweeter than hers. Yea, with these ears hast thou heard it, and therefore cut them off, for they have caused thy sorrow. Nay, Strumbo, kill thy self, drown thy self, hang thy self, starve thy self. Oh, but then I shall leave my sweet heart. Oh my heart! Now, pate, for thy master! I will dite an aliquant love-pistle to her, and then she hearing the grand verbosity of my scripture, will love me presently. [Let him write a little and then read.]
My pen is naught; gentlemen, lend me a knife. I think the more haste the worst speed. [Then write again, and after read.]
So it is, mistress Dorothy, and the sole essence of my soul, that the little sparkles of affection kindled in me towards your sweet self hath now increased to a great flame, and will ere it be long consume my poor heart, except you, with the pleasant water of your secret fountain, quench the furious heat of the same. Alas, I am a gentleman of good fame and name, majestical, in parrel comely, in gate portly. Let not therefore your gentle heart be so hard as to despise a proper tall, young man of a handsome life, and by despising him, not only, but also to kill him. Thus expecting time and tide, I bid you farewell. Your servant, Signior Strumbo.
Oh wit! Oh pate! O memory! O hand! O ink! O paper! Well, now I will send it away.

Appendix 7:

KYD, MARLOWE, GREENE, PEELE, SPENSER, LODGE AND *LOCRINE*: INFLUENCES OR CO-AUTHORS?

In examining the text of *Locrine* I was presented with a puzzle as to who might be influences and who might be co-authors. I present here what I have found as a basis for further research.

Kyd and *Locrine*

The Spanish Tragedie and *Locrine* share many things. Both are revenge tragedies influenced by the Latin playwright Seneca. Both have ghosts which call for revenge and a personified figure of Revenge as a Chorus. *Locrine* resembles *The Spanish Tragedie* in the constant appeal to, or tirade against, Fortune and in the countless references to the horrors of the classic underworld, with its three judges, Minos, Aeacus and Rhadamanth. Both have Latin verses. In *The Spanish Tragedie,* Horatio and Lorenzo strive against each other for the possession of the captured prince of Portugal; in *Locrine,* two soldiers dispute over the captured Estrild. The outraged Hieronimo's appeal to nature to sympathise with him in his sorrow is echoed in the speech of the ghost of Corineus.[52] None of this proves Kyd was the author: just that the author was influenced by Kyd, which is certainly true of Shakespeare. *The Spanish Tragedie* was probably written between 1585-7 and so, in my dating of *Locrine,* pre-dates the latter (*The Spanish Tragedie* was published in 1592). Lucas (1972, 116) however stated that *Locrine* was much more Senecan than *The Spanish Tragedie* and *Titus Andronicus* was more Senecan than any other play of the time.

Marlowe and *Locrine*

Marlowe's *Tamburlaine* also influenced the play. In *Locrine* Humber, the invader, says he will teach the English, "that the Scithian Emperor leads Fortune tied in a chain of gold" (2.2.14). This seems an echo of Tamburlaine when he brags that he has "the fates bound fast in iron chains, and with my hand turn Fortune's wheel" (1.2.174). Tamburlaine was a Scythian Emperor; Humber is King of the Scythians. Furthermore in *Tamburlaine* part II the King, like Brutus in *Locrine*, crowns his son on his deathbed.

---

[52] From: http://www.bartleby.com/215/1002.html [Accessed 2008]

Greene and *Locrine*

In 1592-3 there were six performances of *A Knack to Know A Knave* at the Rose (beginning June 10th 1592) recorded in Henslowe's diary. It was printed in 1594. It contains a passage about Locrine:

> For Locrin being the eldest sonne of Brute,
> Did dote so far upon an **Almaine** maid,
> And was so ravisht with her pleasing sight,
> That full seven years he kept her under earth,
> Even in the lifetime of faire Guendolin:
> Which made the Cornish men to rise in armes,
> And never left till Locrin was slain...

This then was printed the year before *Locrine* was published and probably written about 1591-2, possibly by Robert Greene who died in 1592 (September 3rd): it was certainly influenced by his earlier writings. Arthur Freeman (1962, 326-27) ascribed the authorship to Greene and Thomas Nashe. If it does refer to *Locrine*, and not a chronicle source, then *Locrine* was probably written before 1591. What the reference to 'Locrin' in *A Knack to Know A Knave* tells us is that the writer did not recall the name 'Estrild' (calling her just "an Almaine maid"). This suggests the source could be the play *Locrine* rather than any Tilney play called *Estrild*. Geoffrey of Monmouth refers to 'Estrildis' as **German** so his account may be the source of the *Knack to Know* passage which refers to her as "an **Almaine** maid" (Thorpe, 1966, 76). In *Locrine* Estrild is called "the Scithian queen" (4.2.76).

However as he died in 1592 and *Locrine* was not printed until after his death, if Greene was referring to that play it must have been performed or he had access to a manuscript copy, or indeed he had been involved in writing it. If he had access to a manuscript he would have been more likely to remember, or simply look up, the name so perhaps this is evidence of him imperfectly remembering the story from seeing a performance, unless he was just using a poetic sobriquet.

In *Locrine* the King keeps Estrild hidden underground: the text includes the words "underneath the ground..." (4.4.22), "seven years" (4.4.1) and 'earth' (4.4.9). So we can see how Greene might have rendered this as: "That full seven years he kept her under earth..." It seems however more like a memory of the gist of the text heard in performance than a quotation from a manuscript. This reference then to *Locrine* in *A Knack to Know A Knave* might give us help with the dating of the play: it could have been in performance in 1591 or earlier.

Some have credited Greene with the authorship of at least parts of *Locrine*. (If this were the case it is little wonder that he referred to it in *A Knack to Know A Knave* if indeed he was part-author of the latter.)

The evidence comes in the vocabulary used. "In flashes of poetry, in classical allusion, in high-sounding phrases, the play is sometimes astonishingly in the temper of *Orlando Furioso* and *Alfonsus of Arragon*." (Dickinson, 1909, lv). Dickinson lists words and phases that occur in *Locrine* as characteristic of Greene such as: "parti-coloured flowers", "shady groves", "silver streams", 'straggling' and "rascal runnagates". However these words were used by other authors: Peele in *The Arraignment of Paris* (1584, earlier than all these plays) uses "parti-coloured flowers" (1.1.54); "parti-colour'd" is also used in *The Merchant of Venice* (1.3.83). Marlowe has "straggling runagates" in *Tamburlaine 1*, 3.3.57; Shakespeare uses 'runagate/s' three times in *Cymbeline* (1.6.137, 4.2.64 & 65), a play I will later link with *Locrine*: just 18 lines after the last of these is the word 'rascal' (4.2.83). In *Richard III* there are "rascals and runaways" (5.5.45). The writer of *Locrine* loved the words "silver streams", using them 4 times: Shakespeare used the words "silver stream" once in *Much Ado About Nothing* (3.1.27) and in *Richard II* we have "silver rivers" (3.2.107), "silver fountain" (5.3.59) and the words 'silver' and 'stream' in adjacent lines in (5.3.59-60).

In Greene's *Orlando Furioso* we find: "**I'll pass the Alps**, and up **to Meroe**...that **watery** lakish hill..." (4.2.13). In *Locrine* Albanact says, "**I'll pass the Alps** to **watery Meroe**..." (2.6.48). At first this would seem to be conclusive (certainly if *Orlando Furioso* had been written before *Locrine*), however we must be cautious. If *Locrine* was written first (and it may date back as far as 1585) then we might note that Greene is an inaccurate copyist: **Meroe** is on the Nile delta and cannot be called a "watery **hill**". It is possible that Greene, if he was plagiarising, was confused by the reference to the Alps. It is Greene who uses the word '**up**' here, as if the person were climbing the Alps **up** to Meroe. However the fact that the speaker is Orlando, who is mad, may suggest an element of extravagant parody in deliberately getting the geography wrong, rather than an error[53]. Greene has transposed the word '**watery**' from 'Meroe' to "lakish hill": Shakespeare never uses '**watery**' in relation to a hill, nor does he use the word 'lakish'. All this points to Greene being the borrower. '**Watery**' is used six times in *Locrine* and 23 times in Shakespeare's canonical works. Of the uses in *Locrine* two refer to eyes and one to the sea. Of the Shakespeare usages, five refer to eye/s and eight directly or indirectly to the sea. '**Watery**' is used of eyes in *Edward III* (16.153). "**Watery** eyes" occur

---

[53] Brenda James however suggested that these could be the Abyssinian Alps as the plot involves Charlemagne in a war with Agramante, King of Africa, and referred me to Bell (1827, 287: personal communication 12/7/08).

in Peele's *Battle of Alcazar* (1.1.16). 'Watery' is used by Alice in *Arden of Faversham*, referring to the Goddess Diana's bower (5.1.157). As Diana was a moon goddess it is interesting to note that four of the canonical references are to the moon (which in governing the tides can be seen to link back to the sea). Greene also used '**watery**' in *Alfonsus of Arragon* (2.1.44: of the sea); in *Orlando Furioso* (4.1.7, again of the sea, just one scene before the "watery lakish hill") and in *A Looking Glass for London* (5.3.5) but none of these are in relation to eyes. In the novel *Pandosto* Greene did write of the king bewailing his misfortune with "watery plaints" (Orgel, 1996, 249).

Greene's *Pandosto* possibly provides us with a significant text here as it was published in 1588. We cannot be sure when Greene wrote his plays: the earliest recorded performances were in 1591-2 (in Henslowe's Diary). We do know Greene was writing prose works from 1580 and published several in the period 1588-9. Allowing perhaps a year between the writing and performance, the plays might have been written from 1590 and so if my dating of *Locrine* is accurate either Greene copied the vocabulary or was involved in a revision of the play at some time. In *Pandosto* I have found the following words that echo the vocabulary of *Locrine*: 'frowns', 'falsehood', 'cedars', 'sore', 'ghastly', 'brutish', 'bewail', 'amours', 'cockatrice', 'dainty', 'opportunity', 'pretence', 'mishap', 'plague': but being common words these hardly amount to evidence of authorship. The dominant Goddess of *Pandosto* is Fortune who is named 15 times in *Locrine*. In *Pandosto* Greene writes 'straggled', in *Locrine* 'straggling' occurs six times. Furthermore in *Pandosto* we have a wife confronting a husband about his fidelity: "his wife...began to crow against her Goodman, and taking up a **cudgel**... sware solemnly that she would make **clubs trumps**..." In *Locrine* Strumbo tells us how, "at night I came home... my wife ... snatched up a **faggot stick** in her hand, and came furiously marching towards me... thundering out these words unto me: Thou drunken knave, where hast thou been so long? I shall teach thee how to beknight me an other time; and so she began to play **knaves' trumps**" (4.3.28-40).

Perhaps the similarities are simply commonplace and coincidence: there are actually more differences between *Pandosto* and *Locrine* than similarities. Two favourite Greene words, 'brat' and 'dump', that are in *Pandosto* and in his plays, are not in *Locrine*. *Pandosto*, of course, was the source of *The Winter's Tale*: the word 'brat' occuring twice in that play (2.3.92; 3.2.85). 'Brat' is used in *Edmund Ironside* (1.1.236), in *Henry VI* part 1 (5.4.84), twice in *Henry VI* part 3 (1.3.4 and 5.5.27) and in *Titus Andronicus* (5.1.28); 'brats' in *Richard III* (3.5.102). In other words Shakespeare-Neville was perfectly capable of using any vocabulary used by Greene, before or after Greene employed the word!

We must however consider the possibility that Greene had a hand in *Locrine*. Thomas Creede, who printed *Locrine*, also printed three of Greene's plays. Brenda James has wondered whether Greene was the unnamed 'man' Neville had with him on his continental journey (1578 - 83) because these are the very same years Greene was away on the continent. Greene would have had to obtain a passport, and as he was not rich, it is likely he tagged along with a rich traveller in just such a way as the 'man' connected with Neville. Dickinson (1909, xxv) stated that Greene "took his bachelor's degree in 1578 and thereafter toured the continent, probably after the 3rd of October 1580, at which date the first part of *Mamillia* was registered; that returning he took his M.A. at Clare Hall (Cambridge) in 1583." Neville left England in 1578 and returned in 1583. We do not know if they ever met or travelled together.

Robert Greene's earliest plays were *Alphonsus King of Arragon*, *Orlando Furioso* and (with Thomas Lodge) *A Looking Glass for London*: these were possibly written between 1587-90 (printed 1594-99). Thus if the date I suggest for *Locrine*, 1587-9 is accurate then Greene had only just turned his hand to playwriting. *The Tragical Reign of Selimus* (attributed to Greene, written between 1588 -1592 and printed in 1594) plagiarizes *Locrine* (rather than the other way round). Some of its verses reappear almost unchanged in *Selimus*. If he had been involved in writing both plays this could explain Greene's borrowings from *Locrine*, though of course one can borrow without ever having been involved in composing the original. That Greene might assist with a play by other writer(s) at that time was not unusual. It is clear that he did not write the whole of *Locrine*, as the over all writing is quite different from his other extant plays. Greene may have been the reviser of *Locrine*, although this contradicts the title page's ascription of the revision to W.S.. The alternative is that Shakespeare-Neville was the sole author and Greene copied phrases and words from him. There is evidence of at least a two way relationship between these writers, each borrowing from the other and possibly co-authoring.

Gaud (1904) however demolished the case for Greene's authorship of *Locrine*. He did this by analysing the language, especially redundant prepositions such as "that if", "as that", "for to", etc. "The totals are striking. Of the expressions noted, 11 instances are found in Peele, 6 in *Locrine*, and 160 in Greene" (Gaud, 1904, 3). He found vocabulary and imagery in the plays of George Peele and in *Locrine* that did not occur in Greene's plays. Gaud made a case for Peele being the author of *Locrine*.

Peele and *Locrine*

Peele's first extant play, *The Arraignment of Paris*, which may have been written as early as 1581, was printed in 1584 so we can be confident it was written before *Locrine*. The play is opened by Ate: the same infernal goddess who introduces each act of *Locrine*. There are words that the writer of *Locrine* may have picked from this text such as 'guerdon', "parti-coloured flowers", "burnished gold", 'dazzled', 'unpartial', 'uncouth', 'unworthy', 'shady' and 'luckless'. Peele's *The Battle of Alcazar* was a possible source for *Locrine* but with the uncertainty about the dating of all these texts it is difficult to know for sure which way the influence is flowing. *The Battle of Alcazar* was written after *Tamburlaine* as it refers to him, so we can be sure it was written between 1588-90. *The Battle of Alcazar* was printed in 1594, the year before *Locrine*. It is possible therefore that either play could be a source for the other.

In *Locrine* Humber orders his son:

> Hubba, go **take a coronet of our horse**,
> **As many** lancers, **and** light **armed** knights

(2.5.1)

In Peele's play *The Battle of Alcazar* (Bullen, 1888, 235) the Moor orders his captain:

> Pisano, **take a cornet of our horse**,
> **As many** argolets **and armed** pikes...

(1.2.1)

After his defeat in *The Battle of Alcazar* the Moor asks:

> Where shall I find some unfrequented place,
> Some uncouth walk, **where I may curse** my fill,
> My stars, my dam, my planets, and my nurse,
> **The fire, the air,** the water, and **the earth**...
> All causes that have thus conspired in one,
> To nourish and preserve me to this shame?

(5.1.74)

After his defeat by Locrine, Humber seems to recall the Moor's speech:

> Where may I find some desert wilderness,
> **Where I may** breath out **curses** as I would,
> And scare **the earth** with my condemning voice;
> Where every echoes repercussion
> May help me to bewail mine overthrow,
> And aide me in my sorrowful laments?
> Where may I find some hollow uncoth rock,
> Where I may damn, condemn, and ban my fill
> The heavens, the hell, the earth, the air, the fire,
> And utter curses to the concave sky...

(3.7.1)

What this reveals is that whilst the writer of *Locrine* has perhaps taken ideas from Peele he has improved on the speech. He also repeats the word 'where' five times (see chaper 3 for the use of rhethorical repetition in the play). Having read Peele's plays I am not impressed by the suggestion that he was the author of *Locrine*. The playwright who wrote *Locrine* used many more rhetorical devices. Indeed Gaud's analysis of vocabulary reveals the scores for *Locrine* are different to those of Peele's plays: in the prepositions listed by Gaud (1904, 4) those used in *Locrine* are not used by Peele (except for 'whereas'). I also note that Peele generally uses few of the Phaeton sonnet words (see chapter 2, Appendices 1 and 2). His *Edward I* (printed in 1593, after the Phaeton sonnet and before *Locrine*) has the largest number, yet only one of the five particularly rare words, whereas *Locrine* has three, and those are words that are used more often by Shakespeare (see Appendix 1). I have also looked at the imagery used in *Locrine* and found it is Shakespearean (see chapter 3). Whilst Gaud listed twelve passages scattered amongst Peele's works that are parallels to passages in *Locrine* there are far more parallels in the works of Shakespeare. From my study of the texts it seems Peele may have influenced Shakespeare-Neville and/or vice versa. I suggested in chapter 2 that Peele was copying *Mucedorus* in his *Old Wives' Tale*: so it is possible the influence was two way. Scattered amongst Peele's plays there are a number of rare words which occur in *Locrine* including: 'scoured', 'unsheathed', 'untamed', 'untimely', 'unwieldy', 'enthronised', 'princox', 'pigsney', 'runagate', 'adamant', 'lukewarm'.

Peele was at Oxford from 1571, gaining his BA in 1577, his MA in 1579: Neville was at Merton College, Oxford in 1574-8. We do not know if they ever met but it is certainly possible. Peele provided a comedy, *The Rivals*, and a tragedy, *Dido* (both in Latin) for the June 1583 visit of Albert Laski, a Polish Prince, to Oxford University: an occasion when Giordano Bruno and Sir Philip Sidney were present. Neville had arrived back from his continental travels in 1583, which had included a visit to Poland. We do not know if Neville was in Oxford in June but he was in England.

Spenser and *Locrine*

Previous scholars have suggested a relationship between *Locrine* and Spenser's *Faerie Queene*. However the first three books were published in 1590, probably after a first version of *Locrine* was written. The section on Locrine in *The Faerie Queene* (Book 2, Canto X, Stanza 13) is brief and does not mention that Locrine kept Estrild underground.

Indeed Spenser only mentions Estrild once and does not make any link between her and Humber (in this he is following the sources). In Book 5, published only in 1595, Spenser tells the story of the trial of Mary Queen of Scots and does so using the mythical figure of Ate (Book 5, Canto IX, Stanza XLVII): Spenser makes no connection between this section and the earlier Locrine story. It is possible he was influenced in his turn by the play. However this could all simply be coincidence as Spenser was in Ireland 1579-89 and so could only have seen the play when he returned to England in 1589, when he had already written the section that mentions Locrine. Alternatively the writer of *Locrine* may have had access to manuscript copies of Spenser's works. Spenser used the names Trompart and Debon in Books 2 & 3; these names occur in *Locrine*. Debon does not appear in any other source (Gooch, 1981, 4). In the *Faerie Queen* (2.3) Trompart is "wylie witted and grown old in cunning sleights and practrick knavery." Trompart in *Locrine* is simply Strumbo's servant and lacks any character definition. Strumbo is perhaps based on Spenser's Braggadocchio (Trompart's master). The word 'Braggadocchios' is used by Canutus in *Edmund Ironside* (1070): as I believe this was the bard's very next play this suggests he had access to Spenser's poem in manuscript at least three years before it was published. Gooch (1981, 7) pointed out that all the borrowings from Spenser come in the first half of *Locrine*.

There are quotations from Spenser's *Complaints* in *Locrine*.[54] This was entered in the Stationers' register 29th December, 1590, and contained, in *The Ruines of Time,* a reference to the death of Sir Francis Walsingham (6th April 1590). The *Complaints* were published in 1591 but were circulating in manuscript during the 1580s. But, if *Locrine,* as verse, diction and plot construction lead us to suppose, was written before 1590, it is probable that the lines borrowed from Spenser do not belong to the original edition, but only to the revised published version of 1595.[55] This fits with the suggestion that the play was written, re-written and revised over time before publication.

It is interesting to note that Spenser also influenced the *Henry VI* trilogy: thus recognised works by the bard show he was aware of Spenser and used passages from *The Faerie Queene* in *Henry VI* part 1 (1.1.11; 1.1.124; 3.4.19: Cairncross, 1965, xxxvii).

The author of *Locrine* quotes from Spenser's *Visions of the World's Vanitie*. Spenser describes a dragon thus:

---

[54] http://www.bartleby.com/215/0419.html [Accessed 2008]
[55] http://www.bartleby.com/215/1002.html [Accessed 2008]

An hideous Dragon, dreadful to behold,
Whose back was armed against the dint of spear
With shields of brass that shined like burnisht golde,
And **forkhed sting** that death in it did beare,
Strove with a Spider his unequall peare;
And bad defiance to his enemie.
The **subtill** vermin **creeping closely neare,**
Did in his drinke **shed poison priuilie;**
Which through his entrails spredding diuersly,
Made him swell, that nigh **his bowels burst**...

(2.77)

Although Spenser mentioned a crocodile earlier in the poem the creatures here are a dragon and a spider. In *Locrine* the Act 3 Prologue shows a crocodile and poisonous snake:

High on a bank by Nilus' boistrous streams,
Fearfully sat the Aegiptian **Crocodile,**
Dreadfully grinding in her sharp long teeth
The broken bowels of a silly fish.
His **back was armed against the dint of spear,**
With shields of brass that shined like burnished gold;
And as he stretched forth his cruel paws,
A **subtle** Adder, **creeping closely near,**
Thrusting his **forked sting** into his claws,
Privily shed his **poison** through his bones;
Which made him **swell, that** there his **bowels burst**...

(3.1.2)

Thus we can see that although the writer is quoting Spenser he changes the word order and the animals - from dragon/spider to crocodile/adder, even transposing the "**forked sting**" from the first creature (the dragon) to the second (a snake). We can then see an echo of this in *Henry VI* part 2 when Queen Margaret speaks of:

Gloucester's show
Beguiles him as the mournful **crocodile**
With sorrow snares relenting passengers
Or as the **snake** rolled in a flow'ring bank
With shining chequered slough doth **sting** a child...

(3.1.225)

We have the same order of ideas here: crocodile - adder/snake – sting. Shakespeare later referred to Spenser's *Teares of the Muses* in *A Midsummer Night's Dream* (5.1.52).

Thus the writer of *Locrine* can be seen not merely to copy his sources, to use 'imitatio', but as Bate (1993, 105, 143) has shown in Shakespeare's works, to change the poetry he is imitating, using 'similitudo', 'dissimilitudo' and 'contrarium': in other words the poet deliberately transforms the material he is copying. Shakespeare was a master of this, imitating and transforming Ovid.

Lodge's *The Complaint of Elstred*

Thomas Lodge's poem was circulating in manuscript from 1591: it was printed in 1593. If my dating of Locrine to 1586-9 is accurate it must have been written after the first version of the play. In his poem Lodge used a number of rare words to be found in the play: 'forage', 'bereft', 'countercheck', 'burnisht', 'waterie' and 'dazeled'. However the differences between poem and play are greater than the similarities (including the way Lodge spells these rare words). Some of the differences highlight significant elements in the play so I will outline these. We know Shakespeare was aware of Lodge's work because he used his *Rosalynd* as a source for *As You Like It*. However whilst Maxwell suggested Lodge's *Complaint of Elstred* might be a source for the play I suggest it was the other way round: that witnessing the play prompted Lodge to write his poem. Amongst the differences between them are the following:

1) Humber dies by drowning immediately after his defeat: he does not linger for years, starving in the wilderness, as in the play. (Lodge follows the historic sources.)
2) Lodge seems to suggest that Locrine marries Guendoline at the same time as falling in love with Elstred. (In this Lodge is following the *Historia* of Geoffrey of Monmouth.)
3) There is no deathbed scene with Brutus.
4) Locrine builds a 'labyrinth', a 'maze' for Elstred (not an 'arch' as in the play).
5) Guendolyn binds Elstred and her daughter together after her victory and drowns them: Elstred does not commit suicide as in the play. (In this Lodge is following the *Historia* of Geoffrey of Monmouth.)
6) There are no comic scenes in the poem.
7) Lodge spells his heroine's name differently: Elstred instead of Estrild.

Yet there are traces of the play in the poem and not only in the occasional rare word. Despite there being no Strumbo providing comedy, a cobbler is mentioned as one of the men going to war. Furthermore Elstred says she was presented to Locrine "by unhallowed hand" (stanza 31). She does not explain what she means but in the play Estrild is captured by two soldiers who argue over which of them can claim her as their prize. We are therefore seeing brief memories of the play in the poem. In the play we have: "...all our life is but a Tragedy" (1.1.17). This line is borrowed from Spenser's *Teares of the Muses*. In *Locrine* we find:

> Let him **behold** poor Estrild in this plight,
> **The perfect platform of** a troubled wight.
>
> (4.2.50)

Lodge has Elstred say:

> **Behold** in me the **tragedy** of fate,
> **The true *Idea*** of this worldly woe.

(Stanza 39)

The word *Idea* is italicised in the text: I understand the words 'platform' and '*Idea*' to mean example or archetype. If the writer of *Locrine* accurately transcribed a line from Spencer then this would suggest it is Lodge who echoes but does not exactly copy the play rather than vice versa.

One significant difference however points to Shakespeare's authorship of the play. In the poem Guendoline immediately takes the moral high ground as outraged wife (and so is justified in her cruelty to her husband's mistress). In the play however Guendoline has to build herself up to this point: she begins by lamenting Locrine's abandonment of her yet when Thrasimachus counsels revenge she recalls their love, saying Locrine was:

> More dear to me than the apple of mine eye,
> Nor can I find in heart to work his scathe.

(5.3.33)

Thrasimachus persists and then Guendoline draws herself up, like a proto Lady Macbeth, to be cruel:

> Then henceforth, farewell womanish complaints!
> All childish pity henceforth, then, farewell!
> But, cursed Locrine, look unto thy self,
> For Nemesis, the mistress of revenge,
> Sits armed at all points on our dismal blades...

(5.3.42)

The playwright shows a woman feeling and changing whereas Lodge presents us with a static, revengeful queen. Guendoline's conversion from grief to vengeance is reminiscent of Queen Margaret in *Henry VI* part 2:

> Oft have I heard that grief softens the mind,
> And makes it fearful and degenerate;
> Think therefore on revenge, and cease to weep.

(4.4.1)

Maxwell (1969) takes the view that Lodge's poem influenced the play. He thinks the slight echoes of the play in the poem are hints that the playwright developed more fully. The principle evidence he puts forward is the fact that "when Estrild is brought in captive, her first speech, one of thirty lines, consists of five six-line stanzas of iambic pentameter riming *a b a b cc* – the favourite stanza of Lodge, which he used throughout his *Complaint of Elstred*" (Maxwell, 1969, 37). Given that there are lines in the play taken from Spenser it is strange that there are no lines lifted from Lodge's poem, yet that poem contains words and ideas from the play. I therefore suggest that the poem postdates the play and the use of a stanza form itself is not sufficient evidence of a debt. Indeed reading the poem one gets the distinct impression from the style and language that it is later than the play, which other critics have noted is heavily influenced by Seneca and therefore belongs in the 1580s. Alternatively Maxwell (1969, 44) may be right when he suggests that the poetic passages of Estrild lamenting and Locrine falling in love, in Lodge's stanza form, were introduced into the scene (thus delaying the two soldiers arguing over Estrild) in a later revision, after the poem was written. Given that Lodge was a friend of Greene's and they wrote *A Looking Glass for London* together at some time between 1587-91, it is not impossible that Lodge had a hand in the revising of *Locrine*. It is possible that the play is, like *Sir Thomas More*, the result of collaboration between several writers.

Lodge followed the historical sources in all matters except one: that Elstred was Humber's partner. This is one invention from the play. He does tell of the meeting between Elstred and Locrine, which is in the play but not in the historical sources. He does not use other innovations in the play but reverts to the historical sources. Lodge's poem moreover is non-political. The poem is a tragic, romantic lament that ignores the political issues that are essential to the play: the division of the kingdom, the dangers of invasion and of civil war.

Appendix 8:

CELERITY

The word 'celerity' is found in *Locrine* and the works of Shakespeare. To clarify the usages of this rare word I have listed all the occurrences I have found using the Oxford English Dictionary (OED) and the Literature on Line database (LION) between the first cited in the OED and 1614. It is startling to see that the very first usage is by Richard III who was related to the Nevilles and married Anne Neville. Shakespeare is the writer who uses the word more than any other. Indeed Shakespeare's frequent use of the word, and his frequent use of "effusion of blood" (see chapter 3), both in *Locrine*, is further suggestive of his authorship of *Locrine*. Neville uses 'celerity' in a letter, dated at the very time Shakespeare most often uses 'celerity'. We know that Golding's translation of Ovid's *Metamorphoses* and Preston's *The Life of Cambises, King of Percia* were sources for Shakespeare. *Selimus* is considered as having been derived from *Locrine* so its publication one year earlier is not to be taken as evidence of priority. (Dates in brackets are when the Shakespeare plays were first published.)

DATE	AUTHOR	WORK	SPELLING	SOURCE
1483	Richard III	Ellis Orig lett	celerite	OED
1531	Elvot	Gov.	celerity	OED
1567	Arthur Golding	Ovid *Metamorphosis*	celeritie	LION
1569	Thomas Preston	*Cambises*	seleritie	LION
1570-91?	John Phillips	*Grissill*	celeritie	LION
1591	Horsey	Trav	seleritie	OED
1594	Anon/Greene	*Selimus*	celeritie	LION
1595	**W.S.**	**Locrine**	**celeritie**	**Quarto**
1595	John Trussel	*Rape of Helen*	celeritie	LION
1596	Charles Fitz-Geffry	Francis Drake	celeritie	LION
1599 (1623)	Shakespeare	*Henry V*	celerity	LION
1600	Henry Neville	letter 28/8/1600	celerity	Winwood
1601/2 (1609)	Shakespeare	*Troilus & Cressida*	celerity	LION
1603/4 (1623)	Shakespeare	*Measure for Measure*	celerity	LION
1606	William Warner	Albion's England	celeritie	LION
1606	Nathaniell Baxter	Sidney's Ourania	celeritie	LION
1607	Topsell	Four-f. Beasts	celerity	OED
1608	Thomas Middleton	*Your Five Gallants*	celerity	LION
1608 (1623)	Shakespeare	*Antony & Cleopatra*	celerity	LION

1609	Anon	*Every Woman in her Humor*	celeritie	LION
1613	John Fletcher	*The Tragedy of Bonduca*	celerity	LION
1613-14 (1634) Shakespeare & Fletcher				
		Two Noble Kinsmen	celerity	LION
1614	Arthur Gorges	Lucan's Pharsalia	celerity	LION
1614	John Norden	Labyrinth of Man's Life	celeritie	LION

Furthermore we can compare the usage of this word in *Locrine*:
"The Scithians follow **with great celerity**" (2.6.74) with these works:

1567	Arthur Golding	Ovid *Metamorphosis*	"with the like celeritie"
1569	Thomas Preston	*Cambises*	"with all seleritie"
1570-91?	John Phillips	*Grissill* "with celeritie" and "with all celerite"	
1595	John Trussel	*Rape of Helen*	"with celeritie"
1613	John Fletcher	*The Tragedy of Bonduca*	"with all celerity"
1613-14	Shakespeare & Fletcher 2 Noble Kinsmen		"with that celerity"
1614	Sir Arthur Gorges Lucan's Pharsalia		"great celerity"

(The other works in the main list above do not use either 'with' or 'great' with 'celerity'.) In chapter 3, I pointed out that Shakespeare echoes *Locrine* in *Troilus and Cressida* when Nestor says:

> **with great** speed of judgment,
> Ay, **with celerity**, find Hector's purpose
>
> (1.3.329)

Thus it can be seen that Shakespeare is the closest to *Locrine* in combining 'with' and 'great' with 'celerity'. Neville used the words "**with** vehemency and **celerity**" in his letter of 28/8/1600 (James, 2008b, 252; Winwood, 1725, Vol 1, 248).

Curiously, given that James (2008b, 177-187) has suggested Sir William Davenant was Neville's illegitimate son, he uses the words "with all celerity" in both his play *The Cruel Brother* (1630) and his masque *Luminalia* (1637).

REFERENCES

Internet

I have used these on-line concordances to search texts:

http://victorian.lang.nagoya-u.ac.jp/concordance/ [Accessed 2008]
http://www.it.usyd.edu.au/~matty/Shakespeare/test.html [Accessed 2008]

I have also used the Literature on Line database (LION) at John Rylands University Library of Manchester.

Some of the material in chapter 3 is taken from the following websites:

http://www.wsu.edu/~delahoyd/shakespeare/locrine5.html [Accessed 2008]
http://en.wikipedia.org/wiki/Locrine [Accessed 2008]

Whitney emblems:
http://www.mun.ca/alciato/wcomm.html [Accessed 2008]

32 In poenam sectatur et umbra [Accessed 2008]
http://www.mun.ca/alciato/whit/w032.html [Accessed 2008]

75 O vita, misero longa
http://www.mun.ca/alciato/whit/w075.html [Accessed 2008]

183a Qui me alit me extinguit
http://www.mun.ca/alciato/whit/w183a.html [Accessed 2008]

177 Unica semper avis
http://www.mun.ca/alciato/whit/w177.html [Accessed 2008]

Play Texts

I have used Tucker Brooke (1967) for the Act and scene divisions and line numbering of *Mucedorus* and Farmer for checking the 1st Quarto text. I have used Gooch (1981) for the Act and scene divisions and line numbering of *Locrine*. I have used Sams (1986) and http://www.elizabethanauthors.com/iron1.htm [Accessed 2008] for the text and lineage of *Edmund Ironside*. The edition of *Arden of Faversham* used for line references is McIlworth (1969). I have used Sider (1979) for *The Troublesome Raigne of John King of England* and Melchiori (2001) for *Edward III*.

Double Falshood I downloaded from the Internet version: *Double Falshood* or *The Distrest Lovers*, Transcribed by John W. Kennedy (2004) Transcription from the 2nd London edition of 1728, with notes on all variants in the 1st London edition of 1728 and major variants in the 3rd London edition of 1767:
http://pws.prserv.net/jwkennedy/Double%20Falshood/index.html [Accessed 2008]
I have added my own line numberings to this.

Books

Ackroyd, P. (2005) Shakespeare The Biography, London, Chatto and Windus

A Knack to Know A Knave 1594 (1964) The Malone Society Reprints, Oxford University Press

Bate, J. (1993) Shakespeare and Ovid, Oxford, Clarendon Press

Bate, J. (1997) The Genius of Shakespeare, London, Picador

Bell, J. (1827/1832) A System of Geography, Popular and Scientific, A Physical and Political Account of the World and its Various Divisions, Glasgow, A. Fullarton

Bevington, D. (1962) From 'Mankind' to Marlowe: Growth of Structure in the Popular Drama of Tudor England, Cambridge, Harvard University Press

Bliss, L. (ed) (2004) A King and No King by Francis Beaumont and John Fletcher, Manchester University Press

Bossy, J. (1991) Giordano Bruno and the Embassy Affair, London, Yale University

Bowers, F. (ed) (1966) The Dramatic Works in the Beaumont and Fletcher Canon, Vol 1, Cambridge, University Press

Braunmuller, A. R. (1989) The Life and Death of King John, Oxford University Press

Brooke, N. (Ed.) (1990) Macbeth, The Oxford Shakespeare, Oxford University Press

Brooks, H.F. (1990) A Midsummer Night's Dream, The Arden Shakespeare, London, Routledge

Bruce, J. (ed) (1868) The Diary of John Manningham, Camden Society

Bryson, B. (2007) Shakespeare, The World as a Stage, Eminent Lives, Atlas Books, London, Harper Press

Bucknill, J. (1860) The Medical Knowledge of Shakespeare, Longmans, London

Bullen, A.H. (1888) The Works of George Peele, Volumes I & II, London, John C. Nimmo

Burgoyne F.J. (1904) Collotype facsimile & type transcript of an Elizabethan MS at Alnwick Castle, Northumberland, London (copy consulted at John Rylands Library, Manchester).

Cairncross, A.S. (1967) Kyd: The First Part of Hieronimo and The Spanish Tragedy, London, Edward Arnold Ltd.

Cairncross, A. S. (1965) The First Part of Henry VI, The Arden Edition of the Works of William Shakespeare, London, Methuen & Co. Ltd, Harvard University Press

Campbell, L. (ed.) (1960) The Mirror for Magistrates, New York, Barnes & Noble Inc. (for Cambridge University Press)

Carr, F. (2004) Who Wrote Don Quixote? Xlibris Corporation, USA

Casson, J. (2007a) Evidence for Shakespeare-Neville's authorship in Double Falshood: The 'Lost' Play of Cardenio, Journal of Neville Studies, 1

Casson, J. (2007b) A New Interpretation of Epigram 77 by Ben Jonson, Journal of Neville Studies, Vol 1, No. 1

Casson, J. (2008) Evidence for Shakespeare-Neville's authorship in Arden of Faversham, Journal of Neville Studies, Vol 1, No. 2

Casson, J. (2009) Two Ben Jonson Poems Revealed, Journal of Neville Studies, Vol 1, No. 3

Cawley, A.C. & Gaines, B. (1986) A Yorkshire Tragedy, The Revels Plays, Manchester University Press

Chambers, E.K. (1923) The Elizabethan Stage, Four Volumes, Oxford, Clarendon Press

Clubb, L. G. (1972) The Tragicomic Bear in Comparative Literature Studies Vol. IX, No.1, pages 17-30, University of Illinois, USA

Cockburn, N.B. (1998) The Bacon Shakespeare Question, The Baconian Theory Made Sane, London, Biddles Ltd.

Corbin, P. & Sedge, D. (eds) (2002) Thomas of Woodstock or Richard II Part One, Manchester University Press

Cornish, T. (2007) Unpublished correspondence with Brenda James.

Dickinson, T.H. (ed) (1909) Robert Greene Six Plays: The Mermaid Series, London, T. Fisher Unwin Ltd.

Dorsch, T. S. (ed.) (2005) The Comedy of Errors, The New Cambridge Shakespeare, Cambridge University Press

Duncan, O. L. (1974) The Political Career of Sir Henry Neville: An Elizabethan Gentleman at the court of James I, PhD Dissertation, Ohio State University

Duncan-Jones, K. (1991) Sir Philip Sidney, Courtier Poet, London, Hamish Hamilton

Duncan-Jones, K. (1999) Sir Philip Sidney, The Countess of Pembroke's Arcadia (The Old Arcadia), Oxford University Press

Duncan-Jones, K. (2001) Ungentle Shakespeare, Scenes from his Life, The Arden Shakespeare, Thomson Learning

Duncan-Jones, K. (2002) Sir Philip Sidney, The Major Works, Oxford University Press

Duncan-Jones, K. (2005) Shakespeare's Sonnets, The Arden Shakespeare, London, Thomson Learning

Edwards, P. (1974) The Spanish Tragedy, The Revels Plays, Manchester University Press

Egan, M. (2006) The Tragedy of Richard II Part One: a newly authenticated play by William Shakespeare, four volumes, Lewiston, The Edwin Mellen Press

Evans, M. (Ed) (1987) Sir Philip Sidney, The Countess of Pembroke's Arcadia, London, Penguin Books

Farmer, J.S. (ed) (1910) The First Quarto (1598) of Mucedorus: The Tudor Facsimile Texts

Farmer, J.S. (1911) Locrine, 1595, The Tudor Facsimile Texts

Foakes, R.A. (2005) The Comedy of Errors, The Arden Shakespeare, London, Thomson Learning

Freehafer, J. (1969) Cardenio, by Shakespeare and Fletcher, P. M. L. A., 501-513

Garnett, E. (1991) The Story of the Calverley Murders, Calverley

Freeman, A. (1962) Two Notes on A Knack to Know a Knave, Notes and Queries 207: 326-27

Garnett, E. (1991) The Story of the Calverley Murders, Calverley

Gaud, W. S. (1904) The Authorship of Locrine, Modern Philology, University of Chicago Press, January, 409-422

Gayley, C. M. (1914) Francis Beaumont Dramatist, London, Duckworth

Gibbons, B. (1990) Romance and the Heroic Play: chapter 6 in The Cambridge Companion to English Renaissance Literature edited by Braunmuller, A.R. & Hattaway, M., Cambridge University Press

Gooch, J. L. (1981) The Lamentable Tragedy of Locrine: A Critical Edition, Garland English Texts No. 7, New York, Garland Publishing Inc.

Grady, H. (2002) Shakespeare, Machiavelli and Montaigne: Power and Subjectivity from Richard II to Hamlet, Oxford

Griffin, B. (1997) Locrine and The Babington Plot, Notes and Queries, 44: 37-40

Halio, J.L. (1999) Henry VIII, or All is True, The Oxford Shakespeare, Oxford University Press

Hall, E. (1965) Chronicle: The History of England, New York, AMS Print Inc

Halliday, E. F. (1977) A Shakespeare Companion 1564-1964, London, Gerald Duckworth

Hamilton, C. (1994) Cardenio or The Second Maiden's Tragedy, New York, Marlowe & Company

Hattaway, M. (1993) The Third Part of King Henry VI, The New Cambridge Shakespeare, Cambridge University Press

Haynes, A. (1987) The White Bear, Robert Dudley, The Elizabethan Earl of Leicester, London, Peter Owen

Hicks, L. (1964) An Elizabethan Problem, Some Aspects of the careers of Two Exile-Adventurers, London, Burns & Oates

Holmes, P. (2004) Clifford, George, third earl of Cumberland (1558–1605), Oxford Dictionary of National Biography, Oxford University Press (http://www.oxforddnb.com/view/article/5645, accessed 30 March 2007)

Honigmann, E.A.J. (ed) (1954, reprint 2006) King John, The Arden Shakespeare, London, Thomson Learning

Hubbard, P.G. (1905) Repetition and Parallelism in the Earlier Elizabethan Drama, PMLA, 20

Hughes, T. (1992) Shakespeare and The Goddess of Complete Being, London, Faber and Faber Ltd.

Innes, M. (transl) (1955) The Metamorphoses of Ovid, London, Penguin Classics

Jackson, P. (2001) Shakespeare's Richard II and the Anonymous Thomas of Woodstock, chapter 1 in Pitcher, J. (Ed.) (2001) Medieval and Renaissance Drama in England, Volume 14, Madison Teaneck, Fairleigh Dickinson University Press

James, B & Rubinstein, W.D. (2005) The Truth Will Out: Unmasking The Real Shakespeare, Harlow, Pearson Longman

James, B. (2007a) Shakespeare-Neville, Forests, Islands and Folklore, Journal of Neville Studies, Vol 1, No. 1

James, B. (2007b) The Tangled World of Elizabethan Espionage: Sir Henry Neville and Charles Paget, Double Agent, Journal of Neville Studies Vol 1, No. 1

James, B. (2007c) The Iron Men of the Theatre, Journal of Neville Studies, Vol 1, No. 1

James, B. (2007d) Sir Henry Neville – The Hidden Persuader, article published on website: www.HenryNeville.com

James, B. (2008a) Shakespeare-Neville, Cervantes and the Treaty of Boulogne, Journal of Neville Studies, Vol 1, No. 2

James, B. (2008b) Henry Neville and the Shakespeare Code, Bognor Regis, Music for Strings

Jordan, W.K. (1968) Edward VI: The Young King. Cambridge, Harvard University Press

Jowett, J. (ed) (2000) Richard III, The Oxford Shakespeare, Oxford University Press

Jowett, J. (ed) (2004) Timon of Athens, The Oxford Shakespeare, Oxford University Press

Jupin, A.H. (1987) A Contextual Study and Modern-Spelling Edition of Mucedorus, The Renaissance Imagination, Vol 29, London, Garland Publishing Inc.

Kail, A.C. (1986) The Medical Mind of Shakespeare, Balgowlah NSW, Williams & Wilkins, ADIS Pty Ltd.

Keen, A. & Lubbock, R. (1954) The Annotator, London, Putman

Kermode, F. (1990) The Tempest, The Arden Shakespeare, London, Routledge

Kukowski, S. (1991) The Hand of John Fletcher in Double Falshood, Shakespeare Survey 43 The Tempest and After, edited by Stanley Wells, Cambridge University Press

Lake, D. J. (1983) Three Seventeenth-Century Revisions: Thomas of Woodstock, The Jew of Malta and Faustus B. April, Notes and Queries

Leech, C. (2001) The Two Gentlemen of Verona, London, Thompson Learning, The Arden Shakespeare

Levi, P. (1988) The Life and Times of William Shakespeare, London, Macmillan

LION: Literature on Line database: http://lion.chadwyck.co.uk [Accessed 2008]

Lings, M. (1984) The Secret of Shakespeare, Wellingborough, Northamptonshire, The Aquarian Press

Lodge, T. (1883) The Complaint of Elstred, (1593) in The Complete Works of Thomas Lodge, volume 2 (pages 58-84), Hunterian Club.

Lucas F. (1972) Seneca and Elizabethan Tragedy, Folcroft Library Edition of New York, Haskell House

McIlworth, A.K. (ed) (1969) Five Elizabethan Tragedies, London, Oxford University Press

McLynn, F. (2006) Lionheart and Lackland: King Richard, King John and the Wars of Conquest, London, Jonathan Cape

McVeagh, J. (1982) Tradefull Merchants: the Portrayal of the Capitalist in Literature, History Today

Maxwell, B. (1969) Studies in the Shakespeare Apocrypha, New York, Greenwood Press

Mears, N. (2004) Stubbe [Stubbs], John (c.1541–1590), Oxford Dictionary of National Biography, Oxford University Press, 2004

[http://www.oxforddnb.com/view/article/26736, accessed 11 Feb 2007]

Mehl, D. (1982) The Elizabethan Dumb Show, London, Methuen

Melchiori G. (2001) Edward III, The New Cambridge Shakespeare, Cambridge University Press

Miller, A. C. (1963) Sir Henry Killigrew, Elizabethan Soldier and Diplomat, Leicester University Press

Miller, S.R. (1998) The Taming of A Shrew, The 1594 Quarto, Cambridge University Press

Minto, W. (1885) Characteristics of English Poetry, Edinburgh, Blackwood

Muir, K. (1960) Shakespeare as Collaborator, London, Methuen

Muir, K. (1970) Introduction to Facsimile edition of Double Falshood, London, Cornmarket Press Ltd

Nicholl, C. (1980) The Chemical Theatre, London, Routledge and Kegan Paul

Nicholl, C. (2005) Leonardo Da Vinci: The Flights of the Mind, London, Penguin Books

ODNB: Matthew, H.G.C. & Harrison, B. (2004): Oxford Dictionary of National Biography, Oxford University Press

Orgel, S. (Ed.) (1996) The Winter's Tale, The Oxford Shakespeare, Oxford Universty Press

Peachman, J. (2006) Links between Mucedorus and the Tragical History, Admirable Atchievments and Various Events of Guy Earl of Warwick, Notes and Queries December, Oxford University Press

Peck, D.C. (ed.) (2006) Leicester's Commonwealth, The Copy of a Letter Written by a Master of Art of Cambridge (1584) and Related Documents, Ohio University Press, Athens, Ohio, London, (Reprinted in PDF format, 2006)

Rowse, A. L. (1962) Raleigh and the Throckmortons, London, Macmillan & Co Ltd

Sackville-West, V. (1923) The Diary of the Lady Anne Clifford, London, Heinemann Ltd.

Salerno, H. (2000) Double Falshood Shakespeare's Cardenio: A Study of a "Lost" Play, Xlibris Corporation USA

Sams, E. (1986) Shakespeare's Edmund Ironside: The Lost Play, Aldershot, Hants, Wildwood House

Sams, E. (1988) The Troublesome Wrangle over King John, Notes and Queries, March, Oxford University Press

Sams, E. (1995) The Real Shakespeare, Retrieving the Early Years, 1564-1594, London, Yale University Press

Schoenbaum, S. (1987) William Shakespeare, A Compact Documentary Life, Oxford University Press

Seneca, L.A. (1887) His Tenne Tragedies Translated into English 1589, reprinted for the Spencer Society

Sider, J.W. (1979) The Troublesome Raigne of John King of England, New York & London, Garland Publishing, Inc.

Simonini, R. C. (1977) Second Fruits (1591) by John Florio: a facsimile edition, Delmar, New York, Scholars' Facsimiles & Reprints

Sobran, J. (1996) The Phaeton Sonnet, Summer 1996 Shakespeare Oxford Newsletter, (Shakespeare Oxford Society): http://www.shakespeare-oxford.com/?p=80 [Accessed 2008]

Spurgeon, C. (1958) Shakespeare's Imagery and what it tells us, Cambridge University Press

Sugden, E.H. (1925) A Topographical Dictionary to the Works of Shakespeare and His Fellow Dramatists, Manchester, The University Press; London, Longmans

Sylvester, R. (ed) (1959) The Life and Death of Cardinal Wolsey by George Cavendish, London, Oxford University Press

Tawney, R. H. (1926) Religion and the Rise of Capitalism, London, J. Murray

Thorpe, L. (1966) Geoffrey of Monmouth: The History of the Kings of Britain, London, Penguin

Tucker Brooke, C.F. (1967) The Shakespeare Apocrypha, (first edition 1908) reprint Oxford University Press

Vickers, B. (2008) Thomas Kyd, Secret Sharer, The Times Literary Supplement, April 18th, No 5481

Waith, E. M. (Ed) (1998) The Two Nobel Kinsmen, The Oxford Shakespeare, Oxford University Press

Ward, A.W. and Waller, A.R. (Eds) (1907–21) The Cambridge History of English and American Literature in 18 Volumes: Volume VI. The Drama to 1642, Part Two. II. Chapman, Marston, Dekker, Cambridge University Press

Warren, R. (ed) (2003a) Henry VI part 2, The Oxford Shakespeare, Oxford University Press

Warren, R. (ed) (2003b) Pericles, The Oxford Shakespeare, Oxford University Press

Wiggins, M. (ed) (2008) A Woman Killed with Kindness and other Domestic Plays (including Arden of Faversham), Oxford University Press

Wilkins, G. (1963) The Miseries of Enforced Marriage, The Malone Society Reprints, Oxford University Press

Wilson, R. (2004) Secret Shakespeare, Studies in theatre, religion and resistance, Manchester University Press

Wine, M. L. (ed) (1973) The Tragedy of Master Arden of Faversham, The Revel Plays, London, Methuen & Co. Ltd.

Winwood, R. (1725) Memorials of State in the reigns of Q. Elizabeth and K. James, Volume 1, London, T. Ward

Yates, F. (1936) A Study of Love's Labour's Lost, Cambridge University Press

Yates, F. (1968) John Florio, New York, Octagon Books Inc.

Yates, F. (1975) Shakespeare's Last Plays: A New Approach, London, Routledge & Kegan Paul

Yates, F. (2002) Giordano Bruno and the Hermetic Tradition London, Routledge Classics

Yates, F. (2004) The Rosicrucian Enlightenment, London, Routledge Classics

Other works consulted:

Hasler, P.W. (ed.) (1981) The History of Parliament, The House of Commons, 1553-1603, London, HMSO, History of Parliament Trust

Howard, J.E. (ed) (2003) A Companion to Shakespeare's Works, Vol. II, London, Blackwell.

Roe, J. (ed) (1998) The Poems, The New Cambridge Shakespeare, Cambridge University Press

Authors' Index

List of authors of books cited: writers of poems and plays are in the main Index

Index

Printed in the United Kingdom by
Lightning Source UK Ltd., Milton Keynes
137557UK00001BA/316-348/P